Animal Stories

A Lifetime Collection

Max Evans

Illustrated by Keith Walters

Foreword by Luther Wilson

UNIVERSITY OF OKLAHOMA PRESS : NORMAN

This book is published with the generous assistance of The McCasland Foundation, Duncan, Oklahoma.

Library of Congress Cataloging-in-Publication Data

Evans, Max, 1924–
[Short stories. Selections]
Animal stories: a lifetime collection / Max Evans; illustrated by Keith Walters; foreword by Luther Wilson.
    pages   cm
ISBN 978-0-8061-4366-8 (pbk.: alk. paper)
1. Animals—Fiction. 2. Animals. 3. Western stories.
I. Walters, Keith, illustrator. II. Title.
PS3555.V23A6 2013
813'.54—dc23
                                        2013003772

The paper in this book meets the guidelines for permanence and durability of the Committee on Production Guidelines for Book Longevity of the Council on Library Resources, Inc. ∞

1 2 3 4 5 6 7 8 9 10

Lifetime Dedications

- My friend and compatriot from the long ago "uranium boom," John Beck, for knowing this book was an animal odyssey. A quest.

- Optometrist Randall Carter for all his selfless, very appreciated help.

- Attorney William Marchiondo whose loyalty and long family friendship are treasured.

- Robert Conley, Cherokee author and professor, for our years of fun and frolic, as well as his classic novel *Mountain Windsong*.

- The Witte Family of New Mexico all the way back to my years as a kid cowboy up on Glorieta Mesa.

- Alvin and Barbara Davis for never letting up on promoting the ways of the West.

- My uncle, Lloyd Evans, and his son Corky for overcoming difficult ambitions by laughing at ourselves.

- My beloved parents, W. B. and Hazel Evans, for never giving up on me even when I was so often wrong.

- Luz Martinez, Wiley (Big Boy) Hittson and all the other friends and foes of the Hi-Lo Country.

- Sergeants Milton Rudio and Pick, and Privates Shadow Requenez and Needhi, and the ghosts of all the others who shared with me the bloody infantry months of Normandy when we truly believed we were saving the world.

- Lifetime friend Tony Reyna, governor and always councilor of the eternal Taos Pueblo.

- Lorene and Ernie Mills and their daughter, Joy, of a forever friendship.

- My enormously talented wife, Pat, and our twin daughters, Charlotte and Sheryl, for a life of sharing, giving, loving, and laughing.

Contents

Foreword

Despite having known Max Evans for more than thirty years; despite his being my best friend, a relationship that we both know bears a heavy weight of responsibility; and despite having published or reprinted new editions of half or more of his novels, novellas, and book-length nonfiction works, I find it almost impossible to write anything new or original about Max's writing. Charles Champlin, the longtime great arts and entertainment editor of the *Los Angeles Times,* wrote, "The strength of Max Evans's novels and stories, and of his nonfiction pieces is their authenticity, a foundation in reality as solid as a thick adobe wall." I could write from now until I find myself heading somewhere in a handbasket and not come up with a more perfect, succinct, unique, and accurate description. Champlin's words apply equally to Max's works and to Max himself, except for the "thick" part. Our mutual, and also best friend Robert Conley, award-winning Cherokee writer and Sequoyah Distinguished Professor of Cherokee Studies at Western Carolina University, wrote, "[Max] . . . can dish out stark realism, raucous slapstick comedy, heart tearing tragedy and surreal mysticism equally well and sometimes all in one bowl." I cannot beat those descriptions of Max and his writing, and will not even try. I will try to tell you why you are in for a reading feast from this book, *Animal Stories.*

First, allow me what may seem like an inexplicable aside. I arrived in Albuquerque in August of 1980 as the fresh and somewhat innocent new director of the University of New Mexico Press. An old friend and author, John Donald Robb, retired dean of the School of Fine Arts, invited me to a party at which I was introduced to a close friend of Dean Robb, well-known archaeologist, and, to some, notorious big-game hunter, Dr. Frank Hibben. Dr. Hibben was under fire in the news at the time for having been named the interim director of the Albuquerque Zoo. Some critics claimed that he would use his position at the zoo to add to his already large collection of animal trophies, and that he knew nothing about animals except how to shoot them. At the party I defended Dr. Hibben's selection as interim director of the zoo on the grounds that to be a successful hunter, you have to know the behavior, whereabouts, food and water sources, and thinking of animals about as well as anybody who studies them scientifically. I doubt that I changed the minds of many of Dr. Hibben's critics, but he only agreed to take the interim position until a new, permanent zoo director was named, which came about in a couple of months and the teapot tempest abated.

A couple of weeks later I met Max for the first of what became semi-legendary lunches at Baca's Bar and Restaurant. We met to talk about the UNM Press reprinting several of Max's short novels. It turned out that we grew up in similar circumstances: Max grew up in Depression-era rural and small-town West Texas and southeastern New Mexico; I grew up a couple of decades later in the remote Appalachians of southeastern Kentucky, which had yet to recover from the Depression. I knew from reading several of Max's stories and novels the week before our first lunch that he hunted regularly as a boy to supplement the family supply of meat with small game, something that I had also done, adding fishing to my meat-supplementing skills. We talked about the zoo director flap, and Max and I thought alike: if you need someone who understands animals, you would do well to hire a successful hunter.

I know from experience that Max is a successful hunter, and from reading the stories in this book I know that he really understands animals. Read "The Old One" for a magical, sad, but true look into the mind of an aging prairie dog as she watches her latest litter of pups rolling and tumbling around the mound while thinking of all the things she has to teach them about the world. For a look into the minds of an old cow with a new calf and an old coyote with a litter to feed, as they warily circle each other trying to do their best for their young, read "The One-Eyed Sky." I have rarely read a story that is its equal. "The Cowboy and the Professor," in which I play a minor part, tells the story of a moose, an old cowboy, and his undependable young pardner.

———

After World War II, Max supplemented his small-ranch income by hunting coyotes and other predators for nearby ranchers in the part of New

Mexico that, thanks to Max, has become known as the Hi-Lo Country. Max got to know and respect coyotes so much that he would no longer hunt them. Coyote became his totem animal. In fact, Max gave up hunting altogether for more than forty years. I, too, gave up hunting in general, in part because I no longer needed to supplement our meat supply, but mostly because of the rigors of hunting large game in the high Rocky Mountains. I continued bird hunting for a few more years to supply our traditional wild goose Christmas dinners and to provide feathers that I could turn into flies for trout.

A decade or so ago, some of Max's rancher friends invited him to take up hunting for deer and elk again. Being left-handed, Max told me he preferred to hunt with a Savage Model 99, a lever-action rifle that works the same for a left hander as for a right hander. I found a good one for him from an Albuquerque acquaintance. It was a .308 caliber, which matched the caliber of my long-silent hunting rifle, a Weatherby Vanguard that produced sub-minute-of-angle shot groups for me on paper targets at a hundred yards. I loaded some bullets and took Max to my local shooting club range to test his rifle before he took it hunting. With either rifle Max amazed me. Here was a man rapidly approaching eighty years old (a thousand and eighteen years, according to Max) who with either rifle placed cloverleaf patterns of three-shot groups on the targets at a hundred yards. When Max took his first shot, I saw through my spotting scope that he had hit the target dead center. I could not see his second shot, so after listening to Max complain for a couple of minutes that his eyesight had gone to Hades in my handbasket, I suggested we walk down to the target for a better look. I could see from ten yards away that he had placed his second shot so close to the first that it made a perfect MasterCard symbol. His third shot created a cloverleaf. I could have covered all three with a nickel.

The only problem with his "new" rifle, the Savage Model 99, was that it had a wooden stock, which was just too heavy for Max to lug around all day on a hunt. He asked if he could borrow my synthetic-stocked Weatherby, which was much lighter to carry. Thus began a legend. With Max's shooting accuracy, and what became known as "The Magic Gun," through six hunting seasons, the last well into Max's eighties, six hunts ended successfully using six bullets.

Enjoy *Animal Stories*. If you know wild animals, or so-called domesticated ones, you will find kindred souls in these stories. If you do not know much about them, you will learn from one of the best. As Max would say, "Have fun!"

LUTHER WILSON

Director, Retired

University of New Mexico Press

Introduction

It first appeared to be a fairly routine chore to put together a collection of my fact and fiction animal stories. I knew they must range in length from short-short to my favorite size—both to read and to write—the novella. The collection would cover a sixty-two-year span from the short-short story "The Call" (1950) to this very sentence, written in the summer of 2012.

While going through all this work, I began to realize that although my books and stories don't fall into any given category, it became obvious that all my writing leaned heavily on animal participation. My novels, *The Rounders* (1960), *The Hi Lo Country* (1962), *The Mountain of Gold* (1965), *Shadow of Thunder* (1969), *Faraway Blue* (2005), and even the massive *Bluefeather Fellini* (1993), were animal-oriented to a high degree. All three of my most reprinted novellas were published in the *University of South Dakota Review* at the request of its noted editor, John R. Milton: *Xavier's Folly* in summer 1972, *Candles in the Bottom of the Pool* in autumn 1973, and *The Orange County Cowboys* in winter 1987. *Xavier's Folly* was optioned several times for filming with many noteworthy writers authoring numerous unsuccessful scripts, the latest in 2012. *Candles in the Bottom of the Pool* is my most anthologized story, and *The Orange County Cowboys* has been reprinted in hard and soft covers. All had animals for sure, but the human animal dominated in the latter. So after long deliberation I chose *The Orange County Cowboys* as my human animal story for this collection. A small but critical part of the story involving a baby calf was based on truth. The rest of the story was fictionalized. Although the schemes and instincts of the human animal were very subtle, they were just as savage as a hungry grizzly attacking a newborn fawn.

In the early years of my creative life—the late 1940s and early 1950s—I moved to Taos, New Mexico (a village famous for its many fine artists), with the sole purpose of becoming a serious painter. I met the great Potawatomi Indian artist Woody Crumbo. He became my best friend and mentor. In between paintings, I wrote short stories and magazine articles. The two creative things seemed to complement each other.

Some of the short fiction in this collection—"The Old One," "Don't Kill My Dog," "The Matched Race," and "The Far Cry"—comes from that period starting in 1950, having been published at varying dates throughout my long creative life. (I might have found more polished stories, but I felt that to compile a final, completely honest, representation of my life's shorter work with animals, these were the ones to include.)

Although the two art forms—writing and painting—are compatible, one must finally dominate. The paintings were selling; the stories were not. Financial necessity kept me painting, but when I finally did sell my first article and my first fiction to the Sunday magazine section of the *Denver Post* in 1951, the pull toward serious writing grew stronger. Nonfiction articles outsold my fiction. I have to admit the fiction pieces were not easily categorized; maybe they were even a bit too metaphysical, about the unknown things in our universe. In today's broader thinking world of writing, they would be considered normal by most readers.

During this period, 1950 to the early 1960s, the paintings were selling well, but my writing sales were still very moderate. My survival tactics took on a whole other dimension: I became heavily involved in the mining and prospecting world. Copper, gold, perlite, even uranium—if it existed in the minerals of New Mexico I was in hot pursuit of finding it. My friends were all involved and it was a wild and exciting adventure. We made a lot of money and then . . . we lost it. During this period, for five or six years in the mid-1950s, writing and painting both took a sabbatical; but unbeknownst to me, I was gathering abundant and priceless material for my works of fiction, for the novellas and novels that would govern the rest of my life.

After the mining dust settled and we were in debt over our boots, I went back into writing with a whole new dedication. In 1958, instead of painting or working on short stories, I took the big plunge and wrote a novel: *The Rounders*. It was life-changing. It brought the world of film into our lives, and along with it came the question people often ask writers: "Where did you ever get the idea to write that?" It was easily answered. I wrote *The Rounders* because it was what I knew the most about, cowboying and ranching, but sometimes something I have witnessed just sticks in my mind, hangs around—sometimes for years—and then one day it simply demands to be put on paper. That is true with an incident that inspired "The One-

Eyed Sky," published in 1962 and certainly one of my three or four most recognizable works. The event happened a short while after I returned from infantry combat in World War II in 1946.

I was riding horseback from my little ranch near Des Moines, New Mexico, toward the entrance to Farrel Smith's large outfit to do some day labor. Small ranches and stock farms were still feeling the effects of the Great Depression and having a hard time making ends meet right after the war. Some were still hanging on. During the fighting years, the big ranches had prospered by supplying the high-priced beef that was needed to feed half the world, and they were quietly absorbing most of the smaller spreads.

I had taken a shortcut across A. D. Weatherly's well-watered ranch to the Smith spread (now the T. O. East). Suddenly, as we topped out on a grassy, yucca-covered hill, my mount stopped on his own. I looked where his ears were aimed and saw an old, old cow stopped a ways back from a dirt tank of runoff water. I was stunned to recognize that she was just a short time from dropping what had to be her last calf. She was looking up at the rise just beyond the tank. Here she saw a mother coyote, thin and aged herself with four half-grown pups spotted strategically about. I wanted to run the coyotes off, but then I couldn't stay and wait for the calf's birth. The coyotes would be back as soon as I left.

I rode on to the Smiths', allowing our own survival and my time commitment to prevail. I wondered and I wondered about the results of the standoff for a long time. Suddenly, sometime in 1961, the complete story hit me. I started writing late one afternoon and pounded the old Underwood typewriter straight through the night and into the morning. I was barely able to plunk down "The End."

I took the entire manuscript downstairs from my attic studio. To my surprise it was mid-morning and I found my wife, Pat, sitting at the kitchen table having coffee with her best friend, Betty Mullin. Betty looked at me and sort of gasped out, "Max, are you all right? You're as pale as a ghost." I waved the pages of my novella in the air and replied, "I guess all my blood is on these pages."

It was first published in 1962 in a beautifully printed San Francisco literary magazine: *Contact*. Its editorial board members included internationally recognized authors Evan Connell, Jr., Calvin Kentfield, Walter Van Tillburgh Clark, and William Carlos Williams. That's just about the best beginning a story could dream up. Then the next year (1963) it was reprinted by Houghton Mifflin as the title story in a collection of novellas. In the same collection, another example of my works of fiction that was inspired by a real incident is "My Pardner."

This one started way back in 1928. My father, W. B. Evans, founded Humble City—a town approximately halfway between Hobbs and Lovington in southeastern New Mexico's Lea County. A year later, the stock market crash of 1929 hit, and the next year the great dust bowl started forming. During all the following desperate years, he was trading in whatever came along to hold everything together—his family, his small ranch, and hopefully the struggling new town.

I was about ten years old—that would be around 1934—when he loaded me in his old car along with my saddle, blanket, and bridle and we drove down around Jal, the last little town in New Mexico, before entering the Big Bend Country of Texas. He had acquired a string of what looked like half-starved horses from a ranch there.

Upon our arrival, he introduced me to "an old cowboy friend" named Boggs. It took me a while to realize he had one ear and one eye. I only used the one eye in "My Pardner" to come from our introduction. We stood there in the corral while Boggs—the man with one ear, one eye, and one name—roped me out a horse and I saddled it. Then he roped himself out one and put my dad's bridle on him. He rode him bareback around the corral.

My dad explained to me that Boggs and I were going to deliver these horses to Guymon, Oklahoma, by a certain date and hour where he and his auctioneer uncle, Pit Emory, would be waiting to hold a big horse sale. He said we would have to get them there looking better than they did now. I thought to myself that if they weren't dead the last chore would be a cinch. He handed me three dollars (I'm sure that's all he had) for my total expenses, saying that Boggs would know how to find feed for the horses. And away we went with Boggs on point, bareback. I wondered how a man could be called a cowboy and not own a saddle. Well, I found out a couple of days later when he talked me out of mine.

I held this story inside me until the entire trip turned into one of my own favorite pieces of tragicomedy in the novella form: "My Pardner." It was fictionalized many years later (1961), written and finished about three months before "The One-Eyed Sky." I still recall the way my dad said "Guymon, Oklahoma," as if it was almost in sight already. To that little kid, that day, he might as well have said the sale would be in Singapore, and the way we zig-zagged across the huge West Texas landscape hunting feed for those starved horses, it might as well have been.

About 1998, Joe Lansdale, a writer of southern mysteries with fine humor, asked me to do something for a collection titled *The New Frontier*. I admired Joe and his work so I agreed to come up with something. But what? Simply, "The Mare." Like "The One-Eyed Sky," I had been fascinated by another "old" story. Instead of an old coyote, an old cow, and an old cow-boy coming together, this one was about an old mare who had survived for more than thirty years alone in the vast Gila Wilderness and Black Range area of southwest New Mexico.

I knew the ranch—the F Cross and its owner, my close friend Jimmy Bason—where the mare had roamed a great part of those years. I also knew his skilled foreman, cowboy Randy Lindsey. They had both seen her many times through the years, and Randy had been close enough to her—always by accident—to see the revealing sets of scars she carried that could only have been put there by a bear or a mountain lion.

As close as I ever came to seeing her was spotting her splayed and cracked tracks in the dirt while prospecting for minerals, but I knew there was a major piece of animal fiction here if I could muster the talent to put it together. So the fact that she existed was true, but how she survived had to come from my own imagination.

Finally, I set it down in three passionate, draining sessions. A week later, I read it and was elated. Over the years I had a few people whose opinion I respected call or write to tell me that it was the best animal story they had ever read. Whether it was or not, at least they thought so, and I couldn't help but feel vindicated in my respectful awe at the old mare sur-viving all alone for thirty-three years in an extremely lonely, violent, harsh environment.

Some stories just happen and the urge to share them with someone is overwhelming, but instead of talking about it, I put it on paper. Such was another tale I became obsessed with in Hillsboro, New Mexico. It was related to me firsthand, incident by incident, over a considerable period of time, by a rancher's wife, Sue Bason of the F Cross. Every time she told bits of it, she laughed out loud. I couldn't resist writing it.

I had been over a lot of the rough country where her husband, Jimmy, had pursued this bull from the time it was quite small to when it was really big. Sue casually asked him one day, "What's on your menu for today, Jimmy? Running Super Bull all over the Black Range or taming that colt out in the corral?" That did it. The title "Super Bull" had to be filled out with words.

I never labored any harder to get a story correct. It all worked out. *Southern Horseman* magazine grabbed it up and did profuse illustrations in 1985. It became the favorite of my short nonfiction and even the title story for a book. One film director, Bud Cardos, also became obsessed with it, blocking out every scene even before a script was done. He had just directed a very low-budget horror hit, *Kingdom of the Spiders,* and was sure he could put this together, but as film projects do more often than not, he left it for another offer with a guaranteed paycheck. I was used to this kind of happenstance.

Hollywood and its massive film industry had popped into our lives in 1960 with the novel *The Rounders* and is still there today. We made many wonderful friends, had marvelous fun, and added lots of varied work experiences to our world. Two of the stories in this collection, the novellas "The One-Eyed Sky" and "My Pardner," had been optioned over and over by major directors and producers: Sam Peckinpah, Buzz Kullick, Tom Gries, Burt Kennedy, Marvin Schwartz, David Dortort, Saul David, and others. Some of the actors that at one time or another—some multiple times— wanted to play the lead in either one were Lee Marvin, Brian Keith, Henry Fonda, Robert Culp, Gregory Peck, Morgan Woodward, and Slim Pickens. L. Q. Jones—actor, writer, director—recently said to a crowd at a Western Writers of America convention that he had spent his entire creative life trying to figure out how to do a script from "The One-Eyed Sky."

Beginning in the mid-eighties, 1985, to be exact, I wrote some of my best nonfiction short pieces. One of them, "Showdown at Hollywood Park," came about indirectly when I became a close friend of the once-famous racehorse trainer Lyo Lee. He had news clippings, photos, and personal correspondence on the events of this story, as well as official records on what was a famous race of the time. Lyo had trained the winner, and he slowly revealed the tricks he had used to bring off the biggest win of his life. This story was enlightening, exciting, and, above all, fun to research and write.

In 2004–2007, I wrote some true stories of novella length, based on personal experiences as a kid and a young man. These events had been an obsession of mine over a long, long period of my life. One was "The World's Strangest Creature," and I was a full participant. I was probably eight or nine years old when a traveling show came to Humble City, New Mexico. This barker was hypnotic in his practiced spiel, and he got the last pennies I had in the world. But . . . I did learn a couple of things: to listen carefully to a colorful con and then enjoy it if I was dumb enough to take the hook.

From this same period in my life came another true story, "Cricket," but I didn't write it until around 2007 to fill out the collection of horse stories titled *For the Love of a Horse*. Cricket was the first horse I'd ever owned. He afforded me the transportation and skills to hunt and harvest the small game of far southeastern New Mexico to help feed our family and that of Aunt Pearl, my father's widowed sister with five young stairstepped daughters, during a combination of the Great Depression and the severe drought of the 1930s. This little pony helped so many people survive that I still see and smell his sweat like I'd last ridden him this morning. Even as I'm scribbling right here, I still love and miss Cricket as much as any mother would her firstborn.

During the same time period, when I was twelve, another horse was imprinted indelibly on my mind and soul: a golden sorrel who inspired the story called "Flax." This nonfiction piece was also written for the collection *For the Love of a Horse*.

Flax, in actuality, belonged to Ed Young—my first cow boss up on the vast Glorieta Mesa just south of Santa Fe and east-southeast of Lamy. I had found my first away-from-home job up there on the Rafter EY at the hard-to-jingle sum of seventy-five cents a day. Two years later I was advanced to thirty bucks a month and found that even though Ed Young thought he owned this beautiful great working sorrel, Flax and I, little Max Evans, knew better.

The fiction piece "Old Bum" (published in the *South Dakota Review* in 1993 but placed in my memory box about 1942) includes a short, true scene involving two hunters, several hunting hounds, and a mother coyote and her young pups—an event that changed my life forever. After observing this animal action I could never hunt another coyote, much less kill one. I was derided by some people who said this little event was against all the rules of nature and could never happen. It *was* against all the rules, but it *did* happen. In those days my eyesight was 20/20. This little incident only increased my love and respect for the massive magic of all animals from a mouse to a moose.

Finally, about the year 2000, I decided it was time to gather up a collection of other writers' stories—the other writers being genuine working ranch men and women of the contemporary West. It was to be written half and half by real cowgirls and real cowboys. The director of the University of New Mexico Press, Luther Wilson, liked the idea and gave the go-ahead. It had taken me several years to get most of the men whose lives and writing skills qualified, but I only knew one woman writer and had only one other prospect. I was failing in my dream. Then, in one of those magical moments in life when things somehow work out, I called Candy Moulton of a ranch near Encampment, Wyoming. To my great relief she agreed to help. Not only did this fine writer and maker of documentary films deliver the rest of the women, she also gathered the missing cowboy to complete a volume that I'm still enormously proud of titled *Hot Biscuits*.

Now I had to come up with a story of my own to add to this collection. Thus, "Once a Cowboy" was written. (It was included in the *Hot Biscuits* collection in 2002 and was republished in a 2007 collection titled *Best Stories of the American West,* edited by Marc Jaffe—an editor I deeply admire. He had long before published the first Bantam paperback edition of *The Rounders* in 1965.)

"Once a Cowboy" was inspired by events that happened when I was a very young man, surviving as the owner of a small ranch in the Hi-Lo Country way back in about 1941. A distant cousin, Hooter Mudd, who had cowboyed for years on the Cross L on the southern Colorado border, came to see me with a "cowboy plan." He had used up all his meager cowboy savings and credit to purchase a remuda of locoed horses. He wanted me to help him drive them across the far northeast border of New Mexico, through part of Colorado, and into the Oklahoma panhandle to a stock farm in Kansas where he thought he had them sold. Of course, he would cut me in on the vast profits. I fell for it.

Now, what I planned to do for my part of the *Hot Biscuits* collection was take this misadventure and combine it with others I had personally experienced on a ranch or in town, then add a couple of wrecks by close friends and write a piece about the shared hardships, failures, and successes of these cowboys. I had enough material here for three novellas, but I needed to condense it all into a single short story. I not only wanted to display the life of a real modern cowboy; above all, I wanted to show the wondrous camaraderie that I'd witnessed only among people who lived with and by animals of the soil. I had a plot that included real cowboying, crazy horses and other animals, and the often humorous camaraderie of cowboys, a love story, and some wild adventures in the border city of El Paso. The perfect plot for a novel. I told Candy Moulton that I had just written the world's shortest novel of the West for our collection. I feel today I brought it off in comparatively few words.

In my long trek with the written word, I have written about all nationalities of humans exactly as I had known and became friends and sometimes associates with them. That aspect of my life was fulfilled in nonfiction with "Equine Montage," about the horses and cows my wife, Pat, and I, were deeply involved with, as well as those of a few close friends.

The stories in this collection that begin on page 233 with *The World's Strangest Creature* on to the wrap-up piece *The Horse Who Wrote the Stories* are true adventures that helped form me into whatever person I am as a writer of fiction.

Having been fortunate enough to survive uncountable life experiences, I had all the material I could ever possibly scribble in a thousand odd years.

I did become aware early on that the main difference between true stories and fiction was simply this: fiction sometimes allows you to reveal a greater truth.

Yes, animals, with their beauty and magic, are deeply engrained in all of my writing—and in all my living. I give thanks daily for the food and revelations I've received from these creatures so precious to us all.

MAX EVANS

Animal Stories

The Old One

The grass was short, but growing a fine, virginal green, now that the rain had begun to take effect. It had been cool and windy for some days, the flecked sky racing shadows across the earth. Now the sun was coming through again. The clouds were edging off to the far horizons.

The old prairie dog, a lone figure in the enveloping warmth, sniffed the air for the last time. She beckoned to her young to come forth. Two small heads jerked into sight, beady-eyed, motionless. Suddenly they were on top, scampering about with quick, short jumps. It was their third time above.

The Old One bellied down, watching them patiently as they chased through the curious world. It was her fifth litter. They had so much to learn in so short a time. They must beware of the enemies. The enemies who rode the horses and drove cattle before them. A short time back they had thundered over their home. The ground had quivered under the trampling of a thousand hoofs, and part of the den had fallen in. At first she had thought her young were injured, but out of the dust they had crawled, scared but unharmed.

She shifted her weight, grunted. Her eyes still followed them as she lay head to the ground. The young ones were picking up the track of some new bauble in a clump of grass.

She stretched her flattened form, sighing comfortably in the sun. The hay she had stored away the fall before had made her milk rich and nourishing. They were rolling with fat and bursting with energy.

Soon she would begin teaching them what all young prairie dogs must learn in order to survive. They would have to learn how to cut grass with their sharp teeth. There were small holes to be dug and dirt to be carried. The Old One would show them how to weave the blades of bear grass into mounds of dirt that walled their cavelike homes. The grass would act as a binder, keeping the mounds intact so that the summer cloudbursts would have no way of running into the holes. The young would also have to learn to store grass hay for the long winter ahead. All this was important and necessary. With two as bright and healthy as these, she would have no trouble.

Yet all this was as nought in the face of that one terrifying threat. Old One raised her head, sniffing the air. They were safe for the time being. It was not now as it had been before—many times before—when the two-legged enemy had suddenly borne down upon them. She even would not now be alive if she hadn't known how to disappear into the secret depths of the earth at the first approach of this being whose smell was danger itself.

It was midsummer now, and the days long and hot. The young were more than half grown. In a few days, she would start each of them on a hole of his own. It would then be time to start putting up hay for the winter. She would help them with this task this one summer. The next spring she would have another litter and they would need her undivided attention.

While this was going through the Old One's mind, a figure was crawling slowly and stealthily closer. Suddenly, a warning chatter came from one of the neighboring home holes. With a staccato bark at her young, she dived into the hole. The hole dropped in a fast vertical fall for about eighteen inches. There was a flat place to land before it descended at an easy angle down into the living and grass storage space. Crack. Crack! Crack! Three times the stick spoke, filling the air with the deadly acrid smell. Her heart stood still with terror. There was not long to wait—all were safe. They were learning fast. She felt the ground quiver slightly as the two-legged being came close to examine the hole.

For two days, she didn't come out of the hole. She grew sick with fear for this being, so cunning, so relentless, with whom she had no power to contend except her own awareness.

For weeks after that, the Old One dared venture out to the terrifying upper world only for a few moments at a time. She gathered just enough food for her young ones and a mite for herself. She was starving slowly.

The time to store hay for the cold winter ahead was long overdue but the Old One could not conquer her fear long enough to work at it. Tragedy had been much too close to her young ones. The slightest rustle or off-scent would fill her with trembling terror. She would go scurrying down into the dark hole.

She fought her fear one day after a spring shower. Coming to the top, she worked desperately packing down a new mound. It would bake in the sun to a concretelike hardness, protecting their den from another cloudburst. For this work she did not have to venture far. She felt tremulously safe.

She was aloft some weeks after that, foraging for their food, when she saw the enemy in the distance. She remained for a moment, tensed, watching them. Suddenly she saw they were riding this way again, with cattle.

They were closer now. Down in their hole, Old One crouched in terror, the young ones nuzzling up close. The thundering came nearer and nearer. They were overhead now. The walls quivered. Dust and a few small pebbles showered down into the living room.

The Old One stayed below for two days as she had done before. Weakness and hunger finally drove her to the top. Her small head appeared at the opening, cautiously. She listened for perhaps five minutes. Her nostrils worked busily on a faint, familiar scent.

The hole mound had been ripped off on one side, taking some of the earth with it. A horse's hoof had evidently struck there, tripping the animal.

The little ones sniffed curiously at the damaged mound while the Old One for the first time in almost two months foraged freely in the not unfriendly open. The top of the hole where she had packed the mud had held. They were all safe for now, but there was more knowledge for the young to gain yet. There was the coyote and the bobcat who would hide in the grass or bushes and wait until the prairie dogs were hard at work, then they would dash in with fangs bared. The Old One, wise in her ways, showed the young how to clip the grass near the hole so nothing could hide, and then too, they must never dig near the clumps of speared yucca for that was a favorite hiding place for the coyote.

Once, an eagle dived from the blue sky, claws outstretched. The Old One saw this just in time to chatter a warning to her young ones.

They learned by doing and by experience and were growing into husky, healthy specimens. At the least sign of danger all would scatter to the top of the hole and form a circle so they could watch in all directions. The last golden days of fall were upon them. The Old One watched her young as they carried the grass hay to their own homes. Her job was well done. They would someday have families of their own and the Old One knew they were capable of handling the job.

She reared on her hindquarters and let out a happy chatter. The earth lay peacefully about them.

The One-Eyed Sky

1

The cow lifted her muzzle from the muddy water of the tank. She must go now. Her time was at hand. She could feel the pressure of the unborn between her bony hips. With the springless clicking tread of an old, old cow she moved out toward the rolling hills to find a secluded spot for the delivery.

It was late July and the sun seared in at her about an hour high. The moistureless dust turned golden under her tired hoofs as the sun poured soundless beams at each minute particle of the disturbed earth. The calf was late—very late. But this being her eighth and last she was fortunate to have conceived and given birth at all.

The past fall the cowhands had missed her hiding place in the deep brush of the mesas. If found she would have been shipped as a canner, sold at bottom prices and ground into hamburger or Vienna sausage. Not one of the men would have believed she could make the strenuous winter and still produce another good whiteface calf. She had paid the ranch well, this old cow . . . seven calves to her credit. Six of them survived to make the fall market fat and profitable. The coyotes took her first one. But she had learned from that.

She turned from the cow trail and made her way up a little draw. Instinct guided her now as the pressure mounted in her rear body. It was a good place she found with the grass still thick on the draw and some little oak brush for shade the next sweltering day. The hills mounted gradually on three sides and she would have a downgrade walk the next morning to the water hole. She had not taken her fill of water, feeling the urgency move in her.

She found her spot and the pain came and the solid lump dropped from her. It had not taken long. She got up, licked the calf clean, and its eyes came open to see the world just as the sun sank. It would be long hours now before the calf would know other than the night.

It was a fine calf, well boned and strong, good markings. In just a little while she had it on its feet. The strokes of her tongue waved the thick red hair all over. With outspread legs it wobbled a step and fell. She licked some more. Again the calf rose and this time faltered its way to the bag swelled tight with milk.

The initial crisis was over, but as the old cow nudged the calf to a soft spot to bed it down, her head came up and she scented the air. Something was there. As the calf nestled down with its head turned back against its shoulder, the old cow turned, smelling, straining her eyes into the darkness. There was a danger there. Her calf was not yet safe. Nature intended her to eat the afterbirth, but now there would be no chance. She stood deeply tired, turning, watching, waiting.

2

The coyote howled and others answered in some far-distant canyon. It was a still night. The air was desert dry. It made hunting difficult. It takes moisture to carry and hold a scent. Her four pups took up the cry, hungry and anxious to prey into the night.

She, too, was old and this, her fourth litter, suffered because of it. She was not able to hunt as wide or as well as in past years. The ribs pushed through the patched hair on all the pups. They moved about, now and then catching the smell of a cold rabbit trail. Two of the pups spotted prairie mice and leaped upon them as they would a fat fowl, swallowing the rodents in one gulp. It helped, but still they all felt the leanness and the growling of their bellies.

The old coyote turned over a cow chip and let one of the pups eat the black bugs underneath. They could survive this way, but their whole bodies ached for meat.

They moved up to the water hole as all living creatures of the vast area did. The old one had circled carefully, hoping to surprise a rabbit drinking. But there was none. They had already worked the water hole many times before with some success, but now its banks were barren. They took the stale water into themselves to temporarily alter the emptiness.

The old one smelled the tracks of the cow, hesitating, sniffing again. Then she raised her head to taste the air with her nostrils. The pups all stood motionless, heads up, waiting. There was a dim scent there. Not quite clear. The distance was too far, but there was a chance for meat. A small one indeed, but in these hard times the mother could not afford to pass any opportunity. With head dropping now and then to delineate the trail of the old cow, the old coyote moved swiftly, silently followed by four hungry pups copying her every move.

3

Eight miles to the north a cowboy sixty-years-old, maybe seventy— he had long ago forgotten— scraped the tin dishes, washed them briefly, and crawled in his bunk against the line camp wall. He was stiff and he grunted as he pulled the blanket over his thin eroded body. The night was silent and he thought.

Outside a horse stood in the corral. A saddle hung in a small shed. In the saddle scabbard was a .30-30 for killing varmints. If he had a good day and found no sign of strays in the mighty expanse of the south pasture he could ride on into headquarters the day after next to company of his own kind. It really didn't matter to him so much except the food would be better and the bed a little softer. That was about all he looked forward to now. Tomorrow he, too, would check the water hole for signs. He slept.

4

She couldn't see them, but they were there. Their movement was felt and the scent was definite now. She moved about nervously, her stringy muscles taut and every fiber of her being at full strain. When they had come for her firstborn she had fought them well, killing one with a horn in its belly and crippling two more. But finally they had won. The calf—weak as all first calves are—had bled its life into the sand of the gully. She had held the pack off for hours until she knew the calf was dead and then the call from the blood of those to come had led her away to safety. It had been right. All her other calves, and the one resting beside her now, had been strong, healthy.

The scars showed still where they had tried to tear the ligaments from her hocks in that first battle long ago; she had been sore and crippled for weeks. A cowboy had lifted his gun to relieve her misery. But another had intervened. They roped her and threw her to the ground. They spread oil on her wounds and she recovered.

She whirled about, nostrils opening wide from the wind of her lungs. Her horns automatically lowered, but she could see nothing. She was very thirsty and her tongue hung from the side of her mouth. She should have taken on more water, but the enemy would have caught her during the birth and that would have been the end. She would have to be alert now, for her muscles had stiffened with age and the drive and speed she had in her first battle were almost gone. Then too, in the past, many parts of nature, of man and animal enemy had attacked her.

In her fourth summer, during a cloudburst when the rains came splashing earthward like a lake turned upside down, a sudden bolt of lightning had split the sky, ripping into a tree and bouncing into her body. She had gone down with one horn split and scorched. Three other cows fell dead near her. For days she carried her head slung to one side and forgot to eat. But she lived.

Later she had gotten pinkeye and the men had poured salt into her eye to burn out the disease.

And she had become angry once while moving with a herd in the fall roundup. She had been tired of these mounted creatures forever crowding her. She kept cutting back to the shelter of the oak brush and finally she turned back for good, raking the shoulder of the mighty horse. The mounted man cursed and grabbed his rope. She tore downhill, heading for the brush, her third calf close at her side. She heard the pounding of the hooves and the whirr of the rope. Deliberately she turned and crashed through a barbed-wire fence, ripping a bone-deep cut across her brisket. In that moment the man roped her calf and dismounted to tie its feet. She heard the bawling, whirled, charged at the man. She caught him with her horn just above the knee as he tried to dodge. She whirled to make another pass and drive the horns home. Then another man rode at her and the evil, inescapable snake of a rope sailed from his arm and encircled her neck. Three times he turned off, jerking her up high and then down hard into the earth, tearing her breath from her body until she stood addled and half blind. Then they stretched her out again and turned her loose. She had learned her lesson hard. During the stiff winters and wet spells she limped where the shoulder muscles had been torn apart.

But the worst winter of all was when the snow fell two feet deep and crusted over, isolating the herd miles from the ranch house. During the dry summer they had walked twice as far as usual to find the short shriveled grass. She and the others had gone into the winter weak and their bellies dragged in the drifts. When they tried to walk on top of the white desert the crust broke and they went down struggling, breathing snow and cold into their lungs, sapping their small strength. The icy crust cut their feet and they left red streaks in the whiteness. And the wind came driving through their long hair, coating their eyes and nostrils with ice. They'd wandered blindly, piling into deep drifts, perishing.

Finally the wagons—pulled by those same horses she had hated so much—broke through the snow. They tailed her up and braced her and got some hay into her mouth. Once more she survived.

The old cow had a past and it showed in her ragged, bony, tired, bent, scarred body. And it showed in her ever-weakening neck as the head dropped a fraction lower each time she shook her defiance at the night and the unseen enemy.

The moon came now and caressed the land with pale blueness. It was like a single, headless, phosphorescent eye staring at the earth seeing all, acknowledging nothing. The moon made shadows and into these she stared and it would seem to move and then she would ready herself for the attack. But it didn't come. Why did they wait?

The night was long and the moon seemed to hang for a week, then the sun moved up to the edge of the world, chasing the moon away.

Her tongue was pushed out farther now and her eyes were glazed, but she stood and turned and kept her guard. She saw the old, mangy coyote directly down the draw facing her, sitting up on its haunches panting, grinning, waiting. It took her a while to see the pups. They were spotted about the hills, surrounding her. But these did not worry her. They would not move until the old one did. Nevertheless, she cast her dimming eyes at them, letting them know she knew—letting them know she was ready.

The calf stirred and raised its head and found the glorious world. First it must feed. She moved swiftly to it, watching the old coyote as she did so. The new one struggled up, finding its way to the teat. The cow saw the muscles tense all over the old coyote. Its head tilted forward as did its pointed ears. Then it moved from side to side, inching closer at each turn. The pups got to their feet, ready for the signal. But it didn't come. The old coyote retreated. It was a war of nerves. And because the coyote fights and dies in silence, when the time arrived there would be no signal visible to the cow, only to the pups.

Now the calf wanted to explore. It wanted to know into what it had been born. Already the color and the form of plant and rock and sky were things of wonder. There was so much to see and so little time for it. Again the mother bedded down her calf—a heifer it was—and soon the warm air and full stomach comforted it.

By midmorning the coyote had faked ten charges. And ten times the cow had braced to take the old one first and receive and bear the rear and flanking attacks until she could turn and give contest. She knew from the past they would all hit her at once, diving, feinting, tearing from all sides. But if she could keep the calf from being mortally wounded until she disposed of the old one they had a chance. But with each rise in temperature, with each drying, burning moment of the sun without water, her chances lessened.

By noon the heat was almost blinding her. She felt the trembling and faltering in her legs. All the old wounds were making themselves known now and her tongue hung down, parched and beginning to swell. Her breathing came hard and heavy. The nostrils caked from the powdered dirt of her restlessness and her eyes filled around the edges and watered incessantly. But the coyote waited. And so did the old cow. Life had always been a matter of waiting—waiting for the calf each year, waiting for the greenness of spring, waiting for the wind to die and the cold to quit and the snow to melt. But, win or lose, she would never see another spring. They would find her this fall and ship her away to the slaughterhouse. And if they didn't, the winter, the inexorable winter winds, would drive through her old bones and finish her. But now she had a chore, a life-and-death chore for sure. She would do her natural best.

In the middle of the afternoon she imagined she could smell the water, so near and yet so far away. She bawled out of her nearly closed throat and the tongue was black, and down the other side of her mouth thick cotton-like strings of saliva hung and evaporated in the interminable heat. Her legs had gradually spread apart and she wove from side to side, taking all her strength now just to stand. And right in the pathway to the water sat the laughing coyote, beginning to move back and forth again, closer. Closer. As the sun moved lower and lower, so the coyote came nearer, lying down, looking straight at her.

The coyote lay very still, nothing moving but the pink tongue. Yellow eyes watching, glowing like suns. Ten minutes. Twenty minutes. The coyote came from the ground without warning, straight in and fast. The cow knew the others were coming, too. She braced herself.

5

The mother coyote followed the trail into scent range of the old cow. Her nostrils told her of the new one. Cautiously she moved up now, almost like a cat. The young tried mightily to do as well. It was no use. The quick, intense movement of the cow revealed her knowledge of their presence. They would have to wait. Methodically she went about spotting her young. She ringed the old cow in, giving soundless directions to her pups to stay put.

The scent of birth, the calf, the old cow brought taste glands into action. The natural impulse was to attack as their stomachs drew narrow and craving. But the coyote could tell from the alertness of the old cow that an early assault would be sure death to some. The hours would be long but the cow would weaken. Much of the moisture had been drained from her body in the birth. The sun would be their ally. They could have the early luxurious feast of the tender veal, and the lean meat of the old cow would last for days—even with the vultures and the magpies to contend with. She could fatten and strengthen the pups and make them ready for mating as her mother had done her. Yes, her mother had been a good teacher and she had learned well. She had been taught to hunt under rotten logs, cow chips, and anthills for insects in case of hard times. The field mouse had often saved her from starvation. The lowly grasshopper had filled her belly many times and given her strength to catch larger, tastier game. She learned to steal into a hen yard, to make a quick dash, throttling the fowl and escaping before the rancher could get his guns. All of these things she had taught or was teaching her own. But now must come the ultimate lesson—how to down and kill an animal weighing as much as fifteen of their own kind. Besides, they were desperate in their near starvation.

The old coyote took the main chance in locating herself in the path of the water hole. This was the weak point and she must handle it with care, cunning, and courage. She could not fail, for they too would weaken in the long vigil.

She carried a .30-30 slug in her belly from the past. She only felt it on cold or hungry nights. Her tail was shortened and ugly at the end. Her ear was split and torn. A scar ran across her back. One foot was minus two toes.

The ear and tail wounds had come about at the same time. She had learned a hard lesson from this action. She was almost grown then and hunted with the rest of the litter. They had stopped behind a clump of bear grass, watching the pickup truck circle slowly. They had seen these things before, but no danger had threatened. Suddenly the thing stopped. From its back dropped six large, running hounds. Two teams.

The coyotes moved out too late. Instinct split them in three directions. But the hounds had their speed, and in less than a quarter of a mile each team had downed one of the brood. She alone escaped. On a little rise she whirled watching the hounds bear down on her brother and sister, crushing the life away with their awful fanged jaws. She sailed down from the hill and at full speed crashed into the nearest team, knocking them loose and giving her brother a chance to rise. But it didn't work. Two of the hounds flung the wounded one against the earth again. The third gave chase. She strained away in terror, knowing she could not compete with its size and strength. The hound reached for her throat but missed her and ripped the ear apart instead. They both rolled in a choking spurt of dust. As she rose, the hound clamped her tail. She broke free leaving a humiliating part of herself in his jaws. The chase was more uphill now, and she learned that hounds slowed on that sort of run and never again was she caught on the level or going downhill. She escaped. Alive. Wiser. Alone.

She learned to respect the metallic wheeled things for another reason. She had watched one from a safe distance, as far as hounds were concerned, and suddenly a black something stuck from it and then something struck her in the belly, knocking her over and down. It had been close. She bled badly inside and by the time the bleeding clotted she was very weak from hunger. All that saved her was the finding of a wounded antelope dragging itself into the tall grass of the prairie to die. But now she could smell a gun from a considerable distance. They would not hurt her again in this manner.

Her first sister had eaten poison and died before her eyes. They would not slay her in this vile way, either.

The scar on her back had come from one of those men who whirl the rope and ride horses. She was looking in a sheep pasture for a lamb to carry to her first litter of pups. She was so intent on her job she did not see the cowboy coming through the gate some half mile distant. But as he neared

---

she felt him even before she cast her glance back over her shoulder. He came on full speed on a fast quarter horse, whirling the rope. She did not know what it was, but she felt its danger as she did that of a gun. He was upon her and she heard the whirr of the rope mingled with the ground-jarring thump of hooves. She hit the many-wired sheep fence without slacking speed. She went through, tearing her back on the vicious barbs. Her neck was sore and twisted for many days. But she lived to hunt again.

The worst of all were the steel jaws the men put in the earth. Once, when she had been hungry, the scent of hog cracklings, and also the urine of one of her own, came to her. Bait. This gave her the confidence to inspect even though the faint scent of man was intermingled. The jaws had grabbed her as she vainly leaped away. She struck the end of the chain where it ran up out of the ground and tightened between the trap and the heavy rock that anchored it. She fought wildly and in great pain for a while, gnawing at her foot until exhaustion stilled her violent action.

She studied the rusty, hard, impersonal steel. It had her. But if she was to die she would do it on the mesa—her home. Foot by painful foot, yard by wrenching yard, she dragged the rock. The man had intended her to hang the trap in some brush flexible enough to keep from tearing the foot loose. It hung, all right, hundreds of times, but never for long.

It took her two days to get to the edge of the mesa. The foot was swollen almost to the knee joint now and her yellow eyes were red from suffering. Then the stone hung between a crack in the rocks. She fell off the other side and rolled down the rough boulders. The trap and a part of her foot remained in the rocks.

She lived again, less able than before.

Under the recent rising of the staring moon the coyote studied the old cow. It was obvious she was weakening. Soon she would lie down and then . . . But the old cow stood and at the break of day she suckled her young, looking straight at the coyote and shaking her head in answer to the coyote's slavering jaws.

The coyote moved in now, taunting, teasing, draining another ounce of strength from the old cow.

The sun came soon, hot and red, striking the old cow in the side of her head. The pups squatted and waited with hunger pounding at their every nerve.

By midday the old coyote could feel the muscles trembling and jerking with weakness in her forelegs and the stomach walls seemed glued together, devouring themselves. She now badly needed water and food. At times the earth diffused into the molten rays of the sun and it looked as if the cow had dissolved. At other moments she bunched her muscles imagining the cow attacking. She sat with her tongue out and an eternal laughing expression in all her face except the eyes. They seared through the sun's rays, hungrily, with a quiet desperation and sureness.

The old cow's head was dropping now. She was slipping fast. But still she stood and every time the coyote moved in her snake-track advance the cow raised her head a little and tossed the pointed swords.

There was no backing out now. No changing of plans. The old mother coyote and her brood would soon be so weakened they would surely fall prey to one of their many worldly enemies. Survival now meant the death of the old cow.

The coyote drew in its dry tongue and dropped it again into the dry air and waited. The sun moved on and the old cow's legs spread a little more. The coyote could see her weaving and straining to stay upright. The tender, living veal of the calf lay folded up beside her.

Now the time was present. She sent her message of alertness to her pups. They stood ready, watching, muscles bunched, hearts pounding above the strain of hunger, thirst, and heat. She moved forward and lay down to deceive the old cow. Motionless she waited and waited more. All of her being cried to lunge forward, but still she waited. She had decided on the cow's muzzle. She would dart in between the horns, locking her fangs in their breathing softness, and hang on until the aid of her pups downed the old cow. Then? It would be over shortly. A bit torn here and there and the loss of blood would finish her. Then the feast.

The burning eyes of the old coyote and the old cow were fixed on each other now. They both knew what they must do. The old coyote sent the unseen, unmoving signal to her pups and she came from the ground at the same instant, aiming straight and swift between the horns of the old cow.

6

The man arose from the bunk as stiffly as he had crawled into it. It was not quite daybreak. He clothed himself and pulled hard to get his boots on. He built a fire in the squatty iron stove and put the coffeepot on. Then he washed his face and hands in cold water. He placed a skillet on the stove by the coffeepot. Methodically he sliced thick chunks of bacon from the hog side. He took the last of the sourdough batter, tore small balls from it, placing them in a dutch oven on the stove. This done he rolled a smoke, coughing after the first puff. Soon he had a large tin cup of scalding coffee. Another cigarette, another cup. Then he ate. He wiped up the syrup on his plate with his bread. He washed the utensils and put them back on the shelf. He, or someone else, would be here another time. He went out to the corral.

If he was lucky this day and found no strays he could head for the main ranch house tomorrow morning, or if the moon was good he might ride on in tonight. He had two horses here. One ran in a small horse trap adjoining the corrals. The other he had kept up for the ride today.

He brushed his horse's back with his hand and under his belly where the cinches would fit to be sure nothing was lodged in the hair that would cut or stick. He bridled and saddled, put on his chaps and spurs, and led the horse up a few steps before mounting. He rode him around the corral several times to limber him up. Then he dismounted, opened the gate, got back on, and rode south just as the sun was melting the night.

It was eight miles in a beeline to the water hole. If there were a stray in the huge pasture it would be nearby. He would probably have a twelve-mile ride, what with checking out the sign in the draw and gullies.

The sun was up now, hot for so early in the morning. It was the kind of day that made all living creatures seek shade. Well, he had always wanted a little place with lots of shade trees and water. Especially water. It wouldn't matter how big it was if there was just plenty of water. He would never forget the drought that had sent his family to the final sheriff's sale and moved them from their ranch into a tent on the edge of the little western town to take other folks' laundry, charity, handouts. His pa had already loaned him out to local ranchers. So he just took a steady job with one of them. At first he worked only for his board and blanket. He gardened, he milked, he shov-eled manure out of barns. He patched roofs. He rebuilt corrals. He chopped a whole year's supply of firewood. He ran rabbits in holes and twisted them out with the split end of a barbed wire.

And then the drought was over and the grass and cattle came back to the land. He was promoted to horse wrangler, which only meant one more chore. He was up before anyone in the morning riding into the horse pas-ture, bringing in the day's mounts for the cowboys. But things finally got better. His boss saw him top out a waspy bronc and he was allowed to ride with the men. He got five dollars a month and felt proud. Mighty proud. He learned the ways of the range and the handling of cattle and horses. And at the age of seventeen he could draw down twenty dollars a month with room and board. By the time he had worked on ten or twelve different outfits and reached the age of twenty-five he could demand and get thirty dollars a month. Things weren't all bad.

Then a fellow cowboy with a talent for talk convinced him they were in the wrong business.

"Now look here, Snake" (that was his name at the time from being bitten by a rattlesnake), "we're makin' thirty dollars a month, right?"

"Yeah."

"Well, how much you figure a broke-out saddle horse would bring?"

"Oh, 'round thirty, forty dollars."

"There you are. Now, if a man could ride out say eight or ten a month?"

"I'll have to get a pencil. Besides, where you goin' to get that many horses and how much you got to give for them?"

"That's just the deal. Up north in the rough country there's hundreds of wild horses. Now, I had some experience at catching them boogers when I was a kid. We're crazier than hell stayin' around here when we can get rich on our own."

So he took all he had—two hundred and ten dollars, two head of saddle horses, one saddle, and four used ropes—and moved north with the talkin' cowboy. The money went fast. It was used to buy pack mules and supplies.

They pitched camp and started riding the hills and canyons for sign. The horses were there, all right. But a man could ride all day and never actually see anything but tracks. They were wilder than deer by a whole lot. So the two cowboys set to work building brush corral traps in the narrow part of some canyons on the trail to the watering places. Then they built a round pole corral near camp to break the horses out. It took some wild reckless riding to pen these animals but pen some of them they did. Then they found the horses fought like bobcats and it took some doing just to get a rope on one and snub him up. It was impossible to drive them, so they tied a twisted rawhide garter on one leg. The circulation was cut off and the leg became numb and useless. It wasn't so hard to handle them then.

That was only the beginning of their troubles. When they castrated the studs, half of them died. Most of the rest lost their spirit and became dead-headed and listless.

After a good try they drifted out of the rough country ahead of the winter snow. They had two half-broken mares. But it beat walking because without them that's exactly what they would be doing. Well, they went back—at thirty a month—to the cow-punching job they had left. He started saving again. Finally a rancher offered him a foreman's job at thirty-five a month and he could run as many head of his own cattle as he could acquire.

After a few months, when he had some cash to go on, he made his move. He began trading with the Mexicans. A few dollars down, a worn-out saddle, an old rifle, and so on were his barter goods. In three years he had built his herd up to sixty head of cows, twelve steers, and two bulls. They were a mixed lot and they were his, but the land they ranged on was not. He still couldn't figure why his boss had been so generous. Another thing he couldn't figure out was why the owner and two of his hands did so much riding without him. He didn't ask questions because it looked like a man would be a fool to tinker with good times. They were mighty scarce.

His boss sent him to a roundup over west at a neighboring ranch. His job was to check out any of their strays and deliver them back to the home range. It was a big outfit and the roundup went on for several days. The last of the work was done right at headquarters. The cowboys ate at the cook-house. There was a pretty little brown-headed girl doing the cooking. Fine tasty chuck it was. She was the owner's daughter, Nelda.

Well, he kept eyeballing her and she kept glancing back. He was pretty good-looking at that time . . . in a rough, healed-over way. The aging and scars of the tough life hadn't taken hold yet. On the last day before he started home with his gather he asked her for a date, and he damn near fainted when she accepted.

He borrowed a buggy and picked her up late Saturday afternoon. They went to a dance at the schoolhouse. She was all decked out in a long, flimsy, turquoise dress that hugged her up close around the waist and bosom. Her hair just sparkled like her brown eyes and that was like a fall sun striking new frost on a golden aspen leaf. He was so scared and so cockeyed proud that he danced every set with her, even though he had a heck of a time fending off the other cowboys.

About four o'clock in the morning a little before daybreak when the music was slow, he walked outside and leaned her up against the building. While the coyotes howled out in the prairie he pulled her up hard and said: "I . . . I love you. I sure do."

Although she didn't say anything she let him know how she felt with her arms and her eyes. Sweet.

They went steady then. His luck just kept running. He got into a poker game with a bunch of mining and timber men and won six thousand dollars. That was more money than he had seen all his life put together. He couldn't wait to get over and tell Nelda.

They rode together in the hills and he loved her and she loved him. He told her about the money and how it was not only burning a hole in his pocket but was burning right smack through his leg.

"Snake," she said, "you've got a good start on a herd and the Larking place is for sale. We wouldn't owe more than eighteen thousand."

Eighteen thousand dollars! It scared him. It was beyond him. He would never make it. He just couldn't take on a woman like her, the daughter of a big rancher, owing that kind of money.

Well, he got drunk in town and didn't show up for work. The boss fired him and told him to come and get his cows, at the same time he said there would be no hurry about it. Somehow it didn't make sense.

Snake stayed in town that fall and on into the winter trying to make up his mind what to do. In the meantime the money was going steadily out for whiskey and gambling.

The winter came and a blizzard hit. Most of his cattle walked off into deep drifts of snow and froze to death. By the time he sobered up it was spring and he was broke.

Then the law came and took him. His ex-boss was right there shaking his head and saying he couldn't believe it, after all he had done for him. They railroaded him and now he knew that he had been a blind and a cover-up for the rancher's thievery. He got a year and a day. After three dreary months inside the prison wall he planned to kill the man who sent him there, but then they put him out on the prison farm and he reasoned it wasn't worth it.

He didn't return to the home country for a long time after his release. Nelda married someone else and he kind of regretted he had been so undecided.

He tried a lot of things after that, plunging hard to come back—prospecting, timber leasing, nothing worked out. He was trying to keep from going back to punching cows. He took a job as a dude wrangler in Yellowstone Park. His natural friendliness, his knowledge of horses and everything attracted a lot of business. He had several chances to marry rich widows and cowboy-smitten girls. But he never could decide when the time came. He had heard that all was not roses and sweet violets with the rich dames. A man had to go around with his hand out all the time.

At last, though, he chose to take on this woman from St. Louis. She had come right out and told him she would buy and pay for a ranch, stock it in his name, and put some money in the bank in the same manner.

Then he got drunk in Pony, Montana, on bootleg whiskey. It poisoned him and he was laid up out of his head for sixty days. The doctors almost gave up on him. By the time he came to and acquired strength enough to walk and talk, the widow had disappeared. The wrangler who had taken his job ran off to Mexico with her. If only a man could ever make up his mind at the right time he would have this world singing his songs, he figured.

He kept trying and bumming around into one thing and another. He damned near starved. The years were beginning to show. Finally he returned to his old country and the only thing he really knew—punching cows. The wages were one hundred and twenty-five dollars a month and board. That was tops, as high as he could go in his profession. It was a job that took guts, natural skill, and understanding of the earth and its animals, both wild and domestic, though the present wages wouldn't buy as much as twenty dollars had in his youth. But there he was now riding the draws around the water hole looking for sign and finding none.

It was mid-afternoon and hot. If he turned back now he could make it in a little after dark, saddle a fresh horse, and go on into headquarters. It was three days till payday. He could take his check, go into town, buy a new pair of jeans, a new rope, maybe a new hat. If he was careful he might have enough left over to get a little drunk and maybe even play a little poker. He really needed a pair of new boots but anything worth working in cost between forty and fifty dollars so he would just have to wait till next pay-day—or the next.

He decided to go on and check the water hole just in case he had missed something. It would cost him another night in the line camp but, after all, what was one more night alone to him? He saw the usual sign of wildlife and was surprised to find the day-old tracks of a cow. One lonely cow. She must have strayed in here to calve, he thought. He could tell by the way her hooves splayed out and by the withered cracks around the edges that she was an old cow.

As he followed her tracks up the trail he noticed that a coyote and four pups had been ahead of him. Probably went right on, he thought, and then an uneasiness came over him. Man, it was hot. He pulled his hat back and wiped the sweat from his forehead and out of his narrow sun-washed eyes. The cow had turned off across a small ridge and he saw the tracks of the coyotes do the same. Pretty soon he felt the horse bunch under him. The head came up and the ears pitched forward. He thought he heard a sound, a cow bawling maybe, but he wasn't sure. He got down and tied the horse to a bush.

He removed the .30-30 from the scabbard and started easing forward. He was slow in his movement because of the stiffness from the long day in the saddle and many years of breaks and bruises. Then he was on his belly crawling forward feeling an excitement that he couldn't define. It was more than the hunter's blood surging now.

He raised up carefully from the side of a yucca plant. He saw the old cow first and then, slowly, one at a time, he located the coyotes. They hadn't seen or heard him yet because of the dryness and lack of wind.

He eased the rifle and sighted down it at the old mother coyote as she moved forward. Just as he started to pull the trigger she lay down right out in front of the old cow. For some reason strange to him he held his fire.

7

In the little hollow where the man, the coyotes, the cow, and her calf lay there was concentrated the most life for miles in every direction. Five miles to the north and west in the cedar- and piñon-covered hills twenty-six buzzards circled and lighted on the remains of a cow downed two days before by a mountain lion that lay now in the coolness of the rocks with a full belly; to the east another pack of coyotes was desperately stalking a herd of swift antelope with no luck at all.

A hawk circled curiously above the draw with the man and the animals, smelling meat. The land itself was covered sparsely with buffalo and grama grass and, everywhere, the yucca plants bayoneted the sky. Now and then in meandering, meaningless lines, the land was cut by wind and water erosion forming a rolling, twisted terrain that on the face of a man would have portrayed deep torment.

The man felt the trigger of the rifle with his finger. The hammer was thumbed back. His cheek lay hot and sweating along the stock. The sights were centered on the thin ribcage of the coyote lying so very still. He could tell by the torn, powdered earth around the old cow, standing, swaying so weakly with far-drooped head, that she had held them at bay a long number of hours now.

His eyes raised again and counted the pups. One shot would do it. He must have killed two or three hundred of these animals, these varmints, these predators. He was a good shot. He would not miss. His eyes were in the second sight that comes briefly to older men. He could see almost as good as he could at twenty-one. His stomach was hollow. And he thought vaguely that it had been many hours since he had eaten or drunk. It came to him then that the creatures before him had been much longer without repast.

A sudden admiration came over him for the old, hungry, thirsty coyote and the old, hungry, thirsty cow eyeing each other in the golden blazing, dying sun. His duty, his real job, was to kill the old coyote and as many of her young as possible and drive the old cow to water, carrying the calf across the swells of his saddle for her. In a day or two she would have her strength back, then he could drive her on to the main herd. That was his job. But he didn't move and all of his long life came to him now as he studied what he saw before him.

The old coyote knew what she must do and she was doing it with every particle of cunning, courage, and instinct in her emaciated body. Her pups must be fed and she must, too, if she was to survive and finish their training.

And the old cow had long ago reconciled herself to her fate. She would stand and fight—win or die.

The indecision was not theirs. This trait was his and had always been so.

Time became a vacuum in the floating dust. The bawling of the old cow, just a whisper now, came to him. The coyote lay like dry wood. The pups watched her, their bodies slowly evaporating in the ceaseless sun. It was everything.

His lungs ached from the shallow breathing, but still he could not move the finger that fraction of an inch that would end it. Time. Timeless time.

Then the old coyote attacked as if hurled from the earth. The pups charged down. The man fired but the bullet struck into the shoulder of one of the pups instead. The momentum carried it forward and down and over.

It kicked its life away. He raised the gun and fired again. The hindquarters of another pup dropped. He levered another shell and shot it through the head.

As the old coyote came in, lips peeled back, fangs sharp and anxious, the old cow pulled a tiny ounce of strength from her heart—a little reserve she had saved for her young. She shuffled forward to meet the terrible threat.

The sound of the shot had caused the old coyote to veer just a fraction at the last thrust, and it was just enough. The lightning-splintered horn of the old cow drove between the lean ribs and she made one upward swing of her head. The horn tore into the lungs and burst the arteries of the chest apart. The coyote hung there. The cow could not raise her head again. She fell forward crushing at the earth. When she pulled her head and horns away the coyote blinked her yellow, dying eyes just once. It was over.

The other two pups ran out through the brush. They were on their own now.

The calf got to its feet and sucked a little milk from the mother's flabby bag. The man went back to his horse wondering why he had shot the pups instead of the old one. For a moment he had known. But now the knowledge was gone.

In a little while, as the sun buried itself in the great ocean of space behind the earth, the old cow, her calf at her side, stumbled downhill to water.

Don't Kill My Dog

I would have gone over and killed Marv Jensen right then, but I was too choked up. I just squatted there holding that old white, shaggy dog's head in my lap. He was dead. I knew. It was just that I didn't want to admit it. It's not hard to figure, seeing how much I loved that old half-breed hound dog. I hadn't cried since I was just a snotty-nosed button, but the tears were there now.

I kept saying, "Get up, Rag Dog. Get up and let's go run a coyote. Come on, boy. We'll jump in the pickup and hunt the whole durned country before dark." I should have known old Rag Dog wouldn't believe that, even if he could hear me.

I'd heard some shots while out milking. They came from over west at Marv Jensen's sheep outfit. It sure never dawned on me that it was my dogs stopping the lead.

I went right on and finished milking, let the calf suck, turned the cow out to pasture, gathered up my bucket of milk, and headed for the house. Then I saw Rag Dog coming across the rolling hills between my little starvation outfit and Marv Jensen's. He was pure white and stood out against the golden grama grass like a hole in a saddle blanket. I was sick. I didn't know why exactly. It was just a feeling I had. As old Rag Dog got closer, I could see he was limping.

I set the bucket of milk down and took off afoot toward him. We kept moving closer together. I could see the red smear behind his rib cage running down on his flanks. He dragged one hind leg. He came right on up to me and fell down on the broken leg, looked up, and wagged his tail. Those old honest brown eyes of his stared out around all that shaggy hair and seemed to say to me, "I've had it, Boss. I've had it bad." The eyes dimmed, he swayed and fell over. I dropped down by him and held him a minute or two before he died. I held him for a spell after. He looked at me once and then kicked a little and wagged that big shaggy tail. It looked like he said, "This is old Rag Dog's last run." It was.

Well, I got up and I was mad—just plain killing mad. The other three dogs were missing, too. Killing coyotes was what I did for a living, and they made it possible. It was all I knew. All I ever wanted. Hell, Marv was one of the fellers that helped pay the ten dollars a head for every coyote scalp. That's why I figured Marv had spotted a coyote among his flock and was trying to save ten dollars as well as some of his sheep. I was sure enough wrong.

I walked on back to that little rickety bachelor's shack I called home. I took the .30-30 off the wall and filled it plumb full of bullets. Then I stuffed a box of them in my jacket pocket. There were twelve or fourteen rounds in that box, and I aimed to put every one of them through Marv Jensen's guts. That is one thing I meant. I may not be much else in this world, but I am a sure enough dead shot with a rifle—and that goes for rocks, too.

My thoughts went back to when I was a little kid over on the flat, east side of the state at Humble City near Hobbs. I had a dog called Depression. My granddad named him after what was going on in the world. I didn't savvy any of it. See, I spent all my time with ole Depression running down young jackrabbits and cottontails for food. The cottontails he couldn't catch, he'd chase down a hole, and I'd twist them out with a forked barbed wire. Hard way to help feed the family, some would say, but to me it was fun. I didn't really know the difference.

Then that Sunday, my Uncle Gilt, Aunt Rosie, and their four-year-old boy, Hodge, came to visit. We'd had a batch of blue quail for dinner that I had trapped. They sure went good with the hot biscuits, gravy, and sorghum molasses. Everybody was full and visiting out on the front porch. Ole Depression was lying in the shade, full of dinner scraps, trying to sleep. Hodge kept pulling at his ears and bothering him all over. I told him about five times to quit. Everybody ignored me. Then Hodge picked up my dog's tail and kicked him you know where. Ole Depression jumped up and roared, knocking the kid down. He didn't bite him or nothing, he was just saying, "Let me sleep."

Uncle Gilt jumped off the porch and kicked Ole Depression in the belly as hard as he could. I reached down as naturally as I'd scratch my butt, picked up a rock, and threw it. Thud. It hit Uncle Gilt right between the eyes. He dropped. Everybody, but me and the dog, gathered around to see

if he was dead. He wasn't, but it took him an hour to stand up and a year to quit wobbling. He never did get close to one of my dogs again.

Funny how things from the past pop back into your mind when you're mad about something else. I got in that old pickup truck that I did all my hunting in and set the motor spinning. I almost turned over on the first curve. That little wagon-rutted road was not made for speed. I slowed down. It was mighty hard to do, but I wanted things in good shape when I got hold of Marv Jensen. The breath was coming out of my lungs scorching hot. I gritted my teeth till I could feel the enamel chipping.

Old Rag Dog was seven years old. As dogs go that's not old, but for a coyote-running dog it's just about his last year. I had a five-year-old stag and two young greyhounds. I was using Old Rag Dog to train these young greys. Man, were they working out.

Why, it had only been a week ago that me and the dogs had one of the best days of our lives. Over north about ten miles in a bunch of rolling grass country was where we had hunted. Some homesteaders had moved in here years before. They had one hundred and sixty acres of plowed land apiece. But they starved out. The fields had blown for a while and piled up in drifts, then finally the weeds took over. Some years, when the rains were good, the sunflowers grew up three or four feet high. It was home to Mr. Coyote. It was a fine place for him to hunt field mice, rats, and gophers.

I had this wooden crate built on the back of my pickup, and when we'd jump a coyote all I had to do was reach out the window and pull a rope that ran through a couple of pulleys. This raised a door in the back. Out the dogs would come.

Old Rag Dog knew enough to look in the direction I was driving. He never wasted any time. He just bailed out in a dead run, whirling and heading out in front. Pretty soon he would see the coyote and the race was on. Naturally, the other dogs followed Old Rag, doing whatever he did. They knew he was the lead dog and would keep them out of trouble.

Well, on that great day we were easing along in second gear watching the sunflowers. This old coyote was plenty smart. He stayed down till we were past, then raised up and trotted off in the opposite direction. I spotted him in the rear view mirror. Gradually, trying to keep him from noticing, I fed more gas to the engine. At the same time I started making a big circle. The coyote kept trotting right along. Then all of a sudden, before he knew it, we were headed right back at him. I slammed the pedal plumb to the floor, and that old pickup like to have jumped out from under us.

The coyote caught on then and there. He whirled and headed at full speed toward a canyon about a mile to the northwest. He was too late. We were gaining on him fast. The pickup was bouncing up and down and sideways and every other way as we ripped across the rough prairie. The dogs were bawling to beat hell and jumping at the sides of the crate, wanting out. A hundred—fifty—thirty yards. I slammed on the brakes and pulled the rope at the same time. The dogs hit the ground running. I slapped the pickup into low gear and then back up to second.

Everything was moving at about the same speed now—the coyote out front running for his life, the dogs right behind stretched out in long, smooth, prairie-eating strides, their bellies seeming to drag right on the ground, and me pumping the gas and dodging bear grass clumps. I reckon I would have driven right straight off into a deep canyon if I thought I would be there for the kill.

Just when I was afraid the coyote was going to make it to the canyon, I saw his tail start switching from side to side—a sure sign he was putting out all he had. Then I saw Old Rag move out a little ahead of the other dogs and close the gap. He moved right up beside the coyote and reached over to gather himself a mouthful of neck. They rolled over in a big cloud of dust. The two greyhounds went on past, whirled back, and took hold. The stag had already dived into the breast.

I drove right on up and bailed out of the pickup almost before it was stopped. That coyote was done. Old Rag had the main hold on his throat, and the stag was crushing into his ribs, shoving those broken bones right through his heart. One of the greys was chewing on what little bit of the neck he could find, while the other had a jaw full of stomach—trying to tear it open to get at the guts. What a team of dogs! Old Rag Dog had stayed with the throat, never letting the coyote get a chance to bite one of the young greys. They were getting their confidence fast. A few more hunts and they wouldn't pay any more attention to a coyote's fangs than they would the bite of a baby flea.

I got my breath back, pulled the dogs off, and we all stopped for a little rest. After a smoke or two, I scalped the coyote. Ten dollars it was worth. Good money . . . and a million dollars worth of action.

These things, and more, were jumping back and forth through my mind as I drove over to kill Marv Jensen. Every once in a while I'd reach over and feel the hard steel of the .30-30. In just a few minutes that same steel would be plenty hot. Old Rag Dog dead! He had to go and kill Old Rag! And maybe the others, too.

Seems like the times I'd been in bad trouble in my life it was over somebody abusing my dog. That old dog, Depression, never bothered anything but what I wanted him to bother . . . well, he did chase rabbits on his own, and he'd nip at the milk-cows' heels when I was driving them home. He was just helping and I loved him.

There was a neighbor kid in Humble City, where I was a boy, who had been throwing rocks at Depression for a spell. So far he'd missed. I'd warned him twice. He didn't listen. Then he whacked Depression on the side of the head with a big rock, and just stood there on his front porch laughing. Old Depression headed home just like Old Rag Dog had today. He was slinging his head and one ear was bleeding. I examined him to be sure he'd live, and I took off through the mesquite making out like I was going in the opposite direction. I didn't. I circled around and came up on the other side of the kid's house. He was pulling a rusty toy wagon with a wheel missing.

My granddad had given me a ten-cent pocketknife. It wouldn't hardly sharpen up and the blade would bend when I whittled if I didn't hold it just right. I chased that rock-throwing little sucker up on his front porch and threw him down and got astraddle him. I took that ten-cent knife out of my pocket and opened it, spread his throwing hand out flat, and stabbed. The blade didn't have time to bend and it pinned his hand to the wooden porch like Christ on the cross. While he was kicking and screaming, I told him never to hurt my dog again.

I really got into trouble over that one—even sent me to West Texas to stay with my grandmother. I didn't care. I took my dog with me and we hunted and had a good time.

I was thinking of Old Rag Dog, now, and the day of our great hunt. Old Rag had pulled a jim-dandy. I'd loaded the dogs back into their crates, then drove over to look off a rocky rim. Talk about luck! Just as I slowed down and reached for the door handle, a coyote came jumping up out of the rocks and took off down the rim. All I had to do was pull the rope. Out they sailed right in after him. Up ahead a little bunch of white-faced cattle were grazing. That coyote ran right out through the middle of them. This fooled the two greys and the stag. They got mixed up and lost sight of the coyote. Not Old Rag Dog. I think he gained right then and there. Anyway, by the time I'd circled around the cows, I could see Old Rag straining to latch on.

The coyote knew his time was near. He did just what any animal would have done. He jumped right off the steep edge onto the sharp malpais rocks. Most dogs would have quit right there, or stopped to look for an easier way down. Not Old Rag Dog. He just leaped way out, and when he came down he had the coyote.

I drove up and fell out. There was one hell of a fight going on down there. That coyote was up and then he was down. The white hair was flying where he was tearing it out of Old Rag Dog's hide. They rolled over and over together. Then Rag Dog got hold and held on. I yelled for the other hounds and here they came. They all piled off the rim and down to help Old Rag. It didn't take long then, but I swear I believe that white rascal would have finally killed that coyote by himself.

We caught six full-grown coyotes and one half-grown pup that day. Seventy dollars! In one day, mind you, with my dogs. Only I didn't have my dogs any more. I didn't have anything to talk to and worry over and love. After hunting over all that rough country, the dogs' feet had been sore. For a couple of days I kept the dogs penned up while I soaked their feet in alum water to take the soreness out and toughen them up again. By the fourth day (which was today) they were restless, wanting to get out and hunt some more.

I pulled up at the gate about two hundred yards from Marv's headquarters. I could have leaned the .30-30 over the gate post and waited till he showed up outside the house. I know I could have got him from there. I didn't, though. I wanted to see him kick. I threw the gate back and got in the pickup and headed for the house. I just hoped he was home. I didn't want to wait.

I drove the last hundred yards up to the house kinda slow-like. I was looking hard for Marv outside. Then I saw him out working on the corrals. I drove right up. Marv turned his heavy frame around.

"Marv," I said, and then I couldn't do nothin' but cuss him. I wanted him to suffer just a little before I killed him.

He opened his mouth and said, "The dogs, they were . . ."

That's when I shot him. He was turned sort of sideways like maybe he wanted to run. The first one went through his elbow and side. It knocked him back against the corral. He turned to me, one hand held out in front. I shot right through that hand and saw a finger drop off. Everything seemed to be moving slow to me. Then I shot him through the bridge of the nose. He fell on his face and rolled over. I emptied the rifle into his chest. Every time it hit he jerked a little. When the rifle started clicking empty, I got on out of the pickup. I'd shot him through the half-open door.

I went over and looked down on him. The blood was oozing out all over. Then I heard a scream and saw Maggie, his wife, come running. She ran up and fell down, yelling crazy things. And then she started saying over and over, "Why did you do it? Why? Why?"

I said, "Don't nobody kill my dogs. Nobody."

I got back in the pickup and drove off up the road. About a hundred yards from the house I saw the stag lying stretched out over a clump of bear grass. Then I saw the two greys lying flat and still. I stopped, got out, and walked over to them. Nine or ten dead sheep were scattered out all torn to pieces. One of the grey hounds still had a patch of wool in his mouth. I couldn't believe my dogs would attack anybody's sheep. They never had. Why, they never had even bothered the chickens.

I walked over and sat down on a stump. I could see several hundred head of sheep grazing peacefully off a ways. I had to face myself then. There was nothing to say, nothing to do, just think and look at it the way it was. That morning I'd turned the dogs out for a run and gone to milk. That was the mistake. After being penned up, those dogs wanted to run and kill. That's what I'd trained them for.

Old Marv and his wife had spent twenty-five years building up that flock of sheep. Blizzards, droughts, low prices, coyotes, he'd fought them all. I reckon he felt about those sheep something like I did my dogs. Well, there were still lots of fat sheep out there. They wouldn't do him any good now. I could get me another bunch of dogs, but that wouldn't do me any good, either.

The Matched Race

Mitch Brownel said, "Listen, Jess, that little pony of mine can outrun anything in this country and give 'em daylight."

Just like Brownel, thought Jess Darby, *always bragging that every thing he has is better than anybody else's.* "I've got five hundred that says Dusty can beat your horse."

"It's a bet," came the answer. "Like taking candy from a baby," laughed Brownel.

Later, when Jess told Lorie she said, "Jess Darby after all the years we've worked to get just a little bit ahead and now you . . . you have to go and poop it off on a crazy bet with that braggin' Brownel."

"That's the reason I made the bet, Lorie, everybody's tired of listening to his spouting off." Jess was sorry he'd made the bet now. He knew that Lorie was thinking of the baby she would give birth to in September. To have at least enough money to get a baby started out right is an awfully important thing to a woman.

Lorie had helped make that five hundred—she had helped make the little ranch. Her summer garden had been canned for winter eating. The chickens were hers to feed and care for. The house, small as it was, looked like Lorie to Jess. She had made the curtains, and all the little things that go into a home were hers. But he couldn't welch on the bet now. Win or lose, he had to go through with it.

Jess held the bridle reins up short in his left hand. With his right he swung the saddle over Dusty's back. He shook the saddle around until it was settled neatly on top of the blocky quarter horse. He drew up the front cinch first, then buckled the flank strap. He put on his spurs making sure the buckles were on the outside of his boots.

Then he stood up on his six feet of lean muscle and looked proudly out from under the broad-brimmed, black hat at his buckskin horse. Dusty had a small neat head, short ears, was wide between the eyes, heavy in the hindquarters and forearms. He was a quarter horse, bred for swift getaway and great speed at a fourth of a mile or less.

Jess felt that Dusty would give Brownel's high-powered horse a run for his money. He had to do more than that, though; he had to win for Lorie and the baby. He had bought Dusty four years ago at a horse sale in Clayton, New Mexico. He had given about one-twentieth of what Brownel had recently paid for his horse. Jess had broken Dusty to ride. He knew Dusty would spin on a dime at the lightest touch of the reins. He could catch a cow more than quick and give a man every opportunity to fit a rope around its neck. Dusty was an all-around horse. He had to be.

Jess Darby's ranch was one of those little outfits that was too big for one man to handle without working himself half to death and so small he couldn't afford to hire help. Three grown cows could graze where one horse does, so it was by necessity that Dusty was the only horse on the place.

Jess led Dusty from the corral up to the little three-room frame house. A bunch of chickens were scratching and singing around by the back door. Old Red, their mongrel dog, got up and smelled of Jess Darby's worn boots and then lay back down to sleep.

"Lorie," he called.

"Yes, just a minute," she said as she started for the door. "Taking off, Jess?"

"Yeah, I've got to go over to the old Meyer place and see if that spring rain we had last week washed out that water gap." Jess thought how pretty Lorie looked. Funny, how women seem to have so much color in their cheeks and more sparkle in their eyes when they are going to have a baby. He kissed her and said, "You sure you'll be all right here by yourself?"

"Of course, silly," she smiled. "You act like I was going to give birth to twins any minute. It's four months away."

"Well, okay," he said.

He felt guilty about the horse race Saturday, but as soon as he was out among his cows he forgot it for a time.

His cattle had made it through the winter in fair shape. The buffalo and grama grass was growing fast, thick and green from the heavy spring rain. The calf crop had been good, running about ninety-five percent. The calves stood straddle-legged and watched him. Their clean white faces seemed to say, "Howdy, Bud, it's a wonderful world, ain't it?" One little heifer whirled and bucked several jumps then turned back to look at Jess. "Show-off," he said to it. The cows grazed and lay around in the warm sun. Jess thought that they deserved rest and peace after the long cold winter.

Dusty moved with an easy running-walk. It was a gait that could eat up lots of miles in a day without being too hard on man or horse. Jess hadn't noticed his prize bull anywhere. The bull had cost him half of what last years' calf crop brought at the market, but he figured that the extra weight and quality in his calves would be worth it.

He decided to ride over north to the windmill and look for the bull over there. Besides, he wanted to see if the mill was still in working order. He scrutinized the tracks around the dirt tank. The bull was nowhere around. The windmill pumped water, all right, but he saw that he would have to put in new sucker-rods before long. They were worn thin and if he didn't replace them they would wear in two and then he would have to pull pipe and all.

Well, he thought, might as well ride the north fence since I'm over this far. He found a couple of places where the wire was pulled loose. He stepped off of Dusty and took the heavy wire-pliers out of the holster made especially to hold them. He tacked the fence back up and at the same time kept his eyes peeled to see if the bull had crawled through anywhere.

It was late afternoon when he scrambled into the dry arroyo to check the water gap. That's when he found out what had happened to the bull. The water from the heavy rain had raced down the cut in the earth and broken the wire loose on one side. The wire and the rocks used to weight it down were washed back against one side of the arroyo. There was a hole in the fence big enough for a whole herd of cattle to escape through at one time. Only the bull had found it, however. Jess could see the tracks, rounder and bigger than a cow's, in the sandy bottom of the arroyo.

The bull had wandered out into what people in this area called the badlands. It was rough, eroded country. There was very little for stock to eat. Jess wondered why it was that cattle always went through a break in a fence even if the grass wasn't greener on the other side.

It was too late for him to make the ride today, but he had to get the bull. He was too valuable to take any chances on. He decided to make an early start the next morning. Tomorrow was Friday and he sure hated to ride Dusty hard the day before the race. It cut his chances to win, but it couldn't be helped.

When he told Lorie that night at supper, she didn't have anything to say. He could tell she still didn't feel right about the race. Jess tried to explain, "Look, Lorie, all I've heard for years from Brownel is how good his pasture is, how much better his cattle are, how much faster his automobiles are, and now this bay quarter horse of his can outrun anything in the country. I just couldn't help taking the old boy up on that. Dusty is just as well bred as his horse and I believe he's as fast."

Jess knew that he was talking in vain. It was the baby that Lorie thought of.

Jess rode thirty miles the next day. About an hour before sundown he ran across fresh sign of the bull but he knew he had made his find too near nightfall. His mind had been on the race and how Lorie was taking it. Then too, he was concerned about Dusty. It was just too much of a ride for a horse that was to race the next day. As tired as he was, Jess didn't sleep well that night.

The next morning he shaved while Lorie changed into her town clothes. "Say," he said, "if we didn't win the race it wouldn't be so bad, would it?"

Lorie said, "Jess, quit worrying about it."

He didn't quite know how she had meant the last. As he loaded Dusty in the back of the pickup, he noticed that the horse was stiff from the hard ride the day before. He knew he would have to warm Dusty up a lot more than usual.

The battered old pickup pulled into town about eleven o'clock. Ranchers who had heard about the race were already gathered about. Pete Clemens from over east of Jess yelled, "Hey, Jess, who's gonna win the race?"

Jess said, "The best horse."

They went into the town's only cafe and ordered lunch. Lorie got in a conversation with Mrs. Adams, the owner and operator of the eating establishment.

"How've you been, honey?" Mrs. Adams asked.

"Fine," Lorie said, "except my husband insists on losing all our money on a horse race."

"Now, I wouldn't say that, honey. Some of the boys have been making even money bets. Course," she went on, "there are more of them wanting to bet on Brownel's bay."

Jess finished, fired up a smoke, and said, "Lorie, I'll ride on down to the rodeo arena on Dusty. You can come on down in the pickup in about an hour."

Jess backed the horse out of the pickup. He untracked him before he got on. It was a habit formed during Jess's bronc-breaking days when a horse sometimes untracked straight up in the air.

He gathered the reins and mane up in his left hand. His right was on the saddle horn. It was the way a working cowboy gets on a horse. If the horse bolts, he can pull him around with the reins he has in his left hand. There was no need of this with Dusty but Jess did it from long years of habit.

There was a graded stretch of ground out near the rodeo arena that served as a racetrack for the local ranchers. Jess rode slowly back and forth gradually warming Dusty up. Then he increased his gait. He knew that Dusty had to break a sweat before he could run much after the long ride yesterday.

Several cars arrived. The cowmen were joking back and forth. Some of them were making bets. Then Jess saw Brownel. He was driving a new-looking pickup. The bay was in the back of it.

"Howdy, Jess, working your horse a little early, ain't you?"

"He's got so much wind I was afraid he'd fly right off the ground if I started him fresh," said Jess.

"Well, you'll wish he had wings before this is over," said Brownel.

Brownel weighed about the same as Jess, but was much taller and sharper featured. The bay looked good. He was brushed to a high gleam. As far as his build was concerned, there wasn't much difference in his and Dusty's. It was a close bet but the bay had the advantage of the proper training and rest for the race. Jess knew Brownel would see to that.

The race was to be run with the owners up and plain ordinary stock saddles. A couple of the boys stepped off two hundred and fifty yards. Pete Clemens was to be the starter. His brother and another rancher, who lived in town, were to judge.

Dusty's buckskin-colored sides ran wet with white lather. Jess hoped the stiffness had left Dusty from the workout. It was only a minute or two until time for the race. He wished Lorie would hurry and get there. Just as he was about to give her up, he saw the pickup.

"All set, Jess?" Brownel asked. He had a twisted grin on his face. Brownel was sure of winning this race. Jess noticed that Brownel carried a small quirt. He had forgotten to bring one himself.

"Now, when I bring this hat down and yell 'go' the horse race is on," instructed Pete Clemens.

Lorie walked by. She winked and waved at Jess and said, "I'll see you at the other end." The way she said it sounded to Jess like "You'll be out in front, Jess." Well, I don't have much chance, he thought, but I feel a lot better.

Most of the crowd was gathered at the finish line. Pete's hat swept down. "Go!"

The bay broke a little faster than Dusty. Jess leaned over as far and as low as he could. A horse can run better with the weight of the rider on his withers. He noticed Brownel was riding almost straight up. Jess knew that in a race this short every little trick counts and he would need them all to win.

The bay pulled out to a half-length lead. Jess could feel the burst of power ripple under him. The ground blurred underneath. At the halfway point he had pulled within a head of the bay. The horses' muscles rippled in powerful ground-eating strides.

Jess could see the crowd getting closer and closer. Dusty pulled up within six inches of the bay. Brownel glanced over at Jess and then he started using the whip. It might have been all right, but he was scared now and he was quirting the horse in the flanks about half the time without being aware of what he was doing. This slowed the bay, not much, but a little.

It wasn't over thirty yards now. Jess laid his hand on Dusty's shoulder and there was a feeling between them. Jess was his master. He had broken him, trained him, and used him to make a living for Lorie and himself. They were a team. Jess could feel the tiny bit of extra power that surged into the horse.

Dusty pulled even and then ahead at the finish line. It wasn't over a foot, but as Lorie said later it was as good as a mile.

Both riders let their horses run on a ways before they turned back. Jess eased Dusty into a walk. He let the horse cool off gradually. "You did it, boy. You did it," he said, patting Dusty on the neck. He got off and walked back up to the finish line.

Brownel handed him the five hundred. "You was just lucky, Jess."

Jess said, "Thanks," and pocketed the money.

"I'll take you on for a thousand next Saturday, Jess. If you're not afraid."

It was a challenge. All the men looked at Jess and waited. A couple of them said, "Call him, Jess."

"Well, what do you say?" Brownel asked.

Jess thought about two things then, his horse and his woman. He looked over at Lorie. She was smiling but her eyes didn't say yes or no. She stood there with her hands folded across her first child to be.

Jess thought of the bull that he had to gather. He figured Dusty could daylight the bay with the proper rest, but he had to get that bull and no telling how many miles he would have to ride next week.

No, it wasn't fair to the horse or to Lorie. He looked at her again, then he spoke to Brownel. The words came hard for him: "No, I reckon not. It's like you said, I was just plain lucky."

Then the three of them turned and walked toward the worn old pickup and it was easy to see that Lorie was part of the team.

The Heart of the Matter

The two men were such great friends they would have died for one another. No cliché; it was a fact. They had served in Vietnam together in the infantry. Each had on occasion drawn enemy fire to relieve the other.

They craved safety now. Security. They got it—as much as there is, anyway. For certain, they both had the sweating dreams of violent death and smelling again that exploding, unforgettable stench of war. They had their turns cringing at sudden, sharp noises and trying to make foxholes out of their mattresses. Even so, after all their miserable close calls in that tormented land, it would still be the guns of the Hi-Lo Country that would create their greatest grief.

Upon their return from the unpopular war, they gravitated to work on the steel tracks. Both their fathers had railroad backgrounds, and like their fathers, who had both fought in World War II, they were dominated by the duty of making the trains run on time. Simple.

Knowell Denny became section foreman at Hi Lo, New Mexico, in the northeast corner of the state. Luz Martinez started as a gandy dancer (spike driver) at Pueblo, Colorado, but soon advanced to also become a section foreman under the experienced tutelage of his father.

The friends met each fall—three years straight—in Walsenburg, Colorado, to hunt deer together. The fourth year, after celebrating a successful deer hunt in the Roundup Bar, Luz became sad. Knowell noticed, because his closest friend was a happy imbiber.

Luz finally confided that his wife had run off with his rich uncle. She had taken their only child, a girl, Lucia, and Luz was too brokenhearted to put up a fight for custody. He had left too much of his soul in the bloody, loamy, root-entangled earth of Vietnam.

Knowell took it on himself to have his friend transferred to Hi Lo. It was easy. There was a recently vacated section house six miles southeast of Hi Lo, so Luz moved in.

Knowell lived alone, as well, across the tracks at Hi Lo. His former wife had tired early of the isolation of the little town. She had stayed until their two girls and one boy were all of school age, then one day she took the railroad pass, all their savings, the children, and moved to Oklahoma near her parents' farm. Knowell's kids came to see him for one week each summer. He took it well. He still cared about, and stayed in contact with, his wife. She remarried. He was glad. The only sign that anything bothered Denny was the slow, permanent bending of his skinny, six-foot body until he was five foot ten.

Luz was five feet seven inches of flexible muscle. At times he seemed twice that size. On other occasions he could shrink into himself and become almost invisible, like a shadow in an unlighted cave. He had a Hispanic/Apache face of bones that Rodin would have killed to sculpt, and his dark eyes gleamed from it like rare black pearls, sometimes as sad as slavery, sometimes as threatening as ingrained vengeance, and often as tender as the sigh of completed love.

He loved living just at the foothills of Sierra Grande. Some say it is the largest lone mountain in the world, because it is just under nine thousand feet high and takes a whole day to drive around it in a pickup. Knowell Denny was Luz's best friend, but the mountain was his twin soul.

Luz exulted in the moods of the mountain. The wind-scoured mass of rock dominated millions of surrounding acres with widely scattered malpais mesas like long, flat-backed snakes spewed from the fiery center of the earth, and mighty expanses of rolling grama and buffalo grass–covered rolling hills in between. Space in place. Chaotic order. The mountain would often gather all the clouds in the sky and draw the same fire and thunderous noise that had formed its own bulk from underneath.

Timberline is above twelve thousand feet on most of the mountains of the world. Here it was eight thousand. The reason? The wind. Ceaseless. Hot. Freezing. At different seasons, the mountain was green, then golden, then white, but the canyons were always deeply shadowed in blue and purple mists of grayish ghosts. The deer in its high parts, and the antelope in the foothills, were tough and cagey. They had to be to survive the mountain's turbulence, its coyotes, its cougars, and the hunting season. The season of killing.

Knowell Denny and all the other three hundred inhabitants of Hi Lo were actually on the northern foothills of Sierra Grande. The widely scattered cattle and sheep ranchers looked at it every day of their working lives for location, for hints of coming weather, for a companionship of terrible loneliness. No matter. Most were not conscious of these facts.

The volcanic mountain's base made such a wide, erratic circle that its gradually appearing slopes deceived the viewer. The cattle workers and the true hunters knew well it had thousands of hidden crevices and canyons. Endless secrets. It was a huge place of adventure and relaxation, a place that provided the winter meat Luz and Knowell loved so much. It was a place of destiny.

Just three years back Knowell had wounded a buck. He trailed it into rock-surrounded brush by following its stumbling tracks and scattered drops of blood. He had felt confident as he parted the bushes.

With lowered antlers, the buck made its last run. He struck Knowell in both thighs, hurling him back and down. One antlered point had ripped a gash in his right thigh. He was shocked, shaken, and astonished, but he would heal to hunt another season because the deer died with its head in his prone lap. Since that was the two friends' only kill that fall, they shared the venison with thankfulness and respect.

Just the season past they had hunted a uniquely formed rimrock canyon with Knowell working the top and Luz hunting the bottom, carefully staying several yards behind his friend's progress. If a deer was there, one or the other would get a shot. Care and skill. Slow and quiet movements. Hunters' blood working. The ancient way.

Luz felt a shot would open up—no, he knew it would. The canyon ended and he was alone. He was driven on up, on up the mountainside, by an old, old instinct. He could not see the tracks, but he could smell buck deer in the nostrils of his mind.

Luz entered the last rocky glade before timberline, and there he stood, broadside, majestic, in the autumn light. The mighty antlers caught the sun and made golden slivers against the blue background shadows. The regal head turned toward Luz. Their dark eyes met across the short distance. Luz raised the 300 Savage and placed the sights right behind the shoulder at the unmarked bull's-eye—the spot where the bullet would find the heart. His finger smoothly pulled the trigger. There was no jerk. The bullet exploded, the lead spiraling at immense speed through the barrel and out to the eternal kill.

Luz was so experienced, so skilled, he knew the bullet had been aimed and fired true. He lowered his rifle and started to move to the fallen animal. The mighty buck still stood. Unmarked. Motionless. Instinctively, Luz levered another shell into place, centered, and fired again. Smoothly. Accurately. The deer's stance and stare remained unchanged. A statue.

As Luz shoved the next shell into the kill position, he looked at the breech of the gun as if seeking an answer. When he raised the weapon to his shoulder, the animal was gone. Vanished.

Luz numbly moved to search for its sign, determined to track it until the soles were gone from his hunting boots if necessary. He could find no sign. Totally trackless. He circled wider and wider. No marks. Not a single vestige of disturbed earth or vegetation was visible. Then the one-fourth of his blood that was Apache told him what he had encountered. He had been greatly honored. Luz Martinez had been exposed to a spirit deer. He knew this extreme rarity carried a message of import. No matter how he concentrated and strained his mind, the omen escaped him. No matter how he struggled to relax and become open-minded to the portent, he could not recognize or receive it.

He told no one—not even his best friend. If so, he would be deemed crazy or worse. A quandary. Then, in the cycles of life, before the next hunt a year away, the mystification slowly eroded.

Unlike many, who were still tormented—even destroyed—by the graceless war and the loss of their immediate families, the two friends enjoyed more each year the wonder, the miracle of having been born.

Some of the ranching families successfully intermarried their young to breed and carry on their hard-lived traditions—a built-in security to ward off loneliness. However, a couple of railroaders had little chance of finding a wife or girlfriend in the tiny southwestern hamlet of Hi Lo. It was mostly populated by the very young and the very old. They solved this problem by splitting their vacations into four separate weeks instead of the usual month.

Luz and Knowell used their railroad passes to go to El Paso, Texas, then a cab would get them across the border to Juarez, Mexico. A week of debauchery three or four times a year sufficed.

They also enjoyed trout fishing a few miles east at Weatherly Lake. And on holidays they often made the three-hour drive southwest to Cimarron, at the foot of the Rockies, and fished the cold, fresh mountain streams nearby.

Knowell had a big television set that allowed him to have picture contact with the world. Luz felt such an instrument of imaginary travel and ceaseless information would break the silent understanding of shared souls he had with the mountain. He much preferred reading—Jack London and Camus were his favorites—but he kept this as closely guarded as the spirit deer. However, on those weekends when the Denver Broncos played, Luz would go into Hi Lo and share the game with Knowell, who loved football only when the Broncos were winning.

Next to their annual hunt on Sierra Grande, the Saturday night poker game in the back of the Wildcat Saloon was their greatest recreation. The game had been going on as long anyone could remember. As long as Hi Lo's existence. Sometimes it would last all night and on through the small Sunday church services. The game often included a couple of merchants, cowboys, ranchers, railroaders, pensioners, and then, of course, there was Emilio Cruz.

Emilio was the best poker player in this Hi-Lo land. In fact, he had won his well-watered sheep ranch west of town in a single hand of the region's favorite poker game—high low split. So everyone played against Emilio. There was unspoken relief when he was busy and absent. Nevertheless, at the end of the year Luz would be about even, and Knowell would be a little ahead.

But as Luz said, "What the hell? We've had a million dollars' worth of fun."

Knowell had replied, "What else is there to do anyway? Besides, it gets everybody in out of the cockeyed wind."

The last poker night before deer season came about, and it was different. It was Luz's evening. He even took out Emilio Cruz early on with a 2, 3, 4, 5, 6 straight spade flush and bet it both high and low, winning against Emilio's three aces. Luz could not lose that night. He bluffed. He played cautiously. He played randomly. He was a winner. Luz had even run Knowell dry of cash, so Knowell was forced to sit out the game or write a check—which he never did.

The usual repartee of long-standing poker games varied off occasionally to the upcoming deer season.

Knowell was only slightly irked when he said, "Hey, Luz, if we both get bucks this year, I'll bet you a hundred-dollar bill mine's bigger than yours."

Luz, being silly from constantly winning as anyone would be, said, "You got it, partner. For a hundred extra I'll break a Boone and Crockett record."

It wasn't just the money. It was the ancient hunting pride. Everybody heard and knew. Luz was mostly a quiet, contemplative man, and this did seem a little braggadocio in a country where deer hunting was often from need, and had always been a religion.

Luz broke every card player before sunup. A few even had time to get ready and attend church with their families. Luz did not even count the money. He was already looking forward to being on Sierra Grande with his best friend in just five days. A long, long five days.

Knowell always went to Luz's section camp house to spend the night before the hunt with his friend. They slept little. At daybreak they headed across the foothills. The antelope grazing, running here and about, made their nerves swell in anticipation.

An hour after sunrise, they stopped to rest their lungs a moment. They stood. Sitting would stiffen them in the cold air. But what a day. The wind was blowing at only thirty miles an hour. Just a pleasant breeze in the Hi-Lo Country.

As their breathing subsided, they stared across the vast land to the southeast and north. They could see into Colorado, Kansas, and the Oklahoma panhandle. Although their psyches were on deer, there were millions of other specimens of life herein, mostly invisible to their cursory, wide-sweeping glance.

There were thousands of steers, calves, and lambs fat and ready to be rounded up and shipped to meatpacking plants around the nation. There were scores of horses in corrals and home pastures ready to be saddled to gather that production of beef made fat from the rich grama and buffalo grass. And there were unseen humans to make all this work as a business, a way of life.

There were uncountable coyotes, bobcats, skunks, raccoons, badgers, foxes, eagles, owls, hawks, and rattlesnakes who had hunted that night and, if unsuccessful, were still doing so. There

were rabbits, quail, doves, field mice, prairie dogs, ground and tree squirrels, sparrows, injured or sick calves and lambs, as well as barnyard chickens and turkeys that had been pursued, killed, and feasted on that night—or were still being hunted for another hour of this early light. There were vultures, ravens, magpies, and double-duty coyotes and innumerable insects and worms moving about to clean up the remains of the nocturnal kills. But to their own naked eyes it was infinite golden-grassed prairies and hills and the dark mesas with tops flat as aircraft carriers.

The two friends moved on up the mountain. They split apart to begin their hunt in deadly seriousness. If unsuccessful, they would meet at the bottom mouth of the strangely formed rimrocked canyon.

Luz almost got a shot in at a three-by-three buck, but he disappeared into some high oak brush, moved on into a gully and out of sight. Both men jumped several bounding does—three with fawns.

The timber on the mountain was sparse except in canyons and swales, where their roots were slightly protected from the eternal winds and they got more water from summer rains and snow melt-off of early spring.

All was quiet. Neither hunter had heard a shot. Each one was pleased by the silence of the other's gun. Hope and anticipation. Pride, at times as fateful as jealousy, insinuated itself unacknowledged into their beings. The bet was on and every step brought each one closer to a win.

Knowell, having a longer greyhound stride, reached the canyon first. He climbed on up to the rimrock and waited in an opening. For a time even his expert eyes could not see Luz. At last he spotted the movement down below perhaps a half mile. Luz still carried his gun at the ready. He moved methodically, surveying in every direction for movement as he neared an opening.

Knowell waved his arm back and forth from above.

Luz waved back. He silently pointed forward to the mouth of the rough, rocky canyon. Knowell nodded and moved out along the curving rimrock at the proper distance ahead of Luz.

Now both men moved at the same gait they had successfully ventured for so many seasons. Each heard his own heart pounding, pounding, pounding the blood that pushed it to their ears and to their brains, enhancing any sound, any movement. Hunter's blood. Even more. Time reversed and then caught up and reversed again. The earth stopped for an unmeasured spell to give the sun and the moon a brief respite. Then the machine-gun beating of their hearts put everything back in motion.

The huge buck jumped right out from under the overhang where Knowell had carefully walked. It bounded wildly through the brush around and over boulders at an angle toward the bottom of the canyon. There was no instant, sure shot.

Knowell, with all his ancestors' millions of years of hunting genes taking instant control, saw the opening in the bottom of the canyon where the noble creature intrepidly plunged. Everything, every tissue, nerve, and brain cell of Knowell Denny acted with exactness. He was moving his gun sights just ahead of the blurred animal.

The buck bounced into the opening. As he was at the apex of his leap across the clearing, Knowell centered the sights at just the right angle and just the right small area behind the shoulder blades. His hunter's aura left his body, followed the bullet, shattered the red heart into bits, and sprang back into place before the buck hit the other slope. It fell dead with only a slight movement of its hind leg in one last feeble instinctive move to escape.

Knowell was in a fog of the kill now as he, too, plunged recklessly for the bottom. He wanted to be there before Luz was. This action was alien to his surface nature. Even though he and Luz were true meat hunters, the size of the buck's trophy head was beyond anything he had seen before. Maybe in the world record category. Maybe.

As Knowell dodged around the last brush-wrapped tree into the opening, he was stunned. Luz had his hunting knife out to gut the deer.

He looked up smiling, saying, "Give me my hundred-dollar bill, amigo. There ain't ever going to be a bigger one killed on Sierra Grande than this one—at least not by a human." Still smiling, his attention went back to the job at hand.

The shock to Knowell's system could not have been greater if he had just witnessed the resurrection of Christ and a spaceship landing to pick up the great crusader at the same instant.

"What? What in hell do you mean, 'me pay you'? You pay me the hundred dollars, old friend."

For a moment Luz did not seem to understand. Then the smile slowly vanished. "I can't believe you, Knowell. You gone crazy on me? How come you're trying to claim my deer?"

Knowell stammered out, "Your deer? You gotta be kidding. I shot that big sucker."

Luz saw now that Knowell was serious. Unbelievable. You know a guy most of your life, you think, and suddenly he is not that person at all, he thought, then said aloud, "Listen, you crazy bastard, enough is enough. Just sit down and shut up while I dress out my deer. He's always been my deer. Always. I met him before. My God, don't you understand that? Oh, I guess I didn't tell you about that. Anyway, he is mine, Knowell."

Knowell sat down with his rifle held across his legs and stared grievously at Luz. His mouth and even his throat were dried up now. He rasped out with strain, "To hell with the money. If you touch my animal, I'm gonna blow your ass off."

"You're gonna what? What did you say to me? Did you threaten to kill me, Knowell?"

"You heard it right, Luz boy."

Luz's naturally brown skin changed to a dark red now and almost as swiftly as a lizard's tongue he grabbed his rifle, whirling toward Knowell. The ends of the two rifle barrels were not over three inches apart when they both fired at exactly the same moment. Being the experienced hunters and fine shots they were, each blew the other's heart apart. They fell with the tops of their heads together, at the rear of the dead buck, where he had expelled several gut pellets that still steamed a tiny bit in the high-altitude cold.

Two days later, Herman Eubank, a lone hunter from Texas, stumbled upon the three kills. He nearly had a heart attack getting back down to his car parked on Highway 87. He drove to a nearby rest stop and called the sheriff's office at the county seat in Clayton.

The sheriff, a deputy, and the coroner drove to Hi Lo and gathered up a party to identify and remove the bodies. All three creatures were frozen stiff from the night's cold that reached near zero. After all the examinations and notes had been made, the deputy asked if he could finish dressing out the deer.

"It's been in the world's biggest icebox. The buck is as fresh as the minute it was shot."

The sheriff, like almost everyone else in the Hi-Lo Country, loved venison. He instructed the retrieval party to go on down and wait for them at the highway, adding, "I'll just help Ol' Roy dress out this deer. No use wasting good meat." Then, giving his full attention to the deer, he continued, "I'll flip you for that head, Roy. Damnedest rack I ever saw. An absolute record-breaking head, no question about it. But"—he paused—"it'll never make the record book. Who'd get the kill credit?"

"You're right. Who would get the credit?"

The deputy shrugged his shoulders and continued the job that Luz had started. When he had just about gotten everything cleaned out, he discovered that the deer had been shot twice: one bullet had come in from between the shoulder blades on top, striking the heart. The other had come in from the side just behind the shoulder, also striking the heart. There wasn't enough left of that organ to fill a shot glass. The two best friends had fired perfect rounds at exactly the same instant so that neither had heard the other.

The deputy pushed his Stetson back, staining it with smears of deer blood without realizing it. He stared at the palm of his other large hand that held fragments of metal. Puzzlement.

He raised his head, saying, "Look here, Sheriff."

The sheriff squatted and stared at the upturned hand.

The deputy continued, "I'm holding more than one bullet here. The fragments were all in the heart area."

The sheriff asked, "What are you trying to say, Roy?"

"Aw, it can't be, no, sir, it just can't be. It looks like one of those bullets struck the other one right in the center of the heart. Course, that's impossible. Ain't it, Sheriff?"

The sheriff spoke softly, "I reckon the odds would be . . . oh, 'bout forty billion to one."

"Yeah," finalized the deputy.

It took the sheriff two weeks of sleepless nights to figure out what had happened. He enjoyed the free venison every day while he pondered the peculiar point of it all.

Blizzard

It was at least an hour before sundown when the coyote howled from the rolling hills north of the house. A little farther on another answered and another and another. The way it sounded to me, every coyote in the world was having a say about things. I knew what that meant—blue norther. Besides, the leg I'd cracked up in the Cheyenne rodeo back in my better days was stiffening up. That was a sure sign.

Well, I had it coming, I reckon. I'd been down here on the lower camp for three winters, up until now the quietest winters a man could ask for. There were times when I began doubting how much longer I could hold out.

I remember when I'd first asked old Joe Rivers for the job. He'd said, "Mr. Manners, I've been running this outfit for over twenty-five years."

I interrupted. "Dave. Just call me Dave."

"All right, Dave. As I was sayin'. Twenty-five years of hiring men to work the lower camp has made me just a wee bit leery about the matter. Some make it through the winter and pull out in the spring, but most leave in the late fall when we need 'em the worst. Always throws us in a tight. Have to hire some no-good and give him double pay to sit down there and roast his shins while the cows shift for themselves. I suppose a man gets lonesome thirty miles from the nearest living soul. I'll hire you if you'll stick out the winter."

"You've got a hand," I said. And he did have.

They'd furnished me good horses and fair grub, and that grub was what I was thinking about when I saw Sandy Malone riding up. Although he was a quarter of a mile away, I knew it was Sandy by the way he sat in the saddle. Besides, he nearly always rode the bald-faced sorrel he was on now. I rolled a smoke and waited there by the corral gate.

As he pulled up, he let out a war whoop that to my mind must have answered all the howling coyotes at once, and then some. "Howdy, Dave, you old worn-out, soul-seeking hermit. How about some frijoles?"

"Just took the thought out of my mind, Sandy. Turn your horse loose and we'll see what we can do about the hollow place in your belly. How are things at headquarters?"

"Fine," answered Sandy. "The old man sent me down to check on you before snow flies."

"You're too late, Sandy. She'll hit in the next twenty-four hours."

"Aw, come on, Dave. You know better than to predict the weather in this country."

"You'll see, Sandy, my boy. You'll see."

Sandy had put his horse in a barn stall and pitched him a little hay and corn. We headed for the house. The sun was doing its last do over in the southwest where it went to sleep this time of year. I put the beans on the potbellied heater as soon as I had a fire blazing. I fetched a chunk of venison from the only other room in the lower camp house that I used for storing things.

"I've got to go over north and get another deer right away," I mentioned, as I dropped slices of the dark meat in the skillet. I had a little two-hole iron wood stove that I did most of my cooking on. It had a reservoir on the side that kept hot water whenever I remembered to keep water in it. The venison was juicy, tender, the beans just right. We washed it down with hot black coffee, and settled back for a smoke.

That's when it hit.

It got a little hard to breathe all of a sudden, as if all the air had been knocked out of the house. A window rattled warningly. Then, wham! It was upon us. Sandy got up and went over to the window to look out.

"Looks like you've got company for a while, Mr. Weather-Prophet," he said. "The old man will be worried silly, but from the looks of things, I can't do much about it." Sandy was right as rain.

By morning, everything was white—the ground, the air, the whole world, it seemed. The wind was getting stronger and stronger. I went out to let the horses into a haystack. I was covered with the white powdery stuff when I got back to the house.

"Perty rough," I told Sandy. "I reckon the cows will drift down to the brush country east of here."

"Yeah, they'll make it all right, if it doesn't last too long," Sandy said encouragingly.

Sandy was a good-natured boy and laughed a lot. The two of us usually made payday in town together. That wasn't often, three or four times a year.

We passed the day off talking and eating. There's something about northers that makes a man hungry as a starved grizzly. Sandy was saying, "Remember the time we got in that fracas over at Santa Fe? That hombre thought you were trying to horn in on his gal because you said 'Excuse me' when you brushed her elbow, and took a sock at you."

"I'll never forget it," I said. "He missed me a mile and knocked his Suzy as cold as a judge's voice."

We got on stuff like that and talked for hours. And ranching, too—just about everything in the game. It was warm inside, our bellies were full, and there was plenty of black coffee. With the resulting comfort, many memories came back—some sad, some so funny we'd laugh like idiots. Finally, way in the night, we played out.

The trouble that was going on outside had taken voice now. We could hear it howling like some lost animal.

I pulled out a folding cot and made it up for Sandy. Then I set out my own bedroll. I was sitting on the edge of it, pulling off a boot, when I heard a mouse gnawing in a little cupboard off the kitchen. I went over to the shelves where I kept my few eating utensils. On top, I found a couple of mouse traps. I set 'em, using a bean for bait, and went off to sleep in a hurry.

I've been in the habit for years of getting up with the sun. There wasn't any sun this morning, just grayness. I lay in bed for a couple of extra hours.

The wind was playing a tune to my memories. Neither the tune nor the memories were pleasant. I remembered the blizzard of my childhood. My father, mother, and myself were traveling across country in a covered wagon. The blizzard had struck with terrible force. Father had tried to pitch camp, hobble the horses, and gather firewood. The horses had become lost in the storm. The snow had driven so fast and hard, Father couldn't see to hunt for firewood. The three of us had huddled almost freezing in the wagon. The second day, Father had tried to go for help. He had frozen to death less than a hundred steps from the wagon. Mother had covered me with her coat. The storm finally played out. Some trappers found us almost frozen and starved to death. Mother died a few hours later. I knew I wouldn't be here listening to the wailing wind now if she hadn't given me her coat.

Max Evans

I dreaded to get up. The room was cold. I could hear Sandy snoring away. Well, it had to be done. I raised myself to a sitting position, when I saw a mouse over there in the cupboard doorway. It was a big mouse, bigger than I'd seen since camping down here. Lighter in color, too. I had set the traps up against each side of the doorway. The mouse was standing there looking at me, eyes crystal-black and cunning. He was quivering all over, twitching his nose now and then like a rabbit. I wondered why he wasn't in one of those traps. Maybe he doesn't like beans, I thought. This irritated me a little because I've eaten more beans in my time than I've breathed fresh air. When I reached for my pants, the little dickens scooted back out of sight somewhere into the cupboard. I got up and shivering plenty had trouble getting my boots on.

Sandy woke up, yawning. "It's too cold for a fire to burn, Dave. Better get back in the sack."

"It's not polite to sleep when you've got company," I replied. "Besides, I don't want you to lay there and starve. Ground is frozen too hard to dig a grave. You're not the only company we had last night," I added.

"What do you mean?" asked Sandy.

"There's been a mouse moved in with us."

"Well, he's not getting my bed, even if he thinks I'm not polite to company. He can sleep on the floor or crawl in the bed with you, Dave."

I finally got the fire started. Slowly at first, then faster. It was really melting wood by the time Sandy got up. I told him I was gonna try to make it out to the barn and corrals to check on the horses. So maybe he could mix up a few biscuits and slice off some venison. Sandy agreed.

I put on a heavy sheep-lined coat and tied on a bandana around my face; then with another I tied my hat on. I put it over my hat and under my chin. I'd lost good hats in this kind of weather before. When I opened the door, the storm didn't wait for me to ask it in. The icy blast nearly knocked me down and I could barely pull the door shut behind me. I thought I'd never

56

make it to the barn. The air was made of ice with a million flailing arms to drive its coldness through a man. Here and there I could tell I was on a spot where the ground was swept bare by the whirling wind. Then I'd hit a drift waist deep. Once I fell, numbed . . . and it suddenly seemed warm and almost safe down in the snow. That's when I knew it was bad. It must have happened to my father that way. The memory flashed through my mind. I shivered, the cold rushing back into my body.

I made it all right out to the horses. They were bunched up on the south side of the haystack, heads down and painted white with snow. I managed somehow to get them into the barn. I paused for a moment's rest. When I had gotten my breath back, I started for the house.

The return trip wasn't so bad. I guess maybe because I knew there was a fire and warmth at the end of it. Sandy had venison on the table and was just putting the biscuits into the oven.

"Have a cup of coffee, Dave, and thaw out your clinking old bones."

"Man!" was all I could say as I took off the frozen coat. The coffee worked wonders, and Sandy's bread wasn't bad, although I thought I could've made better. We enjoyed the meal and were talking about the possibilities of the cows making it through the storm when the mouse made a dash across the cupboard and into the "junk" room. The crack under the door looked too small for him to crawl through, but he made it.

"That baby's too smart for my traps, but I'll get him tonight," I told Sandy. I got up from the table right then and set a different kind of trap. I got a bucket and melted snow until it was about half full. I then laid a piece of firewood so that it sloped from the door right out over the middle of the bucket. I took thin splinters of wood and laid them at the end of the firewood. I tied this down with a worn piece of string. On one end of the splinter I stuck a piece of venison. That was sure to get the little dickens. He'd smell the venison, climb the firewood, then crawl out to get the meat. The string would break and he'd take a dive into the bucket. I set the new trap right in the center of the doorway to the cupboard where he'd been standing. I could see where he had gnawed a hole in the floor. I wondered what kind of nest he had down there.

The day passed quickly. The wind had settled down to a steady roar now. Once in a while it hesitated, then blasted forth as before. The old wooden frame house was shaking a bit now and then. We didn't talk as much as before. We'd sorta talked ourselves out the past night. I got to sitting there waiting and watching for that little mouse. He showed up a couple of times all right. I wondered when he had crossed over again from the "junk" room to the cupboard. He ran right under the piece of wood on the trap and peeked at me from the side of the bucket. The little devil was ignoring the trap. This riled me a little, especially when Sandy said, "You've got to be smarter than a mouse to catch one."

Darkness had now spread its dim blanket. I moved my chair over by the cupboard. I held a stove poker in my hand, determined to bash in the mouse's brains if he took another peek at me from the cupboard. I waited and waited, getting stiff and uncomfortable sitting there. Sandy had gone to bed. I was about to give up when I saw those dark, gleaming, beady eyes fastened on me. This paralyzed me for a moment. Then I let fly with the poker. There was a loud ringing noise, and Sandy jumped up like he'd had a rattlesnake for a bed partner. The mouse was gone. I'd knocked over the bucket and spilled the water. The ricocheting poker had sprung one of the traps I'd first set. I felt like an idiot about it all. I suppose from the way Sandy stared at me, I looked like one, too.

Sandy crawled back in bed and didn't say a word. I went to bed, too, but I was a little shaky and lay there looking at the ceiling and listening to the song of the wind. I don't know what made me do it, but I got up and took my old .30-30 off the hooks above the door and laid it by the bedroll within easy reach.

I was just dozing off when I felt something run across my chest. I bolted upright in bed and grabbed the gun. At that instant, Sandy said, "What in the world is the matter, Dave? That mouse get in bed with you?"

I cut him short angrily, then felt sorry about it. I realized too late that I needed someone to talk to. I didn't sleep a wink the rest of the night. I kept thinking I could feel that mouse scratching my head or crawling down my back. Part of the time I lay there with sweat breaking out all over me. I was afraid to move, even to breathe.

I rose before daylight the next morning, taking all the nerve I could gather together to do so. When Sandy woke up, I was sitting over by the stove drinking coffee and smoking cigarettes about as fast as I could roll them.

I was thinking about what the boys at headquarters had told me less than a year ago. Another man like myself, except that he had a wife, had been trapped here at lower camp. Their food ran low; then there was none. They'd been so hungry, he had finally dashed out into the blizzard carrying his rifle, screaming repeatedly to his wife that he'd get food. The boys found him sometime later with his hands frozen to a barbed-wire fence. His gun was lost.

The memory depressed me. I didn't see why exactly, except that I began to have a sort of dread about being here alone most of the time. I suppose I didn't feel too kindly toward Sandy either when I thought he would skip out as soon as he could. Well, damn him, let him. As for grub, I certainly wasn't worried even if we did have to make it for a while on beans.

By the time Sandy got up, it was daylight, and I felt better for a while. I even began wondering at myself for going off the deep end. But when I saw Sandy looking over at the .30-30 by my bedroll, and then looking at me on the sly, I got into a rage inside of me.

The mouse made several trips back and forth from the cupboard to the "junk" room. I sat down on the bedroll, picking up the rifle. I'd wait. My head began to pound. I thought I could hear the mouse laughing at me in a screeching voice that seemed to keep time with the wind outside. I don't know how long he'd been standing there in the middle of the floor when I saw him. I jerked the trigger of the .30-30, working the lever feverishly. The noise sounded like a thousand sticks of dynamite going off at once. I stopped after the hammer clicked empty several times. I'd had genuine buck fever over a mouse.

I was standing now in the middle of the room, with nothing to show for my outburst except some holes in the floor and a loss of breath. I looked foolishly around at Sandy. He was standing over there by the cot with his .45 in his hand. I knew that a moment before it had been pointing right at my back. His gun belt was hung across a corner of the cot. It hadn't been there the last time I looked that way.

I hunted up some shells and reloaded the .30-30. I also got my .45 and stuck it in the waist of my pants. Sandy was lying on his side on the cot making out like he was asleep; but I knew he was awake and was watching me through the slits of his eyelids. I thought the storm had got him—driven him out of his senses. I figured he was planning to kill me.

The day went slowly. By nightfall, I was shaking inside and out. I didn't eat another bite, just sat and stared at the cupboard door. I even forgot Sandy. When darkness did come, I was afraid to go to sleep. I kept thinking things were crawling on me. Once in a while I'd think something was slipping up behind. It didn't matter which way I sat. I was scared silly. I kept the fire going and it cast funny lights about the room where it shone through the vent in the front of the stove door. It had been hours and hours since I'd slept. Finally, against my will and from sheer exhaustion, I dozed off.

I dreamed that my arm was hanging off the bedroll and the mouse was eating my fingers. I struggled and strained with all my might: I couldn't move my arm. He ate my fingers, my hand, my arm. His belly was getting bigger and bigger. I kept looking for it to burst. The little devil had started talking to me now. He said I'd been mean and tried to trap him, tried to drown him, tried to shoot him. He said he was going to eat my arm off and then go get a hundred more mice and let them have the rest of me.

I woke up screaming at the top of my voice. The mouse was crouching there in the flickering light. I hurled the covers back and dived at him with all my might. The world turned into flashing lights—all of them red, some in circles and some in straight lines that went off into space out of sight. Then it was soft purple and hard black and that was all.

———————

The light was in my eyes. It would have been sunlight except that sunlight couldn't get through the windows for the frozen snow. I was covered up in bed. My head was heavy and when I raised myself, pains shot all through my body. I struggled to a sitting position. I felt my head. It was swollen on top and there was a little dried blood.

Sandy's cot was empty. There was a note lying on it. I could tell by the broad line that he'd written it with the lead of a bullet. Guess he couldn't find a pencil. It said that he was going to try to make it in, as the old man would sure be needing him. I'd bumped my head and he'd dragged me back to bed. There was something else, but he'd scratched it out. Well, anyway, I wasn't scared any more. Maybe I was too sore and too cold to be.

As quickly as I could, I got myself into the rest of my clothes and stepped out into the world of glaring white light. It was still and quiet. I saddled a horse and rode down east to check the cattle. They were all right, browsing about in the brush in search of food. I felt good, not having any losses. Soon the horse was tired from moving about in the deep snow, and I headed back for the lower camp house to get another.

As I unsaddled, I realized how long it had been since I had eaten, and how hungry I was. I built a fire in the cookstove and put the last of the venison on. Now I set about stacking the few plates on the table, getting the crumbs together. I reached for the half biscuit left over on the bread plate, intending to finish it, when it fell from my fingers and rolled to the wall just by the door to the cold room. Suddenly I knew that's where I wanted it to be. "That's your grub, little feller," I said half aloud.

I thought I might as well get some beans to soak for future meals. They were in a hundred-pound sack in the "junk" room. I took a pan with me and stepped into the icy place. There in the middle of the barren floor was the little mouse. I could tell by the stiffness of him that he was dead. He looked a lot smaller than before, there by himself.

Even with the fire going and the venison sizzling, the house seemed unaccountably cold.

A Man Who Never Missed

G us Morgan was the best deer hunter in the Hi-Lo Country. There was no question about it. The meat was the proof and Gus always brought home the venison. As to Gus Morgan's other qualities there was doubt. Some folks called him lazy, others worthless, but they all meant the same.

Gus lived out a ways from the small mountain village of Hi Lo on a little one-section, starvation outfit, as he was prone to call it. He kept there a few head of poor cows and one or two half-poor hogs. In other words Gus only had one thing to brag about and that was his deer hunting. He didn't even have a wife to brag about beating the dickens out of.

Now every year when deer season opened you could bet your bottom dollar that Gus was out in the hills with his .30-30. And if you had another dollar beside that one, you could bet and win that within three days Gus would have his deer. He usually hunted alone, but occasionally someone would join him while out on a hunt and they invariably had quite a story to tell. It seems that Gus always put the bullet right where he was looking and that was through the heart.

This season something had gone wrong. Gus had hunted nine days of the ten-day season without bringing in a deer. He deserved credit for trying, though. He had walked what seemed like a thousand miles. He had tried all the old familiar game hangouts and trails. But no luck. Gus, big man that he was in size, couldn't take this sudden departure of luck.

Evenings, when he came back through Hi Lo, he stopped at Lollipop's bar. Always before he had Lollipop's to show off his kill and hold up his reputation as the best deer hunter in the country. Now, however, he stopped and hung his elbows over the bar and drank all the alcohol he could pour down his long, gawky frame. That was considerable.

The town barflies had begun to gather every night in Lollipop's to watch the proceedings. Only one of them said anything; that was Carl Adams. The others just watched, figuring that was the wise thing to do because of Gus Morgan's size and his foul humor over the present situation.

Carl Adams, a Hi Lo merchant, reasoned that Gus would be needing some credit before the winter was over, so he ventured a remark. "Don't let it get you down, Gus. There's lots of has-beens around."

Gus just humped up a little more, turned a mite redder in the face, and kept on drinking.

Gus went home that ninth night feeling confident of success the following day, but upon awakening the next morning, what with a hangover and one thing and another, he didn't feel so lucky.

He drove the old 1939 pickup as far into the mountains as he could. Then he climbed out and took off afoot. About a mile and a half up the mountain slope was an oak brush–covered canyon that he had dragged many a deer out of. He had hunted it the first day of the season and saw only two does. Knowing the way of the deer, though, Gus figured that surely there were some bucks back in there now.

He walked faster than usual, feeling the limited time slip away from him with each step he took. His breath frosted in the cold mountain air and his boots crunched into the crusted snow of Johnson Mesa. He caught a glimpse of something dashing through some small cedars. It was a coyote. Breathing hard, Gus lowered his gun. He couldn't afford to shoot now and chance scaring a buck up and out of the canyon before he got there.

"By damn," he muttered to himself, "I've got to get one today. That's all there is to it." He had never been known to go through a deer season without a kill. This thought made him lean over and walk even faster. The dark edge of the canyon was near. Gus bent low and eased his way up behind a clump of cedars on the brink of the canyon. The last few yards he crawled on his belly, not minding the snow that rubbed up into his coat sleeves and into the top of his pants. There it was—the canyon. There had to be a deer—a buck deer—in it or the reputation of Gus Morgan as a hunter was gone. He would be gone as well for that's all he had.

He scanned the canyon with narrowed eyes, gradually getting his breath back. He knew he had to quit blowing so hard or he might miss. His eyes ran up and down the little breaks that dropped into the canyon. Not even a doe.

Then suddenly his eyes were pulled back to a brush-covered hump in the middle of the canyon. Something was there. It was a buck. Gus's heart pounded at his big chest. He eased the gun into firing position. Over two hundred yards downhill, it was a hard shot. He knew he had to make the first one good. His cheek lay over against the .30-30. His eyes lined down the barrel and set the front bar in the rear V.

Just at that instant a shot rang out. Gus was so taken aback by this that for a moment he thought he had fired. Then he saw the deer thrashing around in the snow and the red blood of its life pouring out on the whiteness.

Gus lay there paralyzed as a man walked down from the other rim and up to the deer. It looked like Carl Adams, the merchant.

"Old Carl, huh?" he muttered out loud. A sickness rose up in Gus Morgan. For a moment he thought he was going to pass out. The sickness was followed by rage. Gus clambered down the slope. As he neared the scene of the kill, Carl Adams glanced up.

"Well," he said. "What are you doing here?" Before Gus could answer, Carl added, "I must have just beat you to the trigger, Gus."

"Yeah, that's right," said Gus.

"Tell you what," Carl said. "If you'll help me dress this baby and drag it out you can have a hindquarter."

So, offering the greatest deer hunter in the Hi-Lo Country a hindquarter to help pull a deer out of a canyon. What did Carl think he was anyway—a has-been?

Gus raised his gun slowly and took careful aim. At the shot a round black hole appeared in Carl Adams's forehead. The back of his head and half of his brains scattered out onto the snow. The impact of the bullet knocked Adams back on his heels where he was squatted. Then he fell with a limber slump forward on his face.

Gus wasted no time. He pulled Adams over to a crevice in the side of the canyon and in a short time had him covered with dead branches. He wanted to cover him with rocks but they were frozen to the ground. He surveyed the burial and decided it would have to do.

As he walked back over to the deer he picked up Carl Adams's rifle, a .30-40 Krag, and hurled it into the clump of cedars where the deer had stood. Then for the first time he actually looked at the deer. Lord! It was a doe!

Gus stood stiff and dropped his gun into the snow. Even through his fear, he realized that he couldn't have taken the game into Lollipop's. Why, he would have been stuck for poaching. He cursed Carl Adams to the bottom of his heart—the ignorant peddling fool thought that was a buck. He whirled and saw the dead branches that had fooled both Carl Adams and the greatest hunter in the Hi-Lo Country. He saw Adams's .30-40 Krag lying out in the snow where it had passed completely through the cedars.

At that very instant he heard someone yell over on the other side of the .30-40 Krag. "Hey, you seen Carl Adams around here? We heard him shoot a while ago."

Gus stood and watched the three hunting companions of Carl Adams moving steadily toward him. In their path the .30-40 Krag shone black against the snow.

Old Bum

"Hey, Mark, guess what I've got in here," Tom Creswell said, clicking his store-bought teeth and licking his lips as he pointed to the trunk of his old Plymouth. His watery, light blue eyes were almost gleaming.

I figured by all this facial action that he surely must have a forty-pound sack of diamonds in there. It turned out to be almost that rare and priceless to us "great white" hunters—even if I was three-sixteenths Indian.

Tom C. was a sixty-odd-year-old rock mason, and we were partners in the rock-building business; and we were friends in fun, drinking, and coyote hunting. He was a "hound-dog man" from all the way back to the first hunting genes.

He opened the trunk and out jumped this black and tan coondog, and looked all around the wide-open grasslands of northern New Mexico. That was back in the early fall of 1947, when Tom introduced me to this creature that would alter my entire life.

"What do you think about this old hobo? I reckon he's just what we need for our hunting," Tom C. said with a certain pride.

"Why, it's a flop-eared trail hound," I said, surprised. "What in the hell are we going to do with him? He couldn't catch a coyote in a month of hard running."

"Coons, Mark. We'll use him on coons. We can double our hunting and trapping income in no time at all."

I believed him. That's the way it is with mentors. You have to believe everything they say even if it's wrong. Of course, mentors are so seldom wrong you are supposed to just let it whiz right on by. Code of the West, you know?

"Where did you get him?" I asked.

"Found him about a quarter of a mile out of Grenville, walking smack down the middle of the Denver/Fort Worth railroad. He looked like he was on the trail of a fast freight. I just whistled and he came to me."

There is a lot of good hunting in the rolling hills of northeastern New Mexico, and Tom and I hunted with dogs all the time. We hunted for the hides and the bounty. We had never used anything except long-legged, long-jawed running dogs—greyhounds, stags, and Russian wolfhounds. So, this trail hound was something new.

Before I get carried away about this wondrously unpredictable creature, I think it's fair to tell why the ranchers commissioned Tom Creswell and me to hunt coyotes for them.

I have on occasion helped ranchers pull calves from birthing heifers to save the lives of both the first-time mother and the new calf. It can be an agonizing struggle taking hours to inch the calf out of a heifer with bare hands or a pulley. The suffering is often great for all concerned. Sometimes it fails and one or both is lost. After one of those successful deliveries, a rancher will usually ride back the next day to check on the animals that feed, clothe, and give life to his tough world and family. He expects to see a mother-licked-clean, big-eyed calf, bucking and playing around with his little contemporaries; or sucking white liquid growth from its mother's swelled bag; or, having done that, sleeping off its contented fullness in the green grass of spring. However, if this rancher sees buzzards circling before he gets there and then just finds small bits of his protégé scattered about the land from a coyote's fangs, and sees and hears the heifer walking and bawling, looking for her firstborn, her untapped milk painfully filling her udder until it drips out wasted onto the earth, the rancher gets real mad. He has lost part of the family's survival here, and he has lost something he gave his heart and hands to bring to the world.

Once I was sitting, waiting for Tom C. to deliver a load of rocks to a windmill site for building a tank on Jim Ed Love's JL Ranch, when his son Clyde drove up in a pickup checking on things. We were visiting about the lack of rain, the price of cattle, the best bar in Raton, and the best hooker in Juarez when we heard a calf bawl over a hill to the north.

"Something's getting after that calf," Clyde said. "Come on."

So I jumped into the pickup with him and he gunned it over to a gate. I leapt out, opened it, and he slowed just barely enough for me to get back in. Then we ran smack up against a sheer-drop arroyo. We bailed out and scurried to the top of a rise and saw a sight to make a rancher sick.

Two grown coyotes had hold of an early calf. One held onto the tail that was already chewed down to a nub, while the other had it by the muzzle.

They were methodically circling. The calf would drop soon, and then they would tear it into shreds and feast.

We both yelled as we ran downhill. The coyotes turned loose and ran up on a hill where they stopped to watch us. They always know if you have a gun or not. I could tell by their boldness they had a den of pups nearby. The little white-faced—now all red—calf had its tail torn off to the spine. Its eyes were bitten blind and its muzzle hung in shreds of bloody meat. The poor little thing sensed we were not the enemy. Seeking some kind of comfort, it kept rubbing up against our legs, smearing us with blood. It was beyond help. Clyde grabbed up a ten-inch sandstone rock and hit it between the eyes as hard as he could strike. It went to its knees, then rolled over, jerked a couple of times, and died. We both understood that was all that could be done.

We numbly wiped the blood from our Levi's the best we could with wads of bunch grass, then slowly, silently, walked back to the pickup. I looked up on the hill. I couldn't see the coyotes now, but I knew they could see us. In a little while they would come back, satiate themselves, taking a stomach full back to their den to regurgitate for their pups' sustenance—just as natural to them as moonlight. It was just as natural for the rancher to try to kill the coyotes to protect his own family. That is what the ranchers hired Tom C. and me to do for them. A terrible impasse.

I had to explain this distasteful truth so the monumentality of what happened later to make me quit hunting forever can be somewhat better understood.

Anyway, this new dog, this stranger in a lonely land of lonely people, would somehow become the cause of my soul-tearing turnaround. We called him Old Bum, instead of Hobo, but we sure never dreamed that he would live up to his name the way he did and turn into a real out-and-out mooch. We soon found out he had all

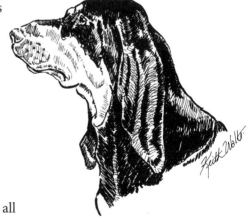

the vices of his two-legged brothers: heavy drinking, staying up all night at poker games, chasing the opposite sex, and finally even becoming addicted to hillbilly music. And with all this going for him, it turned out that he was also a downright snob. However, in the beginning he was a hunter tried and true, even though he was somewhat strange about his methods.

Back when this all happened—in the late forties—my eyesight was perfect, but the totality of my vision was sometimes cloudy. It's hard enough to get a young man to change his mind about a way of life he loves, but to have it altered in one day—with a single mysterious action that lasted less than a couple of minutes—is miraculous.

Now as I look back forty-five—or is it fifty?—years, I marvel at how that old flop-eared hound indirectly led me to such a dazzling enlightenment. And he wasn't even there at the time. Maybe that was part of it.

It was right after I returned from fighting with the combat infantry in Europe, and all that ground-tearing, sky-piercing madness that went on there, that I finally joined up with Tom Creswell. Since he was about thirty-five years older than me, he became my rock-mason mentor. Before the war I had learned the finer points of hunting and trapping from him, and now I was honored for him to teach me how to select, size, smear cement, and lay rocks, so that they could form a water tank, a good horse shed, a milk house, or a fence.

I was able to keep my wife Ortha and four-year-old daughter Connie well fed and clothed and living in a house that sat on a hundred and ten acres just on the edge of Hi Lo. We had a milk cow and laying hens that were fat and producing. It was good to be young.

The cattle ranchers around Hi Lo had been making a lot of money for the first time in quite a spell because of the demand for beef during World War II. The price of cattle just kept going up. Even in those boom times, only a very few had running water in the house or indoor plumbing. Some had electricity supplied by wind motors, but mostly they used kerosene or carbide lamps. The only TV in the whole Hi-Lo Country, that I knew of, was in a bar in Raton about thirty miles to the west. Some people had battery radios for their only worldly communication. In 1947, ranchers still kept milk cows and laying and eating hens, and butchered their own pork. This not only made economic sense but people were still fearful because of the drought and the Great Depression of the thirties, which was still fresh in their minds. Even so, these extra chores made it especially hard on the ranch women who were always overburdened anyway.

In spite of the somewhat primitive living conditions, they were busy expanding and improving their land holdings, which meant the big lizard swallowing the little lizard just like always. Tom C. and I prospered by specializing in building rock stock tanks for them, and since the coyote population was increasing at the same time the calf losses were, it wasn't too hard to convince the ranchers over this vast lonely spread of land to contract us to hunt coyotes at ten dollars a pair of ears.

So, there we were, "settin' purty." We were getting paid for laying rocks way out in the boonies and drawing down ten dollars a kill for the predators we pursued anyway just for the thrill of it. Oh yeah, I almost forgot. On top of the rancher's bonus, we got between five and fifteen dollars for each coyote hide. These extras made it possible for us to support our hunting habit without taking too much out of our construction income.

Coyote hunting was a pretty expensive sport. We had to feed the running hounds, buy traps and gasoline, and replace busted tires, steel springs, and burned-out pistons on our pickups, and also, there were those drinks we had to buy in the bar while bragging about what great dogs we owned and what cunning, courageous hunters we were. We didn't really need drinks to tell these heart-rapping, mind-jouncing tales, but it made everybody more interested in listening. The stories were so wonderful and wild that we had to tone the truth down most of the time. Of course, everybody thought we were stretching things a little—like most other sportsmen have to do. Not us, though. You could bet your sister's drawers on that. This will be better understood after witnessing a few of the incidents that happened after Old Bum came into our lives. To be fair, he entered lots of lives.

Ortha had always been fairly patient with me and Tom C. talking about our adventures until Old Bum came along and we got to making her listen to the endless adventures about him. I really had not noticed it as closely as I should—ain't that a failing in most men? But she had taken to going off in another room and reading Ready Romance magazine when we started up our natural hunting conversation. It wasn't long until she included Romantic Interludes, Always Love, and Hearts the Same on her subscription list of literary pursuits. Since we didn't have any TV and the batteries on the radio were dead half the time, I read some myself. I liked Jack London and James M. Cain the best.

Now, looking back on it, I swear it seems impossible that I didn't see the train coming while I was sitting on the crossing. I reckon I misled myself by the fact she still kept the house, yard, my daughter Connie, and herself neat and clean, the garden watered, the meals cooked, and took care of the cow and chickens. At that time she was getting only one or two headaches a week at bedtime, but when those increased to three and four, any idiot should have caught on that aspirins were going to be useless.

Ortha was a hard-working, loving woman built as well as a quarter horse mare. She had green eyes that could have been worn as emeralds on a queen's necklace, lips as luscious as strawberries, teeth so even and white that brushing seemed like a waste of time, and a voice that rolled out soft words to make warblers and jazz musicians bow down in homage; and I didn't appreciate her as much as I did my hounds. I was a master fool and then some, but I didn't get the illumination until the sun had already set.

I told Tom C., "Blessings be, ole partner, I do believe she almost smiled at breakfast this morning."

He just looked at me blankly, his mind on our upcoming hunt: "Sounds promising."

————

How does the song go? "So far, far away and forever ago." Something like that, I do believe. As I sit here in a comfortable lawn chair looking over the barns and the big house in the middle of four green, landscaped acres that belong to my daughter, Connie, and her husband, Jack Oldham, I can see as clearly as night lightning back to those days before I quit hunting so suddenly, forever.

Yeah, Ortha did leave me, and she took my precious little Connie with her to stay with her folks in Texas until we could get divorced and she could start a new life. No use going on much more about that, except to say that Ortha married a realtor from Fort Worth. Connie grew up beautiful as all the fresh colors sprouting from the earth after a spring rain, and as smart and graceful as a circus pony. Ortha turned back to her naturally decent self and let Connie spend a month or so with me every summer way out here in the Hi-Lo Country. Before I could say "General Patton" or "Holy hallelujah hell" Connie was in her second year in college at University of Texas in El Paso. She wrote and said she would be out in a week to stay a week.

At the time, I was building—Tom C. had finally retired because of arthritis and one short leg—a stock tank for Jack Oldham, a young rancher over south of Raton. I took Connie with me one day. Jack came by to check out the project. I'll never know how it happened, but Connie wound up married to him four months later. Jack was director in a Raton bank, owned some interest in a producing coal mine, and kept this great house just on the edge of the northeast city limits. We got along like coffee and doughnuts.

Since I was so handy with rocks, and not too shabby with wood and nails, either, my son-in-law kept me working on the ranch for years. When I started to stumble over little tiny pebbles and lean permanently to the northeast, he let me have the guesthouse in town, and all I had to do was keep the four acres slicked up some and look after the twin boys, Fred and Ted, whenever Jack and Connie wanted to go off to Acapulco, Las Vegas, Nevada, or Hillsboro, New Mexico, for a little of the so-called rest and regeneration.

Like I said, this very day I was sitting in one of those outdoor chairs Connie kept all over the yard, letting the early summer sun loosen my old muscles so they didn't bend my bones. I felt good. All the family, and a couple of the twins' high school friends, was all out at the ranch, riding and roping to beat seven hundred, I reckoned.

Anyway, I kept dozing some and every time I woke up a little my mind's eyes went traveling into the past about thirty miles east to the lonely village of Hi Lo. For some reason I kept seeing all that malpais, sandstone, wind-ripped country and everywhere I looked I seemed to see Old Bum, who was the critter that led up to my neck-snapping, nerve-cracking turnaround. Like the song goes, "Long away and far, far ago," or something like that.

———

Anyway . . . we were mighty restless waiting for nightfall so we could get Old Bum out in the field. Tom C. chose the Cimarron River country below Folsom for our first venture. Cottonwood trees lined the banks of the creek, and enough perch and other small crustaceans inhabited it to entice the coons. When the coon hunts, that's when we hunted him.

We bailed out of a pickup truck carrying a .22 rifle, a powerful flashlight, two running hounds, and Old Bum. The moon was just beginning to climb over the hill, casting black, night shadows all about. The crickets and a billion other insects sang their eternal songs.

"What's that?" I asked quietly after hearing a noise.

"Deer, I think," Tom whispered. "They come down at night to graze in the rancher's alfalfa patches along the river."

I listened to the whomping noise they made as they ran back toward the hills, and then I said, "Well, that's one thing in Old Bum's favor. He doesn't run deer."

"Yeah. Now let's hope he doesn't take after a porcupine and get his head loaded up with quills."

We shut up then and began to hunt. Old Bum was moving ahead in erratic circles, his nose to the ground and his tail sticking straight up in the air. He acted like a real "cooner." The running dogs just walked along taking a sniff of the air now and then, mostly watching the new, short-legged member of the pack, insultingly, as if they wondered what a snail was doing trying to run with the racers.

Then we heard him bawl. Just once, that's all. The running hounds took off with their long legs eating the ground. I snapped on the flashlight. Tom and I tore through the brush, falling now and then but following the course of the river just the same. Then we heard the hoglike squeal of the coon.

"Here, Tom!" I yelled, flashing the light on the frenzied battle.

It was a huge boar coon. The running dogs had never been on a coon hunt before. They were having trouble deciding on the proper method of attack. The coon was up and down, rolling over and over, slashing with his razor-sharp teeth at the hounds. Finally, Brownie, half stag, half grey, and the heavier of the two, got the throat. Then Pug, the Russian wolfhound, moved in to the brisket, crushing down with powerful jaws. The coon was finished. And where do you suppose Old Bum had taken hold? The tail, that's where, and almost halfheartedly at that. I reckon he figured this end didn't have any teeth.

We caught two more coons that night. Old Bum would work out ahead and jump one. The running dogs would listen for his single squawk, then they would move out fast and down the coon before he had a chance to climb a tree. It was a new and exciting hunting combination—the trail hound to track, the running dogs to catch and kill. As far as Old Bum was concerned, that was just the way it was from the first coon on. He refused to get in close enough to be bitten by the wildly fighting coons. He acted a little stuck-up about it, as if he figured the smelling part of the job was the most important. He wouldn't lower himself to the actual bloody business of fighting.

Overnight, the big dogs had developed a reserved admiration for one whose special talents they couldn't match. The combination improved as the dogs learned to get into the neck quicker by throwing the coon on his back. Old Bum would voice his single bawl. That was like a trigger to the other hounds.

All that fall we hunted up and down the Cimarron with Old Bum, taking about forty coons. We hunted at Weatherly Lake and caught eighteen nice ones. Just three coons made their escape to the scattered cottonwoods that entire season. The eighteen skins brought only about three dollars and fifty cents each, but that was better than a bee in the ear. Hey! Whiskey was thirty-five cents a drink, the jukebox was a nickel a song—six for a quarter—and a loaf of bread cost the same as a shot of the brown whiskey. Two coon hides would finance a small meal, a small drunk, and a big hangover. Those were the good old days and nights—or so it seemed for a while.

Naturally, we began to brag a little about our coon-hunting prowess. Then in the natural process of things, we got to wondering how Old Bum would do on a coyote hunt. I wish we had never thought of that.

We turned the hounds out about a mile and a half from Cow Mountain. It was good rolling country. The coyote had about a hundred-yard start. The running dogs leaped out of the back of the pickup. They sailed smoothly across the grasslands after the coyote, who was now racing madly. If a person had never run coyotes, there is no way to explain how your entire body and probably your boots, hat, and underwear are flooded with adrenalin to the point of feeling as if you were swimming in it. Your heart knocks ribs

apart and causes lungs to swell like helium balloons. We once ran right through a rock wall, actually speeding up before the pile of rubble settled behind us. Crazed. Nuts. A person is instantly hurled back into the time before the wheel was invented and fire was something that only flashed down from the sky in a storm or boiled up from volcanoes. Ancient emotions. Raw. Facts.

Well, anyway, Old Bum hit the ground on his short legs, rolled over about three times in a cloud of dust, then got up and headed in the wrong direction. He had been knocked silly from the fall, causing his inner-head compass to spin erratically.

We could see the running dogs pull up closer and closer on their coyote in long, graceful, ground-eating strides. Then one hound was alongside the coyote. He reached over, took hold of the coyote's neck, and down they went! The other dogs piled on. But where was Old Bum? Well, he had accidentally jumped the running mate to the other coyote and was running as fast as his legs would carry him in pursuit. The coyote just loped along, easily outdistancing him. Teasing.

We drove on to where the other running hounds were scattering the coyote's insides across the prairie. We pulled the dogs off and loaded them into the pickup. Then we started looking for Old Bum.

Way off to the west, we could see two tiny clouds of dust heading into the hills. Old Bum didn't show up again for twenty-four hours, and when he did he was chewed all over, his ears ripped, and his nose was covered with cuts.

It looked like the coyote had led him into an ambush, where several of the varmints had given him a real working over. We felt mighty lucky to have him back alive. He seemed to appreciate breathing, however painfully, himself. We never took Old Bum coyote hunting again. It wasn't the thing to do. I don't think he wanted to go anyway.

We did use him that winter to trail animals that had escaped with our steel traps. He proved invaluable on the trap line, paying for his upkeep many times above and beyond.

I didn't know then, as I've already explained, what was slowly separating me from my family. I started spending quite a number of evenings up on the main street of Hi Lo—which consisted of four blocks split by Highway 87. There was just too much going on uptown, and I didn't want to miss any of it. Well, this move, as it turned out later, didn't do me much good, but what it did for Old Bum was something to sit down with my head in my hands and ponder about.

The first step in his changeover from a damned good coondog to a hard-drinking hound—if not a downright drunkard—came about one Saturday afternoon in the Wild Cat Bar where the sidewalk curb was smack up against the aforementioned highway.

Hi Lo is a little cow town—population of about one hundred and fifty—on a long piece of pavement from way down somewhere in Texas into, and across, northern New Mexico. To the south of town is Sierra Grande Mountain. Some claim it to be the largest lone mountain in the world. It is forty-five miles around the base and about nine thousand feet high. It takes a full day to hunt around its edges. To the north, east, and west is rolling grama-covered rangeland broken now and then by a steep, jagged, malpais-studded canyon—the Carrummpah. There were two grocery stores, Chick Johnson's small hotel, two cafes, an all-night service station, and two bars. The bars are the busiest places in town. The ranchers, cowboys, and odd-job boys—like me and Tom C.—all hang out there when they come to town. They do a little drinking—sometimes a lot of drinking—and catch up on the gossip, find out who won the latest street fights and other such sporting activities.

The bars are directly across the street from each other; the Wild Cat to the south, the Double Duty to the north. It was very convenient for all concerned. If a fight started in front of one, the customers of both places had what you might call ringside seats. If a feller was a little wobbly on his feet and wished to change company, he could just aim himself right straight across the highway and he would be pretty sure to hit a bull's-eye as far as bars are concerned. There wasn't enough traffic in those days to worry about the odds of getting run over.

The wind blows in Hi Lo at least two-thirds of the time. It comes howling around the Sierra Grande Mountain in a grass-bending fury. I think the reason so many fistfights break out is because the people are all on edge from bucking this infernal wind. In fact, after all these decades I've had to think about it, I know that's the main reason.

That Saturday, I left Old Bum in the pickup and walked into the Wild Cat to do a little visiting. It just happened that a friendly pitch game was going on in a booth, and several wind-bent, sun-cured cowboys were standing at the bar giving Lollypop, the bartender, a lot of business. It was a cold day, but the Wild Cat was warm, and the only wind blowing inside was some cowboy bragging about what a bronc rider and calf roper he was. And then, I just couldn't help myself, I began to brag a little about Old Bum.

As the talk got mellower, somebody suggested that it was a dirty, stinking shame to leave such a remarkable dog out in the pickup where he might

catch cold or get snakebit or something. We invited Old Bum inside. He stopped just past the door and looked the place over like General Montgomery surveying a battlefield. For a minute we were afraid he wasn't going to like the place. All of a sudden he trotted over to the bar, wagged his tail just a tad, and stared right straight up at the bartender. That was too much. The thirst pains showed up so strong on Old Bum's face that we kindhearted cowboys, railroaders, and rock masons just broke down and bought Old Bum a double shot.

The bartender set it on the floor in front of him. He looked at it. He looked at me. Then he ran his tongue out and took a lick. Something happened right then and there to Old Bum. Sort of a quiver came over him, and after the booze he went. In his hurry, he turned the glass over, and about half of it poured out on the floor. But it didn't evaporate or get stale, or go to waste or anything like that. He licked it right up, almost taking up what was left of the design from the linoleum-covered floor.

A lot of cheers went up. Over and over the glasses were set up for the greatest of all coondogs; this aristocratic reveler; this friend of man and his vices, as well; this cool cucumber of a canine; this . . . aww hell, there were no words to describe him that first night of his debauchery. As the song says, "Away so far, so long ago."

The pitch players couldn't hear their bids, so they got up and joined the party. After a while somebody punched the jukebox full of nickels, and Old Bum sort of waltzed over and cocked his head to one side. Whenever a hillbilly tune came on, Old Bum would throw that proud, flop-eared head up and join the singing. We all agreed that he sounded better than some of the records. When anything played other than hillbilly, the head came down, the tail stopped wagging, and a sad, sour expression came over his face.

After a time Old Bum wobbled over to the door and scratched to get out. I figured maybe he was sick or something, but it turned out that he, unlike most of us, knew when he had had enough and wanted to get some sleep. This animal seemed to have had experiences we would, or could, only guess at. I helped him into the front of the pickup, not wanting him to suffer from the wind.

About four hours later, I decided it was time to go home. Every time I tried to open the pickup door to get in, Old Bum would snarl and leap at me. It came to me then that he understood himself a lot better than we did. This wasn't the first time for him. Far from it. He probably knew he got mean when he reached a certain stage and wanted to bed down before he got unfriendly and hurt somebody.

I waited down at the all-night station until about daylight. I stumbled back up to my pickup feeling worn out and sleepy. Old Bum didn't make a move. He was lying there passed out, snorting and jerking once in a while as he dreamed his private dreams of the past. And what a past he must have enjoyed. I was certain of it.

I crawled in real slow and careful, and then drove the half mile home just as the sun came up. Since I lived right on the edge of town at that time, I don't know why I didn't just walk on home and turn the pickup over to that dog. But, of course, that would be letting him take advantage of me. Just because Old Bum pulled this one big drunk was no sign he was going straight to hell as fast as he did, but it was a slight indication. Just like it was with my own family, I didn't move soon enough with Old Bum to prevent the sure deterioration. Anyway, I carried his sleeping body into the house with me.

We both woke up lying side by side on the living room floor. For just a minute I felt like running outside with Old Bum and going till we fell off in a deep, dark, secret canyon. It was too late. Ortha was already making extra loud, banging noises cooking breakfast. She saw us both struggling to survive, and she didn't say "Good morning." In fact, she didn't speak at all.

My little Connie made an effort to be her true, sweet self, but soon leapt away from the breakfast table, running outside for an early playtime, shouting, "That dog stinks." I didn't know which one of us she really meant.

When I saw Ortha wash the butcher knife for the seventh time, I got out of there and headed for town. I suppose, for a spell anyway, me and Old Bum sort of got lost in the wicked wilderness. It's hard, all these years later, to realize how thoughtless I could be with the exuberance of youth driving me on and on.

I quit working rocks with my mentor. The reason being, I decided to become a painter—not a housepainter, but the other kind who paints pictures. Tom C. never said much about it, but I could tell he was deeply hurt by the foolish actions of his protégé. I still hunted with him, though. He had to give me credit there.

Levi Gomez, a part Spanish, part Apache, part French, part . . . I don't know what . . . artist friend, was showing me some *bultos* (standing figures of saints) he had carved from cedar. He told me that some people knocked down as much as twenty bucks apiece for such like. I was somewhat amazed at this. A few days later I read in the Saturday Evening Post about a cowboy artist called Charlie Russell receiving thousands of dollars for just one painting. This seemed like a good idea to me. Why shouldn't a rock mason/coyote/coon hunter have just as good a chance at getting rich and famous as a dumb-ass cowboy? I know it sounds stupid now, but during those old times at Hi Lo I believed almost everything was possible.

So Levi and I discussed things over a quart of good brown whiskey and decided we would set up a studio and get rich. We sure did the first, but we missed the last by a country music mile.

Next door to the Double Duty bar (that's the one across the street) was an ugly old building held together by a bunch of brown rusted tin. We rented one end of this for fifteen dollars a month.

I bought a lot of paint in little metal tubes, some brushes made out of camel hair, a sketch pad, and a few canvas boards, and started painting horses and cowboys. You talk about going crazy. For a while it was hard to tell which was the horse and which was the cowboy. Whenever I finished a picture I would tack it up on the wall at a fancy price. I had gone that silly. No one else in that country did any serious painting. We soon found out that the citizens of Hi Lo didn't have much interest in art of any kind, so we went it all alone.

We got an idea then that we might attract a little tourist trade if we had a sign. So Levi painted us a fancy one and we nailed it up on the front of the building. We called our place Ye Olde Masters Art Gallery. Nobody ever stopped by. It took a while for us to catch on to the dearth of cultural interest along Highway 87 at that time.

Our only company was Old Bum. He hung around the gallery with us most of the time. Well, no wonder. We fed him there; it was out of the wind; and it was really handy to both bars. It was also a great place for him to sober up and recover from his hangovers. At these times he didn't tolerate any talk or bother. More than one person in town was snapped at for trying to pet him when he was under the influence. He was a pretty severe art critic, too. Every time I asked him how he liked one of my paintings, he'd scratch on the door wanting out.

In small country towns, cats and dogs roam free. There are no restrictions on a pet's freedom except whatever the owner wants to impose. So it didn't surprise me one day, when I drove into town to do some painting, to see about nine dogs all in a fighting pile. I caught glimpses of what I knew were parts of Old Bum. I jumped out of the pickup and tried to knock them off of him with a long-handled shovel I always carried in the back. When they all left, there lay Old Bum bloody and chewed all over. His tongue was hanging out, and it looked like it had already turned blue. I was sure he was dead.

I laid him in the back of the pickup and started to drive the short distance downtown to tell Levi the bad news. I glanced into the rearview mirror to check for traffic before I pulled onto the highway, and durned if I didn't see Old Bum get up and jump out. He ran across the pavement in pursuit of the same little black-and-white female that had started all the trouble. How Old Bum succeeded in this love affair, against such great and resentful odds, no one could guess, but there was no denying the five little flop-eared halfbreeds born a few months later.

One afternoon I was standing out in front of our "unvisited" gallery, leaning against a telephone pole just soaking up some sun. Old Bum was squatted on his hunkers beside me trying to recover from a little overindulgence of the night before. I studied the condition of our old friend. He was a mess. His eyes were red and watery from his heavy drinking, and there were scars over his whole body. His ears were in little threads and knots out at the ends where they had been bitten so much. But he was tough, and a real mixture of contradiction. A lot of big dogs chewed him up, but none of them ever made him run. He was too high-classed to pitch in and fight an overmatched coon, but when it came to privileges with the female, he would fight any dog in town right to the death.

As much as he admired the women folks of his own kind, he couldn't stand the human breed of female at all. He was strictly a man's dog. I imagine that came about somewhere in his past when a strong, wise woman must have told him to straighten up and do right, or he was going to be shunned. Ortha was telling me the same thing in her own way, but like I said, I'd gone over—way over—the dark crack in the earth and couldn't see any daylight.

Old Bum had been around town long enough now to have a regular circuit worked out for himself. He stayed at the gallery until we began to run out of money and couldn't feed him what he liked. After that, he just dropped by to give the critic's cold eye to our art work, or whenever he was too drunk to make it to his more distant hangouts. Everyone on his appointed route was a bachelor.

Pal England—one of the more sporting lads in town—lived with his retired, widowed, old father. Pal had a short leg from parachuting into a bad landing after his bomber was shot down over the Third Reich, and had spent a spell in one of their POW camps, so the government gave him a small pension for his short leg and long memories.

Pal said, "By all odds, I should be recognized as the town drunk since Vince Moore's unintentional retirement, but Old Bum has more experience, so I'm giving him the title for now."

Vince Moore had held the undisputed title a long time before Pal. He was a part-time bootlegger who had moved his large family into town after being nudged out of his single section of land. He proudly claimed the title of official town drunk. He once told me, "I've been drunk for forty years because I'm afraid of falling dead with a hangover." His worrying all that time was wasted. As he was hurrying to his outhouse one of those Hi Lo wind gusts blew the roof off and knocked him as dead as last year's Christmas tree. If any creature had a chance to match these great accomplishments of the past, it was Old Bum.

Knowell Denny, a foreman on the railroad, lived across the tracks about three hundred yards from Pal. They were close friends, and Old Bum liked them both. They made quiet talk and always had something good cooking on the stove, like venison stew, or biscuits and gravy, and other tasty handouts that appealed to his taster.

Another place the old hound visited was down to the east about a quarter of a mile at Rube Fields's. Rube was an old-time well driller and widower. Rube's specialty was chili and beans. Old Bum kept pretty well fed by making his circuit.

Besides the food stations, he checked on the bars three times a day. The first inspection was around ten in the morning to see if any holdover party from the night before was still going on; then again about three in the afternoon when the pitch and poker games were on the way; and, of course, around nine or ten at night when the more serious drinking was beginning. He would stand up close to the bar and look sad, and somebody was bound to take pity and give him a refreshment.

Old Bum's obvious enjoyment of country music (his favorite singer was Eddy Arnold) would cause somebody else to buy him a drink, so he could relax and more fully enjoy this place of country culture. A couple of drinks and he was well on his way to becoming part of the musical entertainment.

He had a knack for hearing, smelling, or in some way sensing a really jam-up, bottle-throwing, fist-fighting party. Whiskey, female dogs, and fist-fights were the things that excited him most. When a fight would break out, Old Bum would jump around, all alert, not missing a punch. But he never took sides.

The only time I remembered him showing any pity on a loser was when I made a feeble effort to save him from the fun and drinking that was making the both of us wobble and shake like a gravel separator. I told this big cowboy, who worked for the JL Ranch, that I didn't want him or anyone else giving any more drinks to my hunting dog.

He turned away from the bar, looking at me as if I was that sneaky bronc that kicked him in the belly last week, and said quietly, "He's just a dawg."

Talk about foolish, I replied, "No, he ain't just a dawg. He is a first-class coonhound, and you're going to ruin his smeller."

The cowboy grabbed my collar and the seat of my Levi's and hustled me outside faster than thought. That's as fast as it gets.

He said, just as he hit me in the nose, "You got it wrong, partner, it's your smeller I'm gonna ruin."

He did. It always turned to the southwest after that. I went face down in the gutter of the sidewalk with his two hundred and more pounds on top of me flailing away from my kidneys to my ears with fists as hard as horse-shoes. While the old boy had me down where the sidewalk joins the high-way, trying to push my face into the gravel, I kept turning my head to the side to avoid permanent implants. Every time I turned, Old Bum would lick me with a long, wet tongue right across my eyes.

I gasped, "Why don't you get the SOB on top of me by the throat, if you love me so much?"

After a while, Levi came and picked me up and led me over to Ye Ole Masters Gallery and helped me wash the road tar and gravel from my face. He picked up one of the cedar *bultos*—Saint George, slayer of dragons, I think—and said he was going over to beat that cowboy's head into pudding with it. I said, "Naw, Levi, let it go. Killing a cowboy with a saint is not going to be good for our artistic image." He reluctantly saw the wisdom, and all soon became calm.

As time passed, Old Bum's personality changed along with his appear-ance. He was becoming jaded, stuck-up, and more than half cranky. Dur-ing this period, somebody shot Old Bum in the shoulder with a .22 rifle. An amateur horse doctor said to leave it alone and it would heal around the bullet. Which it did, but it gave him a kind of stiff-legged limp in his left front leg. It made him appear to walk in an even more stuck-up man-ner. By this time he had also acquired a big rip over one eye leaving a scar that added to his aristocratic appearance, looking more like a monocle than anything else. He also became very possessive about his territorial rights, as well. Not only did the sidewalks belong to him, but so did four blocks of Highway 87. Sometimes when he was crossing from one bar to the other, he would stop right in the middle of the highway and just stand there with his head up looking mighty important through his drink-blurred eyes. Many times we would hear tires screeching against the asphalt and know some-one was trying to miss killing the current town drunk. He would not move, nor bat an eye, with a ten-ton truck bearing down on him at top speed. It was the greatest wonder in the world that Old Bum didn't get a lot of sober people killed.

Finally, to my great relief, after I had made about a thousand sly hints, people began to worry about him and sort of by mutual consent we decided to cut him off the bottle for a while and try to straighten him out. Trying to be an inspiration to him, I quit drinking myself. Tom C. was thrilled when I said I was ready for another hunt now.

Old Bum had been sober for over a week when we decided it would do him good to take him coon hunting and get him interested again in what he was born and bred to do. We didn't have any trouble finding him, but we were about three hours too late. Some tourist had stopped for a drink on his way up to Colorado, and Old Bum had slipped in, looking kind of lost and pitiful. Before long he had beggared himself a load-on.

Tom C. had spent his long life hunting and handling hound dogs, but this presented a brand new problem.

I said, "We might throw him in the river. It could sober him up."

"It might work at that," Tom C. agreed.

Old Bum loaded into the back of the pickup with the other dogs without any trouble. He was at this happy stage now, but if we had waited another hour to rescue him from the saloon and demon drink, it would have been too bad. The big running dogs gave Old Bum some strange looks, wondering what in the world had happened to their faithful, helpful hunting partner.

When we unloaded, down on the Cimarron, it was dark and cloudy. My flashlight beam knocked a bright round hole in the night. We eased up beside Old Bum and pushed him off into the river with a big, wet splash. He crawled up out of there shaking the water from his hide and struck out for the brush without giving us a glance.

Suddenly we heard him bawl. And bawl again, then again. He had never bawled over once before. Tom C. and I looked at each other. The running dogs were already racing after Old Bum ready for the easy kill.

"What in the world do you think he's got treed?" I asked.

"Well, I sure don't know, but it's bound to be something different. I ain't never heard him bawl twice before."

"Yeah," I said. "I guess he finally had the 'one too many' drinks we all talk about but never believe."

We headed out as fast as we could. The other dogs—always silent hunters before—were barking and growling in sounds of dismay and puzzlement. All of a sudden the light beam found them. A bull! Old Bum had treed a big, white-faced bull. The bull lowered his head and charged Old Bum at full speed. The dog sort of stumbled out of the way, still making that loud bawling noise. The bull whirled, pawed the ground, snorted, and charged again. He didn't miss Old Bum three inches. The other hounds had become so excited they had forgotten their training and were running in circles around the uneven contest like amateur cheerleaders when the baton is dropped.

"A hell of a big coon!" Tom C. yelled.

"Yeah," I answered. "We've got to do something quick, Tom, or that bull's going to kill Old Bum."

The bull charged. We scattered and ran for the pickup. I tried to lead him away from the much slower Tom C. I was successful. He hooked me under one leg with a horn and tossed me like a wet dishrag up on the hood of the pickup. While at the apex of this unwanted fight, I threw the flashlight at a clump of bunch grass. The bull took in after the light until he decided he was in the wrong pasture. We were saved. I rolled over on the ground, my breath knocked loose, wondering if I was dead. I knew I was alive when I heard the bull tearing up brush heading for the hills.

Then Tom C. shined the lifesaving flashlight in my face and asked, "You all right?"

I sat up. I moved. I felt of my legs and all. I couldn't feel any rips in my skin and everything seemed to be in its rightful place. Before I could determine an answer, Old Bum was in my lap licking my face like it was smeared with wild honey. You can say, or think, whatever you want about this animal that had created all the fun and excitement, but he and that slobbering tongue of his always came to the aid of the down and out.

I stumbled to my feet saying, "I'm the luckiest man alive."

"I reckon we all are," Tom C. said with profound truth.

We just breathed in the moonlight a while, not talking. There was a little numbness in my leg where the horn had hooked under and it was beginning to swell a little. I was thanking God and all his kinfolks that that was the extent of the damage. I could have been standing there with my entrails or my privates in my hands. It was at least an hour before we gathered the dogs up and headed for town.

On the drive back home that night, my mentor told me something special. He lifted the wrinkled little tan hat from his head and ran a large, perpetually chapped hand through his thin gray hair. As he tried to push his false teeth solid with his tongue so he could speak clearly, he said, "You know something, Mark? To be conceived is dangerous to life, but being born is even more so."

Later—after my semiretirement in Raton—I would remember what he said, because now all these medical scientists were telling us that just about everything, including ice cream, eggs, beef, and even dreaming, would kill us. The old man's wisdom became even more special by the day. Like I said before, that's what mentors are for, but I didn't understand all he meant back then.

The next day when the boys asked how we did on our hunt last night, we said, "Not much good. Too dark." Old Bum didn't show the least sign of shame.

A few weeks later, Levi and I were working at the gallery while my sore body loosened up. Old Bum hadn't had a drink since the night of the coon hunt. His eyes looked a lot better. All evening, though, we noticed how restless he was. Ever so often he would get up and walk to the door. He didn't scratch to get out, so we didn't pay much attention. Then he started whining.

Levi said, "I believe he needs to hunt a post."

I let him out. I didn't know we would never see him again and it would be decades before I would know all that happened.

—————

Tom C. and I had finished putting some new rigging on the pickup with two compartments in the bed. We had rope pulleys attached to sliding gates on the bottom half of the backend. Each pulley was clamped by opposite windows on the truck cab. When we spotted a coyote, we could jerk the back gate open with the rope and let out one team of dogs at a time. This way we would always have a fresh team ready. We figured we could double our production of coyote ears for the ranchers' bounty. We could hardly wait to try it out. For some unexplained reason, I was determined to take Old Bum along. Tom C. thought I was crazy. Just the same I had the urge for his company; but we couldn't find him anywhere and nobody in town would admit to having seen him. Later, of course, the story would leak out. It always does in these little one- and two-bar towns.

It was one of those days that the poets talk about happening just once in a lifetime. Everything changed forever that day for me. Everything.

I felt a little vacancy for Old Bum as we drove by Weatherly Dam on out to Pete Jones's outfit for our first testing of the fancy-rigged coyote truck. Pete's ranch rolled downhill north to Carrummpah Canyon and creek. We drove on down about a half mile this side of the canyon's rim, knowing from many years of past hunts that most flushed coyotes would head straight toward their protective wildness.

The dogs moved about restlessly in the back, knowing we were hunting, but not yet used to the new setup. In spite of my prior emptiness, because of the missing flop-eared hound, my heart was jump-starting as I stared across the yucca-dotted grassland. I was gripping the steering wheel so hard my hands were almost numb. I could smell coyotes. I couldn't see them yet, but the scent notifiers in my brain already were stirring little squirts of adrenalin all through my body.

The wind was whipping the grama grass in golden rhythms. The electricity that generates somewhere in the brain and the heart was sparking fiery impulses through the flesh of my entire being. Old Tom C. was leaning stiffly forward with both of his huge knobby hands gripping the dashboard with desperate force. They looked as strong and hard as the thousands of rocks they had shaped into beauty and usefulness. His eternally weakening, blue-grey eyes seemed to project tiny rays of light ahead trying to call back the sight of his younger days. I nearly always spotted our prey first, but when the ancient hunter's blood started pulsing and pumping, Tom C. never quit trying. In these few moments out of eternity, it seemed that we were separated from the usual progression of earth, moon, sun, and stars. It was as if our limited chunk of this hard wind-agitated land had been removed to another time and galaxy for our own special events of life and death to occur.

I spotted the mother coyote's ears. They were shaped wider, different from the swordlike blades of the large yucca clump she watched us through. I drove on silently, trying to keep all the tearing turmoil in my body from exuding out so the dogs would not pick up the silent message and start raising hell too soon.

Tom C. had already felt it, but our blood communication was so perfect the only sign he showed was the rising of his chest trying to keep his lungs in place. That's the way it is with longtime hunting partners.

The coyote had four pups, three-quarters grown, lying low in the tall grass, but I spotted their outlines because their bodies created a motion-less little void in the ocean of wind-dancing stems. She was sure we were going to drive on by and miss her, I knew. We were very close to that point you can never return to or from. That immeasurable portion of space where everything will happen.

I kept my foot easing up and down delicately on the accelerator, trying to keep the mother coyote from noticing any untoward movement. I wanted to get exactly between her and the canyon, hoping we could catch her and maybe one of the pups before she could head for the canyon's safety.

Just a few more yards now. The world was a blur of red. There was no breath. The wind had no air for that moment. Then it all exploded at the same precise instant.

I hit the brakes. The mother coyote knew we had spotted them. She whirled, racing east, followed by her scattering pups who looked back at us in a quick hesitation as they tried to follow their mother's lead and at the same time satisfy their curiosity of our movement. It was a fatal half second of hesitation. Tom C. jerked the cage rope and one team of the hounds leapt upon the ground. I jerked the other rope and now two teams were stretch-ing full out. Their long legs were just graceful, ground-swallowing blurs.

Our timing had been exact as a dagger tip. The first team downed a pup—one by the neck, the other at the brisket. The wind had whipped the battle dust away by the time Old Pug and Brownie had caught the mother. Just as hundreds of times before, Brownie raced right up parallel, reaching his mighty jaws out and clamping down on the neck of the coyote. They rolled completely over twice before Brownie would stand up, still crushing the neck. Before the coyote had a chance to rise, Pug was there to secure the prone position and demise of the coyote by crushing the ribs right into the heart and lungs.

Tom C. and I were so caught up in this moment of intense action and sudden death, and the unspoken success of our first hunt with double teams, that we forgot all about the pickup.

I raced afoot across the rolling world toward the kill, driven on by things so old, so deeply rooted, that I would have dived off a twenty-foot bluff without hesitation to be there at the moment of the ultimate. The kill!

Tom C. stumbled along behind, his old heart unable to supply enough air to fuel his movements any faster. Then it happened. My eyes, trained so long to seek out the tiniest form and movement, flashed uncontrollably to the three pups racing for safety over the crest of a hill perhaps an eighth of a mile distant. Two of them disappeared, and thereby lived as their many millions of years of genes instructed them. But one stopped. The universe stopped. Then, as always, it exploded again. The pup, without any hesitation, charged back down the hill, gathering speed in its descent, heading straight for the trio of Pug, Brownie, and its dying mother. It charged with all the speed of its body, with all its ancient fury, into the two hounds whose combined weight and bulk was at least eight times that of the pup. His momentum knocked both dogs loose from the mother. It bounced over the dogs in a complete flip, rolling over several times, stumbling up stunned.

The hounds were also momentarily numbed. The pup's action had no place in their world of directed instincts. For an unmeasured space of time they hesitated. Then all their millions of years of trained genes took control and they downed the addled pup and killed it almost instantly.

All this had happened before our eyes in just under two minutes. But somehow in that tiny space of clock time, a millennium had whizzed by.

I was still standing motionless except for the wind pushing me. The act of the coyote pup was beyond any scientific knowledge in existence. I knew I had witnessed a true sacrificial event against all human knowing. I was numbed and humbled beyond speech.

Old Tom C. finally stumbled up beside me, gasping. He, too, had extended his heart's strength as far as it could be crowded without its own final explosion. He hesitantly reached one of his great old hands out to my shoulder for support. It was trembling so that it shook my body, and myself, back to awareness of this present world. His painful breathing body struggled to keep him upright one more time, through one more hunt. Finally, he was composed enough to stand without using my body as a brace.

Then he said, quietly, "I never saw anything like that in my whole life. Have you, Mark?"

"No," I answered, and the single word was taken away by the wind.

We loaded our dogs and the three dead coyotes—when there should have been, by all the laws, only two. I drove back to town. Neither one of us talked for a spell. We just stared straight and far down the road. I knew I could never hunt coyotes again. Not ever. I didn't.

That same fateful day, Ortha had left for Texas with my sweet little Connie, but I've already told about that. My wife didn't leave me for chasing women. She left me for running coyotes.

———

As I sit now in this comfortable lawn chair thinking back, reliving those days decades ago, I realized how lucky I was to wind up here comfortable and being able to help my loved ones now and then. It had been luck when Tom C. had introduced me to Old Bum. It had been luck when I found out a couple of years back where, and how, that flop-eared wonder had disappeared from Hi Lo. Well, I'm using that word luck a lot, but I know it plays a big part in everybody's life one way or another, but then maybe it isn't just luck. Maybe it's more. I don't know for sure, but I have a feeling it is.

Anyway, back to how I finally got a tracer on Old Bum's disappearance. My son-in-law is sure enough enterprising in a lot of different ways. As a good example, he was the first one around here to make his cowboys use two-way radios as they rode in pickups or on horseback across his hundred and eighty thousand acres of land. The working cowboys checked into headquarters with the ranch manager every scheduled hour of each working day. It wouldn't be long before they would be riding with two-way videos and a little compact camcorder as well. Then the ranch manager could just sit there on his butt watching wall-sized pictures of the ranch and all its operations, giving orders while he had his iced tea or hot chocolate— according to the time of year.

The open-range cowboy was gone before 1900, then the barbed-wire cowboy gave way to the pickup cowboy, and now they were going to be forced to move over for the electronic, high-tech cowboy. Oh, dear Jesus, help us all. So much for the individualism that used to mark the American cowboy.

When the government agency poisoned the coyotes and trapped all the mountain lions, the deer became so thick they were dying of starvation; so my go-getter of a son-in-law just set up a hunting outfit. Every fall, Jack and the entire family, and half of the cowboys, guided, fed, and entertained, charging hunters from Oklahoma and Texas lots of money for each deer bagged. The smart son of a gun was profiting from everything being forced out of balance. It would no doubt teeter and tilt again before long, but right now he was doing a hell of a balancing job with all the misunderstanding going on between the ranchers, the world-savers, and most of the Washington D.C. ding-a-lings. One thing for sure, when the newest technological medium comes on the market, my son-in-law will be there the next day to haul it to the ranch. If politics has become the newest religion, appealing as far left as atheism, and as far right as the most rabid fundamentalist, then television is its pope. Jack knew how the media used these infinitely advancing sciences for ever-growing power. He would always make their knowledge his own.

Mind you, I'm not trying to shovel any of my personal notions off on anybody else. However, revealing the so-called progressive attitude of my son-in-law shows what a vast change has occurred in the world—and, in me—between the time I first met Old Bum and the four-odd decades later when I finally learned what happened to him.

A while back—before Jack got everything organized to perfection on the hunt, two-way radios and all—everyone used to gather here at the Raton house before going on down to the ranch. So now, as much as I enjoy keeping the stock tanks and house all in top shape, about all I contribute to the actual hunts are a few hound dog stories.

I don't hold it against anyone who hunts the right way, don't you know. It's just that I personally never can, nor ever will, hunt again, after that single portentous day when I knew for sure Old Bum was gone, my wife and child were gone, and I had witnessed that coyote pup sacrifice his life over there east of Hi Lo.

It was only two, or maybe three, years back that I was visiting with some of the excited men as they checked guns, bedrolls, and all that stuff before the big event on the oak-brushed mesas and in the canyons of the ranch. I was telling this hunter, Jim from Oklahoma, about some of our adventures with Old Bum when he interrupted with a look on his face like he had just shook hands with God and been assured he had a first-class reservation to heaven waiting with his name on it.

"That dog wasn't a black and tan, was he?" Jim asked.

"Yeah. Yeah, he was," I said.

"That dog wasn't the one whose floppy ears looked like they'd been run through a CIA shredder, was he?" Jim asked and inched forward on his chair.

"That's his ears, all right," I agreed, getting pretty interested in the questions.

"That dog didn't limp from a bullet wound in his left front shoulder when he got tired, did he?"

Now that long-unused hunter's adrenaline and consequent electricity was stirring up in my body. "He did that exactly and for sure," I almost yelled.

Leaning forward with his eyes stretched open, Jim whispered, "And he only bawled once when he treed a coon, didn't he?"

"That's him. That's Old Bum!" I yelled this time loud enough to make the ears spin on a stone statue.

"Old Bum, huh? Well, we called him Old Traveler," Jim said.

"Same thing," I said.

Then we both began to babble, trying to talk at the same time like folks do on those TV talk shows, or when they've been drinking too much. Just the same, I found out Jim's grandfather, and some friends, had stopped in Hi Lo for a beer, and they wound up buying Old Bum from Rube Fields, the well driller. That old scoundrel.

It seems that somehow a party got going, and Rube had started feeling so good he thought everything in the world belonged to him, including Old Bum. After listening to Rube brag, for a total of two hours, about what a hunter the dog was, these guys from Oklahoma just bought him—for an undisclosed price—to shut him up. It didn't matter if it was fifty dollars or fifty million, they still got the bargain of their lives, when I think about what's truly valuable on this circle of fire, air, water, and rock called earth.

With his still-keen ears, Old Bum had heard this party in the making.

Then someone invited him into the Wild Cat. They all broke down and let him join the party, but he fooled everybody—just like he always had. He would not take a single drink no matter how he was enticed. As impossible as it seems—even now—Old Bum had quit cold turkey when he found out that stuff made him pick fights with thousand-pound bulls.

Jim's grandfather had hauled Old Bum back to Laverne, Oklahoma, near the west edge of the panhandle, and gave him to Jim for an early Christmas present, then took them on a coon hunt.

"Traveler didn't stay home a lot," Jim continued, "but he always came back. Seemed like he knew when a man was getting a bad case of hunter's itch." The young man was smiling all the time he talked now. So was I. "I was afraid something would happen to him," Jim continued, "and tried to keep him penned up, but that didn't work at all. He wouldn't take a lick of water or a bite of food until I turned him out of the dog pen. I mean to tell you he would have starved himself plumb to death before he would give up his freedom. I just gave in and let him go his own way. Sometimes when he'd come home he'd be full of new scars from fighting and chasing the gals."

"Wonder how old he was when he died?" I asked.

"Oh, I don't know, Mr. McClure, but we had him seven years. My dad said he was durn sure over a hundred years old in human time. You know, I rode the school bus to and from school, because in those days we lived four miles from Laverne on a farm. Whenever Old Traveler was home, he'd wait for me halfway across the front yard. That's as far as he would come to meet me. He'd wag his tail about one and a half times and give me a glancing lick on the leg. You had to know him to understand that this was as joyful a greeting as he was gonna give anyone."

"Yeah, I remember."

"Then one day he wasn't there. It was nothing unusual, but somehow I knew in my gut he was gone for good. I looked everywhere for him, but found nothing. I guess he just traveled on." Jim paused, and became quieter. Then he added, "One thing for sure, though, I'll forget a lot of people before I do that old dog."

"Yeah, son, I savvy that clear as morning dew." I didn't want to talk about Old Bum the traveler any more right then myself.

———————

Now I sit here enjoying recollecting.

Tom C. went back to his childhood home in Missouri to die and was buried by the side of his young wife. I still miss him very much. Knowel Denny, Pal England, Rube Fields, and a lot of other sporting boys and girls are up on Graveyard Hill north of town.

I remember Levi Gomez telling me one day, "You know what, Mark? Original thinking and doing are deadly. I'm leaving this burg." He moved west over the Rocky Mountains to Taos and became a truly distinguished *santero*. His saints carved from cedar wood were blessed by the pope and his work was collected by rich and famous people from faraway places. He's gone, too.

And me, old Mark McClure? Well, I really wasn't much of an artist anyway, so right after Levi left Hi Lo, I quit painting and started back laying rocks and doing odd-job carpenter work. I kept seeing these people's houses all over whose poor walls were covered with bad paintings forced on them as gifts from friends. Seems suddenly half of America started doing these westerns and scenery paintings—as the locals called them. This world needed a lot of fixing, but one more bad painter sure wasn't going to help it.

I don't know hardly anyone at Hi Lo any more. One of the two saloons is gone and the other will surely follow. Now it would be impossible to get up a poker game in a month of Saturday nights. When Old Bum left, he took part of a spirited era with him. Hell, that wise old dog saw it coming and allowed himself to be sold so he could ride, instead of walk, out of a country soon to turn more boring with each hour. In these little towns, on far-scattered ranches, people were now getting their secondhand thrills from the perversely soul-diminishing, possessive little box called TV; and being told every single second—on one channel or another—how to vote, how to love, how to die, how to everything.

There ain't even any more hillbilly music. It's called country, country western, rockabilly, country rock, country this and rock that. One thing though, there are still hundreds of thousands of acres of grasslands out there broken by lonely malpais and sandstone mesas. Maybe it's even lonelier between the far-spread ranch houses than it was in my time.

There are more raccoons, antelopes, and deer out there now, and, in spite of all the programs of poison, airplane hunters, and all that stuff, the coyotes are still howling when they damn well feel like it, and the Hi Lo wind blows their messages across a deaf world.

Boy howdy, and gobblin' geese, this late spring sun feels good to my old ex-hunter's bones. It is also a grand and comforting feeling to know that dogs and coyotes are equally as important as kings, queens, or cockroaches. Of course, it's probably not, but the sun seems like it is shining just special for me today. I keep looking down the graveled driveway for Old Bum to come limping in from some kind of chase, bringing along his great zeal for life as the most precious of gifts. I don't worry about him because if he doesn't show up today, he will tomorrow, or in a day or so after that, for sure. Like the song says, "Long ago and far away . . ."

Once a Cowboy

You never quite get to know anyone—anyone at all. Most especially how they'll end up. Even if you've been through decades of bar, car, and horse wrecks, like I had with ol' Rusty Carver.

I see him now as I ride this damn forest-line fence that's been kicked down in places by newcomers. They drive their gas-greedy SUVs up as far as possible, then walk the fence line on the U.S. Forest side, kicking weak posts loose so the boss's cows can get out and cause weeks of hard riding to gather. Some we never find.

My mind's image of ol' Rusty was clear as spring water. He was mounting a green horse. He could just barely reach the stirrup. But he cheeked the bridle and swung his body in the saddle, smooth and easy, riding out circling the round pole corral, getting the feel of how the horse moved, how he reined, ready for him to buck if he thought he had to.

As I dream-watched ol' Rusty, I thought of how different we looked. He was about five-foot-eight and had so much hard, round muscle that he didn't seem to have—or need—any bones in his body. Well, except for his hands. The bones sure showed big there.

Everyone in our country dreaded shaking hands with him. He didn't know it, but he was a hand-crusher.

His nose was broken from tree limbs that horses had run him into—and other things, such as rocks, fists, and a skillet his longtime girlfriend Shirley Mae had swatted him with.

He had a round scar on one side of his belly and one on his back where a Nazi sniper had shot him during World War II. I reckon he'd healed up fine because he never said a word about it in all the years I knew him. Not one damned word.

Now me, Roy Barrett, I was six-foot-two of bones tied together with beef jerky. My nose had never been broken, but it did bend over about a half inch to the south from the cartilage being torn loose. I can't recall how it happened, except I was having fun getting drunk.

It wasn't hard to remember most things we'd shared, but some I couldn't call up any closer than a coyote howling in the next county.

I sure remember, and my spine still feels the time I roped the seven-year-old outlawed steer around the neck and he jumped off in an arroyo, jerking me and my horse over the side, where we all fell in a pile. The horse got up before I did, and the steer as well. They both tried to run in different directions. Ordinarily, that would have been natural, except I was in between them with the rope wound around my middle. I felt like I was one of those poor people that magicians put in a box and then drop the blade down, cutting them smack dab in half. Luckily, I was still in one piece, except my waist was pulled down to about thirteen inches.

Now, I reached out and grabbed the rope on each side of me. No matter how hard I pulled, I couldn't get any slack in the rope with a thousand-pound horse tied hard and fast to one end and a thousand-pound steer on the other.

That makes an even ton.

Ol' Rusty had been following on a good bay cow horse, his rope down to heel up the steer if I was unlucky enough to catch the wild shit-splattering son of a bitch.

Well, my eyeballs were being pushed out of my head by all my insides that had been shoved upward from the rope around my middle. I saw things in a blur, but here's how it went when I double-checked it later. Ol' Rusty's double eagle eyes—and brains faster than a war-room computer—saw my entire problem in a glance. He spurred right along the bank of the arroyo and threw his loop over the steer's head, jerking him down hard. He bailed off the bay and flew through the air like a red-tailed hawk, landing rolling in the bottom of the arroyo not unlike a big round rock, and got up pulling his pocketknife out, opening the blade, and cutting the ropes in two, right where they were tightened against the addled steer's neck as he stumbled up to his feet.

Rusty yelled, "Hold the rope that holds your horse," being an efficient cowboy and rescue squad all at once.

I had been doing this with one hand all along, but now I could use two. The well-trained cow horse turned, looking down from the rope where it was tied to the horn like he was supposed to do.

The world was flat full of blurs. One went by me going south.

The steer had charged my savior with his head down some. Our luck just kept on running, and so did the big steer. One horn had gone on one side of Rusty and one on the other. He was trying to shove my best friend toward—and possibly through—the far side of the arroyo bank, but Rusty was knocked down, and all the steer did was step on him with two of his four feet, ripping the back of his shirt for about a foot and removing only a six-inch strip of hide—Rusty's hide, not the steer's.

I want everything clear here.

I also found out later—as we so often do in this puzzling life—that I had a wide belt all the way around my waist that was also missing hide—my hide, not the steer's.

It's a good thing we'd been working in a sandy part of the arroyo or we might have gotten hurt.

When old Rusty got up and looked things over, he said with a good deal of seriousness, "We're gonna have to ride back to headquarters and get some more ropes."

He was twenty years older than me and had been a mentor for longer than that, so I just nodded my head yes, thinking the fifteen-mile ride back over rocky hills, one rocky mountain, and four rocky canyons would be good exercise for both men and beasts. It surely was.

———————

Rusty Carver had saved my life and other little particles so many times I pretty near cried as I looked back on the long years with him. I would have wept a keg-full all right, except the smiling and the giggling got in the way. As a fair example, the long weekend trip we made to the wonderful little hamlet of Hillsboro, New Mexico, and then on over to El Paso would do.

Now, Hillsboro is in the eastern foothills of the Black Range, where the great Apache warriors Victorio, Nana, and Lozen fought to a standstill two thousand U.S. cavalrymen and infantry as well as about six hundred civilian militia. Me and ol' Rusty have worked cattle over every damn battlefield in their wild history. There was big gold and silver booms there and all sorts of other history, too wonderful for me to remember right now.

A feller just naturally favors a place where he has a good time. I would have liked it if I'd spent half my time in jail. You see . . . Hillsboro is a one-bar, two-church town. My favorite kind. You can get in a lot of sinning and saving all in one little place. These little wonderful havens were the foundation, the cement, and glue of the entire West at one time. Now the New West has made them scarce as picnics in a dust storm.

Hillsboro's one great bar, the S-Bar-X, is named after a cow brand. They hardly ever ran out of whiskey, even though I can honestly say that a couple of times the miners, cowboys, artists, and other wastrels have had them down to less than three bottles. I actually witnessed the time they ran plumb out of beer. Some people got real cranky and had little nervous fits.

Hillsboro has two good restaurants most of the time, one gas station, one motel, and a museum or two, art galleries, and antique stores. It was a good place to drink and dance, you see. Ol' Hoss Hogan had a little band that played weekends at the S-Bar-X. He tried to dress like a cowboy, but you could still tell he was a fix-it-upper repairman on the side. However, by nine o'clock at night, he sounded like Guy Lombardo, Patsy Cline, and Hank Thompson all at once.

Shirley Mae taught first grade over at the county seat—Hot Springs. And she was there waiting for us. She was built a little like Rusty, except for her milk glands. They were a half gallon apiece. But she had a kind and pretty face framed in thick brown, curly hair that made her big brown eyes seem to shine like little headlights.

My girl, Cindi, tended bar right here where the fun-havin' people were gathering. She was kinda tall and skinny like me, except for her butt. It was wider than her shoulders. Before I ever dated her, a local miner showed his appreciation for beauty by saying a sort of dumb thing: "When Cindi walks, her butt looks like two corn-fed pigs in a gunny sack." Even so, it was enough of a compliment to make me take notice. Careful notice.

Well, we got us a table and got down to drinking. I hope some of the young will also remember how valuable it is to have a girlfriend for a bartender. The drinks seem to heavy up a bit. The band was playing, most everybody was dancing, and things got louder and louder. Friday night in the high desert makes more than the coyotes howl. It smelled real good—full of spilled drinks, lung-killing smoke, sweaty citizens, and other noisy-scented things.

Now Rusty dances slow with his shoulders all bunched up as if he was afraid his head was gonna fall off, and he looked down at his and Shirley Mae's feet like he was afraid they were gonna cripple one another. Suddenly he stopped, raised his head up, and howled, trying to really get the sound through the ceiling to the moon outside.

It must have worked because everyone in the S-Bar-X caught the howling disease. Hoss Hogan and his Good Boys—that's the name of the band—played louder to be sure they were heard, and the place turned into a yelling, drinking, dancing heaven. There wasn't but one fight that night, and it was outside. People were having so much fun, they didn't even bother to go watch. Now, that's having fun in anybody's town.

Cindi started trying to get everybody out by closing time, which is two o'clock in the morning in New Mexico. By three, there wasn't anybody left but the four of us.

Since it was too near sunup to go to sleep, I said, "Cindi, you got tomorrow off. Hell's fire, let's head down to El Paso."

Rusty jumped in, his little tiny eyes opening wide enough so you could see they were dishwater blue: "That's the best thing I've heard since cattle was a dollar a pound." I couldn't recall when that was, but the girls seemed willing. Cindi had a purse full of tips and got us a bottle of bourbon to keep us awake till we got to the great Del Norte Hotel in El Paso, Texas.

Shirley Mae drove her Ford until we rolled into Las Cruces, where she got sleepy. Rusty took a drink out of the bottle—big one—and decided he'd drive so we'd all be safe for the upcoming adventures in the great Del Norte.

We were on the outskirts of El Paso at daylight when a siren caused me to take both my hands off Cindi and quiver like I'd been shot in the butt with a flaming arrow. Rusty pulled over after the cop drove alongside for about a mile, making mad pull-over signs. He got out seeming somewhat irritated and asked Rusty for his driver's license.

He didn't have one that he could find. He said, "Shirley's got one. Let me have it, hon."

The cop said, "That won't quite work, sir."

"Oh," said Rusty.

"What is your name, sir?"

"All I can remember right now is Rusty."

"OK, uh-huh, OK. Mister Rusty, did you know you were speeding?"

"Speedin'?"

"Yes, sir, ninety miles an hour in a fifty-five-mile zone."

Rusty grinned real appealing-like and bragged: "Sure, I knew it. I was trying to get home before I got drunk."

The cop didn't know what to say for a minute. I didn't know what to say for a minute, but Shirley Mae evidently did. She got out of the car, moved around the back, smiling so sweet you'd think she'd just swallowed a chocolate bar, and motioned the red-faced cop to her. They talked, and they talked some more.

The cop got back in his patrol car. Shirley Mae got back in her car on the driver's side. As ol' Rusty scooted over, he asked, "What did you tell him?"

"Just what I told you the first night we met."

Rusty damn near wrinkled all the hide off his forehead trying to remember what it was she'd said.

Sure enough, we made it through the city of El Paso to the great Del Norte Hotel right at full service, sunup. I emptied Cindi's bottle so it wouldn't evaporate in the upcoming heat of the Mexican border.

———————

We slept until mid-afternoon and had a good breakfast of huevos rancheros in the coffee shop along with a couple of nice bloody Marys with our coffee.

By eight that night, the great round bar was full of visitors mostly enjoying themselves. There were local businessmen, gold and mercury smugglers, ranchers, oil lease men from farther east in West Texas, and even a few plain old working cowboys like me and Rusty.

The tables and booths in the large lounge were mostly full, and a mariachi band was tuning up. So were we four. The air was full of fun and action. Nobody noticed the deadly cigarette smoke in those days. Just goes to show you how easy even the brightest of people are to brainwash. Course, in our own bunch, we only had one genius, and that was Shirley Mae.

I know it's hard to believe, but things got better. The mariachis were strolling and playing. Some people left the famous circular bar, so big that you had to have a hunter's eye to see all around it, but others filled their empty places as fast as popcorn farts. The table next to the bar emptied, and that sharp-eyed Shirley Mae moved and claimed it for us. Now we were set comfortable with a good view of the whole wonderful place.

We had no more than got our second wonderful drink than that crazy Rusty Carver said to me, "Hey, Roy, let's go over to Juarez, where things are really wide open." The rest of us were silent, staring at him like he was a rabid skunk. That ain't a pretty sight to stare at.

Then Shirley Mae broke the crushing silence, sweetly: "Now, Rusty, dear, Juarez is certainly a freewheeling place, a place to let loose, especially for men. However, I don't feel we should crowd our luck driving any more while drinking."

Rusty meekly said: "It ain't but a half a mile. We could walk."

Since Rusty realized there wasn't a single certainty in what he'd just said, he got up and danced with Shirley Mae. I did the same with Cindi. We were snuggling while we moved, and I couldn't see a single hard rock anywhere on the dance floor. Everything was sure keen. We just got mellow as cherry Jell-O, and everything we said broke us up laughing. Everybody at our table was a goddamned comic and had an audience sitting there who knew how to appreciate those flint-edged quips and showed it. Fun. Fun, I tell the cockeyed world.

I said something like, "You know, if we got up in the morning and there wasn't a single chicken left in the world, there would be panic in the streets."

Of course, I was simply observing, seriously, how everybody was going crazy over the fried chicken joints just beginning to sprout up all over the country. Well, not all over. Hillsboro doesn't have one. Anyway, this just rocked everybody back. Cindi was laughing so dang hard she had to put her head down on the table. Shirley Mae was so full of mirth, she was holding her stomach with both hands and had her eyes closed so tight they were squirting out tears. Ol' Rusty was leaning over, slapping at his knees, about to fall out of the saddle. These two big ol' college football players came over to get our girls to dance. That was fine, but the girls didn't want to. And the young men were so impolite as to insist before the girls could stop laughing. After the third "no thank you," one of them pulled Cindi half up, spouting off, "Ah, come on, Slim. It'll do you good."

I don't know what it was that caused me to stand up. Maybe it was him calling Cindi "Slim" before he'd had a chance to see that wonderful big butt. Maybe it was the crude, macho way he butted in. I don't know. Hell, I just stood up in resentment and was knocked down before I could say more than, "Didn't you hear the . . ."

I was a little dizzy, but I rolled away fast to escape the kicks I expected to follow, and even that was too slow.

Ol' Rusty took a shortcut right across the table, spilling a few drinks and breaking a few glasses. That wasn't nothing compared to what he did to the invaders. Rusty was very limited as a bar fighter. He just had two punches. That great big bony hand-crushing left to the belly or ribs and then a sort of overhand right to the cheekbone.

Down the big kid went, flat as a penny on the pavement, and still as a mummy's ass.

There was no way his companion wanted to enter this sudden competition. But being good at competition was how he was getting through Texas

Western University. Besides, what was worse, people were watching to see what he would do.

Whup. Whap. And he joined his friend on the ballroom floor. However, he moved a little bit, and Rusty went down and whapped him on the side of the jaw. Rusty was always a true gentleman, and this last proved it. He could have kicked him instead.

There were evidently folks present who didn't understand loyalty and protecting the hearth and all that.

The El Paso jail for drunks and derelicts was underground in those days. That's where we all spent the night—safe from atomic bomb attacks. Since I had only received and not delivered a punch, this detention was puzzling. Also, when the law arrived we were all trying to explain that we were the pickees, not the pickers. If Cindi and I had shut up and let Shirley Mae do her trick talking, all the trouble to follow could have been avoided. There's no use saying more about the jail. Hell, most everyone who experiences it once decides not to let it happen again. Ever.

The courtroom was full of hangovers. There were other kinds of criminals, of course, but we were with the majority for one of the few times in our lives.

Our turn came. Cindi, Shirley Mae, and me, ol' Roy Barrett, were fined for resisting arrest, drunkenness in a public place, and three hundred dollars in broken glass. We paid up. Even so, I was puzzled by how four whiskey glasses and a cheap little ash tray could mount up to three hundred dollars. Maybe they were imported crystal and I'd been having too much fun to notice.

Then there stood Rusty before the judge, his hat held in front of his chest with his head down like he was praying. I knew better. He was being tried for assault. He was straining his brain matter trying to keep straight all the things Shirley Mae had told him, such as: "Now, dear, don't be afraid. I know this judge. My uncle helped him get appointed, and he's an art lover."

Rusty's little pig eyes opened up so you could tell he heard. "An art lover?" he said.

"That's right, he collects from Tom Lea, José Cisneros, and all kinds of fine artists. He even thinks he's an artist himself. Half the basements and closets in El Paso hide at least one of his paintings." She went on to close the deal out: "Now, you have no doubt noticed how he asked every defendant what their occupation was. Well, when he does that, you tell him you're an artist and he'll be easier on you."

Rusty stared and stared. This was asking a bit much for a hard-rock cowboy and efficient bar-room brawler to actually admit in public that he was an artist.

It was finally Rusty's turn to be questioned.

"And Mister Rusty Carver, what is your occupation?"

Rusty choked. He turned his hat in his hands. I thought the tough old son of a bitch was gonna fall dead as year-old dung right there.

"Well?" Judge Chavez asked.

"Your honor, sir, I'm an artist."

The judge relaxed back in his chair, his hands locked together across his chest, and beamed kindly down on our dear desperate friend.

"I'm a portrait artist, your honor, sir."

"Oh, a portrait artist, huh? Are you good?"

"Well, I s'pose I am."

"Modesty in an artist is very rare, my son. I'd bet you are very good."

"I sure hope you win your bet, your honor, sir."

Cindi and I were hopeful. Shirley Mae was just swelling with pride.

Judge Chavez paused, his nostrils flaring. "Do you think you'd have time to paint me?"

Political machinery was running through the judge's head. I could see it. The thought of a free portrait was perhaps turning the wheels of justice.

"Well, your honor, sir, I'm out of art supplies right now."

The judge leaned forward with serious intent, his pen poised above a blank paper and said, "Well, son, give me a list and we'll see what we can do about that."

My God. We all breathed. It looked like it had worked. Then, my dearest friend and Shirley Mae's closest loving friend said, "Well, let's see, your honor, sir. If I had a broom and a bucket of fresh shit I believe I could get an exact likeness."

The entire courtroom gasped and stared up and down and even sideways as the judge turned that shade of purple you see in mountain crevices as the sun sets in the peaceful West. There was no doubt in my mind that my very best friend was going to be sentenced to hang until he was that same shade of purple.

Shirley Mae became a heroine of the first order as she charged past the guard and the judge's all-around man and pulled the judge's head next to her whispering mouth.

He shook his head at first, still dangerously purple. Then he lessened to red and then to his natural, nice olive. Now he was healthy again and occasionally shook his head in agreement to whatever in the hell Shirley Mae was saying. Then she smilingly glared at us with kind assurance and I for one felt safe and warm.

The judge, amidst slight confusion, calmly dismissed Rusty's case for lack of evidence. There were a few protestations, but simply lifting his manicured hand, palm out, was enough to bring a welcome silence.

We finally followed Rusty's wishes and went to Juarez, and Rusty asked Shirley Mae to marry him. Like the feller said, "In those days you could do anything in Juarez you were big enough to do and still pay for."

Nowadays, of course, you've got the dope smugglers instead of the gold smugglers. But there's a big difference here. It takes many mean and greedy bastards to get the dope for the dopers. It takes good miners to get the gold for the smugglers. Yeah, I miss the miners. Miners ain't nothing but cowboys who can't ride.

We had one hell of a fun time in Juarez, Mexico, before heading back to the Hillsboro country. As I think back on ol' Rusty now, he wasn't near as dumb as some people might think. The first thing he did when he escaped hanging was marry Shirley Mae. That's what I call plumb wise and wonderful.

It was about impossible to figure how a man that smart could suffer such a terrible blow later. You can't build any final forts against the future no matter what the experts tell you.

Shirley Mae and Rusty pitched in their savings, mostly hers, and made a good down payment on a little white-painted, five-room frame house in Hillsboro. He went on working with me on the Ladder Ranch and she continued teaching first grade in Hot Springs. They soon had one cute little daughter, Mary Anne, and another in the chute. A family had been cemented. On weekends in the spring and summer he helped her patch up the place real good and make a good garden of tomatoes, corn, green beans, and, most important of all, chile. And every winter he killed a deer to round out the bounty.

The best I'd done was finally get engaged to the new bartender at the S-Bar-X. Cindi had run off to Tucson, Arizona, with a used car dealer. She'd been fun.

However, my new—and I hoped forever—love had been raised on a ranch until her father lost the place when she was eighteen years old. She was still pissed about that, blaming the U.S. Forest Service, the Bureau of Land Management, and above all the "Do-Gooders." She just said it once so as not to be a whiner. "Five generations of us fighting droughts, blizzards, cow disease, low prices and now, where bear, cows, and antelope roamed there's a bunch of trashy trailer houses and the water's turned sour as cat shit."

I never did know all of it. What I did know was Suzie Lou was a strange but good looker. She had auburn hair worn in a ponytail and oddly enough, considering the red showing in her hair, eyes as black as Geronimo's. She walked back and forth around that S-Bar-X bar like she owned it. She had everything that makes up a young woman a man would want to spend his old age with, moving smooth as water in an irrigation ditch. The mother ditch.

She laughed at all the silly things us humans do and at the same time she could get tough and mean as a badger if you got out of line smart-assing. She also got along great with Rusty and Shirley Mae. That just about cinched it.

I didn't have anywhere to put her on the Ladder, and I hadn't got up the guts to mention it. So when I heard about those forty-eight horses a feller wanted to get rid of over near Hatch, I got ol' Rusty to go with me and take a look.

The man had a combination farm and cow ranch most commonly called a stock farm. The man who owned the horses was over northeast, a ways from Mountainair, and said his name was Tom Nothing, but most every-one called him Nothing Tom. Well, we walked around the corral and looked over Nothing's forty-eight horses. They were every color from bays to paints and every shape and condition from bony to fat.

"What do you want for 'em?" I asked.

"Hell," he said, "I don't know. A couple of 'em ate a little loco weed. The effects ain't shown up yet, but who knows? Huh."

I couldn't give him an answer.

"Some of them is a little green and some of them has been rode hard with a lot of living with dried sweat," he added.

"What do you want for 'em?"

"Some of them has been kid ponies and one or two has been bucked out in rodeos."

I was beginning to show signs of irritation. Even Rusty had taken his five-inch-brim greasy old Stetson off and was scratching his thick-haired gray head.

"For the last time, how much do you want?"

"What you got to trade?"

"Well, let's see, we got ten bred heifers between us that the Ladder lets us run for free."

I looked at Rusty and he looked at me. Then we both looked way off across the desert mesa only a half mile to the west waiting the fatal answer.

"They in good shape?" Tom Nothing asked.

"Yeah," I said.

"Yeah. It's a trade if you deliver them right here," he said.

It was done.

Then we did what all cowboys have to do on their own at least once in their lives. We quit the Ladder, where we had hard but good jobs, and went in business for ourselves.

We owned one good cow horse apiece and the rigging that goes with 'em. Rusty's cousin over at Hot Springs had two pack mules we borrowed. We used most of the little savings we had and with the hesitant blessings of Shirley Mae and Suzie Lou, we headed out across country. We were now cowboy entrepreneurs and aimed to come home in a few weeks with lots of money and other goods to make our women happy and secure. I aimed dead on to ask Suzie Lou for her hand and everything else tied to it.

We headed north along the Rio Grande at first, then angled off northeast later. We had decided to ride a different horse each day and that way we could be testing while we were trading. It didn't take long to realize these horses had spent more time on loco weed than it first appeared. If a tree limb touched them on the head, some of the horses would just fall down and wrap around the tree. We couldn't get them up. So we'd have to tie a rope on their feet and drag them away and then tail them up like a dying cow. It was turning into the damnedest mess a feller ever saw.

I was riding a good-looking sorrel, plumb shiny, and every time he'd see a shadow from a fence post or a tree, it didn't matter, he'd drop his head down and examine it carefully, then jump just as high and far as he could. That sure slowed things down. It wasn't quite so bad if you weren't riding them. Some of them would suddenly see a cow trail and just jump straight up and fall down on it. Sometimes more than once. But the ones that got my total attention were the ones that would lift their heads to a sudden breeze that had blown across a water hole way off somewhere. They'd run around in circles, their heads down, until they found a sink place or a bare patch and just stop and drink. That invisible water must have tasted pretty good 'cause they'd switch their tails and walk away acting satisfied with all that dusty air they'd swallowed. One really did smell water at a farmer's water trough and just fell into it. He must have got water in his lungs. He died. One mare went up to an arroyo bluff and just walked off it, hitting her head and breaking her neck. She didn't hardly kick before she was still forever.

We lost four head before we sort of got the know-how to sort of handle them.

We made our first trade on the fifth day out. A small rancher needed a gentle horse for his kids. Rusty really surprised me. He was a genuinely good liar.

"That little sorrel mare there was ridden by my brothers' kids over at Las Cruces all the time," he said. "Hell, his three-year-old rode her in a Fourth of July parade."

"Well, I'm gonna take your word for it, but this little bay here is a mite too spooky for my kids."

We made the trade and the man had told the truth, mostly. Spooky was not the right word, however. That sucker bucked so hard, Rusty had to run into him three different times with his own good horse to keep me from being thrown hard.

When the new horse finally stopped, I told Rusty: "We made a hell of a good trade there. We'll swap this bastard to a rodeo stock contractor. This is the kind of buckin' stock they're prayin' to find."

"Yeah," the great liar said.

The very next ranch house we came upon was about five miles westerly. The feller took a liking to another sorrel mare we had.

"How old is she?"

Rusty ran up right quick, pushed her lip back, and said: "She shows to be a coming five." Rusty had always been good at teething a horse's age, but now he was also fast, and all those natural muscles stopped folks from doubting his word.

Rusty went on and said: "Why, three of my little nieces and nephews rode this horse to school at the same time down at Nutt." Now, Nutt, New Mexico, is famous for being nothing but a bar between Hatch and Deming. There sure as hell ain't no school there.

We traded that fourteen-year-old sorrel mare for a bull with one nut. That was fine with me. We might have to eat the half-loaded critter to keep going on our trail of riches.

After a trade was done and the handshake made, we'd hear bragging through their laughter such as, "That ol' horse is spavined."

"That ol' horse has been foundered and has a bad ankle to boot."

We heard our victims spout such things as: "That milk cow ain't had a calf in three years. You couldn't get a drop of milk out of her with an oil field suction pump. Ha ha ha."

We got to having a lot of fun out of this. It's always a good thing because the joke was just as much on us as them. Oh, it went on and on for weeks. Course, what these gloating local traders didn't know was this: as soon as we were out of hearing, we nearly fell off our own crazy horses laughing about the shadow-jumping, air-drinking trick horse they now owned.

We weren't gaining much yet, but we knew now we didn't have much to lose, if anything. In the fun department, we were many rocky miles ahead. All this fun puzzles and pains even more when you know what happened to old Rusty later on.

We tried to camp out one night and count up. We had a hundred-and-seven-dollar gain in the cash department. Some few cattle, bulls, cows, and heifers of various colors and conditions. Sixteen new horses—some lame one way or another and four or five that were working real good. We had about half our locoed stock left to trade. Course, they were the craziest of the forty-eight.

When we were trading after three o'clock in the afternoon, we stalled by teething, checking out every joint on the horse, cow, or whatever was on the docket. Rusty and I held endless sidebar conferences and then about sundown we'd make the trade. We'd shake hands in the old-fashioned way that used to hold water better than the tightest contracts you can get now.

Invariably, the traders would ask us to stay for supper and the night. The feed was always better than the crackers and sardines we'd gotten down to.

We had trouble every night, though, when people were so generous. You see, we had so many trading tales to discuss that it was impolite to just bust a gut laughing at midnight or after. Not only that, it would wake up and scare hell out of our host and hostess thinking they had a couple of real nuts in their place. Well?

We spent a lot of evenings planning what we were going to get our women with our profits. Rusty wanted to buy the lot next door so Shirley Mae could have room to raise the flowers she loved so much as well as the vegetable garden they both cultivated. I was heavy on getting a little house like Rusty's and a diamond ring for that special finger on Suzie Lou's hand.

"Hell's fire," I told Rusty. "I may just buy the S-Bar-X for her."

"Well, by damn," he said. "That's what I call a wedding present."

Over by Mountainair in the rolling hill and mesa country, we accidentally ran onto a bootlegger. He was friendly from the start, knowing that if we were any form of the law, we would not have the sad mixture of stock we had.

He was holding a really good .30-30 Winchester. I could tell Rusty really wanted it for a deer rifle. His old .30-40 Krag was about done in.

So we settled for a little tradin' talk over some of the best corn-made white lightning I ever tasted. Damn, we sure had fun. We stayed three days. Old Jake finally got drunk enough on his own concoction that we traded him a beautiful pinto mare that didn't go crazy but every other day—this was her day off—for the Winchester and three crock jugs of homemade whiskey.

Then we got the hell out of there.

Old Jake would have a hangover next day—the day that paint mare was scheduled to go crazy and kick at shadows, sunlight, cedar trees, barn doors, or humans.

When we got to Mountainair we traded another kid horse for a good-looking cow and calf to a feller just west of town. Damned if it wasn't a good old pony. He had six kids, and they all took turns riding him, happy as a fried chicken dinner with biscuits and gravy.

And that's exactly what we had for lunch. Mr. Hawkins insisted on us dining so luxuriously on his wife's cooking. We tried to appear reluctant but damn near knocked one another down getting to the table. We did give him a couple of drinks from ol' Jake's jugs. And we all ate. With the kids and his wife and a visiting sister and her two kids, there were too many to count.

After three cups of coffee and some killer tobacco, Mr. Hawkins said, "I can tell you fellers been tradin' locoed horses and I counted 'em perty close in your"—he hesitated before he said it—"remuda. I was a horse trader for thirty years. That's how I traded for this fine place here. There's a twenty-acre pasture right out there. I suggest you put all the locos in there, and we'll turn the rest of your stuff"—yeah, he called our walking goods "stuff"—"and I'll pass the word around and we'll see what happens. If you get rid of them, you can just give me whatever you like. Locoed horses sometimes get over it in a few years, sometimes minutes. But there's a little shortage of using horses right now."

Rusty pitched right in at this: "They've all been rode several times. We did it ourselves."

"Well, well, well," he said, increasing the volume each time. "That means they'll show better than I thought."

Mr. Hawkins's trading blood was beginning to fire. It took about two weeks, and that was fine with us. Mrs. Hawkins seemed to have an unlimited amount of chickens to fry, and she could cook biscuits and gravy that would make a heroin addict quit cold for just one serving. And that ain't much of an exaggeration.

The horses behaved and reined out pretty good most of the time. There was one day when a skinny ol' gray stud tried to mount the hood of a man's new pickup, and another time a little chestnut mare we'd traded for lit out in a dead run. She did a full circle in the pasture, slid to a stop, and turned around and retraced the whole thing, her ears laid back and her beautiful chocolate mane and tail streaming out in the sunlight.

Now this would have been a beautiful sight to a circus horse trainer, but to a bunch of ranchers, cowboys, and part-time farmers, this was a puzzle. It didn't puzzle me. We'd traded one locoed horse for another. However, when she slid to a stop and looked around, spotting the little gathering, she stood right in front of Rusty.

He smiled as if he knew everything in the world, reached out and patted her on the forehead, saying softly, sickeningly, "My little darling, just like I trained you. Thank you for the fine show." He eased a loop over her head, and a bean farmer bought her for his wife for an astounding forty dollars.

It was time to go home. We were traded out. We had to settle up with Hawkins. He was smarter half asleep than both of us at our best, so we had to cheat a little to even the odds. We took the last gallon of ol' Jake's whiskey and just kept toasting such things as "to the hospitality of the Hawkins family . . . to the beautiful Hawkins children . . . to the best fried chicken in the world . . . to new friends and old memories." If we hadn't had to put Hawkins to bed, we'd have gone on all day and far into the night. As it was, we watched while Mrs. Hawkins threw a cover over him. Rusty asked her if she had an envelope. She did. He stuffed some bills in it, licked and sealed it and placed it on the fireplace mantle. Mrs. Hawkins smiled knowingly. We saddled our own horses—the two we'd left home with—and got the pack mules ready. We gathered our new horses, cows, bulls, and heifers up and headed out across country as far off any trail as we could. We were aiming in the general direction of Hillsboro, way off southwesterly.

————

A few days later, tired, hungry, and with the sardine diarrhea, we stopped, looking down from a hill above our town. We were on the far eastern edge of the Sterling Roberts ranch, I think. We counted up our money. We had six hundred twelve dollars and seventeen cents to split up.

There were twenty-six horses, none of them locoed where you could tell by looking, but a lot of them limping. There were nine milk cows, from Holsteins to jerseys and a couple of brindles. Some of them had even given milk at one time. We had four cold bulls, one hot one and another with one nut, three burros, two mules, and a Rolf collie dog who was about to have pups. Of course, Rusty had his Winchester.

The only thing we could figure out was the split on the money and we had figured hard. Before even facing our beautiful women, we gathered the little courage and energy we had left and pushed this bunch of livestock up the road north past Jimmy Bason's F-Cross Ranch and way on up into the U.S. Forest land of the Black Range, opened a gate and drove them scattered out in the vast Gila Wilderness. We'd lied so long on the trading trail that we now lied to ourselves about how all our livestock would heal and fatten up and then we'd gather them and hold a big sale. What few the lions, bears, and coyotes would miss couldn't be penned in that huge and wild country with a dozen top cowboys and that was about all there was left in the whole of Sierra County. The Rolf collie bitch would turn into a fair cow dog. Shirley Mae fell in love with her, though, and we never got to use her much.

We mounted up, leading the two pack mules. After having spent two days near Hillsboro, we finally headed straight for the S-Bar-X bar. It was all downhill right to the front porch. Then two steps up and four more to the door. We'd made it.

———

It was a Thursday. Shirley Mae would be home from Hot Springs for the weekend on Friday night. So we had time to sip a few drinks and talk over our next move. Suzie Lou evidently had a day off, so we sat at a table and relaxed.

No matter how we figured, that three hundred odd dollars we each had pocketed wasn't going to last long, and it sure as hell wasn't going to put us in business for ourselves. Before we could admit we were going to have to go back to cowboying, Ginger, the relief bartender, came over and handed me an envelope. She turned around and whipped up to get away from our table before I could ask her about it. I unfolded the letter. It was from Suzie Lou. My eyes blurred over as I read it. The gist of it was that she loved me

116

but didn't see any future for her in Hillsboro, and she didn't see any for me anywhere else.

I wanted to yell out about the lonely beauty of the whole damn surrounding country and the fun a fella could have if he worked it right, but all I did was say to my best friend, "Suzie Lou left the country."

Rusty just said, "Awww, shit. What did she do that for?" with disappointment showing on his old broad, busted face.

I don't care what people say, when this happens you get shook up. There was a rock in my throat I couldn't have washed away with a barrel of beer.

Ol' Rusty and ol' Roy were sure surprised when Art Evans, the foreman of the Ladder, told us the boss knew we'd be back and had just hired a couple of gunzels (phony cowboys) to help out until we returned.

Art was a hell of a good cowboy and a fine feller, but he had to issue the orders the big owner gave. Our first punishment was building a mile and a half of fence in solid rock. We got blisters bigger than silver dollars digging those postholes with regular hand diggers and a heavy steel bar. We finally had to use dynamite on most of the postholes.

Then we were exiled to Farber Camp, a powerful forty miles from nowhere. There were a hell of a lot of cows in the Farber pasture to be checked out and a count made.

We pulled six good horses over with the Ford pickup and a six-horse trailer the boss had bought from a broke racetrack runner.

Farber Camp held a pretty fair three-room shack that had actually been painted twenty years back, and it had recently been left vacant by a cowboy and his wife who took off for Montana. Art Evans told us that they had left some grub there, as was customary. He said there was enough for a month.

There was plenty of pinto beans and sowbelly and a starter of sourdough bread. There was also a rare luxury—three boxes of Post Toasties.

The next morning for breakfast I poured us out a big bowl each of the corn flakes. Rusty had our thick bacon ready, but I was still scrounging around looking for some canned milk to eat them with. I looked everywhere but the outhouse. There was no cockeyed canned milk. Rusty seemed a little disappointed, but I was half mad.

"Rusty," I said with much conviction. "We are surrounded by big pastures. These pastures are grazing over seven hundred head of mother cows. All those mamas who have calves have milk."

"Let's saddle our horses," he wisely added.

We rode a long way. It was a nice feeling, though. All we wanted was one cow to give us enough milk for the breakfast of delicious Post Toasties. We'd eaten the sowbelly before we left. A good thing.

The Ladder had over two hundred thousand acres of mostly rough rocky land, but good grass for the cows and brush of all kinds to feed the numberless deer, elk, bear, mountain lions, coyotes, foxes, wild turkeys, and even quail in the lower flatlands. As we rode along side by side, our heads down looking for cow sign, as cowboys do their entire lives, we saw the tracks of most of these wild critters. Then I pulled up and stared a minute across mesas, breast-shaped foothills, and smaller rolling hills where you could find great meadows. I looked all the way across the Black Range, dark bluing the lighter blue of the sky, and into the mighty Gila Wilderness. No, I didn't feel small in this vastness. I *knew* that. I just felt at home, just like old Nana and his little tiny surviving tribe had felt and fought so damn well to save what I so easily viewed.

We saw a lot of cows, but in widely scattered bunches. Most of them had been sucked dry by their calves. Finally we found the cow we were looking for. She and about ten more head of mothers were returning from a drink at a spring down below. She was the only one that had a full bag. The other cows were flabby-bagged, and the reason why was their calves were with them. It was obvious this big old cow had a late calf, and she'd hid it while she went for water.

We were taking down our ropes, angling off so she wouldn't booger, waiting till they hit the open meadow just up ahead.

Now, me and ol' Rusty had made a lot of little punkin' roller rodeos around the country, trying out bulldogging, bronc riding, and calf roping, but about the only thing we'd ever won much at was wild cow milking. Whichever one of us got position first roped the horns. If you caught the neck, it choked them and made a cow mad and harder to mug. Rusty usually mugged because he was a lot stronger than me.

I had brought along an oversize Coke bottle to get our breakfast milk in.

We pulled our hats down over our eyes.

The little bunch of cows hit the opening. We spurred after them. Damned if that old sorrel horse didn't put me just right to fit a loop around her neck just as she hit the brush. Rusty bailed off his horse and was fighting tree limbs and brushy entanglements to get to her head and mug her, so I could squeeze a teat or two and get us a Coke bottle full of milk.

Now several things had already gone to hell and back twice. Not only had I caught her around the neck instead of the horns, but deep next to her chest. Now she could get mad without hardly choking. She did that. She was bellering and bawling in bass. And she ran through the thickest skin-plowing bushes she could find. There were millions of them bushes. Old Rusty was hanging onto her horns with a hand on each, but she was flinging him up and then down. She was dragging him a spell, then turning back and stepping all over his legs with hard, sharp, fast-moving hoofs. Skin ripped off, but Rusty held. I was running after them through that same hide-loving brush. Every now and then I'd stick my head in her flank, grab a teat with one hand, and try to squeeze milk in the small opening of the big Coke bottle.

I mostly missed it because of the thrashing about. My cow horse was trying his best to hold the rope tight, but she twisted and turned so many different ways it was impossible. I must have had about an inch of cloudy milk in the bottle when she got loose bowels. Of course, she was swinging her tail all the time, hitting me all over, but especially in the face. So now, with the added weight on her tail she whopped me across both eyes and I damn near went blind. I was forced to wipe the brown-green stuff out of my eyes, and it made the bottle slick and harder to hold, and some of it was getting into the milk. Course, I was too busy at the time to know it. Then, too, there was a little blood from my scratched face mixed with the cow shit and then into our breakfast milk.

The second time she whopped me across the face with that dirty old tail, I not only went blind; I got mad.

I was calling her names I usually reserved for child molesters, wife beaters, crooked politicians, and road ragers. I used all these expert names and more when I fell down under her and she kicked me in the side of the head. I was thinking maybe she'd kicked my left ear off, but I knew damn well she'd ripped at least half my hat brim loose because it was flopping in my face.

After several years passed in about fifteen minutes, I had the bottle three-quarters full of dark-colored milk.

I yelled, "We got the milk, we got the milk! Rusty, hang on till I get my horse."

He yelled back, "There ain't nothing left to hang on with but my arms. The rest of me is in pieces in the bushes."

I sympathized as I got on my horse with my thumb over the bottle top to save every drop of the precious liquid. It was difficult to believe, but it happened: we hit a little opening, Rusty plowed his worn-out heels in the ground and stopped the old cow. She was getting kind of worn out, herself. I spurred my horse up, loosening the rope. Rusty jerked the loop wide and off over the cow's head. By God, we'd done it!

The cow took off bellering in the direction of her calf. Rusty was standing in the way. One horn grazed a trail on the outside of his rib cage and several hundred pounds of cow knocked him rolling.

He lay still. The cow tore more brush apart vanishing in broad daylight. I got down carefully, so as not to spill our milk, and went over to see if Rusty was dead. My knees buckled and I sat right down by him. With my free hand I tried to roll him over face up. It worked. He sat straight up.

"You got milk?" he said.

I proudly held the bottle out where he could see.

"That there looks like chocolate milk," he said.

"Now ain't that something," I said. "A cow that gives chocolate milk."

He stared at me so hard I got scared.

"Something is wrong with your hat," he said.

Before I could move, he reached out and jerked my hat brim. It all came off. I was wearing a little cap with no bill. What a feeling of inadequacy for a working cowboy. Terrible. By gollies, I got home with the funny-colored milk. The sun had been coming mostly straight down on my face. I didn't know it until about sundown, but I was burned red as a woodpecker's head. My cap that had once been a hat didn't do the job.

And I'm ashamed to admit that my best friend Rusty refused to let me pour the milk on his Post Toasties. I had strained it several times through a dish towel into a little pitcher, but he kept saying there was cow shit in it and always would be. He poured water and a spoon of sugar on his cornflakes and ate them with no expression of appreciation on his face at all.

Of course, one has to make allowances in special situations. Rusty's face looked like it had been pounded for an hour with a steak softener and had barbed wire dragged across it until the barbs wore off. His shirt and even his Levi's were ripped and skinned from the cow's front feet and the strangling brush. There was just no way you could foresee the tough old bastard's futile future.

Anyway, I had strained that milk over and over through clean dish towels until the chocolate had turned plain gray. That was the best I was ever going to do for my Post Toasties milk. And by dogies, I want the world to know that I poured half that little pitcher of semichocolate milk on my cereal and ate every damn flake and spooned what was left out of the bowl, making the most gluttonous sounds. As everyone says, a man has got to do what has to be done, and I'm still here to tell about it.

The second day of actually working cattle for the benefit of the Ladder outfit, we were riding along with our heads down looking for fresh cow sign. Without even looking up, Rusty said, "You look just like a rabbi on horseback with that little skullcap."

I didn't hesitate. I reined my horse around, rode to camp, and drove all the way to Hot Springs to buy me a new hat. I couldn't go to headquarters for the spare hat I had there. I'd have to explain to the other cowboys forever. My face was red as a monkey's ass in every way.

———

The owner finally let us go back working under Art Evans, and the Hillsboro world moved on and on with cattle prices going up and way down like always. A few miners grubbed enough gold from the hard hills to keep their bodies and dreams barely alive. Some of the artists who had drifted here stayed, but most, like the world around, moved on to other little colonies, then still others. But there was an amalgamated core community here that was both solid and bizarre.

A big movie star bought a half serious, half play ranch over across the state border in southeastern Arizona and Rusty got the job as foreman with

Art Evans's recommendation. It seemed far away, but actually it was only a half day's drive. So Rusty got back to Hillsboro to be with Shirley Mae about twice a month. This raise in pay, combined with his mate's teaching wages, allowed them to raise their two daughters perty good. The girls were just one year apart and were both running straight A's in high school. That meant college scholarships would come if the grades held up, and they did.

I kept looking for another Suzie Lou, wondering how many chances at such a woman a cowboy's God would grant. I hated to quit the Ladder outfit, but I had the itch to hunt for something I hadn't found, whatever the hell that was.

I worked up near Hi Lo in the northeastern part of the state for a few years. Here I was catty-cornered completely at the other end of the state from where I'd come. It's really good cattle country, but old Jim Ed Love, who owned the JL outfit, was so cockeyed unpredictable I finally had to pull out of there to keep from throwing a rock or something at him. One minute he was sweet-talking you into doing twice the amount of justified work and the next second he was sweet-talking you and meant it. Course, that was his way of keeping us dumb-ass cowboys confused and doing what he wanted.

I worked up there for several years—on three different outfits—and still had the same saddle and maybe a hundred fifty dollars more money than I'd had the day I left the Hillsboro country. I told ol' Wrangler Lewis and Dusty Jones who had worked for Jim Ed most of their lives, "This cowboyin' has got me stiffened up all over, but the one place that counts."

Dusty said, "Me, too."

Then he looked way off at the sky for bird migrations and sadly went on, "However, I sometimes wish my dinger was as stiff as my neck."

That was too much truth for me to handle. A week later I quit the Hi-Lo Country and started working dude ranches in Wyoming and Colorado. The dudes were only there in the summertime, and these dude outfits kept their play cattle in the barns in the winter. I didn't have to go out in sixty-mile-an-hour blizzards and feed freezing cattle with a freezing cowboy riding a freezing hay wagon. Why in hell hadn't I figured this out before my temples turned gray?

It was easier work for sure. There was more women available, as well as more whiskey. Some of these women, even rich women, seemed to like me, but even if I could have put up with holding my hand out behind me with my palm up, I never seemed to be able to hook up with one that suited. I sure fought my head to do it, though, but the money didn't make them anywhere near Suzie Lou.

Cowboys, unfortunately, aren't much on writing letters. Me and ol' Rusty mailed about one a year for a while, then none. Shirley Mae wrote me three or four times a year, no matter what. The girls were going to graduate from New Mexico State University on the same day this year. Time flies faster than falcons. Before Art Evans and his wife retired, he got ol' Rusty a sort of easy horse-wrangling job on the Ladder. I went back and thought I'd finish up with Rusty there. Twenty years' age difference isn't so much when one of you is twenty-five and the other is forty-five, but now it was like a thousand years.

The first thing I noticed was certain crazy things we'd done in our youth had gone missing in Rusty's head. He covered up real quick by answering, "Well, yeah, whatever" and such like.

Shirley Mae had been retired for five years and with Rusty's faltering help had their little place in town pretty shiny. She was sure wanting Rusty to retire with her, but for plain working cowboys, there was no such thing as retirement pay. Finally, Ralph Moon, the new foreman, had to let him go. Shirley was sure happy to have him home, even if he was getting a little forgetful a mite more than most. Rusty had gone to wrangle the horses every now and then without his pants on. And once he'd even gone out barefooted and no shirt. Course, he never forgot his hat.

A famous TV mogul and his movie star wife—at the time—bought the Ladder and were turning the whole damn thing into a buffalo ranch. That is right. Over two hundred thousand acres of buffalo. I don't have anything against buffalo. I just wasn't raised to work them. I was goin' crazier than I was natural born. That is crazy. I had to go.

Then, luck finally hit me right between the horns. A Texas oilman had bought a play-pretty ranch a few miles southerly from town and to everyone's surprise, his wife, Dottie Eastman, took to it and went and started raising and breeding Arabian horses like she'd been born to it. She wouldn't hardly ever go back to his Midland, Texas, headquarters with him.

One day, he had a hunting party of longtime, rich friends driving and climbing around after elk. Carl Eastman fired on a big five-by-six and just as the elk fell, so did he, both deader than a bleached cow skull.

I went over one week later. I sat in that big fancy kitchen and had coffee with that big fancy woman, stayed all day and stayed all night, and had me a top-paying job helping raise and train them Arab horses on this big fancy ranch before the sun came up that next morning.

A week after I'd been employed on the Dottie outfit, she took some meat out of the freezer and cooked us up the best damn elk steak I ever tasted. I was sure enjoying life like never before. I silently thanked old Carl Eastman for being such a good shot.

Course, my tires was flattened a little every time I visited Rusty and Shirley Mae. He was always so happy to see me that he'd forget and crush my hand. He might be old and getting soft everywhere else, but those damn hands could still turn a chunk of steel into baking powder. But it was getting damn near impossible to talk about the old days and great times we'd shared. He would remember a snatch or so, then his eyes would go to a place unknown. Finally, it hurt my heart so bad, I told Dottie this would be the last time I could take watching him disappear like that. To her credit, she said, pushing at her dyed red hair, with those wonderful fifty-year-old blue eyes wide as a baby's, "No, darling. You have to see it through. He would, for you."

She was right, of course, and at that moment, I realized I had finally moved up from Suzie Lou.

When I got to their house and parked the pickup, I knew something was wrong. There wasn't anybody in the house and their dog was gone. Ol' Rusty had just wandered off out of town, walking across the foothills west toward the F-Cross Ranch and the Ladder on beyond. With the help of their little mongrel dog, Buckshot, Shirley Mae and several more citizens found him. I met them walking back into the edge of the one and only main drag of Hillsboro. Shirley Mae was holding his hand, leading him slowly along with the little black-and-white dog by their side. The rest of the townfolks walked respectfully behind.

When she saw me, she smiled a tiny bit and said, "Buckshot trailed him . . . or I might never . . ."

I took his other hand and tried to visit on the way back to the house.

"That old bay horse is hiding in the outhouse," I told him. That's all. He didn't even know I was there or anywhere else as far as that goes.

It got worse almost daily now. One of their daughters lived in Portland with her husband and two grade-school kids. The other one was divorced in San Diego, working at a computer firm trying to support three stair-step boys alone.

They managed at great hardship to come for a couple of days, each a month apart. About all they could do was clean everything up and cook several meals ahead and put them in the freezer. Then they had to get to El Paso and take flights back home and hold their worlds together there. That's just the way of it.

I brought up to Shirley Mae about putting him in a good permanent care home in Las Cruces. I'd checked it out myself. Shirley Mae finally said "no" for the last time. "Not while I can move." A month later, she fell dead, just wore out. The girls came. The cowboys from all around came. Most of the town of Hillsboro came. We buried her up on the windy hill where all cow-mining towns have their graveyards. The wind blew like hell.

The daughters dressed Rusty up in a suit he'd only worn twice in twenty years. One held his hand on one side, her sister did the same on the other. He smiled and said something unintelligible every now and then.

Some black yearling steers with white faces lined up along the fence, all in a row, staring at the people at the cemetery. A red-tailed hawk shot down out of the huge sky, screamed once, and whirred off out of sight over the hills.

We all went down to the S-Bar-X and got a little drunk telling great stories on and about Rusty's wonderful wife. The girls stayed home with their dad, and the next day, Dottie and I went with them to Las Cruces and got all the papers done to keep him there. I told them, "Don't let the nature of things ruin your families. Just come when it's really possible—not impossible. I'll go see him every week. All we need to know is how he's treated. He doesn't recognize any of us anymore."

They took off to the El Paso airport, and I drove me and Dottie back to the ranch.

Dottie and I went to visit him once a week. I could sit there and tell stories about all the cowboy wrecks, all the drinking, all the rodeoing, and more, for a while. Then his not hearing, not knowing, began to wear on me. I told Dottie not to come with me anymore. It was doing more harm than good. They kept him clean, but his pajamas were hanging on his bones where all those muscles used to be. He looked backward into his head, seeing nothing in front. I don't think he weighed a hundred pounds.

Then I started falling behind on my visits. I only went twice a month now, and feeling guilty about it. I hadn't been to see my best friend in a month. But somehow this day I felt better. I didn't dread it so much. Maybe looking at the varied landscape around the ghost town of Lake Valley caused this. It sure was beautiful with all the odd-shaped little canyons and valleys that you come upon like a surprise present. The golden fall grass was up a foot high. It looked like patches of ripe wheat on the rolling hills, and what cattle I spotted were fat.

Just before I got to the three or four buildings on the left of the road, I could see a great grouping of those breast-shaped hills that were scattered all over this country. To the left, near the road, was the opening to the old Bridal Veil Mine that once had silver ore so rich you couldn't even blast it properly. They had run a rail line into the mine and backed the cars in, cutting the silver loose with double handsaws, dropping it directly into the ore cars.

On around past the three or four buildings, all on the left side of the road, if you looked carefully up on the right-hand hill, you could see another windy graveyard. A little distance on from there was Skeleton Canyon, where Victorio, Nana, and the great female warrior and medicine woman, Lozen, had lured a bunch of drunken miners and soldiers into a destructive ambush.

I wondered why I'd never really looked at all the detailed beauty and history here before. I decided right there that folks go all the way through their little lives and miss seeing the things that matter most.

————

Lately, I'd gone into Las Cruces on Saturday to miss the Sunday obligatory rush to these places of the old and the stricken. I was stopped at a red light near the university when I saw something that would make an old-timer pray for total darkness. The last few years, I'd noticed cell phones grafted on most folks' ears. A man stood there holding one in each hand, talking first into one, then the other, so fast it appeared he was watching tennis. By God, I couldn't wait to report this sighting to Rusty.

I'd usually arrive just before lunchtime and push Rusty in a wheelchair to the dining room to eat. Well, he had to be fed by the nurses, by hand, so I did that, too, when I was there. The only thing in his room was pictures of Shirley Mae and his daughters hanging just above the table by his bed. About a year earlier, I'd fixed a place to hang his best hat below the pictures. I was a little early for lunch, so I started off talking about the fun we'd had on our wonderful loco horse-trading trip. There in the wheelchair, he never even moved. He was gone way off in another world that didn't belong to me yet.

Just the same, I went on about him tradin' a good-looking locoed horse for an even better-looking outlaw. I reminded ol' Rusty about what he'd said: "All right, it's a deal if you'll throw in a paid-up doctor bill with the horse."

It was time. I got hold of the wheelchair to take him to lunch. Suddenly he started whining and trying to turn his head. It wasn't a complaining whine—just a desperate one, a solid little cry from long ago. I thought he might hurt his neck straining back. And one fist—the bones still big, the only thing left on him that wasn't shriveled to mostly nothing—reached out for the wall. I was puzzled. But then without a thought I took his big old Stetson hat from the wall, placing it on his head as near as possible to the way he'd worn it all his life. Rusty's whining stopped instantly. He put both his hands back in his lap, leaning forward some as if he wanted his horse to move out.

I pushed him through the halls of smells you never forget. The old. The dying. The urine. We rolled on into the dining room. A couple of the service ladies who recognized me waved. There were others at his table. Some were awkwardly feeding themselves. Others were spoon-fed by impatient employees.

I pulled an empty chair over by Rusty, intending to place his hat on it. To my astonishment, he beat me to it. He set the hat upside down so as not to tilt the brim out of its natural line. Then Rusty settled down in the wheelchair, not moving anything but his mouth as I scooped the soft food into what seemed to me an untasting, unfeeling body. Afterward, I wiped his mouth and chin carefully and replaced the hat properly on his head at the exact right angle, and I pushed him back to his room.

I sat on the bed where the sidebars had been dropped. Then I took his long, bony hands in mine. I looked as hard as I could straight into his eyes. I strained. Nothing. Absolutely nothing.

Just as I was standing up, I thought I felt the tiniest squeeze from each of his once-powerful hands. But I got nothing else from any part of him. He had gone to the place beyond the planets. I got up and left. I knew I'd never see him again.

————

Back out in Lake Valley, I drove leisurely along enjoying the wonderful land all over again. Then I remembered that a large fifth-generation rancher had been unable to hold it together with all the bureaucratic conditions put on his lovely land. Impossibilities had descended from many sources. He either had to sell it or lose it, thereby becoming an old worn-out pauper.

Suddenly I saw the first development house going up on the fresh-torn earth. How had I missed it on the drive down this morning? How? Then I knew. I'd just on this very day learned to see without looking down at the ground for animal tracks.

A lost sadness covered me, and penetrated inside, seizing every particle of my being. Then I was no longer here. I was worse off than Rusty. Then from somewhere I realized he would never know about the residences and residents to come. He would never have to bear seeing this special landscape smothered with dwellings or know that the deer, the cattle, the coyotes, and the mountain lions would soon be gone to that other place he now inhabited.

My eyes blurred with wetness so thick I could hardly see the road. I wiped them with my shirt sleeve as clean as I could. At just that second I looked back visualizing both sides so gleefully thinking we'd skunked one another when actually we'd broken even, unknowingly trading one locoed horse for another. Then I smiled just before I laughed out loud so hard I damn near ran off the road and had another wreck.

The Far Cry

Strangely, Jim Tatum wasn't tired when at last he finished the hard job of hazing his small herd of cattle up the steep, winding trail to the top of Piney Mesa. His saddle horse was nigh worn out, but Tatum was buoyed up with the satisfaction of knowing that the strong grass here in the high country would put flesh on his stock and give them plenty to eat all summer long.

How lucky Frances and I are to control this fine forest grazing land, he thought, and if only we now get a good crop on our flats ranch . . .

"What's that over there?" he said aloud. "Heavy storm clouds building up. I'd better head for home."

With this, Tatum turned his black gelding back down the crooked trail on the malpais-studded and brushy slope that led to open country far below the mesa's top. But as the man let Blackie pick his own way, his pleasant thoughts ran on: If mid-June rains came, the dormant, empty pastures below would grow and ripen. He'd cut several stacks of hay and there'd be grazing left for the long winter!

Down, down the trail horse and rider moved, around and over the rocks; through sweet scented cedars and piñons. This morning cottontails had scurried through the underbrush; blue jays had squawked and a magpie had shrilled his resentful cry. Now it was quiet. A still, ominous quiet.

Tatum looked across the intervening miles to his home. He could see the smoke coming from Frances's old iron range. It lapped over the house and seemed to move slowly toward the earth. A good sign of rain. His wife would be as glad as he about the moisture. She had sweated out the long, lean years right by his side.

He looked up and back at the clouds. They were twice as big now—twice as close. Man, they were heavy with water! This rain would fix the pastures for the whole summer. A few showers in August, and his grass would be made. The bills would be made. He and his family would be made for one more year.

He would sure be glad when Billy got a little older so he could help with the ranch work. It wouldn't be long. At six, the boy was already riding, but he couldn't hold out for a cattle drive. Jackie was only three and would be with his mama quite a spell yet.

Tatum felt the sudden stir of air and saw the cedars sway and the sparse grass of the hillside move. He pulled at his hat from years of habit. Then he noticed the pastures far below him turn dark under the shadow of the clouds. They were swiftly spreading over all of the sky.

"We're goin' to get wetter'n a baptising, Blackie," Tatum told his gelding. "It's goin' to rain catfish and big fat bullfrogs in about three minutes . . . I sure hope Frances remembers to turn off the windmill!"

The coarse mane of the horse flapped in the wind. The clouds were shredded and torn now, breaking away in parts and then sweeping back as if by call. The wind pulled harder at Tatum's hat, and it seemed as if the clouds began to roar, louder and louder.

"It looks bad," Tatum said grimly. "Blackie, old boy, we better move out. This could turn into a twister." As he spurred the horse faster on toward the bottom of the mesa, he saw the funnel dip and return and then dip again. It was still above the earth, mixed with the white fangs of lightning.

"I sure hope Frances turns off the windmill and puts out the fire in the stove. A twister might burn the house down, even if it didn't blow it away."

A black tongue snaked from the sky and lapped at the earth. Even in the beginning rain, Tatum saw the puff of dust where it had torn the earth. The thunder and lightning overlapped one another until it was solid, continuous sound and light.

"I hope Frances has taken the kids to the cellar."

The wind pulled the horse sideways and almost swept Tatum from his saddle. Blue-purple sheets of rain were streaking from the clouds as the storm moved out between Tatum and his ranch.

"Blackie, I sure hope Frances thinks to stash some meat in the cellar. I wonder if she'll think to save some extra clothes, and a couple of lamps and some kerosene. It looks to me like the cellar's going to be our new home, old horse."

Eight gut-busting, muscle-stretching, sweating, hoping, praying years it had taken to get the little JT outfit where it was now. Only this past year

they'd finished paying for the windmill. Both of them—he and Frances—pulling against the traces together like a good wagon team.

"I hope Frances and the kids ain't gone to sleep and let this storm slip up on them."

Tatum pushed out of his mind her soft brown hair and eyes, her tender voice, her patient, constant care of the young'uns. The love they made together. He must think of other things.

"Man, that windmill sure saves lots of work." They had had it only three years now. Before that, they had hauled all the water for drinking, washing, and the milk cow from a spring four miles to the east. It seemed as if nearly all Tatum's time was spent hauling water. They had to use a wagon and team most of the time. The old Ford truck just ran when it wanted to, and that was seldom.

But he'd improved the ranch these last three years. The fences were now tight with strong water gaps and gates. The roof on the house was patched and didn't leak. He had built a good round-pole corral for breaking his horses.

What a day when the well driller had told him, "You've got a good well of water, Jim. She'll never go dry."

It had been an even greater day when workmen swung the shiny new wheel in place on the windmill, set the pipe, screwed the sucker-rods together, and turned it over to the wind. The water came bubbling out in a sweet, clear stream. And the harder the wind blew, the more water the well furnished. But now that same life-giving wind, whirling and growling, could take it all away!

The funnel came down out of the seething blackness and stayed. It ripped at the earth, tore the grass from its roots, and gathered up the soil, the twigs, the insects, the life of the land, and hurled it up, up. All Tatum had, all he would ever have, was down there on the flats. The whirling beast meant to suck his own from him as he rode, helpless.

He screamed instructions to his wife into the wind. He knew she couldn't hear him—but maybe if he felt hard enough, strong enough, she'd hear. She would feel.

"Blackie! Come on, Blackie." Tatum spurred the horse's heaving sides, and Blackie responded. Once he stumbled and fell to his knees. Tatum yanked back on the reins, and the horse rose, hurled himself down over the rocks and out onto the flats and into the storm.

The wind, the rain, the thunder and lightning, the horse and his rider, all were one. The sky and the earth welded themselves together and ripped off into the great spaces above. Tatum grabbed his hat from his head and stuffed it inside the Levi's jacket. A good hat cost a lot of money. He could feel the horse under him, somehow harder to ride against the force of the wind than a bucking bronc. The wind pulled at his arms where he held the reins and gripped the saddle horn. Now and then he felt the horse wrenched sideways as if he were a dry weed.

The man's eyes were so full of dirt he just clamped the burning lids tight and held on. Hard objects driven by the wind struck him in the head and all over the body. A mighty vacuum sucked and pulled at the rider and his horse, sucking the very air from their lungs and nostrils.

"Oh, if she just remembered to turn off the windmill."

With chest heaving, Tatum strained the thought from himself. "Frances, honey! Git to the cellar! Git the kids in the cellar! Turn off the windmill, Frances." He felt he would burst apart from the force of his will.

Then for a timeless spell he felt nothing, saw nothing. The blackness was deeper than the darkest night had ever been. Maybe they were right on top of the storm and would come crashing through to the torn earth when it quit. Or would it ever quit?

"It's been blowing for a month now, Blackie. Frances, turn off the windmill!"

Something was changing. He could hear his own voice. Louder, he yelled, "Frances, Billy, Jackie!" and all the time his voice became clearer. At last he could see the ruptured barren earth. The wind was dying, He watched Blackie's mane gradually settle.

Then he knew the storm was past. The earth was wet and muddy. He was drenched and cold. Water and sweat ran from his tangled hair in tiny arroyos through the grime down into his stinging eyes.

It cleared fast then. First he saw the barn. It was still standing! But where were the corrals? They were gone. He spurred the staggering horse forward. The house was still there. And Frances stood in front of the cellar with the door pushed back. He jumped down and stumbled the last few steps to her. He held her close, saying nothing.

"The kids?" he asked.

"They're still in the cellar. I told them it was a game. It's the most fun they've had in ages."

Tatum plunged down into the cellar.

"Daddy, look here," cried Jackie. "I've got a frog!"

"It's half mine," said Billy, his large brown eyes gleaming in the light of the kerosene lamp.

"Can we stay down here and play, Daddy?" Billy asked.

"Yes, son, you can stay all the way to chore time if you want to."

Tatum looked at the rifle, the canned food, the meat, and the extra clothing Frances had brought to the cellar. He walked slowly, thoughtfully, up the stairs. Close. Very close. Only the corrals were gone. Had Frances heard his far cry?

When he saw the fan of the windmill pulled tight against the wheel, motionless, he knew.

My Pardner

1

After twenty-odd years, the image of Boggs is just as clear as the day he came walking toward me with his head leading his body a few inches. His skinny legs were bowed like a bronc rider's, but he wore the bib overalls of a farmer and a dirty old brown hat that flopped all over. Both boots were run over in the same direction, so he leaned a little to the left all the time. His nose was big and flat, and his mouth so wide it turned the corners of his face.

As he moved closer, I could see that there was only one crystal in his thin-rimmed glasses. A funny thing, though—he had one eye gone and the crystal was on that side, leaving a single blue eye beaming from the empty gold rim.

He swung the heavy canvas bag from his back to the ground and stuck out a hand saying, "Reckon you're my pardner Dan. Well, it's shore good to meet you. I'm Boggs."

"Howdy, Boggs," I said.

"Why hell's fire, boy, you're purty near a grown man. Your pa didn't tell me that. How old are you, boy?"

"Twelve goin' on thirteen."

"Hell's fire, I was punchin' cows with the top hands when I was your age. By the time I was fifteen I was out in Arizona mining gold."

Suddenly I felt real small. Course I didn't weigh but ninety some-odd pounds. But I'd felt pretty big a while ago when Papa had handed me the map and the three dollars and said, "It's up to you, son. I'm dependin' on you and Boggs gettin' those horses to Guyman, Oklahoma, by ten o'clock July nineteenth." He had gone on to explain that we'd be out on the trail nearly sixty days because every other day he wanted the horses to rest and feed so's they'd get in looking good and ready for the big sale. That was the key thing to remember: balance the moving and the stopping so the horses would pick up weight.

I looked over at the corral and counted five mules and sixteen starved, ragged-looking horses of every color. Well, Papa had more confidence than I did, but I couldn't help swelling up a little when he shook hands and said, "I ain't worried a peck." But then Papa had lots of guts. Here we were on the edge of Starvation, Texas, living in a shack that was held up by hope, on land that the drought had singled out to make an example of. Half farm, half grassland, and only half enough of either one.

At heart Papa was more of a trader than a land man. He'd traded for a hotel once in Starvation, but when the drought came a few years back, everybody left Starvation except the pensioners, the postmaster, and a few others too broke to go. Then he traded the hotel for a herd of goats, and the goats for some dried-up milk cows, and the cows for a truck, and the truck for a car. Somehow or other I liked the old Ford better than the hotel. Anyway, in between he kept something to eat on the table and Ma made it taste good.

Well, lately Papa had done some more figgering. The drought of the thirties had broken and people were putting a lot more virgin land into wheat and cotton. They'd need lots of horses to plow with. Most folks still hadn't gotten used to the idea it could be done cheaper and better with a tractor. The way Papa looked at it was this: by July 19th all the wheat farmers would have their wheat in and by then the grass would be made for the stock to finish fattening on. People would feel like buying horses for the next plowing. That is, if it rained in early July. The spring rains had already been good. So Papa had started trading for livestock, and finally come up with this ugly bunch. He and Uncle Jock would head up north about a week before we were due and get the sale handbills out and so on. Uncle Jock was an auctioneer, so it wouldn't take much money to pull it off. If everything worked right, we might be able to pay the mortgage, buy some seed, and put in a crop of our own the next spring.

Boggs said, "Let's git goin', boy."

My horse was already saddled and I'd thrown the rotten old pack on the gentlest of the mules. I had two blankets, a jacket, a stake rope, and a sack of dried apricots tied on it. That was all. Papa had said we could find plenty to eat along the way. He hadn't explained exactly how.

Boggs hung his canvas bag on the pack and fished out an old bridle. Then it dawned on me he didn't have a saddle.

I said, "Ain't you got a saddle?"

He grunted, caught a bay out of the bunch, grabbed his mane, and swung up bareback. We turned them out and started across the mesquite-, shinnery-, and grass-covered pastures to Oklahoma.

Boggs rode out front and led the string. They weren't hard to lead, because they were in such poor shape, but riding the drag was something else. They just wanted to stop and eat all the time. I was riding back and forth every minute yelling them on. All the same I felt great again—sorta like a man must feel on his first ocean voyage.

Along about noon I could feel my belly complaining. We rode up to a windmill and watered the horses. After my horse had finished I got down and took a drink. Then I reached in the pack and got a double handful of apricots, and handed some to Boggs. He spit out his chew of tobacco, wiped his mouth, and threw in the whole batch and went to chewing.

When he finished, he said, "Boy, get up on that horse. I want to show you something." It took me kind of by surprise but I crawled up. "Now look here," he said. "Look at your knees. See how they kind of bend when you put 'em in the stirrups? Now look here," he said, walking off. "See them pore old bowed legs of mine? Why, you could run a grizzly through there without him even knowin' it. Now ain't that a disgrace?" he said.

"I don't see as it is," I said, having always felt bowed legs to be some sort of badge of honor.

"Well, by jingoes!" he said. "You don't see, boy? You don't see? Do you realize that I'm a highly educated man—havin' traveled far and wide and knowin' all about the isns and ain'ts of the world? Young feller, I'll have you know that at one time I was made a bona fide preacher. Yessir, a man of the Lord dwellin' in his own house, spreadin' the true and shinin' light. But what happened?" And he jumped around in his runover boots waving his long arms in the air. "What happened?" he shouted, putting that sky-blue eye on me. "Here's what happened," he said as he squatted down and pulled off his boots and overalls and waded out into the dirt tank. "Look," he said, "look at them legs. By jingoes and hell's fire, boy, how would you like to be baptized by a preacher with a pair of legs like that?"

I burst out laughing, even though I was half scared I'd made him mad.

"There you are," he shouted, running out of the water. "That's another thing that happened . . . peals, barrels, tubs full of laughter burstin' across the land. You see, Dan"—he suddenly lowered his voice and it was like dragging satin over satin—"a young boy like you with his bones still growin' and shapin' should never ride a saddle. Otherwise your legs will get bent like mine. A long trip like this will doom the young sapling. Let me have that saddle, son, and save you this terrible disgrace. Grow up straight and tall like Abe Lincoln. And besides"—he leaned at me with his hand in the air signaling for silence—"besides, when our duty is done I'll buy you the fanciest present this side of the pearly gate."

Well, that was fancy enough for me. I just crawled down, unfastened the cinches, and handed him my saddle. He threw it on his bay horse, then went over to the pack and took out a half-gallon crock jug.

"Cider," he said, tossing it over his arm and taking a long pull. "Ain't good for young'uns," he said, corking the jug. "Cures the earache. Always got an earache." He rubbed one ear and put the jug back inside the bag. Then he took out a long plug of tobacco and really bit him off a chew. "Let's git goin'," he said, and we struck out.

About five hours later the horses quit. There wasn't any way to keep them all moving at once. Well, I had an inkling why. My belly was just plain gone. It had lost confidence in ever being fed again and had just shriveled up to nothing.

Boggs rode back and said, "We'll pitch camp right over there." He pointed to a dry lake bed with a heavy growth of mesquite most of the way around its edges. Off to the northeast I could see a clump of trees sitting like a motionless prairie ship in a green grass sea. I knew there was a ranch house there with beans and bacon and good black coffee, but it would be late the next day before we'd make it. Tonight we'd dine on apricots. Dried.

We unsaddled the horses. I took my rope and staked out one for a night horse. I wasn't worried about the others running off. They were too hungry. Besides, they would be easy to hem up in a fence corner about a quarter of a mile off.

I spread my blanket out and Boggs reached in his canvas bag. He had another pull of ear medicine. He fished around in the bag and came up with

a coffeepot and a little Dutch oven. Then he said, "Gather some wood, boy. I'll be back in a minute." He struck out in that rocking-chair walk of his, leaning to the west.

I started picking up dead mesquite limbs, watching every now and then to see what Boggs was doing. I could see him twisting some loose wire on the corner post. I didn't know what he was up to, but if a rancher caught him we'd sure be in trouble.

He came back carrying a six-foot strand of barbed wire and said, "Come on, let's git goin'."

I followed. We walked out through the mesquite. All of a sudden he yelled, "After him! After him!"

I saw a cottontail rabbit shoot out between us. I took after him feeling like a damn fool. The fastest man on earth can't catch a rabbit. Well, that cottontail wasn't taking any chances on it. He ran and jumped in a hole. I stopped, breathing hard, but Boggs just ran on past me, right to the rabbit hole. He squatted down, took one end of the wire, and spread the strands about two-thirds of an inch apart. Then he bent about ten inches of the other end out at forty-five degrees. He put the forked end into the hole and started twisting the wire. To my surprise the wire went right on down, and even passed the spot where the hole turned back. Then I could see him feeling his way. His eye was bugged out in concentration. His face was red and sweating. Then he gave another couple of twists and said, "Got 'em, boy. Now the secret is not to bring 'em up too fast or you'll pull the hide out and they're gone. If you bring 'em up too slow then they'll get a toehold and the same thing will happen."

He backed up now and I could see the rabbit.

"Grab 'im!"

I did.

"By jingoes, he's a fat one. A regular feast," he said, and he wasn't joking.

We built a nice fire and Boggs scraped the fat off the rabbit hide, then we cooked him in his own juice. I'm telling you that rabbit woke my stomach up and really put it back to work. We finished it off with a cup or two of black coffee and half a dozen apricots. The world was all of a sudden a mighty fine place.

I leaned back on my elbow and watched the flat rim of the prairie turn to bright orange. High above, some lace clouds got so red for a minute I thought they would just drop down and burn a man up. Then the cool violets and purples moved in and took over. Bullbats came and dived in the sky in great swift arcs, scooping the flying insects into their throats. The crickets hummed like a Fordson tractor, and way off the coyotes started their singing and talking howl.

Then Boggs said, "Boy, you ever been to Arizona?"

"No."

"Course you ain't. But you will. That's a great country, boy. That desert and all that gold just waitin' to be dug." He went on a little while and I looked at the sky full of stars and my eyes got heavy just trying to see past the first bunch. Then his voice came again, "I'll tell you all about Arizona one of these nights, boy, but right now my ass is too tired."

I could hear the horses grazing nearby, snorting now and then, slowly in contentment. The fire was a small red glow teasing the night good-bye. I slept.

2

"Let's git goin', boy."

I sat up in my blankets.

"Here." He handed me a cup of hot coffee and kicked dirt over the fire.

It was just breaking day. I swallered the scalding stuff and tried to stand up. This took some doing. I was sore and stiff in every joint, but that wasn't what bothered the most; it was my hind end. The rawboned back of the saddle horse had rubbed my rump like grating cheese. I had to walk with my legs spread apart. It was not a good condition for horseback riding.

The sun got hotter. My setter got rawer. Every little bit I'd slide off and walk, but the insides of my legs were galled so bad I couldn't keep up with the slowest of our horse herd. There was nothing to do but get on and go.

By eleven o'clock I was hurting so bad, and the sun was so hot, I got somewhat ill-tempered. I was cussing Boggs, not altogether under my breath. "You old liar and conniver. You old nitwit. You old . . ." It eased my pain.

By two that afternoon we pulled up to the trees. There was a water tank about fifty yards long and a windmill pumping at each end. But the ranch house had long been unoccupied. It looked like now it was occasionally used as a temporary camp for cowboys. It was a disappointment. While not thinking about my sore bottom, and when not cussing Boggs, I thought about the beans and bacon, hot gravy and biscuits we'd have had at the rancher's table. I just got down and lay in the shade and listened to my belly growl.

After the horses watered we turned them all loose in a little horse trap where the grass was coming good.

"Reckon there's any rabbits around here?" I asked Boggs, chewing on an apricot.

"Might be," he said, looking in the tank.

"There ain't no rabbits taking a swim in that tank," I said.

"You're right, boy, but I'm tellin' you there's some catfish in there."

"Catfish?" I said, bolting up out of the shade.

"Yessirree Bob."

Then I settled back down. "Well, we ain't got no way to catch 'em. Guess we better get to lookin' for a rabbit."

"Now look here, boy, you're givin' in too easy. We're goin' to have an ample amount of rabbit before this trip is over anyway, so let's try doing a little thinkin'. It's all right to go through life just plain feelin', that's fine, but when your old gut is cryin' 'hungry' to your soul, it's time to think, you hear? Think!"

Well, we walked around the yard. If you could call his bowlegged and my wide-straddled motions walking. We went into the ranch house: nothing but an empty table, cupboard, and four chairs. Out in a shed, we found some tools, old and rusty, a can of axle grease, and a stack of empty feed sacks tied in a bundle.

Boggs said, "Look here, the great gods above done smiled down on us poor sinners. By jingoes, boy, we're in for a treat." He gathered up the sacks and out we went.

After untying and splitting the sacks, he spread them out on the ground and began sewing them together in one big sheet. Then he tied some rocks along the bottom, put sticks on each end for handles, and we had us a dandy good seine.

Boggs went back in the shed for a minute. "Here, boy," he said, handing me a can of axle grease.

"What's that for?"

"Rub it on your hind end."

I just stood there holding it in my hand.

"Well, go on," he said, "we ain't got much time."

I rubbed it on. It was sticky and left me a little embarrassed when I walked, but it did ease the pain.

"Pick you out a couple of them sacks to ride on tomorrow." I did.

"Now, come on, boy. We're wastin' time."

Boggs told me to go to the deep end and start throwing rocks into the tank and yelling. He said this would booger the fish into the shallow water so we'd have a chance at them.

About middle ways down, we shucked our clothes and waded in. I sure was glad I had applied the axle grease in the right place. That water would have really finished chapping me. I pretty nearly choked to keep from laughing at Boggs's bowlegs until he got them under water. The seine was spread and he told me to keep the bottom just a little ahead of the top so the fish couldn't get underneath.

"Now, boy, move in steady to the corner and when I yell, come out with the bottom first and hold tight. Then give a big heave out on the bank."

We moved along.

"Haawwww!"

Up we heaved. Sure enough, there were seven or eight nice cats, three perch, and a goldfish. I didn't heave quite enough and two of mine fell back, but the next trip through we got another good catch and Boggs said, "Hell, that's all we can eat, so let's go swimming." He put the fish in a wet gunnysack and we took a cooling swim.

When we crawled out the sun felt good for a change. Just when I thought I was going to faint from hunger and the extra exercise, Boggs said, "Boy, get out there and get a bunch of mesquite wood."

I went after it. When I got back with the first load he had dug a hole about a foot deep and a yard long. He built a fire in this hole and I kept packing wood for it. After the fish were cleaned and wrapped in some pieces of brown paper sacks we'd found in the shed, he mixed up a batch of mud and rolled them in it. When all the wood had burned down to glowing coals, be buried the fish in them.

We waited and we waited.

"Don't you think they're done, Boggs?" I asked, feeling the saliva run into my mouth.

"Not yet."

"Lord, I'm starving. Looks like to me those coals have done gone out."

"Not yet."

Finally, he took one out and broke it over a rock. The baked mud fell away and there it was, the juicy white meat of the catfish. Everything was soon gone but a pile of bones cleaned as slick as crochet needles.

All the next day we let the horses rest, water, and eat. We did the same. Then on the move again. The wide green tablecloth of a prairie soon turned to shinnery bushes and sand where the sun was meaner and the earth drier. We ate rabbits and apricots until the apricots were gone, and that left just rabbit.

Then we could see the little clumps of trees increasing in the distance, and we knew we were finally on the edge of the farm country.

We checked our map. If we were lucky, we could make it to a Mr. Street's farm before night. He was supposed to be a friend of Papa's. Papa said Mr. Street was a pure farmer and wouldn't have any pasture grass for our horses, but he would have plenty of cane bundles to give us. It was here I was to buy two hundred pounds of oats out of the three dollars and start graining our herd.

As I followed the old white horse into Mr. Street's road I finally figured out why he was behind the others all the time—one ankle was twisted just enough to make him slower. He was a stayer, though. I was getting to feel friendly toward him and wouldn't have liked any of the other horses back with me.

I went up to the front of Street's house, leaving Boggs out in the road with the horses where they grazed along the bar ditch. It was a neat, white house with a paling fence around it, and a few elm trees scattered about the place. I could see a big barn, several corrals, and feed stacks. Down below the house was a shack for the Negro hired hands. Mr. Street was rich. I could sure tell that.

I tied my horse at the yard gate, went up to the door, and knocked. It didn't feel as if anyone was home. I couldn't hear a sound. Then I knocked again and waited. Just as I raised my hand, the door opened.

"What'd you want?"

I looked up and up and sideways and all around. That door was full of woman. I felt like I was standing at the bottom of a mountain.

"Well, what'd you want?"

"Is Mr. Street in?"

"What'd you want?"

"My papa . . ."

"Your papa? What about your papa? Come on, boy, speak your piece."

"Well, uh, my papa is a friend of Mr. Street's."

"Who is your papa?"

"Ellis Thorpe."

"You know any Ellis Thorpe, Nate?" she said back over her shoulder.

"Yeah, used to," he said. "Ain't seen him in years."

I never saw such a woman—little bitty ankles with massive muscular legs above to hold up the rolls and rolls of blubber that ran right up under her ears and spread over her cheekbones so it made her eyes look little and mean. Sure enough, they were.

"Well, what do you want?" she asked again.

"Papa said you might put us up and feed our horses for a day."

She went in and talked to Nate in low tones. Then she filled the door again.

"Nate says times have been hard what with overcoming the drought and all, but he says you can bunk down at the shack with the help and you can have all the bundles you want at a nickel apiece."

"I, uh . . ."

She started to shut the door.

"Just a minute," I said, and pulled out the three dollars. "I guess we'll take two bundles apiece for the horses. How much'll that be?"

"How many head you got?"

"Sixteen horses and five mules."

"Forty-two bundles at five cents." She counted on her little short fingers. "Two dollars and ten . . . er . . . twenty cents."

I handed her the three and she brought me eighty cents change. She slammed the door.

I felt sick. There went the grain money. I'd already started letting Papa down.

We took the horses to the corrals and started pitching them the bundles. Then Nate came out and counted them. He was a little man with a quick, jerking motion to everything he did. When he was satisfied we hadn't cheated him he said, "Tell your pa hello for me," and walked off.

Over on the other side of the corral stood four big, fat Percheron work-horses. They made ours look like runts, and I began to wonder if Papa had a good idea or not.

It was almost night when we walked down to the workers' shack. Three little Negro kids grinned at us from the steps. Boggs spoke to them and a man came to the open door.

"Howdy. What can I do for ya?" he asked.

"Well, Mr. Street said we could bunk with you tonight."

"Sho, sho, come in," he said. "I'm Jake."

He introduced us to his wife, Telly. She was almost as big as Mrs. Street, but somehow in a different way. There was something warm about the place.

Boggs sent me to get our blankets and his cider jug off the pack saddle. Telly sat out three cups and they all had a drink.

"Sho fine," said Jake.

"Better'n fine," Telly said.

"Best cider in Texas," said Boggs, winking at them, and they all busted out laughing.

Then Telly fixed us a big stack of hotcakes and set a pitcher of black, homemade molasses on the table. I smeared a big dip of churn butter between about six of them and let the molasses melt all over. I forked three strips of sowbelly onto my plate and really took me on a bait of home cook-ing. Then two tin cups of steaming coffee finished it off.

A while after the eating was over the three grown-ups went back to that cider jug.

Every little bit Boggs would say to Jake, "Ain't you got a bad earache, Jake?"

"Sho nuff, Mr. Boggs, I do. I ain't never knowed a ear to hurt like this'n."

Telly said, "Well, you ain't sufferin' a-tall. Both my ears done about to fall off."

The only earache I'd ever had hurt like seventy-five. I never could figger out how these people were getting such a kick out of pain. I spread my blankets on the floor and lay down to get away from all this grown-up foolishness.

It was soon dawn again, and it was Boggs again.

"Let's git goin', boy. Leave the eighty cents on the table for Jake."

I was too sleepy to argue.

We moved the horses out fast. Then I said, "Boggs, where's the pack mule? We forgot the pack mule."

"Shhhh," he said. "Shut up and come on."

In a little while, maybe three-quarters of a mile from Street's, I saw the pack mule tied to a fence. On each side of the pack saddle hung a hundred-pound sack of oats.

"Where'd you get 'em?" I asked, bristling up.

"From Street."

"That's stealin'!"

"No, it ain't, son. I've done him a real favor."

"How's that?" I said smartly.

"Why, boy, you ain't thinkin' again. This way him and your pa will remain friends."

I studied on it all day, but I was a full-grown man before I figured it out.

"Well, anyway, that's too much for that mule to carry," I said.

"That shows how little you've been around the world, boy. That mule is plumb underloaded. When I was mining out in Arizona we packed four hundred pounds of ore out of the mountains. Mountains, you hear. This mule is at least a hundred pounds underloaded."

"Oh," I said, and we moved out with me staring that old white horse square in the rump.

3

After a while we stopped at a little grassy spot along the road and poured out some oats. Those old horses were really surprised.

"You know something, boy?" Boggs said, filtering a handful of dirt. "This here's sand land. Watermelon land. They come on early in this soil. Fact, just about this time of June."

He raised his head kind of sniffing the air as if he could smell them. Then he got up and ambled off through a corn patch that was up just past knee-high. I sat and watched the horses eat the oats thinking what a damn fool Boggs was for figuring he could just walk off across a strange country and come up with a watermelon. I'd stolen watermelons myself, and I knew better than that.

The ponies finished their oats and started picking around at the grass and weeds in the lane. I began to get uneasy. Maybe somebody had picked Boggs up for trespassing. Then I heard singing. I listened hard. It was coming through the corn. I heard loud and clear, "When the saints . . . Oh, when the saints go marching in. Oh, when the saints . . ." closer and closer till I could see the long stringy figure of Boggs, and the watermelon he had under each arm.

"Had a little trouble finding two ripe ones. Most of 'em's still green."

I didn't say a word.

He took out his long-bladed barlow and stuck her in a melon. It went riiiiip as it split wide apart like a morning rose opening up. I knew it was a ripe one. He cut the heart out with his knife and handed it to me. I took it in both hands and buried my head plumb to my nose in it. Good. Wet. Sweet. Whooooee.

I ate every bit of that watermelon except the seeds and rind and my belly stuck out like I'd swallered a football. Boggs didn't waste much of his, either. It was a mighty fine lunch.

When we stood up to mount our horses, I said, "Boggs, sure enough, how'd you know them watermelons was over there?"

"Look right there in them weeds under the fence."

All I could see was a bunch of flies buzzing around. I walked over. Sure enough, there was a half-ripe watermelon that somebody had busted open the day before.

"I just figgered nobody could carry one any further than that without seein' if it was ripe. Knew they had to be close by."

"Oh."

We got our horses and rode. We soon came to the main highway to Brownfield, Texas. According to Papa's map we'd be riding along this bar ditch for a long spell now. It was late afternoon and that watermelon belly had disappeared and the usual holler place was making itself known.

We looked around and finally found an old fallen-down homestead out in a cotton patch. It was vacant, and there was a lot of weeds and stuff growing around the barns and old corrals for the horses to feed on. But we still had to water them. The windmill was cut off and if we turned it on in the daylight somebody might see it and maybe have us arrested for trespassing. We had to wait for dark.

Boggs said, "Let's see if we can find a rabbit."

We'd already lowered the rabbit population of West Texas a whole lot but I was willing to thin it out some more. We rode along the fencerows, all around the old place, but there wasn't a cockeyed rabbit to be found. About half a mile from the homestead we looked out over a weed-covered fence. There was a farmhouse with chickens, milk cows, chickens, some white ducks in a little pond, chickens, and dogs.

"By jingoes, boy, how'd you like to have some roasted chicken tonight?"

"Sure would, Boggs, but we ain't got any money."

"Money? Why, only a sinner against mankind would pay money for a chicken."

"What do you mean?" I asked, feeling fingers made out of icicles grabbing my little skinny heart.

"I mean we'll procure them chickens. Now you know the lady of that house is overworked. She's probably got six kids to look after besides her old man. All them ducks to feed, and the churnin' to do after milkin' those cows. Now it's just too much to ask of her to take care of that many chickens and gather that many eggs, ain't it?"

I started to say it was stealing, but my belly set up those growling noises again and I felt my legs trembling from hunger weakness.

"What about the dogs?" I asked.

"No bother a-tall. I'll take care of the dogs while you steal the chickens."

"Me?"

"You."

"Now listen . . ."

"Now you listen close and I'm going to tell you how to get the job done. Why hell's fire, boy, you're just the right size for such an operation."

I wondered how in the world it could make any difference to a chicken whether I weighed ninety pounds or two hundred.

"Now, about them dogs. I'm goin' to go off to the right of the house and howl like a coyote. The dogs will come out barkin' and raisin' cain at me. It'll throw everybody's attention in my direction. Get it?"

I swallered.

"Now the minute you hear me holler and the dogs start barkin' get to that henhouse. Here's the secret of chicken stealin': first, a chicken sleeps pretty sound. About the only thing that will wake 'em is one of their own taking on. That you have to avoid. Be as quiet as you can gettin' into the henhouse. When you're used to the dark so you can see a chicken, grab her right by the throat and clamp down hard so's she can't make any noise. Then just stick her head under her wing. A chicken's so dumb it won't make a sound. Now as soon as this is done carry her outside and do 'er round and around in the air," he said, and made a circular motion with his arms held out. "Like this. She'll be so dizzy, it'll take 'er ten minutes to stand up again and that much longer to get her head out from under her wing. You can steal a whole hen-housefull in twenty minutes."

"Do we want 'em all?"

"Hell's fire no, boy. Just one apiece."

Darkness came and the lights went on in the farmhouse. Every once in a while the dogs would bark. I think they heard us.

Boggs said, "Let's git goin.'"

He circled off to the right of the house and I eased along to the left behind the henhouse. When the dogs started barking, I stopped. They quit for a minute and I heard that coyote Boggs hollering his head off. I dashed up to the henhouse with my breath coming in quick gasps and cold prickles just breaking out all over. I was scared but at the same time thrilled. I slipped around to the door and fumbled for the latch. The noise pierced the night like a runaway wagon. It was too late to back out now. Besides, I was too durned hungry.

I heard the chickens stir and talk a little as I went in. I stood still just a minute. My heart thumped louder than the chickens. I could make out a dark mass over on the roost. I moved as quietly as I could with my hands outstretched. The dogs were really raising the dickens over on the other side of the house. I wondered if maybe they had Boggs down chewing on him.

Then my hand touched a chicken neck. I squeezed tight and holding her with one hand I stuck her head under her wing with the other. Outside I went. Whirl that chicken I did. I plunked her down and she just sat there like Boggs had said. This gave me confidence. In a half a minute I had another one outside on the ground all dizzy and still. Then I relatched the door. That Boggs had started me thinking tonight. I grabbed up a chicken under each arm, and sailed out of there.

Boggs got back about twenty minutes after I did.

"What took you so long?" I asked, feeling kind of important.

This seemed to rock him back for a minute, then he said, "A funny thing, boy. Just as I raised my head to let out that coyote yell, a sure-enough live one beat me to it. I just hung around a few extra minutes to see what'd happen."

The cooking took place.

The eating took place.

The sleeping with a full belly took place.

And I dreamed.

4

We went through Brownfield before sunup, right into the heart of cotton country. It stood up straight and green everywhere. In a few more weeks the hard, round boles would form. Then in the fall they would burst open into the white white of ripe cotton. The fields would fill with bent-over pickers dragging long canvas bags behind them and their hands snaking cotton from the vine to the sack. Wagons by the hundreds would pull it to the gins, and the gins would hum day and night for a brief spell, cleaning and baling the cotton for shipping and sale all over the world. Now, it was still, and hot, and green.

The people in the autos traveling parallel to us all waved. I guessed it had been a long time since they had seen a remuda of horses on the move. All the horses, except the old gray, were beginning to pick up flesh; just the same, I couldn't help worrying some. In the first place, if that thieving Boggs got us in jail, our time schedule would be thrown off, and one half day late would be just the same as a month. I couldn't figger Boggs out. One minute he'd be preaching and the next he was stealing. Sometimes his speech was like a school professor's, and then like an uneducated dunce. On the other hand, I would have starved nearly to death without his help. We were hungry most of the time anyway. Besides worrying about letting Papa down, all I could think about was getting enough in my belly to last a whole day.

We moved on through Meadow, Texas, and then out to the edge of Ropesville. We had a two-day holdup here if we wanted it. There was a patch of heavy grass by the road where a sinkhole had held back some extra moisture from the spring rains. We decided to take a chance on the horses grazing alone on the road while we did a little exploring. This was risky because if someone took a notion to impound our horses, we were done. It'd cost five dollars a head to get them out. That would be impossible to raise in time to make the sale, but Boggs had said, "Our luck's holdin', son. You can't beat luck—even with thinkin'. The odds are that no one'll think but what the owner is keepin' his eye right on 'em. You got to be willin' to take chances. The way to survive this world is knowin' when to duck. That time generally comes when a man has made a mistake while takin' a chance. Now you take my whole durn family. Ma, for instance. She died having me 'cause she didn't reckon she needed a doctor. Now my brother got killed robbin' a bank. He walked in when two plainclothesmen were making a deposit. He should have watched everybody instead of just the guard. That sister of mine jumped in the Rio Grande to save a drowning boy. The boy caught hold of a limb and swam out—she sank. Pa didn't do so bad. I don't reckon you can hold it against a man for gettin' choked on a piece of bear meat. By jingoes, boy, you can't hold that against a man, especially since he killed that bear with his own hands swingin' an axe."

"No," I said, "you cain't."

"You're right, boy."

We cut across a pasture looking for a place to hide the horses for a couple of days. The nearest house was about a half a mile away, and we had to get out of its sight.

"Looky there!"

"What?" I said.

"A rat's den!"

It was a whopper—three feet high and six or eight feet in width and length—made up of broken mesquite limbs, thorns, bear grass leaves, and cow chips, with numerous holes woven in and out.

"Rats!" he screamed into the air, throwing his long arms up as if seeking the help of the Almighty. "Rats! Rats! Rats! Oh gracious and powerful Lord, give me the strength to wage battle against these vilest of creatures. Pass on to me a small portion of your power so that I may stand strong and brave through the conflict about to come upon us. Lend me some of your skill and eternal magic while I slay the carnal beasts. Guide and protect this innocent young man as he follows forth the bugle's glorious call."

I was getting boogered and looked all around to see what might be fixing to tear us in pieces when he jumped from his horse and handed me the reins.

"Here, boy, this is your duty. Hold the mounts that we may yet escape to wage war another day."

He raced to the large pile of trash and put a match to it. A lazy rope of smoke rose, then the pile burst into flames. Boggs had secured a long, heavy mesquite limb and he had it drawn back in a violent gesture.

"Ah, you four-legged offspring of the devil, I have turned your own fire and brimstone against you. Seek ye now the world of the righteous."

Well, they started seeking it. Rats were fleeing the burning nest in every direction. Boggs was screaming and striking with fury. Dead rats soon covered the ground.

"There, pestilence!" he shouted as he bashed one to a pulp. "Die, evil creature of the deep. Return to your ancestor's wicked bones. Bring the black death into the world, will you? Destroyer of man, his food, of his life. Die, rats, die!"

When he could find nothing else to strike at he turned to me breathing heavily, still waving the stick.

"Rats have killed more people than all the wars combined. Did you know that, boy?"

I shook my head "no," trying to quiet the nervous horses.

"Well, they have. They are man's one mortal enemy. They live off man's labor, off his love for other things. They can't survive without man. It's a battle to the great and final death. People shouldn't fight people, they should fight rats. Here, give me my horse."

He dropped his stick on the dying fire and mounted.

"We better get out of here," I said. "That smoke will draw some attention."

"Just the opposite, if it's gone unnoticed till now we'll be safe in pasturing our horses here. Let's git goin'."

I was in such shape after the last few minutes of action that I just rode obediently along and helped gather our horses. It was almost night and that same old weakness of all day without food was upon me. It never seemed to bother Boggs, or at least it didn't show. He rammed a plug of tobacco in his mouth and chewed on it a while. He seemed to be studying hard.

Turning to me all of a sudden, he spoke. "Boy, I'm takin' you out for a steak dinner."

"We ain't got any money."

"That's right, boy."

"Well?"

"Don't ask so many questions. Would you like a steak dinner? It's too late to catch a rabbit."

"Yeees," I said meekly.

Ropesville, Texas, had two tin cotton gins standing huge and sightless like blind elephants. The cotton lint from the ginning last fall still hung in dirty brown wads from the phone and light wires and in the weeds and grass around the town. It was a small place, maybe a thousand or twelve hundred people in and around the town. But it was a big town to me this night.

We tied our horses in a vacant lot off the main street. I was scared plumb silly. I had no idea how Boggs was going to get us a steak dinner without stealing it. And I just couldn't figger any way to steal it without a gun.

We marched right around to the first restaurant we came to, stepped in, and got us a table.

A woman came over smiling like she meant it and said, "Good evening."

"Evenin', ma'am," said Boggs.

"A menu?"

"It's not necessary. My pardner and I desire one of your finest chicken-fried steaks."

There wasn't any use ordering any other kind of steak in the backwoods of West Texas in those days. They all served the one kind.

"Would you kindly put a little dab of mayonnaise on our salad? And pie? What kind of pie you want, boy?"

"Apple?"

"Apple for me, too, ma'am."

"Coffee?"

"Coffee for me and orange soda pop for the young'un."

"All right." And she went away writing.

In a little bit there was a whole table load of stuff. I stuck my fork in the steak and sawed my knife back and forth. I put a great big bite into my mouth. Whoooeee! Was it ever good. Before I hardly got it swallowed I took a big bite of the mashed potatoes on the plate and another of salad. Then when I got my mouth so full I could hardly chew I'd wash it down with a big pull of orange pop. Great goin'! For a minute I quit worrying about how we'd pay for it.

The time came to face up to it. Boggs was finished and so was I. The lady came over and asked if there'd be anything else.

Boggs said, "Another soda pop, coffee, and the check please."

Well, I drank on that soda and watched Boggs. I'd been scared plenty on this trip already, but he was really headed for the deep end now. Every once in a while he'd grab out in the air like he was crazy. Then I saw him put his hand over his coffee cup like he was dropping sugar in it. But the sugar was in a bowl.

All of a sudden he straightened up and said seriously, "Lady. Lady, come here."

The lady walked over smiling. Boggs pointed silently into his coffee cup. She looked. The smile crept off her face.

" I . . . I . . . I'll get you another cup."

"Lady," Boggs said under his breath, "I don't want any more coffee—that ecstasy has been denied me now and probably forever. One of the true pleasures of life will now raise only a ghastly memory to my mind at every thought. I feel I should bring suit against this café." Boggs rose now and so did his voice.

The other customers had stopped eating and the woman ran to a man behind the counter. He looked up, listened, and walked over to our table.

"Please, please," he said. "Just quiet down and leave. I'll take care of the check."

Boggs stood a minute with his gleaming blue eye on the man. "Very well," he said, standing there with his head thrown back, "but you haven't heard the last of this yet. Boy, let's git goin'."

As I walked around the table I leaned over just a minute and looked in the coffee cup. There were two big, fat flies in there and only one had drowned.

5

Boggs woke me up praying. I'd slept late for once; it was nearly noon. All we had to do this day was feed and water ourselves. It didn't sound like much but it could turn into quite a chore. Anyway, I heard this voice taking on. I raised up in the blankets and tried to rub my eyes open.

"Lord, now listen to me close. We're goin' to be in the land of plows and man-planted things for over eighty miles now. It's goin' to get harder and harder to live off the land. We made a promise, me and Dan, to deliver these fine horses on time and in good shape. We got to keep that promise one way or the other, Lord. All I ask of you is to help me think. And listen, Lord, if I mess up, which being one of those so-called human bein's I'm liable to do, I want you to know I ain't blamin' it on you. Amen, Lord." Then looking over his shoulder at me he said, "Mornin', boy. It's a great day. Care for a cup of coffee?"

"Uh-huh." I looked at it to see if there were any flies in it.

Then he said, "When you finish, let's go to town."

I swallered. We went.

We were riding along the highway when he spotted a big piece of cardboard leaning against the fence. He got down and cut out a couple of eight-inch squares. Then with a stubby pencil he wrote on one: I'M DEAF AND DUMB. This one he hung around my neck. On the other he wrote: I'M BLIND.

This one was his. I didn't need any explanations this time to figure out what we were fixing to pull.

He took off his glasses and put on a pair of dark ones he had in his canvas bag. He put his floppy old hat in the bib of his overalls, pulled his yellow hair down over his forehead, and rubbed some dust on his right eyelid. When he closed it, it looked sunken like his blind one.

We tied our horses in the same alley, and started down the street carrying a large tomato can he got from the bar ditch.

"Now, boy, if anybody tries to talk to you just shake your head and make Indian sign language."

"I don't know any Indian sign language."

"They ain't nobody goin' to know the difference. Here, boy, hold my hand. Cain't you see I'm blind?"

I took his hand and walked into the lobby of the town's only hotel. I held the tomato can out in front. An old lady put down the newspaper she was reading, reached in her purse, and dropped fifteen cents in the can. She rubbed me on the head saying, "What a pity."

I blinked my eyes real hard for her.

The man at the desk gave me a dime and on our way out a man and his wife stopped and watched us. The man fetched a nickel out of his pocket but his wife glared and gouged him in the ribs with her elbow. He came up with fifty cents this time.

The drugstore was next. We left there with nearly two dollars. Boggs dragged his feet along, not only looking blind but acting like it. The grocery store was good for eighty-five cents. Then a garage for forty. A little girl with a nickel in her hand kept following us around from place to place, running out in front once in a while to stare at us. All of a sudden she ran up and dropped the nickel in the can and gave me a kiss. If my knees had been trembling before they were going in circles now. Boy, I sure wished I had time to get to know a girl who would give up a bar of candy and a kiss for a dumb boy and a stranger at that.

We made it on down to a red brick building at the end of the street. There was a bank and a dry-goods store. The bank was closed but the dry-goods was worth ninety-five cents. By the time we'd covered the entire north side of the street we had fourteen dollars and sixty-three cents. We went into the alley to count it.

"By jingoes, we're rich," I said. "I ain't never seen so much money."

Boggs smiled clean around his face. "I used to make this much in a day when I was panning gold in Arizona."

"How come you left?"

"The gold was gone."

"All gone?"

"Hell's fire, no, boy, not all of it, just all of it in this one spot. I'm goin' back some day. Besides, I decided to try to find my gold already coined in the form of buried treasure. So I left Arizona and went treasure huntin' up at Taos, New Mexico. You ever been up there, boy? Course you ain't. I keep forgettin' you ain't been out of West Texas. Well, Taos is one of them adobe towns full of Mexicans, Indians, gringos, and nutty artists. A feller had sold me this treasure map and told me to look up a bruja. You know what that is? Course you don't. Well, it's sort of fortune-teller and witch combined."

He gave that tomato can full of money a good rattle and went on, "Well, I found her. Yessir, by jingoes, I found her all right, and she said the map was true and the treasure was buried there, but a lady had built a house over it. So we went to this lady and she said she could tell by the map her bedroom was right smack over the treasure, and if we'd split we could tear up the floor and dig it up. Well, I tore up the floor. The bruja said, 'Dig there,' and I dug. I had dirt piled all over the place. Pretty soon the bruja said, 'The devils are at work and they have caused us to dig in the wrong place.' Well, sir, she grabbed a poker hanging by the fireplace and rammed it about three inches into the dry hard ground and said, 'There! There it is!' Hell's fire, I stood right there and pulled on that poker, trying to get it out of the way so I could dig. And the harder I pulled, the deeper in the ground it went. When it went out of sight I naturally couldn't hold on any longer. Now I ain't the kind of feller to scare easy, but I broke into a run and I ain't been back to that insane town since. Ain't hunted much treasure either."

"What about the floor?" I asked.

"I never did write to find out."

He would have gone on for two hours telling me yarns, but I suddenly remembered how hungry I was so I said, "Let's go over to the café and buy us a big dinner. I'm starvin.'"

"Now there you go, not thinkin' again. We just can't go in there like this. If they catch us faking this blind act, to jail we go. Come here," he said, and ducked my head under a water faucet and washed me off. Then he pulled out a dirty comb and slicked my hair back. "Take off your shirt and turn it wrong side out. Now," he said, "you can go over to the store and get us some grub. Hell's fire, you look just like the mayor's son. Don't hardly know you myself."

He handed me a list and I walked over to the store. I got cheese and crackers, a loaf of bread, and four cans of sardines for tonight. Then I got us another big bag of those dried apricots and a slab of cured bacon. We could take these along with us and they wouldn't spoil. Besides, we had lots of money left. I went all the way and bought Boggs two new plugs of tobacco and me a Hershey bar.

We rode out to our camp that night with Boggs singing "When the Saints Go Marching In," just chewing and spitting between notes.

6

The next day we just loafed around and watched the horses graze. It was the first time we'd been sure of eating for over one day at a time.

Boggs said, "Boy, you ain't wrote a line to your mother since we've been gone."

"She don't expect me to."

"That's right, boy, she don't. But that ain't keepin' her from hopin'. Now is it?"

"I reckon not," I said, getting scared again.

Boggs tore a piece of brown sack up and handed it to me along with a stub of pencil.

"I ain't never wrote a letter home," I said.

"Might as well start now," he said. "It ain't much work and it'll do your ma a lot of good. It'll even make you feel better. You can drop it in the mail when we ride through Ropesville."

Well I was out of arguments with this man Boggs, so I wrote my first letter home.

Dear Ma,

I'm sending this letter just to you cause I expect Pa is gone off somewhere on a deal. He generally is. How is old Blue and her pups? I sure hope we can keep the brindle one. He's going to make a real keen rabbit dog. I can tell because the roof of his mouth is black. That there is a sure sign.

Did the old red hen hatch her chicks yet? I hope she saves all of them so we'll have fried chicken this August.

Me and Boggs are making it just fine. Ever time he talks it's about something different. He kind of puzzles me.

Is the cow giving lots of milk? I bet her calf is fat. Are you going to try and can everything in the garden like you did last year? Don't work too hard on the garden or the canning either.

This man Boggs is a funny feller. Sometimes I think he's the smartest man in the world and sometimes I think he's the dumbest. Are you getting any sewing done? Don't worry about patching my overalls for school. I just plain know we're going to get into Oklahoma with all these horses and make us rich. The horses are looking better.

Love,

Your son Dan

There was no question now, the horses were putting on good solid meat. I could tell by looking and I could tell by my sore hind end.

Ropesville had been good to us. We fed regular—regular for us, and the horses had done the same. Besides, we had some money in Boggs's pocket and some sowbelly and pork and beans in that pack. Things looked better all the time. That's what I was thinking about five miles out of Ropesville when I noticed the old gray horse throw his head back and stop. The horse in front of him had also stopped and was holding up one foot.

"Boggs," I yelled, "come here. Something's wrong with this bay horse."

Boggs reined back and we both dismounted. He picked up the forefoot and examined it. I could see it was a bad cut.

"He stepped on a piece of glass, looks like to me," Boggs said.

I walked back a few steps and sure enough there was a broken bottle.

"What do we do?" I asked, fearing what he'd tell me.

"There ain't a thing to do, boy. With the best of care this horse is going to be lame for a month or more. The frog is cut deep. We'll just have to leave him. I'll go up here to this farm and see what we can work out."

He was gone maybe ten minutes before he returned with a man. They both looked at the foot again.

Boggs said, "He's yours if you'll doctor him."

"I'll give it a try," the man said, looking worried.

"Now listen," Boggs said, "soon as you ease him up to the barn throw some diluted kerosene on it. It might burn him a little but it'll take a lot of soreness out quick. Then make a poultice out of wagon grease and churn butter. The grease will keep the flies from getting to it and the butter will take out the fever."

"I'll give it a try," the man said again.

I wanted to say that my hind end could still use some of that butter, but I felt too bad about the horse. Now we were falling short on delivering the goods and we had a long way to go yet.

"Let's git goin', boy."

I rode along now feeling blue and upset. After a while I thought I might as well try to cheer myself up so I started trying to guess what the fanciest present this side of the pearly gates would be. Maybe Boggs would get me a new hat. Or even better, a new pair of boots. I'd never had a new pair of boots—just old brogan shoes. It was a disgrace. Why, I'd be thirteen my next birthday. And that birthday was tomorrow according to the calendar in the Ropesville café.

All of a sudden Boggs rode back. "Look there, boy, there's Lubbock."

"I was there once," I said, blowing up a mite. But I was really too little to remember. The tall buildings stuck up out of the plains so's you could see them for miles around. "Man, that must be a big town."

"Naw, it ain't nothin', boy. You should see Denver, or San Francisco or Mexico City."

"You been all them places?"

"Hell's fire, yes, and a lot more besides."

I still wasn't going to give up on Lubbock. "How many people you reckon lives there?"

"Oh, maybe twenty-five thousand."

I whistled.

"See that building? The tallest one?"

"Yeah."

"Well, that's a hotel. I still got a suitcase in there. One time I was driftin' through here and went broke as a pullet bone. I figgered and figgered how to get out of that hotel without paying."

"You was thinkin'," I volunteered.

"By jingoes, you're right, I sure was. Well, I took a shirt and put all my other clothes, all my shaving equipment, and some crooked dice I happened to have with me in this shirt. Then I tied it up in a bundle so's it would look like a bundle of dirty laundry. As I stepped out into the hall, one end of that shirt came open and dice and razors and all sorts of stuff fell right out on the floor. A porter and two maids just stood there and stared while I gathered it all up and tied it back tight. That was where they let the hotel down. Before they could get to a service elevator to squeal on me, I was already down three flights of stairs and asking the desk man where the nearest laundry was. Well now, once ole Boggs got outside I was gone. That little Ford car just purred me right out of town."

"Ain't that cheatin', Boggs?"

"Why, Lord, no. What's the matter with you, boy? That's what you call tradin'. I left them a sure-enough good, empty two-dollar suitcase for a week's rent and feed."

The closer we got to Lubbock the more my eyes bugged. It sure was a whopper. We skirted around the west side of town next to the Texas Tech campus. Boggs pulled up.

"Here's a nice little pasture to hole up in. I've got to get on into town and do a little shoppin'. You'll have to stay here with the horses, boy. Part of my shoppin' you wouldn't understand anyway."

Well, just as we were unloading the pack mule, we heard a truck coming. There were two men in it and one of them said, "What the hell you think you're doin' turnin' a whole herd of horses in my pasture? I'm a notion to impound 'em."

Well, my little skinny heart was tearing my ribs out. That was all we needed to fail Papa completely.

"Why, my good sir," said Boggs, "let it be my pleasure to inform you kind gentlemen that we have merely paused a fleeting moment in our travels to relieve for an instant the burden of this fine pack mule. I am a preacher of the gospel. Myself and my young apprentice are heading north—our eventual destiny to be deepest Alaska. There we intend to bring about a revival of the Eskimos that will shake the northern world. Our horses we shall trade for reindeer upon our arrival. There are some things a reindeer can do that are beyond the capabilities of the American horse. Suffice it to say that with another moment's kind indulgence we shall wend our way over the great horizon to far-distant shores."

One of the men just stared, puzzled, and the other one said, "Well, I don't know about that."

"And what, my beloved fellow inhabitant of this celestial globe, can I inform you of?"

"Jist git out, that's all, jist git out." They drove away mumbling under their breaths.

"Well, we shall skirt on around town, my boy. There's a canyon full of grass to the north of town. Yellow House Canyon by name. We shall perhaps find a better sanctuary there."

I was wishing he would shut up that silly talk and quit practicing on me. Hell's fire, I was ole Dan.

It took us another hour to skirt town and sure enough there was a nice little canyon with lots of grass. We pulled up and pitched camp.

Boggs said, "Now get a good rest. There's plenty of grub for a change. I'll see you after a while." He rode off on a black, leading the pack mule. I had me a nice meal. Worried a while about losing the horse and finally fell to sleep.

It was getting somewhere close to ten o'clock the next morning when I heard a heck of a yell. I looked up and there came Boggs down the other side of the canyon. He kept yelling and singing. And that mule was having a hard time keeping up with him. There was stuff hanging all over the pack.

"Happy birthday, dear Dan'l, happy birthday to you." He was really singing it out and swaying in the saddle till I was certain he'd fall off. He jumped off his horse and shook me by the hand so hard I thought he was going to unsocket my arm. He lifted the jug from the pack and said, "Here's to you, Dan'l, and a happy birthday it's goin' to be. I got no more earaches, Dan'l. Whooooppeee! Happy birthday to you!" He ran over to the pack and grabbed a secondhand No. 3 washtub. "Gather the wood, boy."

I knew better than to do anything else. But since the mesquite was thin here I had a devil of a time keeping him supplied.

He dumped a ten-pound sack of flour in the tub. A five-pound sack of sugar followed. Then he threw in a can of baking powder, and I don't know what else. He wouldn't let me stay to watch. Said it was going to be a surprise. I watched for a minute from off a ways. He ran down to a little muddy spring with a rusty bucket and got some water. Then he stirred it all up with a mesquite limb.

Well, when I got back with my next load of wood, the fire was blazing under this tub, and he said, "Here's your surprise, boy. It's a chocolate cake. Now what boy on this earth ever had a chocolate birthday cake like that?"

I had to admit that I doubted if there had ever been such an event take place before. Well, I kept carrying the wood. And he threw it on the fire and stirred. After a while the cake started rising. He kept shushing me to walk quiet.

"Hawww, boy, watch your step, you'll make this cake drop."

Well, I figger that nine hundred buffaloes could have stampeded right past and that cake would not have dropped. In fact it rose up in the air about eighteen inches above the rim of that tub and just ran out in all directions. Boggs had taken his earache medicine and bedded down.

For a while I thought I needed his help when it looked as if the cake would fill the canyon, but when it finally cooled and I took a bite I was real glad he was asleep. I choked for thirty minutes. After I got finished choking, I hauled most of it off and fed it to the magpies. I didn't want to hurt his feelings. I should have had some consideration, though, for the magpies, but in those days I was just a growing boy.

<h1 style="text-align:center">7</h1>

We worked our way north of Lubbock through country spotted with cotton fields, sorghum—thick and heavy leafed—and here and there the brown stubble rectangle of an oat patch already cut and stored. On past Plainview we got into some grassland again, and that's where something happened.

We were moving out of a small draw through some cutbanks when the old gray horse pulled out of line reaching for a special clump of grass. I reined over to the edge of the sharply sloping cutbank and yelled "Haaarr" at him. Just as I did, my horse bolted to the side and I went down hard against the ground. I was sort of off balance lying on the slope of the cutbank. I reached up to get hold of a thick clump of grass to raise myself, when I heard the rattle. The snake lay coiled on a level patch. That's what had boogered my horse.

We looked each other right in the eye. I strained my left arm where I held the grass clump. The snake struck out right at my head, but he was short an inch or two. Now, I was in a fix. I could tell the grass roots would give way if I put any more weight on them. If they did, I'd slide right on top of the snake.

His little black eyes looked at me over his darting tongue, and suddenly they seemed as big as light bulbs. And that forked tongue popping in and out was nothing to make me happier. I could feel the sweat all over, and a ringing in my head. For a minute I nearly fainted. Then for some reason I thought of Papa and how he was depending on me. If I panicked and got snakebit the whole thing would be blown up. Everybody's hopes would be done in. But I didn't know what to do. If Boggs just knew, but of course, he couldn't. He couldn't see me. I'd just have to hold on as long as I could, and maybe the snake would go away. It wasn't advancing, but it wasn't backing up, either. It just lay there coiled, its head in striking position, shaking those rattlers a hundred miles a minute. I kept feeling like I was sliding right into those fangs. I couldn't move, but just the same I pressured my belly into the dirt hoping to hold.

Then I heard the voice coming, easy and sure. "Don't move, Dan boy. Boy, you hear me, don't you? Well, keep still now. Just a little longer, boy."

I didn't even twitch an eyeball. I saw him crawl into my range of vision. He had a stick held out in front of him and he was kind of humming the same note over and over and twisting the end of the stick in a slow circle. Closer, closer, hum, hum. The stick circled near the snake's arched neck. Nothing but the tongue and the rattlers moved now. Then the head shot out and Boggs scooped the snake onto the end of the stick and hurled him way down to the bottom of the draw.

I was paralyzed another moment. Then I leaped up screaming, "Kill him! Kill him, Boggs!"

Boggs sat down beside me and said, "Now, just calm down, boy. You're fine and the snake's fine."

"Ain't you goin' to kill him?"

"Lord a mercy, no, I ain't goin' to kill him. Why, that poor old snake's in the same war we are."

"War?"

"Sure enough, boy, he's fightin' those pack rats harder'n we are."

I forgot all about the loss of the horse, and when I found out that Amarillo was a bigger town than Lubbock I even forgot about the rattlesnake for a while.

I did wish I could go uptown and see all the sights, but Boggs said that would come for me soon enough; besides, we had to stay on the march and take care of our horses now.

8

Between the towns of Amarillo and Dumas, Texas, runs the Canadian River. We drove our horses along the highway until we spotted the long, narrow cement bridge crossing it.

Boggs threw up his hand and stopped the horses. He rode back to talk to me.

"I don't believe we better try to take the horses across the bridge. We're goin' to block too much traffic. And besides we've got to have a permit, as well as the highway patrol to watch both ends. It's too late to get either now. We only have one choice, boy; that's bend the horses back to a gate and ride east down the river till we find a crossing."

This we proceeded to do.

I could see the storm sweeping toward us from the west and north. It must have been over a hundred miles in width. We had to cross the Canadian before it hit. This river is nothing to play with. It is full of quicksand and bogholes, and when it rains heavily to the west a front of water drops down out of New Mexico and West Texas with great force and speed.

Most of the time, though, the Canadian is a quiet river. Many places in its bed are as wide as the Mississippi, but during dry spells only a few small, red, muddy streams trickle through its bottom. Cottonwoods break the tree-less plain along its banks, and cattle come to water from it for hundreds of miles up and down. Wild turkey, quail, coyotes, antelopes, and many other kinds of wild game love the Canadian. But to man it is always treacherous.

For ten or twelve miles on each side are the sand hills—thousands upon thousands of tiny, rough, ever-changing hills of sand—spotted with sage, shinnery, mesquite, and yucca. The yucca was green now, and the pods were soon to open their beautiful, milk-white blooms.

We rode hard, pushing the horses through and around over the sand. The old gray could only be moved so fast. So that I was constantly having to yell and crowd the poor thing. But he did his best for me.

There was no sun as the huge cloud blanket moved on toward us and shadowed the land. The lightning was cracking so fast now that the thunder was a continuous roar, never letting up but varying its sound like rolling waves. Even without the sun it was hot—sure enough hot. The horses were lathered white. And my almost healed-over hind end was sweated to the back of my mount. The Canadian looked fifty miles wide to me but was actually only about three-eighths where Boggs finally chose to cross.

I crowded the old gray down into the clay and sand of the bottom. There were tracks where a cowboy had crossed here. The forefront of the storm clouds was moving up over us now. I kept glancing up the river, fearing that wall of water I knew had to be moving upon us from the west. The wind was intense and the horses' manes and tails blew out almost parallel with the ground. We struck a few shallow bogholes where our mounts went through to the hard clay underneath.

Way up the river bottom I could see the rain reaching out into the banks and I knew a head of water was racing right along with the storm. I saw a small tornado drop down out of the sky for the ground and then return like a hand reaching out of a shawl to pick up something. Several writhing snakes of cloud broke loose in torment. I could hear the roar of the rain above the thunder now and its chorus—the river.

I almost panicked and left the old gray horse. More than anything I wanted to get out of the river bottom and up to the banks above the cottonwoods. Even if there was a tornado there. And there was one just beyond. I could see the inverted funnel ripping at the earth. Black. Mad.

Now we were on a huge sandbar that carried all the way to the bank. There was no turning back. There was no detour. Underneath the slight crust of its top was quicksand. Deep and deadly. The sand shook and quivered like Jello. The bank was nearer now.

The old gray stumbled and the extra force against the ground broke the crust. He went in up to his belly. I rode up beside him and pulled at his mane. My horse was sweated and excited and almost jumped out from under me. For a moment I thought the quicksand would get him. The more I pulled, the more the old gray fought, the deeper he sank. I was crying and begging the old horse now. And it wasn't just because it meant another loss to Papa, but it was a loss to me. He was my friend, this old horse.

And then I heard Boggs. He was riding back across the bar. "Git, boy! Look!"

I saw the terrible churning wall of dirty, red water racing at us. He slapped me hard up the side of my head and said, "Ride!"

I rode on by the old gray and I saw his nostrils almost tearing his face. His eyes rolled back as he sunk to his withers. In his eyes there was an acceptance along with the terror.

We rode up on the bank as the rain hit us harder and the edge of the tor-

nado squalled on by. I got one glimpse of the old gray straining to throw his head above the river's blood, and then he was gone.

It rained for two hours and then the sun came out. We were very cold and very wet. It didn't even bother me. The river would be up all night. We gathered our horses and moved on across the sand hills. I didn't look back.

9

I had a numb feeling as we rode along. We were getting into the last stages of our drive, and we were two horses short. It was just plain awful to let Papa down. I was sick thinking about it.

We reached the edge of Dumas, Texas, on a Sunday. We knew that was the day, for the churches were filled with singing and shouting. I watched Boggs up ahead. I could almost see him quiver, he wanted to get in there and go to preaching so bad. He raised his hand and stopped the horses. They milled about and started grazing on somebody's lawn.

He rode back to me. "Boy," he said, "it's takin' all my willpower to stay out of that church. I'd like to go in and talk that reverend into ten minutes with Boggs. There's a lot of sinners in there and they think they're saved, but ten minutes later I'd have 'em lined up and headin' for a baptizin'."

It sounded like he wanted me to say, "Go ahead." So I said, "I'll watch the horses, Boggs, if you want to go in."

"That's a magnanimous gesture, boy, but I reckon we've got to do somethin' about replenishin' this herd of horses. We just cain't let your papa down. And besides, your ma is staying back there worrying herself sick about the mortgages and all that. Now the way I got it figgered is this: these little West Texas towns all have baseball teams. Today is bound to be Sunday. There'll be a ball game around here somewhere."

Well, he was right. We found the baseball grounds out on the edge of town in a big opening. We turned our horses loose on the grass and rode over where a man was dragging the field down with a tractor and scraper.

"Yes, sir, there's going to be a ball game," he said, taking a chew of the tobacco Boggs offered him. "Spearman, Texas, will be here in just a little while. They've got a good team but we've got a better one."

"Is that so?" Boggs said. "What kind of pitchers you got?"

"One good 'un, and one bad 'un."

"Sounds about right."

I was sure puzzled about Boggs's interest in baseball, but since we were going to graze the horses a while we might as well have a little fun watching a baseball game.

The crowd began to gather early. They came by truck, car, wagon, and horseback. The teams began to warm up their pitchers and everybody was getting excited. Seems like this was an old rivalry.

I followed Boggs around till he found the manager of the Spearman team. This man also chewed tobacco, but when Boggs offered him a chew he reared back and looked out over his monstrous cornfed belly and said, "That ain't my brand."

Boggs said, "How much would it be worth to you to win this game?"

"Well in money, not much. I only got five dollars bet on it. But in personal satisfaction, my friend, it would be a strain for a millionaire to pay off."

I could tell the way he talked they were going to get along.

"Did you ever hear of Booger Boggs who played for the East Texas League?" Boggs asked.

"Sure. Everybody's heard of Booger Boggs. Why?"

"That's me."

"Ahhhh," and he started laughing and laughing. "You're jist a farmhand. Maybe a bronc rider, by the looks of them legs."

Boggs was quiet for once. He let the manager finish out his laugh then he said, "Can you catch a ball?"

"Sure. I am the Spearman catcher."

"Well, go get your mitt and get me a glove and ball, my dear associate."

While the unbelieving fat man went after the equipment, Boggs started warming up his arm, swinging it around and around.

"Now, son," he said to me, and I knew he was really going to get serious because of the "son" bit, "this old arm ain't in much shape and it'll never be any good after today, but I just want you to know I'm going to give 'er all I got."

"You goin' to pitch?"

"You just wait and see."

He threw a few soft ones at the manager and then he let one fly that purty nearly tore the catcher's arm off. I knew he was going to get his chance. He went around and started a few conversations.

"You folks from Dumas don't know when you're beat. I'm goin' to sack you boys out today." As usual when they looked at Boggs everybody just laughed and laughed. That's what he wanted them to do.

One of the sporting boys said, "If you're goin' to pitch I'd like to lay a little money on the line. Now, if you ain't just a blowhard, why don't you put your money where your mouth is?"

"Well now, I ain't got no money, my dear compatriots, but I've got something better," and he swept a long arm at our horses grazing off a ways. "I'll bet any four of that fine bunch against any two of yours."

One man got so carried away he said, "I'll bet my good wagon and team with the grain and laying mash that's in it and a box of groceries to boot."

That was the only bet Boggs called. They shook hands and had plenty of witnesses.

The game started. I watched Boggs fan three Dumas men in a row. Then Spearman got a man on base. The next two up for our side struck out and the Dumas catcher threw our man out trying to steal second. Then Boggs fanned another and two grounded out to shortstop. And right on into the sixth inning scoreless. Then I could tell Boggs's arm was weakening. A Dumas batter swatted a long, high fly that should have been an easy out in left field. The fielder just plain dropped it. The man scored standing up.

Well, Boggs took off his glasses, pulled out his shirttail, and went to cleaning that lens. He took his time about it. Everybody was wondering what difference it could make if he cleaned a glass that fit over a blind eye. So did I.

The Dumas fans were naturally rawhiding him quite a bit and the Spearman team was getting uneasy. I watched him closely. He was up to something. I knew that no matter what Boggs was, I'd never see another anywhere like him. Come to think of it, that's a whole bunch to say about any man. He was at least three different men and maybe a dozen.

When he got through cleaning his glasses he slowly put them back on. Then he took off his hat and his glove and held the ball high in the air. And he shouted so that everybody quieted down.

"Lord, up there in the great universe, heed my call. Lord, I'm goin' to ask you to put some devil on this ball. Just let me use him a little. I want a devil curve and a devil drop and a devil fastball, and I'll guarantee you that the end of the game will belong to you, Lord. What I want is victory. Now I know you heard me, Your Honor, Lord. So it's up to me. And if I don't win this game bring a bolt of lightning down upon my unworthy head and burn me to a cinder. Amen and thanks."

I looked up in the cloudless sky and thought that even the Lord would have to strain to get lightning out of that blue sky.

He pulled his hat back on tight, picked up the glove and ball, squinted out that glassless rim, took a big spit of tobacco, and let fly. No matter what happened to this game it was quite a sight to see him pitch. Those runover high-heeled boots, bib overalls, and that old floppy hat sure were different to say just a little.

That ball whistled in there so solid and fast the batter fell down hitting at it. Boggs didn't waste any time now, just wound up once and let fly. The ball broke in a curve and the batter nearly broke his neck fishing for it. The next one was a drop—breaking sharp and clean. The umpire yelled, "Strike!" and thumbed him out. A great roar went up from the Spearman rooters.

After that it was a walk-in. Boggs had shot his wad on those three pitches. He was faking his way now. The spirit of the home team was broken. The Spearman players started a seventh-inning rally and the way they batted I could have been pitching for them and they would have won.

The game wound up nine to one and we had us a team of horses, one of which was a mare with a colt by her side, a wagon, a lot of feed, plus a big box of groceries.

Boggs was carrying his arm at his side. It was obvious he'd never pitch again, not even for fun.

10

When we headed out of Dumas the next day I was sure a happy kid. As soon as Boggs was up ahead where he couldn't see I just plain let loose and bawled. After that I felt fine.

Now our only problem, if we were lucky, was the time. We were a half day behind. At the same time we couldn't push the horses too hard or it would gaunt them and the buyers wouldn't pay enough. I drove our wagon with my saddle horse tied behind. We'd taken the pack off the mule and so we all moved out pretty good.

Wheat country sprung up all around now. The plowed fields contrasted to the rich green of the sorghum. There was a zillion miles of sky all around. The farms and ranches looked peaceful and prosperous, but every little bit I could see where the drought still showed its fangs—fences buried beneath drifting sand, fields barren and cut to clay beds. But this new idea of contour plowing, so the land wouldn't wash, was sure enough helping. I didn't like to remember the dust that came and choked and killed and desecrated the land like the earth had suddenly turned to brown sugar. I liked to think about the green growing things. But I was young and I know I'd never have appreciated the wet years without the dry ones.

Night and day became almost the same. We didn't sleep or stop much and when we pulled into Stratford, Texas, in the upper panhandle, we were dead tired. We camped about four or five miles from town. It was so thinly populated we could see only one farmhouse close by.

We ate, turned the horses loose to graze, all except the one we left tied to the wagon eating grain, and went to sleep.

As usual Boggs was up before the sun. "Go drive the horses over close while I fix breakfast. That way we'll save a few minutes."

I saddled up and rode out through the mesquite. I was surprised the horses weren't nearby because the grass was good everywhere and they like to stay fairly close to the grain. I tracked them a ways and blamed if they hadn't walked right up to this farmhouse. There they all were in a corral. I felt a hurt come in my belly. A hurt of fear. Those horses durn sure hadn't penned themselves, and we were on somebody's private land. I didn't have long to wait, before I found out whose.

He sat on a big plow horse holding a shotgun, and spoke in a mean voice, "Thought you'd be around directly. Well now, boy, where's your pa?"

"At Guymon, Oklahoma."

"Guymon, huh? Well now, ain't that interestin'. What's he doin' off up there?"

"Waitin' for me," I said, swallering and feeling the tears start to burn. I choked them back.

"Who's helpin' you with these?" He motioned the shotgun at the horses. He was a short man but broad and big bellied. He wore a tiny hat that just barely sat on top of his head and his mouth hung loose around his fat face. I couldn't see his eyes, just holes in the fat where they were.

"I reckon you know you were trespassin'?"

"Yes, sir."

"Well, cain't you read?"

"Yes, sir."

"Well, then how come you didn't heed my 'posted' sign?"

"Didn't see it."

"Well"—he started nearly every sentence with well—"I'll tell you one thing, young man, you'll look the next time you come around my place. You got any money?"

"No, sir."

"Well, now, ain't that too bad. I'm just going to have to ride into town, get the marshal, and we'll have to have a sale to justify the damage to my land. Five dollars a head, that's the law. If you cain't pay, I take the horses."

"But we ain't got anything else, no way to live . . ."

He interrupted, "Well, you should've been thinkin' about that when you rode on my place and started destroying my grass."

"Please."

"Too late for that, sonny."

I had to stall for time. I said, "Look, mister, I know you're goin' to take my horses, but first, before we go, could I have a drink of water?"

"Ain't no harm in that," he said. "But hurry it up. I ain't got all day."

I went over to the horse trough and drank just as long as I could. I thought I saw something moving out near our camp.

"Hurry it up, sonny. Get on your horse and let's go."

I walked up to my horse and picked his hind foot up. I glanced under his belly and I could see Boggs snaking along from one yucca clump to another, and it sure looked like he was eating yucca blooms. The damn fool was going to get himself shot sneaking up this way. My horse heard him and pitched his ears in that direction.

"Here, sonny, what you doin'? That horse ain't lame. Now get up on there before I give you a load of this here buckshot."

I got up on my horse just as Boggs raised up and broke into a wild, arm-waving, screaming run right for us. The froth was streaming out both sides of his mouth. His one eye gleamed right at us just like a wild man's.

That horse under that man with the shotgun just snorted and jumped right straight up in the air. When his hoofs hit the ground, there wasn't anybody on his back. That feller came down hard and the shotgun blew both barrels. The horses and mules broke out of the corral and ran back toward our camp snorting and blowing to beat seventy-five.

I finally got my horse calmed down and when I did I saw Boggs sitting on top of the feller who once had a shotgun. He reached over and tapped him up beside the head with a rock. The man slept. Boggs got some rope from the barn and tied him up.

"Go round up the horses," he said, as he stuffed the man's mouth full of shirttail.

I soon had them cornered, and tempting them with a little oats in a bucket, I made them follow me over to the wagon. By then Boggs was back. We caught our team, hooked them up, and got to hell out of the country as fast as we could.

We rode on now through the day and into the night, and then again. We let the horses have twelve hours on grass and a big bait of grain just before we crossed the state line into the Oklahoma panhandle. The last lap now.

This strip had once belonged to Texas until around 1850, when they sold it to the United States as part of the territory including New Mexico, Colorado, Wyoming, and Kansas. It had been known as the "strip" and "no man's land" until 1890 when the strip was made a part of the Oklahoma Territory.

It was part of the great plains we'd just come across. These vast regions shot northward all the way through the Dakotas, Montana, and into Canada. My hind end felt like we had covered our part of it.

Late in the afternoon of the next day we spotted Guymon. We unrolled the map out of the oilcloth wrapper and studied it.

"The sale is tomorrow at noon," Boggs said. "That means we need these horses in there at ten o'clock like your pappy said. The buyers like to look before the biddin' starts."

"We're late," I said, feeling cold and weak.

"No, sir, we turn up here about a mile and then it's nine more northeast from there. If we ride way in the night we can make it."

"But the horses'll be gaunted down."

"No, we'll feed them a good bait of grain and give them till eight in the morning to graze. If we find grass where we stop we'll be all right."

"If we don't?"

"Like I said, son, there's risks in everything. That's where the fun comes in life."

"Let's git goin'," I said.

We pushed the horses on. They didn't like it and kept trying to graze in the bar ditches of the country lanes. We made them move. I left it up to Boggs to lead, hoping hard he was going in the right direction. For a long time we could see the orange light of the farmhouses sprinkled off across the prairie and once in a while a car light moved in the night. Then all the lights were gone except those of the stars and a half moon. It was enough. I nearly went to sleep several times, but I'd wake up just before falling off the wagon. It seemed like we'd ridden a hundred years to me. My body was still working but my mind had long ago gone numb.

Then there was Boggs. "Take a nap, son. There's plenty of grass for the horses right along the road. I'll stay up and watch 'em."

I crawled in the wagon bed fully intending to sleep an hour or so and then relieve Boggs. It didn't work like that. The sun was up and warm when he woke me.

"Get up, boy, and let's have another look at the map."

I raised up fumbling sleepily for it.

"Here it is!" he cried. "Here it is! Look, two dry lake beds, then take the first turn to the left for one mile. Look—" He pointed up ahead and there were two dry lake beds. A tingling came over me. Boggs handed me a cup of coffee and said, "Just a minute and I'll fix you some bacon."

"Don't want any."

"Let's git goin', Dan boy," he said, grinning all over.

It took us a while to get hooked up and on the move. The colt bounced saucily beside the wagon. The horses were full and although they weren't fat, they had lots of good solid meat on them. They were strong, tough, and so was I. I was burned brown as a Comanche warrior and my hind end had turned to iron.

Papa saw us coming and headed down to meet us in his old Ford. He jumped out and said, "Howdy, fellers. Why, look at Dan. Boy, you've growed a whole nickel's worth. Have any trouble, Boggs?"

"No, sir, not a bit."

I didn't tell Papa any different. Besides, he had such faith in us he didn't count the horses. If he had he'd have found there was one extra.

The sale went over big for us. Uncle Jock really got his best chant going. When it was all over Papa had cleared over twenty dollars a head on the horses and nearly thirty on the mules. Ma could rest easy and go ahead and plan her garden for the next spring. Papa gave me three whole dollars to spend just any way I pleased.

Soon as we got home I went over to Starvation to drink a few orange soda pops and get my present from Boggs. He didn't show up the first day and he didn't show up for a whole week. I was getting a trifle worried but figured maybe he'd had to go plumb up to Lubbock to find me the new pair of boots. I'd made up my mind that's what he'd give me for using my saddle.

Well, on the eighth day I ran into him coming out of Johnson's Grocery, and said, "Hi, Boggs."

"Well, howdy yourself, Dan. How've you been?"

"Fine," I said. "Did you get me the present you promised?"

"Just a minute, boy," he said, and walked back in the store. He came out with a nickel pecan bar. I took it. He said again, "Just a minute, boy," and went back in the store.

I figured he must be getting my present wrapped up pretty for me, so I hunkered down on the porch and started eating my candy bar. It sure was thoughtful of Boggs to feed me this candy while I was waiting. I'd eaten about half of it before I noticed the funny taste. I took a close look. That candy bar was full of worms. Live ones.

I got up and went in the store. I walked on toward the back figuring Boggs was behind the meat counter. Then I saw this table that said: ALL CANDY ON THIS TABLE PRICED ONE CENT. There were lots of those wormy pecan bars among them.

He wasn't at the meat counter and I asked, "Mr. Johnson, do you know where Boggs went?"

He said, "No, I don't. He walked out the back door."

Well, it finally glimmered in my little brain what had happened. I got mad. Real mad. I got me a board and I went all over town looking. I was going to knock his head clean off if I found him. It got dark. I waited at the back of the pool hall looking through a window for him. I waited till it closed. I waited till the whole town closed. I was in such a rage I nearly died.

I never found Boggs. In fact, I never saw him again. I don't know where he came from and I don't knew where he drifted to. But by jingoes I sort of miss him. After all, he was my pardner.

The Sky of Gold

It might take two or three days, but just the same it was upon him. It was the time to die. The legs beneath his thin, shaky body moved with a stiff certainty beyond their strength, for he had been here a long, long time. He must get away from the town. He could feel its pull, reaching out to him. He could hear it say, "Come, Old Pete, sit by my dusty streets in the shade of my trees. Loaf and dream in the sun on my porches and warm your worn old legs. Come and die slowly here, looking out at the far distant hills." He moved out in front of the burros, the voice of the town becoming weaker with each halting step. Up there somewhere in the hills was a secluded spot where he could die without interference from the town, from all the towns and cities, where no one could ask him to recount the tales that belonged to him alone—tales that only he could understand.

Old Pete had lived as he wanted. Surely now he could die as he wanted. Just a hidden spot of hard earth somewhere in the rough hills that had been his home where he could lay his head and depart. Where he could make a meal for the coyotes, those singers of the night who had been his partners in loneliness these fifty-odd years, who like himself had scratched their breath and sustenance from the hills.

He felt no pain. His heart still pumped his blood, and though his legs were stiff and very old they kept him upright. Still it was his time, and he knew, and like a gut-shot wolf he hunted his true home. There it was out ahead—dry, washed, worn, cruel. It was his. That was the difference. He'd long ago earned his place here.

He stopped to rest after a while. The burros grazed about in the thin patches of grass as Old Pete looked back. He had made better time than he thought. It was about noon, and the paved road splitting the village of Hillsboro looked narrow and fragile. He could see the trucks. He could hear their endless drone that spoke of things he felt no part of. Maybe by nightfall he would be free of their sounds.

The packs on the burros were light. Soon he would free them of their

burden and turn them loose. They, too, could roam free and unmolested. But he would need them for a while yet.

"Haaa!" he said. "Let's move out, Old Mary, Old Nancy." The burros raised their heads and followed, their sharp black hoofs pitching tiny balls of dust at each step.

Now they entered the arroyos and the small, rolling, coverless hills. In and out they moved, up and down, around the sage and cactus. Slow, steady, sure.

It had been a good life—and he had found his gold. Four hundred dollars to the ton. He had dug and blasted it out in a month. The vein had narrowed, pinched, and then petered out altogether. He had crushed the quartz a little at a time in a hard mortar. He panned out the gold and sacked it. Eight thousand dollars worth at twenty dollars an ounce. What a time he had! The town was his then—the drinks, the tender women, the feasting, the dice table—they had been his. Then it had ended. The town turned its cold side to him. He went away and though he returned many, many times, he never gave of himself to the town again.

The tiny, sunken, blue eyes pierced out beyond the sharp eroded cheekbones to the land ahead. The great red mesas edged nearer. On beyond, the high, breastlike mountains called.

What had started this search so long ago and kept him at it all those years? Was it the gold? Was it? He couldn't answer that. He had been young when he started. He was strong then, and he was strong for years after. Before his strike there had been moments of indecision. One summer, far, far past, he had dug and panned nine hundred dollars worth of gold. "We can start a feed store," the woman had said. "You can settle down. You can sleep in a feather bed every night. My body and my heart will be yours, and I will cook and sew and raise your kids, and we will grow old together happily." That was Mary. Every burro he had ever owned had been named either Mary or Nancy.

He must have been about thirty-five or six when he met Nancy. That was the time he had failed to raise a grubstake for months, he now remembered. Nancy was a dancing girl. Every young man wanted a dancing girl—this one wanted him, though. "Now, look, Pete," she had said, "I've been everywhere and done everything, I know men, but I don't really know you. You want my love—well, here it is, Pete, take it, but don't throw it away. Come with me. I'll show the tricks of the cards to you, and we can tour the world. Just you and me. You'll never have to worry about the grubstake again."

She had made it sound so good, so easy, so sure. But the great secret magnet of the mesas had pulled at his life fibers, and he had been drawn back to the rocky slopes of the hills. Again and yet again.

He was growing very tired. The sun lingered just above the hills. He hadn't looked back for a long time. He would not look back until the night was upon him. It came swiftly and all at once. He knew that the sky just before had been filled with gold, but he couldn't make himself look.

He built the fire from a few sticks of wood on the pack saddle. They were still some distance from the scrub timber of the mesas. He fried the bacon and took the hard, sourdough bread into himself with little taste. He could hear the whish of the night owl's wings and the cry of the coyote. In his lonely wail, his old partner sang to Pete of the Marys and the Nancys and the warm firesides. Of the things only they could understand—the things Old Pete had missed, and the things he had found.

Now Pete looked back and listened. There it was still—the drone of the mighty trucks. He was not nearly far enough into the hills. It would take another day, maybe two. He could see the tiny flickering red and blue lights blinking from the village below like a small cluster of earthbound stars.

Old Pete slept little that night. It was the longest night of his life. He lay in his blanket and stared and felt the earth throb beneath him. This earth was his. It was his love. He craved to have it devour him. But he must live the night out and move on beyond those lights and noises below. The voice of the coyote kept him company, crying into the night from one valley, then the next. Raising his head atop the hills and voicing his concern for his compadres who sleep alone on the desert sands.

It was almost noon the next day before the stiffness left Old Pete's legs. It only proved how right he was. He could no longer roam these wastes searching for his treasure. The burros threw their long ears forward and shied sideways. The diamondback lay coiled, black tongue flickering, quivering in tenseness. The rattles were a blur on its tail as it shook its warning.

"No need for that," Pete muttered. "I'll give you back your land very soon. I will walk far around you. You were here first. It is yours."

He climbed on up through the scattered timber above the desert floor, the burros following slowly in single file behind. His stooping shoulders ached, and it was now a great effort to put one foot in front of the other, but on upward he moved. He saw the deer and the bobcat tracks in the soft sand of the washes, and he saw the fresh droppings of the coyote matted with rabbit hair.

He turned and looked behind him, taking his ragged old hat from his head so the light breeze could blow through his grayed and tangled hair. He looked close. It was gone. The village was gone. He strained his ears. No sound but the distant calling of a magpie. He was beyond it, but they still moved on up—the three of them.

They topped the high, long mesa and struggled up into the thicker timbers. Pete could feel the blood beating hard on his ears now. His breath rasped through his worn, broken teeth. The rat-tat of the woodpecker told him they had reached the timberline.

Then he found the game trail into the oak brush. It was very steep. The timber thickened. He saw in the trail the lion's round track as big as his hand. Yes, he was near his destination, for the lion, too, feared the same thing in his own heart and had moved to the outermost reaches. It was just a matter of finding the spot now—the right place to return to his earth.

Pete walked and looked for a long time. Then he found it. A flat place on solid rock. A mighty tree-fettered canyon lay below. He could look down the canyon and out into another desert to the west. He could see as far as his eyes could reach. He could hear as far as his ears allowed. Only the sounds of the desert and the forest above were audible.

He unpacked the burros. He neatly piled up his equipment, his blankets, his pick, his shovel, his gold pans. He yelled, waving his bony, trembling arms at the burros. They looked puzzled for a moment, then seeming to understand they turned and moved down through the brush.

Beyond the purple-bottomed mist of the canyons Old Pete saw the sky redden to the west. Then it turned yellow-red, gold-red, and then pure gleaming molten gold. He lay back slowly and settled himself. The trembling stopped. The breath came slower and slower. Only the sound of the forest was here. The elusive whisper of the night wind soothed his tired old body. The thin chest barely moved.

He looked into the dark blue of the upper sky. His fading sight saw the twin streaks of white vapor forming behind the soaring aircraft, and he heard the harsh, shattering blast of its jets.

Mary and Nancy grazed peacefully back down the hill toward the distant village. Moving downhill it wasn't so far away. They would soon be there.

––––––––

AUTHOR'S NOTE: "Sky of Gold" was written in 1950 and is the nucleus of the massive and major works of my life: *Bluefeather Fellini* and *Bluefeather Fellini in the Sacred Realm*. The *South Dakota Review* published "Sky of Gold" in the spring of 1995 as part of a dissertation on my two major works.

The Orange County Cowboys

If a person's whole world was going to end within two weeks, very few people would spend this precious time tying barbed wire around sandstone rocks and dropping them into a gully, but that is exactly what the two weathered, battered cowboys, Dusty Jones and Wrangler Lewis, were up to. They were repairing a water gap, three or four strands of barbed wire strung across a draw to keep the cattle in a certain pasture. Instead of being firmly anchored to fence posts, the bottom wire is tied to suspended rocks so they swing freely instead of breaking in a minor flash flood.

Dusty made a wrap around a ten-pound rock and secured it with a tight twist of the wire. As he dropped it, he turned to Wrangler saying, "Ever since those Japanese people looked at this ranch with the idea of buying it, I've felt like one of these rocks was barb-wired to my balls."

"Awww, I think they'll probably like George Haley's place better than this'n."

Jim Ed Love, owner of the Hi Lo, New Mexico, ranch was definitely serious about selling it to a group of Japanese investors. He had shown his usual wisdom in allowing his foreman, Dusty, to be their escort guide. The interested buyers were led by Mikio Reynolds. She was the divorced, thoroughly Americanized sister of Mr. Yakahami of Tokyo and other worldly places. Dusty had given the tour all he had even though it had hurt him deeply knowing that his bragging about the ranch might cost him the only home he'd known as an adult.

Dusty pushed his hat back on his head and said, "I'll tell ya, Wrangler, I never wanted to lie so bad in all my life, but this is a great ranch and . . . that Japanese lady, Mikio . . . well . . . nobody could ever lie to her and get away with it."

Wrangler grunted and said, "Maybe they won't like it at all. Maybe they're just winder shoppin' like folks do in town. Maybe Jim Ed don't really want to sell. Maybe if you'd run off with that perty Mikio lady, that'd stop the deal. Maybe if . . ."

Dusty interrupted a little tautly, "Like they say down at Lubbock, Texas, maybe if the dog hadn't stopped to shit he'd of caught the rabbit. If ... if ... if ..."

Wrangler only grunted this time.

Dusty rambled on as they finished repairing the water gap. "Two weeks. That's what we got left to make a too-late, brand-new beginning. If you'd just married that rich old Myrna Hopwell over at Santa Fe that time we wouldn't be havin' these worried notions."

"Now let's don't start that agin. I can't help it if she thought I had that terrible epidemic disease."

"You couldn't help it?" Dusty snapped his head in Wrangler's direction, then said through clenched teeth, "If you hadn't been so damn drunk you wouldn't have sent that poor, old, toothless wino to take your blood test for you. Whaddya mean you couldn't help it?"

"Sounded like a hell of a good idea at the time." Wrangler began gathering up the tools. Then he smoothly added, "Seems like that Japanese lady took quite a likin' to you, Dusty, ole pard." He waited for a smart-ass answer, but when it didn't come, he continued, "I can see plumb through a mountain of malpais that she's the marryin' kind." He snorted a couple of laughs through his flattened nose and added, "I reckon it's your turn next."

They tossed the wire stretchers, wire pliers, staples, and hammers into the back of the pickup and drove off down a rocky, rutted, bumpy road in a cloud of powdered dust.

Dusty rubbed his sleeve across his dry mouth and suggested, "Why don't we stop at Vince Moore's and have a cup of his bootleg belly burner?"

Wrangler cheered up. "Yeah, why don't we? I never seen a drink of whiskey I didn't like."

––––––––––

Two tall businessmen, dressed up to play cowboy, sat in the John Wayne Airport lounge in Orange County, California, and raised full glasses of Scotch, toasting one another.

"Here's to fourteen days of freedom," said Ed Mason.

"Here's to escape," said Al Goodspeed, smiling for the first time in a week.

They were on their way, this time without Al's family or Ed's girlfriend, to Al's vacation ranch in northeastern New Mexico. This vast, rolling, canyon-gashed land was called the Hi-Lo Country. From the high mesa top, twenty miles east, three other states could be seen on a cloudless day. It was an ideal place for Al to build a ten-room log cabin.

Goodspeed's land was surrounded by large, working cow ranches, but he didn't run cattle on his spread. Deer, bear, cougar, and an occasional stray elk had that privilege. They wandered freely across his place and drank from the small trout lake formed by a thin stream. The coyotes howled nightly, and during the day the hawks circled the sky looking for rabbits or rodents. It was a choice place to entertain clients in the fall with big game hunting. In the spring it was good for trout fishing or just watching the grass grow and the neighbor's newborn calves leaping and frolicking in a nearby meadowland pasture.

Al Goodspeed, an international manufacturer of precision machine parts, headquartered his company in high-tech Orange County. He had just turned a heavy-framed fifty-five. Ed Mason, his best and longest-lasting friend, owned a small but elite advertising agency in the same county. Ed was about to finish out his skinny forties. Because of Ed's independent nature he operated the agency alone and had, by his own choice, limited his clients to only three—but they were good ones. Al Goodspeed was his best. They looked forward to talking things over out at the ranch—heavy things that had been bothering them—but right now they had just enough time for one more fast drink before catching the plane to Albuquerque where they'd rent a car and drive north.

Al said, "Do you think these people here," he motioned around the airport bar, "believe we're real cowboys?"

Ed answered, "Well, last time we were up there, your rancher friend George Haley said we looked 'perty much' like the real thing, but I have a feeling he was being very, very kind."

Al laughed aloud now, his blue eyes beginning to visualize things other than his factories and sales offices in Orange, Sweden, Germany, Belgium, and Switzerland.

"Hey," Ed said, "it's time to go, and this is one plane we don't want to miss."

If the two had just joined the first wagon train to pioneer the Santa Fe Trail they couldn't have felt more excited or adventurous. When the plane finally reached thirty thousand feet, and each had a drink of Scotch in hand, the friends knew they were finally "away."

Ed said, "I can already feel the freeway bullshit dropping off my back."

"I'm somewhat lighter myself," Al said as he settled in for the ride.

Ed Mason and Al Goodspeed weren't the only part-time residents on their way to the high-altitude ranches of Hi Lo. Jim Ed Love's shiny, twenty-six-year-old secretary-companion, Shirley Holt, drove him in his Cadillac along the highway between Clayton and Raton as if she owned it. She and Jim Ed had left the ranch headquarters near Andrews, in far West Texas, early that morning.

Jim Ed had inherited the shinnery, the sand- and mesquite-covered Texas ranch, in the mid-thirties from his father, along with a foreclosure mortgage, the Great Depression, and a searing drought. He would have lost the whole forty thousand acres except an oil company leased the mineral rights and drilled, bringing in a thousand-barrel-a-day well on the first location. Now two hundred and fifty pump jacks, looking like great steel blackbirds, pushed their bills deep into the earth and forced his liquid wealth to the surface. The drop in oil prices shouldn't have bothered Jim Ed much, but it did, even though all it meant was his income changed from three and a half million to two million a year. He'd also diversified into high-tech stocks, real estate, and businesses in San Diego, Beverly Hills, and other expensive places. Even so, Jim Ed had decided to trim his huge holdings and take life a little easier. He was somewhere in his seventies—the quiet country years—but was in good shape physically and his mind could slice up granite.

He picked up the car phone and called his son, Jason, who had privately jetted to the Hi Lo ranch two days earlier from Midland, Texas.

Jason answered, "How you doin', Dad?"

"Fine, son. I woke up this morning with nothing to do and I believe I got about half of it done."

"Glad to hear you've been so busy. Did you get any of that good rain at the ranch that we got up here?"

"Awww, maybe four drops and a squirt."

Jason knew that it had, in fact, rained an inch and a half just two days back, but he wanted to hear what his dad would say about it, knowing that if one of these old ranchers had just received two feet of moisture they'd swear a dust storm was already blowing the grass dead.

"Well, Dad, the Tokyo people are still here. I got your price within three dollars an acre on the Hi Lo ranch."

"Hey, that sounds okay. What about the cattle?"

"Market price on the day of closing like you said."

"Mineral rights?"

"They want three-quarters of those."

"Oh boy, they know there's a huge coal deposit under the north half of that ranch, don't they?"

"Yes, and they're also aware of those hundreds of CO_2 gas wells Amoco has drilled all around us."

"Well, that's the big trap. There's always a trap to watch out for. Always."

"And that's not exactly all. I've been dreading to tell you this. They want George Haley's ranch, too, because our coal deposits extend over on his land. And . . . if they can't get George's they say they don't want ours."

"What's the hang-up then? Have you talked to George?"

"Yes, and so have they. George swears he'll never sell."

"Ever'body says that, son. We'll have to see what we can do to change George's mind. Won't we?"

"Guess so. Say, Dad, there's something else that's bothering me. What are we gonna do about Dusty and Wrangler? They've been up here on this outfit for over half their lives."

"Well, we can move 'em back to Texas on the Big Lake Ranch. They oughta like that."

"But then we'd have to demote Dusty from foreman to just plain cowboy, and that don't seem fair to me."

"Hell, maybe the Japs'll keep them both on. They'd sure be smart doin' it. Nobody alive knows that spread like ole Dusty and Wrangler."

"Yeah, but . . . they're gonna feel like . . ."

"Listen, son, don't go gettin' sentimental on me here. There's nothing in this world as pitiful to gaze upon as a broken-down cowboy with ambition." He gave a quick chuckle, then added, "We'll be there soon. Bye."

Jim Ed hung up the phone and was thoughtful for a few minutes. Then he reared back in the cushioned seat and said to Shirley, "They're trying to hang us out to an early frost on the mineral rights and they're making the deal subject to Haley selling his outfit under the same terms, and he doesn't want to sell."

"You'll handle it, Jim Ed. That's for sure," she said, smiling warmly at him.

Jim Ed was quiet a spell as the car moved over the graveled road. He thought to himself how many generations the Love family and the Haleys had been friends. Fine people the Haleys, but just as tough as they were kind.

"Tell you what I'm gonna do, Shirley. We'll toss a party for those Oriental folks that they'll never forget. We'll invite ever'body in the entire Hi-Lo Country. Hell, we'll have us a big fiesta. We'll throw so much bullshit, booze, and music into the air that old Haley can't help but discover he wants to sell. I know the Japanese are smart traders, but they haven't lived through a Jim Ed Love fandango before."

"See? I told you, you would handle it."

"Awww, Shirley, you know this ol' boy don't know thin brush from firewood." He gave her a sly wink and the two Cadillac jockeys shared a comfortable laugh.

––––––––

George Haley was watching his wife, Doris, comb her auburn hair with the streaks of gray at the temples. To him, she was even more beautiful now at forty-five. Her figure was slightly fuller, but better, and her blue-green eyes seemed deeper and more caring. He found it hard to believe they'd been married twenty-seven years. Sometimes it seemed like last week, and at other moments it seemed a thousand years. Where in hell was time, anyway, and what was it to deceive them like this?

Haley forced his mind out of the past back to the present and said to his wife, "Well, Goodspeed was supposed to come in from Orange yesterday and here we are taking off for Albuquerque."

Doris replied, "Don't worry about it, hon. He's bringing Ed Mason with him and they'll probably appreciate being alone to rest up for a few days. We'll have plenty of time to visit them when we get back from the Cattleman's Convention."

"You're right. Anyway, we really don't have a choice. I feel like we have to go. There are lots of issues on the docket this year besides the low cattle prices. There's the high land taxes and those fees for the grazing permits sure have to be talked out, and I darn sure want to be there to put in my two bits' worth." He paused for a minute, thoughtfully, and added, "Besides, I'll be kind of glad to get away from here for a few days. It'll give us a little time to think. We've got quite a bit to sort out in our heads."

George was, in part, referring to the prospect of selling their ranch to the Japanese investors. It would be a difficult decision to make.

Life on the Haley ranch had been tough, but full, and they liked it here. Together they had fought all the natural disasters that befall ranchers—droughts, blizzards, and currently it was low cattle prices and mounting debts. Somehow, up to now, they had kept the place afloat.

George and Doris were partners, and Doris had done more than her share. Without her, Haley could never have made it go. Besides making her family a comfortable home, keeping them well fed, neatly dressed, and healthy, she also helped George with a lot of the ranch work—branding and fencing. The bringing up of their two children, sixteen-year-old Terri and twelve-year-old son Douglas, had been mostly her responsibility. She was proud of the results her dedication had brought.

The Haleys loved their land and the lives it gave them, even though the years of increasing debts were wearing them both down to the marrow. They fought on, still losing ground by the day. Now they could change it all if they chose to. They could get out with a livable nest egg, enough that the monthly check they were now receiving from Al Goodspeed to look after his place wouldn't have the same importance. That money had kept them off the edge, and they were grateful for it.

George found himself wondering if Doris would, in her heart, really want to change everything, or would she just go along with what she thought he wanted? Guess he'd never really know that for sure. Anyway, they wouldn't deal with the Japanese unless Jim Ed went along as well. He'd be in from Texas anytime now and they'd have to decide, but they could think about all that later.

"Well, while you're gettin' ready, I'm goin' down to the barn and talk to the kids."

Today his daughter and son, and some of their friends, were going to move a herd of cattle from one meadow to another. George believed in rotating his stock regularly in the lower country. Then in early summer he'd turn the cattle out into the high-timbered pastures until fall. This kind of rotation would let the meadows near headquarters grow lush and tall to make hay for the winter.

He found Terri and Douglas warming up a couple of quarter horses. In an hour or so, five neighboring ranch kids would arrive and they'd move the three hundred mother cows and their calves from the Francis meadow to the adjoining north pasture. It wasn't much of a cattle drive, but the young cowhands would be doing it without their parents, so it couldn't have been any more exciting if they were driving thousands of head from Texas to Dodge City.

George checked things over, gave a few last instructions, and said good-bye. He felt completely trusting of the youngsters. All of them had been working cattle since they could climb on a horse. He and Doris were ready for town!

———

Ed Mason and Al Goodspeed arrived at the playhouse ranch on the kind of summer day God would have bragged about. The early afternoon clouds had gathered, rumbled, rained, and moved away east. The slanting sun drank the moisture from the meadow grass so swiftly that damp ghosts of steam rose lazily into the freshly washed air.

Three hundred head of George Haley's white-faced cattle grazed in the meadow about a half mile west of Al's place. The biggest-boned, best-conformed, five-year-old "boss" cow nursed her three-week-old calf and

chewed nonchalantly on her cud. The bull calf was so full from the plentiful milk that he slobbered and gasped for breath. Even so, he hunched at her bag so hard she kicked at him from the pain. His tail whipped back and forth like a contented puppy. Then he heard, and saw, the blur of a frolicking little heifer race by.

He let the teat slip from his mouth, turned his head to watch as she ran away, jumping and twisting. She whirled and charged straight at him only to veer off at the last second. The young bull pursued her, kicking and bucking even higher. They circled and chased one another, stopping to playfully butt heads. They were so full of life on this one perfect day that they had to expend it in joyous celebration. They went running, weaving, teasing across the meadow, strengthening their muscles and improving their agility.

A few years back, this meadow had been cleared of timber except for one huge pine tree. George Haley left the giant as a remembrance of how mighty the forest had been. Since it had no others of comparable size to act as buffers against the strong winds, a violent gust had toppled it. There it remained with its roots in the air higher than a horse's withers and a hole in the earth as big as a cellar.

The two calves, faces as white as the top of Pike's Peak and their deep-red body hair complementing the emerald-green grass, raced almost side by side now, heads stretched out, tails arched. The baby bull jammed his front feet into the ground to whirl back and away, but one hind leg slipped off into the hole left by the fallen tree. His momentum whirled him like a top and he fell thumping on the bottom dirt.

He was addled, but swiftly recovered and attempted to climb out on the only slope possible. It was still muddy from the rain and his hooves cut and churned at the earth as he struggled upward and slid back down over and over. Soon the ground was smoothed slick so that it was impossible for him to climb out. He was trapped.

He smelled around its sides. At one end where the topsoil reached down to clay, a small basin of water drained in and was captured from the recent rain. He dropped his muzzle down into the puddle, took a couple of sips, and then found he couldn't turn around in the narrow end of the hole. There was nothing to see but the water, the banks of brown dirt, and blue sky above where a couple of buzzards circled floating on updrafts looking and smelling for anything dead or dying.

———

The young cowhands did a good job rounding up the modest-sized herd. The cattle were moving along smoothly now, with the kids yelling like old-timers, popping hands on chaps and snapping the end of catch ropes at the slackers. They were making a lot of noise, but they were also being careful not to chouse the stock too much so the weight loss would be kept a minimum.

There was only one problem. The "boss" cow, who usually led the bunch, kept cutting back out of the herd, bawling. Terri noticed that her bag was so full it was dripping milk from each teat. It was obvious that she was looking for her lost calf.

Terri searched among the cattle for the little bull. Not finding it, she left the herd and loped back through the meadow. She made a wide circle in the well-fenced pasture, but there was no calf to be seen.

She finally decided it may have been killed earlier by a mountain lion or a bear, or even a coyote, and dragged off into the brush. After a while she accepted the loss of the calf as ranchers always do, with a minute of pain and a necessary forever of forgetting. She'd tell her parents the moment they returned, but for now there was a job to finish, and after that came the picnic, the flirting, and the "horse bragging" with the other young wranglers.

————

Mason and Goodspeed were finally relaxed. The winds of the Hi-Lo Country had blown the particles of concrete and plastic from their bodies and erased the computer programs from their heads.

Yesterday they fished, and feasted. Last night they enjoyed a relaxing meal of venison and quail out of the freezer and the fresh trout they'd caught by Al's lake. Now, today, after a good night of sleep, they sat out on the porch sipping drinks and nursing a semi-hangover.

Al got up and focused the powerful telescope, perched on its tripod, down on the meadow where they'd heard the cattle bellering and the kids yelling the day before. He moved the scope around, as he loved to do, looking for wildlife. He moved it up the slope, through a forest of rocks and then back down. He saw a sudden movement. A badger was chasing a ground squirrel. He watched as the little squirrel twisted, turned, and leaped, avoiding the jaws and claws of the predator. It dived into its burrow four inches ahead of death. The badger rammed his head down into the hole, backed out, looked around, then jumped down and started digging—the thing badgers do best.

Al was hypnotized by the life-and-death action occurring across the quiet, resting valley. Ed was reading a book by William Manchester on World War II—a somewhat larger, but no deadlier, struggle than Al was watching.

The dirt flew out behind the badger's claws like he had shovels on his legs. He was digging down out of sight now until he backed up for a moment to kick the surplus dirt away. Al could tell by the excited posture of the animal's body that he felt he had his prey ready to pluck from the deep dirt trap. Then, to his eternal amazement, Al saw the squirrel's head rise from a tiny escape hole a few feet from the main entrance. The squirrel looked swiftly around, leaped out, and dashed frantically for the large rocks above.

There was a blur as a hawk dived from the air, scooped up the ground squirrel in its claws, and flew to its nest on top of the pillared rocks where she ripped it apart and fed the pieces to her young.

Al's thoughts flashed back to the nursing home and the last visit he'd had with his uncle Carl. He was devastated when the old man didn't recognize him. Al's mind just wouldn't accept that this man he loved so much, who'd been so vital, so full of spirit all his life, had in two short months lost the use of his brain, his body, and possibly his soul. It didn't matter that Uncle Carl was ninety and had enjoyed a full life. No, it just wasn't right. After all, he didn't retire until he was eighty-five when he was still going strong. Al was only fifty-five now, and Carl had gone on producing for decades after that age, but still the visit had really turned Al's head around. All he could recall was the vacant stare from the man in the wheelchair, and in his mind he put his own body there. He was thinking like the song says, "Is that all there is?"

He stood back from the telescope and stared off at the mountains. He ached to describe the drama in the dirt to Ed. His feelings had been filtered to their purest form. Words would have to wait for the proper progression of time. Instead, he quietly moved into the house and got them each another drink.

The two old friends talked about the good times for a while. They reminisced about the camping trips to Baja before the tourists discovered it— when they had once driven for hundreds of miles without seeing a human. How they'd loved the desert, the camaraderie with a couple of other friends, the Mexican beer, the long, empty beaches, and the quail chirping their cheerful sounds across the precious stillness. They spoke of their drinking and business bouts on Sunset Boulevard twenty, even twenty-five, years ago. Ah, how their youth had laughed at hangovers, business setbacks, and how swift the recovery from broken love affairs. They elaborated on the trips to Europe as Al's business expanded, the great museums they'd seen, and the grand hotels they'd stayed in. My God, they'd had a lot, and now, this moment, they felt incomplete. They believed their clocks had stopped and the winding keys had been lost.

Ed tried to convince Al that he had pulled it all off. "Hell, old pardner"—
he reverted to the local way of speaking—"you've put it all in a box and tied
a bright red ribbon around it. You've got a pretty wife, two healthy, educated kids, and business around the world. You have the ballets, the clubs,
the boats, money, position, and power that goes with it all. Seems to me,
you've done damn well."

"That's just it," lamented Al. "It's not what I thought I wanted. Now I feel
vacant . . . and . . . ah, hell, I don't know. There's just got to be more. Something . . . something else that really matters."

Ed Mason looked out across the meadows where the late sun had turned
the green pastures to soft gold and said, "There is, Al, if you want to pay the
price."

"What's that? Just tell me how I get out of this . . . get rid of this feeling of
doom. Go ahead, tell me."

"Think of all the things you can enjoy when you have the time. The time,
that's the catch," Ed said. "That's the one thing you can't buy. You love art.
You love reading good books and watching fine films. You love the outdoors and sometimes the isolation. There are dozens of things, except the
time to do them. Sell the goddamn factories and go do all the things you
love. You've got enough to take care of you and your family from now on.
What in hell is holding you back?"

Al's face turned deep pink as he rubbed at his graying blond hair and
said, "I know you're right, but I just can't call up the guts to do it. I can't
seem to make the break no matter how much I want to. I keep thinking of
all the reasons why I shouldn't—my wife, my kids, my employees."

"Okay, then. Okay," Ed said, shrugging his shoulders. "Go ahead and
work yourself to death. What will anyone really care—and which will be
remembered the longest, you or your properties? Everybody'll start fighting
over them in about three seconds after you're gone anyway, so everything
you've worked like hell to put together will crumble and turn into a beautiful pool of diminishing, confused crap."

Suddenly Al decided he resented the very thing he'd asked to hear.

"Okay, look at yourself. You've sold out to a comfortable house full
of paintings and books. You never work on the novel you constantly say

you're going to write. Why don't you just quit and follow your heart like you're telling me to do?"

"You got part of it right. I could have stayed up on Sunset Boulevard with that advertising agency and lived in a castle in Beverly Hills, but I chose to come down here and do just enough work for you and my other clients so I can live well, buy some good books, hang a Couse and some Icart paintings on my walls, and now old friend, just like you, I want to get to work on my novel and the Hollywood and European stories I've dreamed of writing. I feel just as miserable and cowardly as you do, believe me."

"Well then, why don't you follow the advice you gave me? Just quit and do it," Al said smugly.

"That would be about as fruitful as irrigating concrete. I don't have any income except what I earn each and every month. None. So don't try to put me in the same Rolls Royce you're in, old buddy. I'm coming on fifty, you know?"

"You're just a kid," said Al with a grin, and then they both laughed and touched their drinks together. Al added, "You know, Ed, the truth is, we built our own big trap and jumped in it with both feet."

"And eagerly . . . too damned eagerly, if you ask me," Ed agreed.

"Let's go into Raton tomorrow and celebrate the fact that we've got the problems of the universe solved."

"No, no. Raton has about ten or twelve thousand people. Why don't we drive over to Hi Lo where the population is about a manageable three hundred?"

"Of course," Al agreed, "that's what Uncle Carl would have done."

As the sun set they heard the yapping of what seemed like all the coyotes in the world—but there were only six. The coyotes stayed up, but Al and Ed went to bed early.

———

The old mother coyote sat on the hill and stared down at the calf in the hole. She was confused. So were her pups. If she meant to attack right now she'd have spaced her three pups out like a military formation, but they stood and squatted by her sides because no definite signal had come from their mother. Now, two grown dog coyotes had joined them and also sat staring down at the baby calf. It stood motionless except for the occasional nodding of its tired head.

The coyotes had never experienced a setup like this and their genes had no guidance to give. The sun said good-bye behind the western mountains and a half moon came up. They howled at the sky and at the top of the earth. Now, however, the wind was moving just right to blow the scent of a mountain lion down to them from where it had gorged on a freshly killed deer. It was dragging the victim's remains to some brush to hide it for recovery later when it, in turn, caught the scent of a four-hundred-pound black bear shuffling along, clawing at rotten logs for insects. Because of the wind's direction the bear didn't smell the lion, the lion didn't smell the coyotes, but the six coyotes were getting it all—as well as the blood scent of the dead deer. It gave them enough to puzzle over so that they delayed, for a while, their attack on the calf in the hole.

The Hi Lo wind had once again altered life and death here this night.

———

The next afternoon Mason and Goodspeed drove optimistically down from the rim of Black Mesa toward Hi Lo. This entire vast area had at one time exploded into a flaming, searing, molten hell. Scores of malpais mountains had formed, most of them spaced apart and of greatly varied shapes. These vistas and historical happenings always stirred their receptive minds.

Off to the west, eighty or a hundred miles, the Sangre de Cristo Mountains shoved thick, white spear points into the tender turquoise sky, and just on the other side of them was the old art colony of Taos and the multistoried Indian pueblo that was still very much inhabited.

Ed pointed southwest toward the distant Eagle Tail Mountain. "It's sure plain to see why that was the main lookout point for the Comanches, and all those other tribes, who were planning attacks on the wagon trains and all the white settlers that were invading their land along the Santa Fe Trail."

Then he switched his attention due south, toward the national monument, Capulin Mountain. He waved his arm in a circular motion at the hollowed-out edge of the recently extinct volcano. "It's so perfectly formed

it looks like it might explode any moment just for the hell of it. It kind of takes you back in time, doesn't it?"

Al agreed. He enjoyed the atmosphere of the surrounding country almost as much as he liked hearing Ed expound about it every time they came. They always arrived in Hi Lo almost transported back into the Old West.

About twenty miles easterly was one of the largest lone mountains in the world, Sierra Grande. It would take a rancher in a pickup truck from sunup to sundown to encircle its base. Highway 85 wove around its edge approximately halfway between Clayton and Raton. There, hovering like a neurotic child pulling its mother's skirts in the presence of a stranger, was the village of Hi Lo.

The Orange County friends could observe, from their present position, over a million acres of land. They wheeled down to the little town of Folsom where that important primitive, archeological man's ancient remains had been discovered.

Shortly, south of Folsom, they drove close to the railroad where it made a very sharp curve next to a huge volcanic cinder mine.

Ed pointed with elation: "Now there's where a bit of Western history took place. See? Right there."

Al glanced at the railroad.

Ed continued: "That's the very spot that Black Jack Ketcham, the famous Western outlaw, jumped on to rob the train."

"Yeah, I've read all about it. That's where he got shot up and was later hanged over at the county seat of Clayton. Right?"

"You got it." Ed spoke with enthusiasm. "And when they dropped him through the trapdoor it jerked his head clean off."

Being in the core of such a mighty circle of bandits, train robbers, pioneers, and cowboys hastened their natural desire to reach the village of Hi Lo and associate with those who presently lived and survived right in its middle. They speeded up the car, humming down the eternally corrugated road.

––––––––––

The wind was laying the grass flat outside the Hi Lo Bar, but inside the jukebox was playing, the cowboys were drinking, and Dub, the bald-headed, ex-horseshoeing bartender was a little edgy. Even though he was built to take care of any trouble, this grizzly man with his belt-stretching belly and forearms like fireplace logs knew in his lower brain that the ceaseless winds did more than bend trees and drive tumbleweeds against the fences; it bent people's minds as well, and on a high-wind Saturday night in a cowboy bar it could get dangerous.

"Shut the goddamned door," cowboy Dusty Jones yelled when someone opened the front entrance. "The wind's blowin' the whiskey outta my glass."

Wrangler looked at his glass and said through his flat nose, "Shoot, with the door shut tight the wind's still makin' waves in my whiskey."

The two had been telling tales about their long-gone horse, Old Fooler. They never got tired of talking about him, or so it seemed to Dub. He'd heard so much about that danged horse that he wished Old Fooler was still alive so he could kill him, even though he had been the "greatest" roping horse, the "greatest" cutting horse, and the "greatest" rock-working horse that ever lived.

In reality the old roan horse had done everything he could in his twenty years to disable these two cowboys. He'd run under tree limbs with them, banged them against tree trunks, bucked them off in the middle of nowhere miles from headquarters, bitten, kicked, and otherwise declared all-out war on the whole human race.

It puzzled Dub that they never talked about how Old Fooler died. Wrangler had been riding him as he and Dusty worked a small bunch of cows off a rimrock. Old Fooler thought he'd caught Wrangler napping and he started pitching. Wrangler grabbed the saddle horn with his right hand and locked his right elbow over his hipbone and rode him. It made Old Fooler so mad and mean he bucked off an eighteen-foot bluff, breaking his neck and dying instantly. Wrangler ended the fall with a cracked arm, a broken leg, and a fractured skull. It was several months before he could mount a horse.

Still, he remained their favorite topic. In desperation to change the conversation before it drove him berserk, Dub bought his two best customers each a double shot. It worked. They were so shocked by this unheard of event they forgot all about Old Fooler.

After downing the precious gift in a couple of swallows, Dusty said, "Give us another'n jist like it."

Wrangler raised two fingers and said, "Make that two to save time."

Dusty tried to get serious, "I was just wonderin' if we've been so busy keepin' up with the changes in the way to handle horses and pickup trucks that we got about three steps behind the violin. That, and the VCR Jim Ed bought for the bunkhouse, is enough to make a man lose the path to the barn forever. Don'tcha think."

Wrangler didn't really want to strain his jumbled grey matter, but realizing that Dusty had something bothering him, tried to help, "Seems to me like you done saddled the mule."

"Yeah . . . well, I was just, uh, wonderin', too . . . that maybe, just maybe, them new owners . . ."

"Them Japanese don't own it yet," Wrangler insisted.

"Yeah, well, what I was thinkin' was that maybe they'd leave me on here as foreman. Whaddya think? Reckon we both oughta try stayin' on here? Wouldn't it be better than goin' to Texas where Jim Ed would be looking down our collar all the dang time?" He wasn't getting the response from Wrangler he was expecting. He straightened up his chair and rearranged his whiskey glasses and the ashtray and continued: "Well now, Wrangler, when you get right down to it, no matter how the deal turns out, it's either Jim Ed Love or the Japs. Take your pick. It's like my ole Uncle Slim once said, We got our asses between a landslide over here and a flash flood over there. Soooo, what do you think?"

"Whatever suits you just tickles me plumb to death," Wrangler answered in a low voice like ball bearings rolling over velvet. "I didn't come here tonight to wear out my thinker. Let's get to dancin' and havin' fun."

Al wheeled the car to a dusty stop in front of the white, stuccoed building. They had arrived at their happy destination—the Hi Lo Bar. Several older cars and pickups were already there.

Ed and Al opened the front door and were blown inside just as Dusty was on his way to the jukebox.

They all three stopped, shook hands, and said how glad they were to see each other again.

"Is Wrangler here, too?" Al asked, looking around the dimly lit room. About that time Wrangler let out a yell that made the paint want to peel off the walls.

Dusty answered, "Yeah, I believe he is."

Wrangler waved at Delphino Mondragon, from Folsom, and ambled over to the table to ask if he could dance with Mrs. Mondragon, their two daughters, and Mrs. Mondragon's widowed sister.

Delphino said, "If you're loco enuff to try 'em all four, I'll pay you by the hours."

They all finally got seated around the table and Ed asked Dusty, "How's everything going over at the Love ranch?"

"Perty good fer now. Got some early rain, but we'll have to have more moisture quick or we'll start turnin' to desert. How's big ole California treatin' you fellers?"

Ed and Al gave each other a look, trying to figure out an answer. Finally Ed said simply, "All right."

Al ordered another round of drinks in lieu of a proper reply.

About that time, young Eddie John from Kim, Colorado, made his entrance into the room. He took his time shutting the door. He was so big that the wind barely made him weave even though he was already drunk. He walked up to the bar and said in a noticeable voice, "Give every other person in the joint a drink, cuz I'm gonna whup all the rest."

All that prevented the front wall from being torn apart by about twenty escaping people was the fact that Eddie John was laughing when he said it.

Dusty leaned over the table and quietly relayed vital information to Al and Ed. "Them Kim, Colorado, bastards are sure 'nuff bronco riders, bull-doggers, and fistfighters. And right there's the toughest of 'em all. I seen him take on a whole bar in Raton. A bunch of 'em got him down and kicked in about six ribs and other things and drug him over in a corner. They left him for dead and went on with the party. But Eddie was hurting too much to die, so after a while he got up and whipped all their butts."

"I'm glad he seems to be in a good humor right now," Al said.

At that instant Eddie John spotted Dusty. "Hey, Dusty, I ain't seen you in seven hundred years. You still shoveling cow shit for good old Jim Ed Love?"

Dusty swallowed, and said, "Naw, Eddie John, I'm about caught up for the summer."

"Bulls beller and cows bawl," Eddie yelled for no apparent reason and then introduced himself to Ed and Al, asking them, "Where you two fellers from?"

"California," they answered.

"California, huh?" he repeated, and he went back toward the bar muttering "California" over and over.

Dusty Jones never claimed to be the world's brightest cowhand but he was smart enough to know that Eddie John coming back to their table with a full glass of whiskey in one hand and the grin gone from his face meant trouble. He said quietly to Ed and Al, "Get ready to turn on the tough."

Dusty knew there was nowhere to go. If he was going to get killed it might as well be indoors out of the wind.

Eddie John stood towering and glowering above the table. Ed grasped a heavy ashtray. Al had moved one hand around to clutch the back of an empty chair.

Just as Eddie John said, "California, huh?" again, Dusty stuck his whiskey glass in Eddie's free hand, saying, "Here, hold this a minute, please."

Eddie stared first at one glass, then the other, and somewhere within that open space, Dusty rammed a fist. Eddie went back and down. Wrangler jumped over and kicked Eddie in the ribs and then stomped up and down on one hand until he figured there was no way he could close it into a fist. That still left him with one hand to hold a pain-numbing drink. This time Eddie accepted his loss. He even bought "every other one that he was going to whip" a drink.

Wrangler and Dusty rejoined Al and Ed at the table. They were trying to get their breath back and have a drink all at the same time.

Dusty said, "Course ol' Dag Oakdale might've taken Eddie John by himself."

Wrangler said, "I wouldn't 've known who to root for."

Dusty agreed. "Me neither. You ever met him, Al?"

Al answered, "I know his outfit joins Haley and me on the south, but I've tried not to meet him."

Wrangler said, "Mighty good judgment. The first time I ran into'm was nose first," and he rubbed at the flattened appendage in painful remembrance.

Everything returned to normal fun. Everybody there, including Delphino, danced with all available women. The party was on.

"Black Jack Ketcham and the Wild West live again," Al yelled at Ed as he whirled Teresa Mondragon off her feet.

Ed returned the shout, "We're home, Pardner. Hot damn, we're home."

———

The next morning the Orange County boys decided to walk off their hangover. They wore their cowboy duds proudly today. Hell's fire, they'd survived a real Western showdown last night and were about to go to another one coming up soon. Shirley Holt had called and invited them to Jim Ed's big DO. They would have to get back in shape for that one.

Al wanted to show Ed an old cabin beyond George Haley's cow meadow. A shootout had occurred there in the late 1880s between Indians and late-blooming mountain men who were trapping the Indians' furs. There were a few artifacts lying around and the bullet holes were still visible in the cabin walls.

They got into their Old West attire and mood. Bears had been prominent in the area recently so they had a good excuse to strap on a couple of pistols. Al chose a collector's old Colt .45. Ed wore a new .357 Magnum.

Today the wind had let up, the clouds didn't come, and the sun had a free shine at this part of the earth. By the time they'd crawled under or between the wires of several cross fences and stumbled over the main meadow, they were soaked in their own brine. The thick grass looked like the carpet in the Royal Suite at the Dorchester, but in reality it was a rough, ankle-twisting, tendon-stretching jaunt.

Ed stopped a minute and said, "Al, when are you going to get some horses on this ranch?" That, of course, was the missing element of their "cowboying."

"The cabin's not too far now," Al said, stopping to catch his breath.

Ed didn't move, but said, "Ah shit, I can see it good enough from here."

Al was not difficult to convince. They took what looked like an easier and more interesting way back. As they walked within perhaps a hundred yards of the great downed pine, they saw six coyotes lope off over the hill out of sight. Both men wondered what so many were doing together.

They walked toward the massive fallen tree and looked down into the hole at the swaying back of the calf. They were suddenly confused by the helpless feeling permeating their beings.

"My God, it's trapped," said Al.

"I can see that."

They both stared for quite some time until Al broke the silence.

"That poor little thing must have been down in the hole since the kids moved those cattle. It's been standing there for four days." His voice was filled with disbelief and admiration. He took action.

He leaped down into the hole with the intention of lifting the calf out to Ed.

He picked up one end, but the other dropped back down. After a short struggle, he tucked both arms under the calf's middle and, with Ed's grunting help, they hefted him out of his four-day torture chamber. They felt an elation now. So did the calf, but he was starving. As nature intended, he tried to nurse. He rammed his muzzle between Al's legs first and shoved upward. As Ed stood wondering why Al was bent over moaning, he found out. The calf would take any mother it could find. Ed was bent over, holding his crotch, gasping for air. Finally he choked out, "That little bastard is a karate expert."

When both men regained most of their composure, Al said, "We better take him to his real mother."

They moved across the rolling, cedar- and piñon-spotted hills toward the county road to Haley's ranch. The calf followed behind like a puppy, except it kept rooting them in the back of the knees, occasionally almost knocking them down.

"Ed, do you realize that we can build up a herd with this bull? He's high quality, you know."

"A one-bull, no-horse ranch sounds about right for us to handle."

Then they got serious about the little creature. There could be no doubt about it; it was fate, their finding him at the last moment before his demise. By the gift of life it must become theirs. They wondered how much money their neighbor would want for him and pondered on the cost and care of several head of cows with their new companion as the no. 1 herd bull.

They had walked at least two tortuous miles, with blisters forming in boots that were made for riding, when they spotted a road grader growling toward them.

Al said, "That noise is going to scatter our herd."

Ed, by now completely unsound of body and mind, agreed, and offered up the supreme sacrifice for their ranch. "I'll go ahead alone and have a showdown with that herd-buster."

Al was relieved, but another thought flashed into his head: "Oh Lord, what am I going to do with this Colt .45 when I get there? It'll embarrass me to death for that driver to see me wearing this thing."

Ed was now so involved in his "Western" part that nothing could deter him. "Here," he said grandly, "give it to me." He strapped it across his own gun belt and started walking valiantly down the road. This very tall, slim man with very long legs tied to very sore feet walked straight at the iron monster moving relentlessly toward him cutting wide swaths in the earth with its massive steel blade. Ed, just for a fleeting moment, thought that not even John Wayne, nor any other gunman for that matter, had ever topped this. The "walk-down" music thundered in his head and the palms of his fast-draw hands itched for action. Man and machine edged closer and closer together for the final confrontation. Ed stopped spread-legged in front of it.

The driver braked the machine and leaned out, asking politely, "What can I do for you?" Who wouldn't be polite to someone armed with two pistols and all dressed up like he was playing cowboys and Indians for the first time?

"You can stop the goddamned noise for a few minutes," Ed the gunslinger said.

There was no doubt in the driver's mind that this person was deranged and he instantly agreed to move the machine from the road until the "herd" had passed.

Ed motioned for Al to proceed. "Move 'em out," he waved and screamed.

When they neared, Ed took up the "point" position while Al held up the "drag." The three-part trail drive didn't last long because the calf just couldn't go any farther. All attempts at verbal persuasion—"Here, baby.

Come, pretty calf"—failed, as did whistling, finger snapping, and hand clapping. The calf's wobbly legs finally gave out and it sank to the ground.

They cautiously, tenderly, lifted him up several times, but nothing worked, so Al sat down on the road and held the calf's head in his lap, stroking its neck and telling it encouraging stories while Ed bravely walked the two miles to the ranch for help.

George drove Ed and his blisters back to Al and the calf, marveling that it was still alive and agreeing with Ed that it was saved by the trapped rainwater.

When they reached the ranch, Doris fixed a big bottle of warm milk for the calf. He drank and drank, even though he was so weak they had to hold his head up. Soon he was miraculously looking around for a mother again.

Al rode in the back of the pickup and held him while they drove to the new meadow to reunite mother and child. Jim had warned them that the "boss" cow might not accept her offspring because her bag would be swelled tight and sore now and about ready to start caking before finally drying up.

All the cows ran away except the "boss." She stood and waited. Even with the excruciating pain, she let her excited, tail-switching calf nurse as she licked at his red-haired coat.

It was just part of a lucky day's work to George and Doris. To Al and Ed it was a miracle. It was part of both.

When talk finally moved onto other subjects, they discussed Jim Ed's fandango. The Haleys told Al and Ed about some of the other parties that had taken place at the Love ranch. It was definitely not to be missed.

The Hi-Lo Country was rapidly weaving together its basket made of minerals, cows, cowboys, cowgirls, and varied and sundry other wet and dry things.

———

At one point or another, Wrangler Lewis had bucked off horses onto rock piles, cacti, concrete highways, barbed-wire fences, pole corrals, and other similar things. He'd broken legs, arms, ribs, one nose, one neck, two hands, and mashed his balls ninety-nine times, but he'd never had even a minor twitch in his ankles. These appurtenances had been magically immune from harm until this very morning.

Walking from the bunkhouse to the corral, blind sober, on smooth, rockless ground he'd stumbled, farted, and fell in screaming agony at a brand-new pain. He had sprained his ankle at last . . . and just one day before Jim Ed's big celebration. It was cause for a quandary.

Dusty saw the whole thing. "You want me to tail you up?"

Wrangler answered without getting up, "Why don't you quit your blabberin' and saddle me a horse. I want to get up off this dangerous ground."

Dusty saddled two horses and after much moaning and cussing Wrangler pulled his stocky body into the saddle and they rode off for the day's duties. Checking out the windmills nearest headquarters was at the top of the list.

It was unheard of in recent Hi Lo history—the wind had been still for two consecutive days. The temperature, however, was normal—very hot. So far all the windmills were pumping because Dusty had to climb them every one and whirl the wheels by hand to test them. As much as they hated the usual 310-days-a-year blow, they could have made use of a little breeze today, but the fact was, they spent so much of their time justifiably bitching about the mind-zapping winds that it would have seemed ill mannered to do so this morning. Wrangler didn't mind the stillness nearly as much as Dusty because he was badly wounded and hadn't dismounted all day for fear his friend the foreman might suggest he climb up on one of the windmill towers.

They always kept a coffee can tied to each windmill to drink from. Because of his climbing exertions, Dusty dipped a can full of water for Wrangler and then one for himself at every stop. After several windmills Wrangler felt a desperate need to get down and relieve his kidneys of the generous and bountiful liquid that his old pardner had been supplying him. However, if he dismounted before they arrived back at the home corral it would look as if he'd been slacking off all day. At the last windmill he could control it no longer. He felt like the liquid would soon start draining out his ears.

He waited until Dusty was up on top of the crow's nest of the mill. Then he suddenly had only three choices left: go in his Levi's, get down and risk endless ridicule, or stand up in the stirrups and relieve himself while still in the saddle. Like any sensible cowboy, he chose the latter, twisting and aiming the best he could, while trying to achieve the greatest possible distance. He certainly didn't want to get anything on the horse, the saddle, or himself. He certainly didn't want Dusty to observe the carefully calculated procedure.

The first part of the plan worked. The wet jet did arc out to the side of the horse's head by about six inches and for just a fleeting second he'd kept the saddle and himself dry. It will probably never be known why the horse dodged sideways at such a harmless little stream, nor why he ducked his head way down to look at the spot where it splashed, but he did, and he didn't raise his head for about twenty, belly-whomping, ground-pounding jumps.

One can't fault Wrangler for turning loose of the vital instrument that had sent the horse up and down and round and round, and grabbing the saddle horn instead. Of course, there had been no time to put it back into his pants, so it just kept spewing on the horse, on the saddle, and on himself. Some of it even sprayed out into unoccupied space.

Dusty was observing this from the top of the windmill, but his vision wasn't as clear as his fine eagle eyes would dictate for they were full of laughing tears. As he leaned over to hold his hurting belly, he tripped on a loose board and fell off the windmill into the water tank some thirty feet below. It didn't kill him, but did knock the laugh out of his lungs and replace it with pure mountain water.

The horse quit bucking and Wrangler got the rest of his middle self back into his Levi's. He just sat there on the winded horse praying for a fast, burning wind to come dry him out before his good and jovial friend Dusty rode up. He looked out across a peaceful, green valley carpeted with deep, rich buffalo and grama grass where sixty-five head of Hereford cattle grazed and lay about contentedly chewing their cuds. A calf bawled, a squirrel chirped, and a bird warbled, but Wrangler Lewis didn't see or hear any of them. His ears were sensitive only to the sound of an approaching horse to his rear. He felt that the recent dampness he'd absorbed had shriveled and shrunk him down to the size of a baby skunk. He seemed so naked between his shoulder blades that he wondered if there was a bull's-eye painted there.

Dusty, still dripping, rode up behind him and looked across the draw at the peacefully grazing cattle for three or four years and then said in an extremely soft and pleasant voice, "Not a cloud in the sky. Looks like we're in for a looooong dry spell."

They reined off into a valley on the trail heading back to headquarters and the upcoming grand get-together. It had been just another average romantic day in the life of a working cowboy.

———

Delphino Mondragon got his tall, powerful body up early, checked the sheep, goats, and cattle in his hay meadow, fed the pigs and chickens, took a bath with rainwater from a cistern, shaved, combed the hair on his corrugated skull, and put on the only pair of blue dress slacks he owned, a white Western shirt, and a silver and turquoise bolo tie. By Jesus and his disciples, Delphino was ready to go have some "parties."

He sat out on the porch of his rock house taking a sip of homemade chokecherry wine out of a fruit jar. He was getting conditioned for Jim Ed's big day while he waited for the women. He could hear them chattering excitedly in Spanish and was struck for the thousandth time with wonder at how they could all talk at once and still understand one another.

Delphino had heard rumors that the Japanese, and even the West Germans and British, were trying to buy up some ranches around Hi Lo.

He petted the black-and-white bushy-tailed old dog stretched out by his chair and said to it, "Well, thees place is probably too leetle to even interest them, but eet doesn't matters, ole dog, because, eet ain't for sale. Never. You don't have to worry your leetle head about thees, Pedro."

His ranch was fully paid for. He had subirrigated meadows as well as a variety of livestock and he didn't mind milking a few cows, feeding chickens, and slopping hogs like so many modern-day ranchers. His wife could raise a lush vegetable garden every year and they had some fruit trees. All these thoughts ran through his head.

"What a paradise we have here, huh, amigo?"

Pedro raised his dark eyes to let his master know that he was completely aware of the importance of his words. His soft tail brushed the porch in affirmation.

Delphino was a very secure man. He was a skilled rock mason and could pick up extra money building tanks, fences, barns, and sometimes even a small house.

To hell with these business thoughts. He wanted to get on over and grab a taste of Jim Ed's generous hospitality, sing a few songs, do a dance or two, and raise a little hell if he got the smallest excuse.

———

Delphino wasn't alone in his thoughts that day. Al Goodspeed had gotten up at dawn and gone fishing at his lake. The trout were biting salmon eggs this morning, and by an hour after sun he had six browns from ten to fifteen inches long. He was surprised when he got back to the lodge and found Ed was up drinking coffee and reading the World War II book by Manchester.

While Al cleaned and cooked the trout, fried some potatoes, and baked a can of refrigerator biscuits, Ed finally finished the book he'd been reading. He closed it with a look of satisfaction.

"Well, I got that done."

Al said, "You make it sound like a difficult job."

"No, no. It was a great pleasure to read and I'm sorry there's not more. It's just that I wanted my head free to enjoy Jim Ed's party."

Al served the hot food and poured each another cup of coffee.

"I tell you what, Ed, fill your belly now, and then again after we get there. That's the way to prepare for Jim Ed Love." Al took a sip of the brew, halted his cup in midair, and said, "You know, it rips my guts out to think of the Haleys having to sell their ranch, and it also tears me apart to think they might keep it and risk losing it all. They're the kind of people we're damned short of in this world."

Ed was surprised at the depth and sincerity of his friend's feelings. He was mute for a moment and then replied with what he instantly felt was an inadequate statement. "Yeah, it's a tough decision for them to make. It seems everyone and everything gets in a trap. You just have to figure a way out."

Al nodded his head in agreement. "Right, look at us."

———

People from all over the Hi-Lo Country were talking and preparing to attend the grand happening. Others had already landed out-of-state jets and prop planes at Jim Ed's private airstrip. They were all moving toward the center of the circle, from the air, in limousines, cars, and pickup trucks, and a couple of neighboring cowboys came horseback even though they'd had to sleep in their bedrolls the night before. The entire area would forever be changed in this day and upcoming night.

By noon, droves of people had arrived. They were simply astounded at what they saw and heard. There had never been anything to touch it around here before and it's doubtful if there ever would be again.

Jim Ed and associates had the grounds set as large and colorful as a state fair carnival. Brightly colored tents with the sides rolled up were scattered over a 300-yard circumference. There were whole beeves and pigs turning on spits over barbecue pits. Great iron pots held steaming pinto beans, red and green chile, and posole. Long tables would soon be filled with chickens cooked in a variety of ways. There were even imported seafood delicacies, fruits, vegetables, and melons.

The music was as varied as the food. The entertainment groups were set far apart so the audience could choose their favorite. A mariachi band, dressed in colorful native clothing, strummed and sang all the old Mexican favorites. A country western group from Austin supplied the cowboy atmosphere, while a pop band from Albuquerque kept the younger generation entertained. A special section was reserved for Indian dance groups from Laguna, Zuni, and Taos pueblos.

Near each musical group, bars, with several attendants, were set up to serve drinks. The beverages ranged from plain whiskey to the fanciest liquors found at the Algonquin or Polo Lounge.

People were feasting, drinking, dancing, and visiting. Every age group was represented, from babies in strollers to great-grandparents who could barely toddle around. The wide spectrum of nationalities provided an international flavor to the gathering. The totality of the colorations of their clothing, the tents, and decorations added up to a kaleidoscope of rainbows.

As the cacophony of sound grew, the musicians unknowingly played louder to compensate. At first the children were in awe and fairly quiet, but soon with their bellies full of food and soda pop they sensed that their parents were occupied with many different wonders and they proceeded to invent their own amusements and to run wild as outhouse rats, as the Kansas wheat farmers used to say.

By two o'clock in the afternoon everything was at full volume. The number of dancers gradually increased with each song and drink as the stomachs negotiated the alcohol into the bloodstreams and hearts pumped it on to the brain, and the steps grew faster. Jim Ed Love had certainly pulled off a grand shindig, but he would have a lot of anxious hours before he would know the final result of his calculated munificence. Right now, though, his luck was running—the weather was just right. It had been practically windless for the two previous days and now it was about seventy-eight degrees with just enough breeze to keep the sweat down, the men's hats on, and the women's hairdos in place. Yes, if there was one thing important to the mood swings of the Hi Lo inhabitants, it definitely was the weather. The gods had smiled, however briefly, for Jim Ed Love.

There was so much more going on, besides the party, that was unseen to most and hidden by the knowing few.

Mr. Yakahami and entourage had come out of Jim Ed's large guest house with all the men in dark dress suits and their women wearing high-fashion apparel. However, after mingling a while and sampling the rich, varied foods and beverages, they had quietly retired to change into more casual, comfortable clothing.

Mikio was the exception—she came dressed in Levi's, boots, and a custom-tailored silk shirt right from the beginning. She was different from the rest of her countrywomen. She had been married to Jackson Reynolds, a wealthy land developer from the San Francisco Bay area, while she was there lecturing at a university about the changing cultural phenomena between Japan and the United States. On the night of their twentieth wedding anniversary celebration, Mr. Reynolds fell dead. Mikio inherited the entire thirty-eight million dollars' worth of bonds, stocks, cash, and real estate. Since they had no children, she also inherited an awful lot of free time.

Mr. Yakahami, knowing that his sister was thoroughly Americanized and experienced in business world transactions, gave her the challenging job of handling all his U.S. investments. She had happily and admirably delivered. It was Mikio who first brought the geologist, agriculturist, and several other kinds of experts to inspect the Love and Haley ranches. Her report had been thorough and confident. Her decision: buy at the proper price. Since the yen was so low against the American dollar, and cattle, oil, and hard minerals were depressed, she suggested that they utilize carefully directed haste to gain the full benefit of proper timing.

The preliminaries had come off without a flaw. Jim Ed's son, Jason, had fronted for his father, as Mikio had done for her brother. Dusty Jones had been sensibly appointed official guide and driver of the large van. It was all perfectly logical and well organized.

Mikio walked over to talk with Dusty. He was happy to see her again and flattered that she treated him with such warm respect as she introduced him to all her people. She thanked him again for the kindness and efficiency he'd extended on her last exploration trip. Dusty felt a pleasant glow as she and her friends moved on toward the mariachi bandstand.

Jim Ed was everywhere, shaking hands, slapping backs and rears, succeeding at making the guests feel wanted and pampered. He had several people seeing that Mr. Yakahami and his associates were looked after properly. They had reserved seats at each event.

While all the merriment was taking place on the grounds, it was quite a different happening in Jim Ed's redwood-paneled office. Jason and Mr. Yakahami's lieutenant, Akiri, and their secretaries, were missing the party altogether, except they had enough food on the table between them to feed a highway building crew. There was no alcohol. Only soft drinks and herbal and Indian teas filled that void. They were politely trying to cut each other's throat while smiling and without the blood showing. The final results could possibly create far greater ripples than a contest to the death of two great samurai warriors.

The first major plans for the final battle were taking place in these rooms, but those who would sharpen and hand over the swords were outside mingling with the uninvolved, and acting as if they were on their first picnic.

When the Taos Indians did the war, wind, buffalo, and eagle dances, the Orientals were ecstatic with applause. Their appreciation was genuine. Then Alfred Two Lions, age seven, did the hoop dance to the rhythm of a drum beat, passing more than twenty hoops up his legs and back down, then up and over his arms, back, and shoulders in whirling, twisting, smooth, complex moves, without a moment's pause. The audience stood fascinated and with a measure of awe as they unknowingly felt ancient vibrations through this Indian child.

When the performance ended, Ed, Al, Doris, and George strolled back toward the bar for refills. The Haleys were talking casually about the party as if their entire world wasn't on the sales block. The two friends respected this and left the subject alone.

Dusty, walking unusually stiff in all joints, and Wrangler, who was limping noticeably, moved into the circle of friends.

Haley asked, "What happened to you boys? Did you both get run over by a hay baler?"

Dusty answered, "I think ol' Wrangler got on a horse he couldn't get off of, but me," he hastened to explain (he wasn't about to confess falling off a windmill to anybody), "I'm just walkin' like this so it'll make him look better."

Wrangler snorted with what authority he could through his flat nose and said, "If I looked any better they'd cast me in bronze and stand me up in a beauty parlor for all the ladies to admire."

Delphino Mondragon walked up overhearing this last and said, "My eee-ars they are so full of bullsheet it weel take a gallon of wheesky to wash 'em clean again. Give us all a two shotter for starters."

The bartender complied. Al asked for another round. Dusty politely duplicated the procedure. Business was improving rapidly at Jim Ed's free drinks bar.

Jim Ed, the big man himself, arrived on the scene. "Now, it's good to see you fellers enjoying yourselves. That's what we're all here for. A man's got to pour a little gold dust on the rust of life once in a while out of appreciation for this bountiful earth and the wondrous opportunities it offers us all. Right, friends?" Jim Ed took only two bourbons in the evening, but he raised his hand cupped around a ghost glass in a toast to his own words. Everyone else did the same with the real thing without even noticing the illusion.

Jim Ed took Haley firmly by the arm and steered him away from the crowd at the bar. "It's lookin' good, George. Mr. Yakahami and his sister know that the price of oil and cattle has started easing upward. It gives us an edge. They're gonna want to get this deal over with before the prices go too high and while the dollar is cheap against the yen. I tell, you, George, if we'll hang tough another hour or two we'll get four more dollars per acre and get to keep three-quarters of the mineral rights. I tell you what, George, we're not just sittin' in plain clover, we're harvestin' four-leaf clover and makin' pure honey out of it."

Haley dug a toe of one boot in the dust, pushed his hat back, and scratched his head with the same hand, saying, "Jim Ed, I know you're tryin' to make a good deal for us, but I've told you twice I just can't bring myself to sell at any price. Even at four dollars an acre more, all we'd have left is enough to barely squeeze by on. That ain't no good and you know it. We ain't made that way."

"I know how you feel, George, but it's a whole lot better than starting over with nothing. Nothing, you hear? That ain't gonna sound, or feel, too good to your family, George. Think about that now. What're you gonna tell them when it all goes under?"

Haley left Jim Ed and returned to the bar. None of his friends had heard a single word that had passed between the two but somehow sensed the essence of the conversation. Jim Ed didn't have a deal without the Haleys, and they all knew that Jim Ed would drop his only son out of an airplane into an erupting volcano if it would help make a deal.

Ol' Wrangler yelled out, "Give us another glass of that hero juice and save the last ten dances for me."

With some noise and a great deal of joy the group of friends totally agreed with Wrangler's whopping wisdom.

Ed and Al had talked earlier about the difficulty of George Haley making a decision that would alter his family's destiny on land that had passed through several generations. Ed had reminded Al of the agony that must be going through the souls of Dusty and Wrangler. He was so right. This day was filled with multiple, hidden emotions for many people. Dusty and Wrangler were at the top of the list.

The two old partners had been with the Jim Ed Love ranches since they were kids in far southwest Texas. They started work on the Big Lake Ranch. Then they were moved to the Andrews, Texas, outfit right after the first big oil well was hit on that sand and mesquite bushland. As soon as Jim Ed bought the Hi Lo ranch, they were transferred again. At that time, they were still in their teens, but they made good ranch hands. They'd been here on the JL since then. Every so often, they'd get their "neck hair up" at Jim Ed and take off. But they would either wind up broke or in jail. Jim Ed would always bail them out and they would always have to come back to him.

It had been home to them for most of their lives, and they'd made Jim Ed a considerable profit over the years. There was no question about what they had given to the JL Ranch. They had left a lot of freezing breath in the high-wind blizzards of the Hi Lo winters, along with dust-burned eyes and scratched lungs from the blowing sands of many dry, eroding summers. Pieces of their flesh had been left on rocks, trees, barbed wire, and the hard land itself for decades now. Most of their bones had been broken and a lot of their joints almost welded solid from the strings of bucking horses and the jolts of working cattle in both thick brush and sharp boulders. They had dug postholes in miles of hard rock and fixed windmills and put up hay. They'd fed cattle in snowdrifts taller than a Jeep in below-zero weather and chopped ice from water tank after water tank so the cattle could drink instead of dying. All this and more—not to even count the various times they had left their blood on barroom floors trying to get out of the god-damned wind and forget the constant pain that wracked their battered bodies of which they seldom spoke.

They had no retirement funds or insurance plans and they were getting old for working cowboys. Today. Today they could be cast out into the street like any wino, the plain shiftless, the government spongers, or the truly unfortunate. Their lives had been spent in the wide-open outdoors. The streets to them would look like Dante's next dream. They'd put in a long, rough time, and now they had absolutely nowhere to go and nothing to say about it.

Dusty gathered up his cowboys for a meeting. He knew they had heard all the rumors concerning their futures, but hadn't been told anything to give them any reassurance. So, being their foreman, he felt it was time they were told the true situation.

They were a select group that could handle the old, or modern, ways of cowboying. Besides Wrangler, there was Sonny Jim, a Modoc Indian; a

Mexican named Pat Flores; and Big Timber Smith, a one-eyed black who was the greatest outlawed horse breaker in the entire country. They all stayed at the lower camp. Dusty had spent a lot of time there when he was young and knew that few men could handle the loneliness and isolation, much less the real ranch work. Elliot Calhoun was the headquarters fix-it-up man. At one time he had been a top rodeo cowboy. Dusty had always thought that Sonny Jim could easily have taken those honors, even bigger, better than Calhoun, if he'd wanted it badly enough.

Dusty explained as best he could about the Japanese negotiations, adding, "If the deal goes through, fellers, we may all be pecking shit with the buzzards. If the deal falls flat I reckon we'll go on just like we are for Jim Ed."

"Is there a hell of a lot of difference?" Sonny Jim quipped.

Big Timber Smith said, "Well, I shore don't want to go back to pickin' cotton."

They all laughed and then Sonny Jim got serious again. "How does it really look to you, Dusty?"

Dusty said, "I can see a cow on the other side of a mountain, but I'm plumb blind on this. One good thing about it, though, we ain't gonna have to hang around frettin' about it after tonight." Then he added, "Now don't you boys say one goddamned word about this till I tell you. Hear?"

Pat Flores said, "We ain't opening our mouths for nothing but brown whiskey and red chile."

Dusty felt better and walked the whole bunch over to the country western bar and ordered them a free drink. He didn't feel like they were free—he'd already paid for them a thousand times or more.

Dusty spotted Mikio and her companions in the crowd. All day long he'd been watching her from afar. However, he tried to hide his interest from everyone else. He'd been a little in awe of her from their very first meeting. There was something else there that he couldn't explain, especially to himself. The way she walked with little short steps, or the delicate way she moved her hands and tilted her head slightly to the side, affected him. She made his hands and feet go cold and the rest of his body feel like it was melting and running down into his Tony Lama boots.

He turned his attention back to his cowboy helpers, lifted his glass gesturing a toast, and said, "You fellers have fun. I'll see you later." He looked in the direction of Mikio's group but now she wasn't among them. He strained his eyes through the hundreds of moving people but he couldn't see her. Then, like a good cowboy spotting cattle in brush, he saw her coming from the bunkhouse. She was pulling a straw hat down on her head.

Dusty watched her. Even in cowboy boots she walked as gracefully as a professional dancer. She wove her way through the erratically moving crowd. Dusty realized with a start that she was coming straight toward him. If he'd been on horseback he would have reined around and spurred for the highest mountain and the thickest timber. Instead he grew roots.

She came right up smiling with her entire face and said in unaccented English, "Mr. Jones, could we have a private visit?"

"Dusty, that's me. Call me Dusty," was all he could get out.

Mikio took him by an arm with such a gentle touch that he could barely feel it, yet he was guided as firmly as if he'd been tied by the neck to a bull-dozer.

"Is there somewhere we could have privacy? There exist some matters I'd like to discuss with you."

Dusty's brain waves flashed around like a ricocheting bullet. She had said "private." He couldn't take her to the bunkhouse. It might be miscon-strued, and if Jim Ed and Mr. Yakahami failed to deal, they would blame it on Dusty claiming as sure as hell that right in the middle of the trade Dusty was trying to slap the make on Mr. Yakahami's beautiful sister. And that is how it would look. On the other hand, he wanted desperately to be with her even if all she needed to know was how long it took a cow to raise a calf.

There was only one choice. It was a big risk. He took her by the arm and guided her to his pickup. He started to open the truck door for her.

Mikio thanked him, but refused. "I may have to get used to opening my own truck doors. So I will start now."

As they drove past the horse pasture, Dusty slowed the vehicle to a crawl as he pointed out special mounts and explained each one's specialty. An old Indian camp was the next stop. They picked up a few potsherds and she found an almost-perfect arrowhead. She was childishly thrilled with this. On the rock bluffs he showed her the petroglyph carvings of deer, moun-tain sheep, cougars, medicine men and women, the sun symbols, and more.

Mikio suddenly became very solemn as she studied the pictures and said there must be a link somewhere between the American Indians and the Orientals because the drawings on the rock face somehow reminded her of old Japanese textiles.

Dusty didn't exactly understand the last, but was happy she was observing and absorbing part of his private world.

As they drove along now, he became more comfortable. He showed her spots where he had bucked off horses and had many assorted adventures.

They were talking and laughing where the only noise was the muffled hum of the motor in the quiet stillness.

Dusty and Mikio weren't the only ones to stray away from the fiesta. Terri Haley and Luke Fremont were secluded in a patch of brush on some thick vega grass about a half mile below Jim Ed's headquarters. They had grown up on neighboring ranches and had always cared for each other. Luke was eighteen and would soon be enrolling as a freshman at Highlands University in Las Vegas, New Mexico. They were desperately in love, and today he was going momentarily blind as he touched her. But his mind would soon be cleared by her reluctant, but successful, repetition of "No. No. No."

The revelers at the party weren't saying "No" to very much of anything. Their enthusiasm seemed to be growing.

Al and Ed walked slowly through the mob in the direction of the Indian drums. On their way there they caught pieces of conversation as varied as the nation they lived in.

"Oh, darling, there is just no place in Mexico except Ixtapa, don't you know," said a blonde with a distinct southern drawl. Ed gave Al a "What do you think?" look.

Two housewives were exchanging ideas: "Well, I don't care what you say; the vegetables are always fresher at Safeway."

"It won't matter before long. Walmart will probably put in a grocery department and put them all out of business, anyway."

Several seasoned-looking cowmen were talking about horses. One said, "That ole sorrel horse of my boy's can turn on a penny an' give you back twenty-nine cents change."

"Boy, I'd like to have a look at him."

Al and Ed smiled as they passed someone saying, "Listen, I'm trying to tell you gentlemen a truth. There just isn't any choice. The United States, Mexico, Canada, Great Britain, and Japan must form a solid alliance now. I mean now, while there is still time. We're all so interlocked by history, art, intermarriage, intertrade, borders, banks, oil, and the absolute and final need for one another that the blindness not to do so will lead to all of our eventual destruction."

Al said to Ed, "We might ought to join that group." One jovial fellow slapped his leg and said, "I had to buy me a country club. That's the only way I could join one."

As Ed squeezed past a couple of wildly dressed women, one of them was saying, "I desperately need a cyanide . . . and . . . a root beer."

Then out of nowhere came, "Well then, if you're so damned smart, who gave birth to God?"

"Hey, bartender, give that man a shot for rabies."

They were almost to the circle of Indian dancers, then were stopped by thick crowd congestion.

"It'll never work. You see it's too round on this side and too square on the other. Besides, it'll swell up and burst in cold weather and tip over in a high wind, and you couldn't even see the damn thing in a thick fog. That's not all. It has so many holes in it the darkness will leak out."

Ed turned to Al. "Well, like the man said, it'll never work."

A female voice drifted out to them: "Well, Jim Ed sure knows how to throw a party, even if he is making a fool out of himself over that Shirley Holt. Why, she couldn't be a day over twenty-five."

And in the same group, someone said, "I don't care what everybody says about Jim Ed trying to take his money with him when he goes. I've never seen a Brinks truck at a funeral."

The drum stopped just as Al and Ed arrived at the dance circle, and the dancers started mingling with the guests. The Indians were being very polite and answering, with myths, the stupid questions and laughing quietly to themselves. They didn't need, or want, sympathy from anyone. They were professionals and had received adulation all over the United States and Canada. And they really didn't like all the interference from the outside "do-gooders."

The business procedures were gaining in momentum as two jets landed on the airstrip. One carried two lawyers from Midland, Texas, and one from Dallas, to represent Jim Ed. The other contained two lawyers from San Francisco and one from Tokyo to take care of Mr. Yakahami's legal needs. Numerically the samurai were evenly matched. The dice were still spinning.

Wrangler had been discovered by Charlene, an Odessa, Texas, oil widow who had gone to school with one of Jim Ed's kin. As they danced less and drank more, she somehow got the facts mixed up. She decided that Old Wrangler was Jim Ed's cousin instead of working for him. So anybody kin to Jim Ed was her flesh, blood, and full partner.

Wrangler had favored his twisted ankle so long that he had now numbed the other one. So he walked Charlene over to the bunkhouse without a limp and got her bedded down in the lower bunk. The trouble was his ankles had swelled so much that he couldn't pull off either boot. Therefore he couldn't pull his tight-legged Levi's off, either. He got them down about halfway over his hips where they rolled into a jam. He went back to his boots, pulling and straining till it looked like his eyeballs were going to fly out and smash the wall.

"Goddamned, son of a bitch, bloody-nosed bastard, stupid puke-headed, frog-eyed, badger-nose, skunk-assed, shit-eatin' dog." Even though he used the correct vocabulary for removing tight boots, they wouldn't come off.

Charlene was getting a cramp in her thighs from trying to hold the waiting position on the narrow bunk.

She made a practical suggestion. "Darling, why don't we just do it with your pants on. It's fine with me."

This was one wonderful shortcut in what was left of poor Wrangler's mind. He said, "Whatever suits you just tickles me plumb to death." Whereby he attempted to stand up, turn around, and jump on Charlene all at the same time. What he did was step, stumble, and fall, ramming the top of his head into the leg of a heavy oak table, knocking him as cold as an arctic night. Charlene waited a spell for him to regain his composure and finally realized that her anticipation was being wasted. She pulled her dress down, got up, and staggered past Wrangler on the floor, saying to herself, "I keep hearing what great lovers these cowboys are and that one there can't even get his pants off."

As Charlene bounced out of the bunkhouse, Delphino came around the corner where they collided into a hugging match. He gathered her up and took her to the tack room at the barn. Delphino's ankles were in perfect condition.

Al was now sitting at a table with all four of Delphino's women. He had been dancing with one right after the other. The Latin music, along with a bottle of scotch, had made him nostalgic about the old days in Baja, California. He was telling his dance partners some Baja stories and they were laughing and having fun.

Ed had been captured by a supposed lady clothing designer from Santa Fe and they were regaling one another with sharp and cynical quips between dances at the pop group location.

The party showed no signs of slowing down nor was anyone considering abandoning it for the peacefulness being enjoyed by Dusty and Mikio.

Dusty drove the truck as far as he could into the rocks and timber. He told Mikio they'd have to walk a short distance to get to something he wanted to show her. She reached out and took his hand as he wove his way carefully through the trees and brush protecting her from springback of branches as he pushed them out of the way. Then they were there.

They looked down on a horseshoe-shaped cliff formation of reddish-brown sandstone surrounding an emerald pond about sixty feet across. Its overflow formed a stream that ran down a steep slope of rock and created another pool perhaps a hundred feet below.

Dusty carefully led her down through the rocks to the edge of the water. In the soft mud along the bank he pointed out the arrowhead-shaped tracks of a coyote, the bearlike prints of a raccoon, and the round impressions of a bobcat. He showed her the pronged prints of several wild turkeys.

Mikio was touched by their sharing of a lifetime of knowledge and the special private pool. They moved back up from the sun-jeweled water to a rock outcropping with a grassy spot underneath. They sat next to one another and looked out across the quiet, far-spreading spaces over the top of the Rockies where great castles of clouds climbed so high they became lost white wonderlands that faded into the mists of eternity.

After a while Dusty said, "What was it you wanted to ask me?"

"You've already answered," she said softly. "There is one thing though

. . . if you'll forgive me . . . why didn't you present these special things to me when we were here before?"

"I only showed you the parts that make money. Besides"—he paused before he confessed—"I didn't really want you to buy it then. It's the only real home Old Wrangler and me have ever had. I didn't want to leave it. Not ever."

He wanted to tell her they had no other place left to go at their ages. No place worth living on, anyway. He didn't have to.

She took his hand and said so quietly he had to strain to hear, "If we acquire this ranch, I'll need you . . . need you very much. You know so many more things than I."

This time he was speechless. He looked at her and she turned her head half to him, but her black eyes were on his. He reached over with one battered-up hand and touched the back of her head, and then they both fully and completely touched the earth together.

———

Ed, Al, and Delphino had wound up together at the country western bar, and, of course, the band was playing "On the Road Again." They all three felt "plumb keen," as Delphino would say. The sun was only an hour high and the party had mellowed to fewer and fewer cowboy yells.

Ed observed, "Free booze gets the festivities going fast, all right, but it also thins out the tame ones rather quickly."

Al added, "The musicians are getting a little woozy from all the booze these kind and thoughtful music lovers have been bringing them."

Jim Ed and Mr. Yakahami had now moved inside along with the lawyers. The closing, or the "cut and run" period, was coming to a collision point soon. All of America was condensed here at Jim Ed's this day. The rich, the poor, the strugglers and stragglers, the big winners and the little losers. All colors and combinations, all attitudes and affections. All. It was judgment day as well and the major decisions were about to be handed down.

———

Wrangler had been too busy pursuing his own sources of R and R that he hadn't noticed Dusty's absence, so he wasn't surprised when Dusty returned to join everyone. He was surprised to find that Dag Oakdale was sitting with the group.

Dag was big and dumb and mean. A dangerous combination in any society. He owned a ranch to the south of both Al and Haley. He was a nat-ural-born, greedy, son of a bitch and he was jealous and furious because no one had contacted him about buying his ranch. It had been on the market for three years without a taker. Dag didn't express any of this verbally, but he said something else in a loud and penetrating voice:

"The thieving Texans came in and bought up all of eastern New Mexico, and now the car-makin', computer-punchin' Japs are movin' in and buying out all the egg-suckin' Texans. Wonder who'll come and kick-ass the god-damned Japs."

Dusty and Wrangler started to attack the offender because there was a group of Japanese and at least thirty Texans within insulting distance. They all were hoping that the hands on the grandfather clock in Jim Ed's office were approaching the moment of final and momentous decision.

Al said, "Gentlemen, shall we do our Boy Scout deed for the year?"

Delphino had waited patiently all day for an opportunity such as this. At the same instant that Ed and Al each grabbed an arm belonging to Dag Oakdale, Delphino got him by the crotch and they led him away to avoid any more embarrassment than had already occurred.

Ed yelled back at a stunned but grinning Dusty and Wrangler, "We owe you one from the Hi Lo Bar."

Dag would have been screaming like a parrot with his tail feathers on fire from Delphino's powerful, rock-mason grip, but Al Goodspeed had his free hand clamped over Dag's mouth. All Dag could do was snort like a fresh-saddled bronc.

They marched him behind the main barn and Delphino said, "Turn thees mad dog loose." They did. Delphino stayed with Dag's crotch but added a new and helpful move with his other hand. He grabbed him by the throat, charging the barn with him, bending Dag's head down as they gained momentum. Delphino had hoped to run Dag's head all the way through the barn wall, but since it was made of corrugated steel, he failed. Delphino didn't give in easily, though. He tried to accomplish his mission three times before he dropped Dag to the ground and gave up.

Back at the bar, Dusty was saying to Wrangler as they got a new glass of brown "hero juice," "Nice fellers, those three."

Wrangler grunted. He asked few questions in his life, but now he just couldn't hold off any longer.

"How . . . how're we doin', ole pardner?"

Dusty grinned real big and said, "The barbed wire with the rock tied to it has finally been removed from my balls."

Old Wrangler forgot all about his twisted ankle and jumped right straight up in the air, yelling, "Jesus wept, Moses crept, and Peter came a-crawlin'. Hallelujah and wild horses!"

They toasted their plastic glasses together so hard it squashed out all the contents. It didn't matter because Jim Ed had a plentiful supply of whiskey and everything else.

Delphino, Ed, and Al returned triumphant. Delphino casually remarked, "Dag Oakdale ain't gonna bother nobody till mornin' no more. Savvy, amigos?"

They did.

Goodspeed saw Jim Ed and Haley walking along in a close-headed discussion. Haley reached out and touched Jim Ed on the shoulder, signaling him to be left alone for a minute. He walked over to meet Doris, struggling within himself. Then he looked up and saw Al. Haley's eyes said, "Help."

Al walked over wordlessly. Then George cleared his throat and strained out, "They've come up the four extra dollars an acre Jim Ed was trying to get. He said they would. Of course he's got a hundred and twenty thousand acres and that adds up to lots of money. It's not that much with our place. Not anything like that . . . but . . ."

Al interrupted: "Would there be enough left over to have all your debts erased and all the cattle and horses paid for?"

"Yeah, and a little bit more . . . but . . . what good is that without land to put 'em on?"

Al said, "Well, George, I've put considerable thought into this. I've got a deal for you. But you can't stall around like you've done with Jim Ed and the Japanese. You'll have just ten seconds to make up your mind. That's all."

George Haley looked at Doris and then back at Al like he was witnessing the resurrection.

Al said, "I'll buy Dag Oakdale's place and lease it back to you until you're in a position to purchase it."

Haley stared at Al about three seconds. It took two more to ask, "You mean it, don't you?" Then at about the nine-second mark he looked at Doris for her answer. She nodded, "Yes." George and Al shook hands.

Al said, "It's done." Then the industrialist leaned over and whispered a private thought to his rancher friend. "You're doing us all a big favor, George. We've got to get that chickenshit Dag Oakdale to hell and gone from our part of the country."

Haley laughed out loud for the first time in days and he and Doris walked toward the main house to make the Jim Ed Love and Yakahami families—as well as a few working cowboys—very happy indeed.

The fun lasted until the sun shone new again. It turned out to be the greatest party ever held in the Hi-Lo Country, and it was certain that people from many diverse worlds would look back on it with some fondness and eventually noble nostalgia for as long as they could remember.

All arrangements had been made for the purchase of the Oakdale Ranch. Al and Ed drove up to the old Haley place, as it would be known from now on, to tell them good-bye. They were invited inside, but declined, wanting to get on the tedious road home.

George said, "Say, I sure want to thank you boys for saving that calf. I'd already picked him out to butcher this fall."

Al was shocked. "You're going to kill him? We'll buy him from you. Why, he'd make a great breeding bull."

"Not now he won't. We've done cut him."

At Al's puzzled look, Ed got to show off his western knowledge once again. "They castrated our calf, Al," he explained. "He's a steer now and forever."

"Oh," Al said softly.

They said their good-byes and solemnly started south. Soon they were on I-25 headed toward Albuquerque and an airplane that would take them back to Orange County. Ed looked off left toward Eagle Tail Mountain and said, "Quite a trip."

"It sure was. We'll have to do it again before long."

"Yeah, and if we ever do get horseback . . . hell, Al, there's just no telling what we might do."

"Right," Al said, suddenly in very high spirits.

The Call

The old man stood stiffly washing at the tin plates as the wild game digested inside him. His chores done, he sat on a sawed stump in front of a rickety, unpainted table, slowly smoking a pipe, staring at nothing, and only occasionally blinking his tiny sunken eyes. Then he took a tattered Bible in hand and read . . . Genesis: . . . TILL THOU RETURN UNTO THE GROUND; FOR OUT OF IT WAST THOU TAKEN; FOR DUST THOU ART, AND UNTO DUST SHALT THOU RETURN . . .

Then he heard the scream. He bolted from his chair, dropping the Bible. Standing with his head held taut, high, and turned to the side, his eyes rolled white and wild in their sockets. His nostrils flared in and out like a beast scenting fresh blood. One mighty rusty hand clawed at the long grey-streaked hair.

The scream—it came at him again now, piercing his eardrums, slicing into his inner skull and vibrating there like pounding gongs and exploding cannons. The hound dog cowered against him, trembling. The hair bristled along his spine.

This was the sixth night now. It came at the same hour of darkness. It broke away just as suddenly. It did not die gradually but stopped with startling abruptness, as if a sword as long as a pine tree had been swung by a giant and severed the scream in one swift cutting instant.

He stood a spell, as yet tense and waiting, but it did not return. His drawn old muscles slackened, and the dog lowered his bristles. What was it? What could it be? His ears were trained, as the hound's at his feet, to the sounds, the smells, the signs of the wild. A long time before he had rejected his own kind. He was one of these creatures of the forest. He had joined the animals and he had lived from them.

For over twenty years no one had been allowed in his canyon. No one except the fur trader who came once a year to pick up the winter's catch and leave the year's supplies in exchange. Even he was stopped at the very mouth of the canyon and waved back down the moment the transaction was complete.

Yes, the hermit knew the bearlike track of the coon, the round, padded ones of the bobcat and the cougar. He knew intimately the arrowhead-shaped print of the coyote and the three-pronged track, like one-fourth of a broken rimless wagon wheel, of the wild turkey. He knew these wild things so well he could outwit them and exist from their furs captured by his swift-closing steel traps. He knew the pointed track of the doe and the wider-spread ones of the buck, and he could trail them and down them with one shot in the heart. He knew their sounds, their night calls, their cries of death. He knew them better than they knew themselves.

But he didn't know this scream that came pealing down from the rim-rocks at the first touch of darkness. What was it that clung to the rocks and yet vibrated forth with great gusts of sound that struck at him like a flaming arrow? It seemed to be an infinite part of the rocks releasing the sound itself to torture him, to drive him mad with its unknown stabbing horror.

Strain as he might, he could not place it in his canyon. It was new here. It was not one of his animals. Was it some strange unknown beast invading his sanctuary? Had it come to challenge his superiority, to destroy his mind with sound alone? He could not say how long the sound lasted each time. A minute? An hour? An eternity?

Each evening from sunset on he stood poised, his hound rubbing against his bent legs, waiting. No matter how he prepared himself, he was always caught unaware. It was on him, around him, in him, before he could brace his being for the shock.

He moved back to his log cabin. As he opened the door, the hound dashed past him and crawled under the bed, growling and whining. There was no sleep now, only a numb listening through the night. He lay with the rifle at hand waiting . . . waiting. Would it always come at the same time, or would it break loose in everlasting sound, blanketing his canyon and stilling the movements of his animals? Would the maker of the scream leap from the bluffs and devour them all in an orgy of blood and hair?

The night turned into day, and the sun came up above the rimrocks and shoved shafts of yellow light between the piñon and the pine. The dog stood at the door sniffing carefully, wanting outside. The day was better. They could see now. But there in the atoms of their bodies, the dog and the hermit, the two hunters, lingered the knowledge that night, too, would return.

They breakfasted hurriedly on dry jerky. The trap line had not been run in four days now. The trader would soon be here for the winter's catch. Taking the rifle and putting a leash on the hound the hermit headed up the canyon to follow out his trap line.

He saw no fresh sign along the trails—not of the deer nor the furred creatures. Not even the rabbit. No birds moved among the trees. The forest was still. Yet he felt them there, waiting, listening, watching him. The first trap was undisturbed, as was the second, and the third. He circled widely around them. No animal had been near. All tracks were old and crusted. The hound hardly dropped his head to the ground at all. There was no scent there for trailing.

On a promontory in a little clearing he stopped and studied the rimrocks. What deep shadow hid the scream? In what crevice did it crouch with huge hollow eyes staring at him, waiting to leap? For a moment the idea of leaving the canyon struck him. No! The beasts of the outer world lurked just as dangerously. If the thing would attack now in the light of day,

he would make his stand and fight to the death. But no movement came to his vision. No sound. The hawks that usually circled above the rocks were gone. Not one flew in search of food. The sky was barren.

The sun moved on over the heavens and reached for the bluffs above the scream. There was only one more trap on his line. Each had been empty. The hound stiffened against the leash and moved toward the set in a little clearing. Something was in it. It had been a double set. One trap had caught a cottontail rabbit. The rabbit was half eaten. The ribs showed white through the dried meat. In the other trap was a foot—a large foot of a bird. It was a vulture's claw. The tendons strung out hard and yellow where the bird had pecked and torn free. It had eaten the heart out of the rabbit before it had stepped into the other trap. Where was the vulture now? Up in the rocks, perhaps, nursing its crippled leg.

The hermit stared again. The sun was resting on top of the rocks now, and he felt the first cold touch of wind that day. It brushed at him with ghostly fingers, and the goose bumps popped out like measles over his body. It would not be long now until the terrible sound would shoot forth and flail him into trembling fear.

Where was the coyote's sunset howl? Where was the haunting, raucous call of the magpie? Utter stillness, muffling, smothering, quiet prevailed.

Suddenly, he whispered to his dog to come. He could bear it no longer. This seventh night of terror had drained him of the power to wait. It must be faced. He must see this screaming thing and look into its eyes and slavering jaws. It called to him silently now, as if the rocks were magnetized for flesh. He moved on toward the bluff. The hound turned with his tail between his legs and ran down the canyon toward the cabin without looking back.

The hermit's heart beat at his body and pushed his blood hard, forcing it through his veins in a swift, artery-straining surge as he climbed. His lungs were pained to handle the air drawn back and forth in struggling gulps. But he moved and clambered through the rocks. The sun had set, and the last rays weakened in the sky. He must be there at the instant of the scream. It drove him, this decision, beyond his actual strength, and the rocks jabbing and tearing at him were forgotten. Now every act of his life became as nothing compared with the desire pulling him higher and higher.

The orange sun and its beamed rays were gone. Twilight lingered a moment. On he struggled. There was only a faint glow now. The mighty boulders swelled around him, and the crevices split them sharply on each side. And then it was dark, and a crevice deeper than any he had ever seen was before him.

He leaned over, staring into its depths, searching. This was it. He could not see, but he could feel it. He leaned farther and fell down into the blackness. His mouth flew open, and a sound of terror hurtled from his throat. He knew now what the scream was and where it had come from, but it was too late to do anything about it. It had always been so.

The World's Strangest Creature

The boy had pulled off a good day for an eight-year-old. It was just past mid-sun and he was already back in town loaded with success. Unbeknownst to him his whole world, very shortly, would widen. His little bay horse, Cricket, moved under him, eagerly anticipating home and the early removal of the saddle, plus a good feeding. The two brown-and-black shepherd dogs followed, smelling at the ground now and then, but knowing the hunt was over. Three cottontails were tied to the old four-dollar saddle. The dogs ran the rabbits into holes and the boy twisted them out with a forked barbed wire. It was the middle of the Great Depression and drought. The rabbits were for human consumption and the few so-called inedible parts fed the two dogs.

Then the boy spotted the funny-looking wagon. That was easy because most of the ground around Humble City, in far southeastern New Mexico, was so flat you could shoot a marble and all it would do was spin in circles looking in vain for a downhill slope. The frame houses of the tiny town were scattered about one to an entire block. Some even had several empty blocks between them. The odd, out-of-place wagon was on one of these.

The boy's father started up a town on what once was their cow ranch. He purposely set the houses far apart in a vain attempt to make the town look bigger, and as he said, "give it room to expand." His idea worked for a while. There was a one-room school; a combination filling station, general store, and drug counter; and the post office was in the former ranch house because the boy's mother was the postmistress.

Between the Great Depression and the mid-thirties drought, Humble City's existence was a miracle of the highest order. All that kept it there, squatting scared, scattered, and lonely, was the fact that his dad had accidentally struck an irrigation well while hand digging a cellar. Hope. Folks believed there would come a day when the bounty from the watered land would bless them all. It did. A couple of decades after most of them were gone, the land was covered with irrigation and oil pumps, and finally the oil-rich ranching town of Hobbs grew around Humble City, and left its actuality only on road maps.

They were hard times, but the sandy-haired boy didn't know the difference. Supplying wild meat for their empty bellies was all an adventure to him. Fun. The fun was over today and Cricket was heading for the corrals of home when his rider reined him toward the new wagon in town. The tired dogs, not realizing the new adventure they were about to miss, went on to the house.

The boy rode up hesitantly, but so full of curiosity that his ribs were spreading. He'd never seen a wagon rigged up like this one. There was a big wooden crate with doors that swung to reveal its hidden treasure. A crudely painted sign was haphazardly lettered across the sides, saying:

THE WORLD'S STRANGEST CREATURE
MIXTURE OF TEN ANIMULES IN ONE

A man built like a thin, winter tree was feeding the team of horses. He spotted the freckled-faced visitor and smiled big with a mouth that seemed to run all the way around and hide behind his turkey neck. Yes sir, he had a smile, and not only that, it was mostly full of teeth. There were only two vacant spots to mar the perfect gleam of charming promise. His small blue eyes were something to think about as well. They could hardly be seen when he was smiling, but when the stretch came out of the mouth, the eyes flew open wide as a sunflower, and as blue as a painted sky. The boy could just tell that these were eyes that had seen many rare things.

With a voice as smooth and slick as new shoes on ice, he said, "Well, haaaalo there. How are you, Button? My, that's a fine-lookin' steed you're mounted on, and I see you're quite a huntsman, too. Rabbits are gettin' scarce during these days of culinary disaster. Our stomachs may despair now and then, but I have here in this wagon a creature that will make the gray matter twitch and twirl for days. It's obvious a young gentleman of your upbringing and outdoor talents could never pass over gazing upon one of the wonders of the world. Huh? Huh? Whaddya say, Button?"

"Uh . . . uh . . ." The boy's mind was mush, then he managed to utter, "What . . . what is it?"

"What is it? Can't you read? It's an animule. You got a quarter? That's all it'll take to feast your starving eyes upon this marvel of the universe."

The boy knew exactly how much money was in his pocket. "Gosh no, I ain't got but four cents."

"Well, this ain't no four-cent look . . . not this . . . this is a twenty-five-cent look and the price might just go up in the next ten seconds." Sadness must have registered on the boy's face, for great pity came over the man's as if he'd just heard of his best friend's death, the spread of the plague, and the permanent cancellation of the Second Coming all at one time. "Well, I'm not one to keep knowledge from the young . . . far from it. It's within the nature of my sympathetic soul to give, not deny. Just hand me the four cents and that rabbit hanging on the right side and we've got a deal."

The right-side rabbit was the plumpest of the three, but the huntsman handed it over along with the four coppers and crawled down from his steed. He wanted to feel if the earth shook when the great vision was finally revealed.

The man stepped to the wooden crate. Stretching his long neck longer and twisting his head at the youngster as if he were going to show him how to make gold bars out of chicken droppings, he jerked the flaps back and said, "Cheapest education you'll ever get, Button."

The wide-eyed observer was speechless. His horse pulled back on the reins and snorted. There was a critter ceaselessly pacing back and forth behind iron bars.

"Just look at this, son. Can you believe your staring eyes? Hump like a buffalo. Ears like a fox. Hind legs like a dog. Front legs like a tiger."

The man reached into a separate compartment of the cage and pulled out a large bone. He swiftly shoved it between the bars, and the creature snapped it in half with one crack. The man slammed the flaps shut then, and said "Makes an alligator's jaws look like a mousetrap."

The boy's throat was dry as sand but he managed to stutter, "Could I . . . coulda . . . I'd like . . . Could I see . . ."

"Now, now, Button. You mustn't get greedy. I've done given you a fifty-cent look. Tell you what . . . you spread the word all over and you can look FREE . . . free, I say, all day long."

The dazed boy crawled back on his little bay horse and made a ride Paul Revere would have done deep knee bends over. He raced from house to house informing the occupants of the greatest animule of all time.

"Everybody's coming." He enticed the inhabitants of the land. He did have one piece of luck—several ranchers and farmers, along with the townsmen, were cutting mesquite bushes and building a brush arbor for a big religious camp meeting on the edge of town. While their husbands labored for the Lord, the country wives visited with the town ladies.

"You ain't never seen nothin' like it. It's made outa coyotes and elephants and bobcats and . . ." The boy was getting a little carried away, but who could blame him?

The crowd gathered. They arrived afoot, horseback, by wagon and team, and then there were three Model T Fords and a shiny Model A. Even the boy's mother closed the post office and walked over. He was sure sorry his dad was on a trade on the other side of Hobbs and would miss this phenomenon.

The man was masterfully keeping the gathered crowd mesmerized. Finally he figured that he had about all the people Humble City, New Mexico, could provide. While he was collecting the looking money, the boy couldn't help saying proudly to a couple more of his age group, "I done seen it."

The man pocketed all the money he was going to get. He stood poised a pulsating second, then swung the doors open as if he were unveiling a Michaelangelo. There was a low gasp from the crowd. The man never gave them a chance to recover.

"See there! He's got teeth like a grizzly bear . . . and have you noticed those spots? Why, those are the spots of a leopard. And that head . . . why, that head belongs to a wolverine."

A woman said, "Whew, it sure does stink."

"There you are. Now, that's real observant of you, ma'am. This animule is even part skunk."

One old man interrupted, saying, "I seen a picture once and that there's a hyeeeni."

The man, sensing a slight murmur of rebellion in the crowd, recovered swiftly. "You got 'er there, old pardner. 'Hyena' is an ancient Persian word meaning 'animal of many parts.'" Then he motioned to the front of the animal, saying, "He's high there," then he pointed at the animal's rear. "And eeny beeny there—like a buffalo." Then he threw another bone into the cage, and while the crowd was in slight shock from the loud snap of its jaws on the bone, he swung the doors shut again.

The beginning murmur of possible danger from the crowd was short—very short—when the man explained that he now had to let the creature out of the cage for its daily constitutional. He went on to tell that he had a strong leash, but with such a beast one could never tell. The crowd scattered like wild dogs after a shotgun blast.

The boy, having twice been exposed to one of the eight wonders of the world, was courageously the last to leave. He was finally summarily dismissed with, "You did a good job, Button. Don't ever forget it, you hear? Now you can go home and eat your rabbit . . . the rest of the folks can chew their crow."

It was a lot of years later before the boy fully understood what he'd learned that day from the man with the animule.

As the man buckled the doors shut, he flung a parting question at the boy. "By the way, Button, what's yer name?"

"Max Evans, sir," I replied.

Super Bull

There are all kinds of bulls in the world, that's for sure—Angus, Brangus, Charolais, Jerseys, but Super Bull was a Hereford—and if Jimmy Bason, cowboy and rancher, had known about this particular one, he probably wouldn't have bought the S Bar S outfit. This bull would give him more trouble than a street full of terrorists and drive him as crazy as a bee-stung bear.

The Basons' land starts just west of the historical little mining and cattle village of Hillsboro, in southwestern New Mexico, and goes all the way to the top of the Black Range Mountains. When Jimmy bought the ranch in 1962, it was the S Bar S, but his brand was F Cross and he intended for every animal on his spread to carry that marking.

He started riding and looking for strays. He soon found a bunch of wild Hereford cows and calves enjoying the springtime grass in South Percha Canyon. A few of the cows and all the calves were unbranded. This had to be changed.

Jimmy went for help to three absolutely top-notch mountain cowboys, Joe Wiegel, and Mac and Bill Nunn. They brought with them their best rock horses. These animals could run a cow up a tree and back down a badger hole. And would they ever need them, because South Percha Canyon ranges from seven to ten thousand timbered feet in altitude and is as close to straight up and down as they come and still have a rock roll instead of drop.

In three days of hard riding and skilled tracking, they'd gathered seventeen head. They all agreed that there was at least one waspy old cow and her bull calf left. Jimmy knew that these good hands had work and responsibilities of their own, so he thanked them and said they could go on about their business. It wouldn't be any problem at all for him and his grulla horse, Billy Bob, to finish up.

Well, that old S Bar S cow was a smart one. She turned back on her tracks and over. She'd run up and down the nearly sheer slopes in a zigzag manner and then cut back and hide like a mountain lion in thick, brushy patches. The bull calf followed right along, making the same moves as his mother.

Jimmy and Billy Bob wore down after about four days, and as embarrassing as it was, Jimmy called on Rob Cox, another hellacious cowboy from the Organ Mountains near Las Cruces, to come give him a hand.

Two running, plunging days went by. No cow. No calf. Tired cowboys. Tired horses. Rob had other ducks to race, so Jimmy was once more left alone to face the rugged wilderness.

In this rough country he had to work by sign instead of sight. He looked for freshly overturned rocks and broken brush, but mainly he trailed by tracks and by the squirts and drops of green, mostly digested grass that falls behind a running critter. The way it splashes points out the direction she's going.

This vast land of steep slopes is covered densely with pines, spruces, and all kinds of brush and rocks and is some of the roughest terrain in America. To emphasize how wild it is, the great Indian leaders Geronimo and Chief Victorio chose it as their last stronghold after thousands of soldiers had pursued them for years.

South Percha Canyon stretches along Highway 90 for six miles, and along this whole distance there were only four trails that dropped down from the road. Jimmy finally got the old cow and calf headed up one of these trails. He could tell by the freshly steaming, green droppings that he was right on 'em. Then he saw them top out and vanish on the winding highway. He topped out himself, and the green sign told him which way they'd turned. He had to get her before she reached one of the other trails. Billy Bob charged right down the pavement while Jimmy shook out his loop. He knew he could only catch one of the two, so when he pulled in roping range, he decided to take the cow. He figured the calf would hang around hunting for its mother. He threw the loop. He caught. Billy Bob set up, sliding his hind legs under and screwing his tail in the pavement. If he hadn't been a top rock horse, there would have been a hell of a wreck. The cow was jerked down hard right on the yellow line, knocking enough breath out of her to turn a windmill for thirty minutes.

Jimmy bailed off with his piggin' string to sideline her—that is, tie two feet together on the same side so she could move around and easily get her breath, but couldn't get away. He had slipped the loop of the piggin' string on one foot when she found some lost wind and really started kicking and bawling. A tour bus full of Japanese had stopped on the highway and about fifty excited, camera-toting Orientals were circling around jabbering, scuffling, pushing, and trying to take pictures. Here it was—the wild and wooly West in action right before their shining, dark eyes.

The old cow didn't like one human being much less a whole highway full of folks making more noise than a tenth-anniversary class reunion. Billy Bob was boogered by all the racket, but kept the rope tight anyway. Jimmy was being kicked, butted, and generally abused by the crazed cow. The more Jimmy yelled at the Japanese, the closer they came with the cameras, smiling, pointing, snapping pictures like they were recording the Resurrection itself. At last Jimmy got the attention of the bus driver and screamed at him to get these photographic maniacs out of his way so he could finish his job. The driver finally waved and pushed the crowd back. Jimmy tied the cow. The bus moved out with many smiling faces mashed against the windows.

Jimmy rode down to the pickup and horse trailer, then drove back to take the cow home. The maverick calf with tiny nubbin horns was off the road somewhere out of sight, but probably nearby.

The next day Jimmy rode leisurely back to the spot where he caught the cow, expecting to find the bull calf bawling for his mamma. It wasn't there. He slid his horse off down the trail, confident he'd easily find the calf. They'd cleaned the country of wild cattle so any fresh tracks were bound to be the little baby bull's. Well, he rode for several days and although he found sign, he never saw the calf. The little critter was running the same country as his mama, backtracking and pulling the same tricks she had. Jimmy was getting the first tiny inkling of the marvelous events yet to come. Well, no bother. He had fences, windmills, and other cattle to look after. He'd let Billy Bob rest a while, then come back and get the little feller.

When Jimmy returned to the scene, he found the calf tracks and other damp sign. He saw him with his own eyes. He ran him with his own horse. The little bull would run—no, he would fall—off the mountains at least three times as fast as the best cowboy and horse possibly could.

Jimmy said, "That calf just wouldn't go where any well-thinking animal should. If I jumped him at the bottom of a canyon, he would charge up through bush so thick it would have stalled an army tank and then he'd bounce across piles of rocks so agilely that if a mountain goat had seen it he would have fallen dead from pure jealousy."

Jimmy never got a loop. He did get very tired. After three hours of these games, Billy Bob was sapped out, too. So, Jimmy decided that all his other chores had suddenly become extra urgent, and besides, if he pulled out for a couple of weeks maybe a rain would eradicate all the old tracks and he'd have a clean shot at him.

Rob Cox came back to help again. They both made runs at the calf, but neither got close enough to throw a loop. The anguish mounted. Jimmy was finding it harder and harder to go into town now. The kind and considerate populace showed its deep concern by asking him about the elusive bull every place he went. One morning, as he was walking out to saddle his horse, even Sue, his patient wife, yelled after him, "Are you gonna go play with Super Bull again today, honey?" That's the day the maverick got his name. Jimmy humped up like he'd been shot in the butt with a sack full of rattlesnake fangs, and with a great show of willpower kept his teeth clamped together.

Super Bull was getting bigger and stronger every day. Jimmy and Billy Bob were getting weaker. Sometimes Jimmy would spot Super Bull through field glasses way across a canyon just lying in a flat, grassy spot looking back at him. All the time Jimmy was riding down the canyon and up the mountain, the calf would be resting. He had every advantage.

A lot of people, including Jimmy, had seen Super Bull grazing along the highway where the ditches fostered lots of tender green grass and weeds. He especially liked to graze there at night. He wasn't afraid of cars or pickups—only horsebackers. So? First Great Grand Plan: Sue would drive the pickup while Jimmy rode in the back. He tied his rope to the headache bar, then they practiced driving slowly back and forth past Super Bull. At first the young bull didn't even look up from his meal. Then he started watching them as they passed by. He still grazed, though. Jimmy tapped against the back window and Sue pulled the pickup over closer to the ditch so Jimmy could make his throw. He did. At the first swish of the top, Super Bull knew something was wrong. He'd heard that swishing tune before. He took off. The rope sailed out and barely caught the top of his head and one short horn

enough to jerk him slightly sideways. Sue gunned the pickup after him, but Super found one of the four trails before Jimmy could get his rope ready for another throw.

Jimmy crawled back inside the cab with Sue and said, "If his horns had been an inch longer I'd-a had 'im."

Sue said, "Well, I guess we'll just have to wait until you both grow up." It was teeth- and jaw-grinding time again.

That winter, when the sun beamed and the wind eased, Jimmy made several runs in the snow. If Billy Bob had been a world-class skier, he and Jimmy might have had a chance, because Super Bull busted in and out of the drifts like a dolphin in seawater and lost them every time. Jimmy got more than a normal amount of remarks and ridicule from all his cohorts, which made for an extra-long winter.

One rancher asked him, "Hey, Jimmy, you gonna call in the air force? They ought to get him easy. I hear old Super can't fly over a quarter of a mile without having to land." Just because Jimmy had been in the Strategic Air Command didn't increase his appreciation for this remark.

Then an out-of-work miner volunteered to use his dynamite expertise to close all the trails. Jimmy didn't bother to ask the miner how he would get down into the canyons to chase Super Bull if all the trails were closed. All in all, it was just more than a long-shanked cowboy could listen to without getting a skull ache. Yes, it did make the winter longer and the obsession stronger. Spring came again in all its bird-singing glory, but Jimmy paid no attention to their merry chirping, nor did he smell the wildflowers, or notice how the water sparkled from the melted snow.

Super Bull was a yearling now with nice little horns. Jimmy and Sue tried the pickup trick again, but couldn't get close to him. Well, Jimmy would just borrow a neighbor's pickup and fool the dumb animal. He soon found out that Super had now added all pickups to his list of no-no's.

Then came Second Great Grand Plan. The flash of Einsteinian genius was blinding. Simple. They'd go after him in a car. He'd never expect that. They'd just wait until he was grazing by a strip of highway so steep it would be impossible for him to jump off. Jimmy would leap from the hood of the car and bulldog him. When Sue made her next remark, Jimmy began to suspect that the loyalties of his faithful companion for fifteen years might be wavering in favor of the bull. As he pulled his hat down over his ears to prepare to mount the hood of the car, she said, "Now you be careful, honey, and don't cripple poor little Super Bull. That's getting to be an expensive, valuable animal." Jimmy doesn't remember whether he shortened his teeth or not.

Jimmy tied a rope to the undercarriage of the car, then laid it in a coil on the front seat beside Sue. Jimmy would bulldog the animal and try to sideline him with his piggin' string. Sue was to jump out and hand him the secured catch rope for insurance. If Super didn't tear the bottom out of the car, Jimmy figured they should have him.

They watched and waited until Super was in perfect position. The sides of the road dropped almost straight off for half a mile, and it was at least that distance to the next trail exit.

Sue eased the car along past him, turned around, and passed him going the other way. Super grazed on, ignoring the car. The plan was working to perfection. The young bull, who now weighed around eight hundred pounds, was about to be had.

Jimmy put the piggin' string in his mouth to free up both hands. Closer. Closer. Super loomed up in the car lights like a circus pet. There! Jimmy leaped. Super leaped. Jimmy grabbed both little horns, but had landed so far back he couldn't get enough leverage to throw the bull. Super charged out ahead bellowing and scattering the thin green with Jimmy desperately trying to pull himself forward to brace his feet.

The bull, suddenly and without hesitation, bailed off the side of the impossible drop. Super was really snapping brush in his descent. Sue could hear the racket from the car. She waited. She waited some more with the car lights locked on the spot of sudden departure. Just as she was about to take a flashlight and have a look, two hands grasped the side of the highway. Then the forearms and a head appeared. Then the rest of the battered body arrived on the road. Jimmy's shirt was ripped like it had been run through a

CIA paper shredder. His handsome face was peeled all down one side, and there were knots and scratches from the top of his six-foot-two frame to the bottom of it. He still had the piggin' string in his mouth.

As he stumbled wearily to the car to get a dose of well-deserved sympathy from his admiring wife, she said, "I see you didn't use your piggin' string, so I assume Super Bull is alive and free . . . unless, of course, you broke his poor little neck."

"#*&#@@#&*. . . &&#%@$#&*@@," echoed across the land.

Just the same, Jimmy maintained his vigilant pursuit. He couldn't very well stop. His closest friends, his nearest neighbors, his pretty little wife, and even his four-year-old daughter, Stacy, kept it constantly on his mind. Only Brent, his three-year-old son, seemed to care about his predicament. He had nightmares—he'd catch the bull, but the rope would always break. Once he dreamed he caught and jerked him down tying him perfectly, but that changed and he was tied to the bull and they were sailing through a blue western sky falling swifter and swifter to jagged rocks a mile below. Oh, if he'd never heard of that critter! Oh, if only no one had!

Super Bull was a year and a half old now. He was unbranded, unmarked, and gaining in weight, condition, and brains. Super belonged only to himself. Something—anything—had to be done. Third Great Grand Plan had to produce better results.

Jimmy said, "I figured I was on my third great plan, but Super was on his sixth and probably heading for the seventh. Since it was such a dry year, I decided I could salt Super down the hill with some nice green blocks of hay."

It worked. Jimmy would drop the hay a little farther down the hill each day. Super would eat it and wait for the next batch of bait. He was moving closer and closer to the smaller hills and an open cattle guard gate. Once through that, Jimmy would shut it and capture him at last.

It was June. Jimmy and his neighbors were branding. Jimmy was having to get up at four o'clock in the morning, work all day, then deliver the hay to the bull. Super Bull didn't have a clock, so he was sleeping and fattening up while Jimmy was being worn all over like a ditchdigger's hands.

Jimmy forgot about the work, though, because he now had the bull taking the bait four miles down the canyon and still gaining. Glory, glory, hallelujah, and fried chicken on Sunday! Just one more block of hay and Super should be through the gate. Then it clouded up and started raining, raining, raining. The grass came up green, tender, and delicious all over. Super had no use whatsoever for a dry block of hay. To make matters unhappier, some of Jimmy's gentle cows found the open gate and wandered up the canyon into the wild bull country. It took him three days, riding across the boggy ground, to gather them. He decided, however, the mud would be an advantage. He could run the bull now as fast as he could ride and the tracks would be clear and sharp in the wet earth.

He was giving Billy Bob extra grain and doing lots of talking to him. Since Sue's unfaltering faith appeared to be wavering, he could only share his woes with his horse. Well, Jimmy and his four-legged confidante ran Super Bull with all they had for three days. Even Super was beginning to tire, so he took a trail going to the highway. Jimmy followed the muddy tracks, and with a last surge of energy they were closing in on him. It was three-quarters of a mile to the next trail. Super was almost there. They had to do it now! Jimmy threw his thirty-foot rope when Super was twenty-nine feet away. It just caught one horn and the end of his nose. Billy Bob set 'er down. Super flipped over the side of the canyon and landed in the middle of a ten-foot oak tree hanging upright with his four legs way above ground. Jimmy stood there and looked him right in the eye. He couldn't reach him, but he could have spit on him.

"We got 'im, Billy Bob!"

All Jimmy had to do now was sideline Super with the piggin' string. The dawning. How was he going to get out there to the bull? He was wearing heavy leggings and a brush-popping coat. He couldn't risk the time to take off these cumbersome garments, but he wasn't any ballerina, either. He put the piggin' string in his mouth, stood on the edge of the road, and jumped. He'd forgotten one little thing—a tree that's already holding up about nine hundred pounds of bull might not handle an additional two hundred pounds of cowboy and costume. It didn't.

The bull bellered, twisted, and kicked, and the tree slowly began to bend down. Down. Super Bull's feet touched the ground and when he got traction, he really zoomed out of the tree and down the canyon. With the main weight gone, the relieved branch snapped up—boing! Jimmy clung to the top looking around to see if a squirrel, a pissant, or somebody had seen the event. Billy Bob was the only witness and he would never tell. Super Bull tore through the downhill brush still unbranded. Jimmy climbed out of the tree marked all over.

Jimmy didn't want to be inhumane to the bull so he decided to give Super a few days' rest. During this period of recuperation he met a professional hunter-trapper who used a tranquilizer gun on mountain lions. Jimmy wanted to know if it would work on cattle. The trapper said, "Why, I seen 'em knock elephants down on TV, ain't you?"

The Greatest Grand Foolproof Plan of All.

Jimmy tried to sneak out without Sue seeing him. It didn't work. Not only did she go along, but she brought Stacy and Brent to witness the event.

They picked up the trapper, and he said they'd just need one dart if he found the muscle. Jimmy insisted on four in case he missed. Jimmy drove the car up Highway 90 until they found Super following a neighbor's cow who was in heat. Super Bull was harking to his calling and like many males before him was vulnerable.

Jimmy drove slowly to within fifteen feet of him. The trapper fired. Super Bull just kicked at the dart and went on sniffing the air. The trapper said all they had to do was drive up ahead a couple of hundred yards and wait about fifteen minutes, then Jimmy could just walk over to the snoozing bull and tie him up. Easy pickin's. At last the moment of truth. D-Day. He was glad his proud family was there to witness and verify his success.

One hour later, after some discussion, they decided to shoot Super again with a stronger dose. They did. The fifteen minutes turned into another hour. They doubled the next dose with the trapper protesting that it might kill him. Super kicked at the dart with his hind leg and went on sniffing after the cow. This process was repeated, increasing the dose each time until all four darts were in him. Super maintained his pursuit of the opposite sex. He hadn't been watching TV.

Jimmy turned the radio up loud on Louisiana Hayride trying to drown out the unnecessary comments from the spectators.

He thought the bull must surely be groggy by now. He would make one last valiant effort. He mounted the car hood again, piggin' string dangling from both sides of his mouth, and Sue drove him within jumping distance. Yipppeee, he had the thousand-pound bull by both horns! He held them for about a hundred yards through the dense downhill brush. The crowd waited on the highway. Jimmy crawled back on the road into the daylight to a shattering round of applause. His piggin' string was gone, but no one asked if he'd tied the bull.

The confused trapper had obviously forgotten to figure the difference in weight between a mountain lion and a bull; however, he insisted on ten dollars apiece for his lost darts. Jimmy rode back the next morning and found his piggin' string and all of the brightly colored darts where Super had rubbed them out against tree trunks.

As the weeks went by, Jimmy made many more grand plans but kept them all to himself. He didn't even divulge them to his horse. It was such a rank, snowy winter he couldn't have used them anyway.

Spring came. Jimmy was driving his pickup over low, rolling hills to check some loading pens that had a water tank sticking out on both sides of the corral. The pens were out in the flats not far from headquarters. He topped the hill and suddenly slammed on the brakes, leaned over the steering wheel, and stared so hard his eyebrows joined his hairline. There was Super Bull ambling slowly along, bellering low in his chest, heading straight for the open gate to the corral where a bunch of cows were watering.

Jimmy eased out of the pickup thinking that every move he made sounded like a battery of cannons exploding. He crawled on his belly and crept from bush to rock like one of Geronimo's warriors. Then there was no more ground cover—just fifty yards of wide-open pasture to the corral gate.

He crouched behind the last bush getting ready to take off like an Olympic dash man. It suddenly hit him that he and Billy Bob had done a hell of a lot of dashing without any results. He simply stood up and walked slowly, casually across the open ground like he was taking a course in daydreaming. The calm exterior camouflaged a heart that was pumping all the blood his plumbing could handle and lungs that were overloaded to the bursting point with that clean mountain air.

When at last he placed his hands on the swung back gate his palms were wet enough to fill a sponge. He closed the gate. Simple as that.

The three-year-old bull had already picked out his next mate and was courting her with enthusiasm. As multitudes of males before him, he'd been captured by sex. Why not? He had nothing left to prove in the Gila Forest.

The next person to accost Jimmy with a sarcastic inquiry about his bull-ish escapades got this answer: "Oh, you mean Super Bull? Nothin' to it . . . caught him afoot."

At first Jimmy wanted to shoot him and even worse, castrate him, but instead he branded him with the F Cross and called his special friend, Rob Cox, to come look him over. Rob liked the young bull's conformation. Jimmy was relieved. Even though he couldn't stand to have Super around, he wanted him safe and happy. It was agreed that Rob would take him back to the Organ Mountain Ranch. A lot of bulls don't like the strain of doing their duty in rough, high country. It was plain natural for Super Bull. He was turned loose at 7,500-foot altitude to live out the rest of his days eating and breeding in paradise.

Even now when Jimmy Bason and Billy Bob ride the South Percha Canyon, they instinctively look for the wild bull's sign. They are never going to find any. They just made ONE Super Bull.

A Horse to Brag About

I reckon just about every human in the world that was raised on a cow ranch, worked as a cowboy, or just plain rode for pleasure knew and loved a horse like Old Snip. In the memory of us all there is one old pony that comes to mind more often than all the others. A horse to do a little braggin' about. That's the kind of horse Old Snip was.

The first time I saw the little stocking-legged, blazed-face, snip-nosed bay, a long-legged bronc stomper named Robert Ian was hanging the steel in his shoulders. It was in a big pole corral at Cow Springs, New Mexico, and the dust was fairly boiling from under Old Snip. He bucked hard, mighty hard, with long, ground-bustin', neck-poppin' jumps, straight ahead till he hit one side of the corral, then he turned and put out all he had till he hit the other side. He bucked straight just like he did everything else in his life. But that was the only time he ever bucked.

Gradually he slowed and then quit altogether. Robert Ian worked him in and out around the corral letting him get used to the weight on his back, the steel in his mouth, the rein on his neck, letting him know that these things wouldn't hurt him if he behaved himself. The little old pony caught on quick and by the fourth saddling, Robert Ian decided he'd turn him over to me. He said, "Here, boy, get your saddle on this here Old Snip. He's gentle as a loggin' horse."

I was just a gawky, freckle-faced kid hanging around the outfit wranglin' horses, patching fences, anything Robert Ian happened to think of that he thought I wouldn't mess up. Mainly I hung around to get a few square meals, listen to the tall yarns cowboys have a habit of spinning, and maybe learn a little something.

"You think he's broke gentle?" I asked, cautiously eyeing the bay.

"Why, boy," he said, "this here horse would do to go to preachin' on."

I saddled up, gathered the reins up tight in my left hand, and grabbed the heavy black mane at the same time. I took hold of the saddle horn with my right and stuck my left knee in his shoulder, swung my right leg smoothly over his back, and Old Snip moved out with a nice running walk. Right away I breathed easy again. I've never known a horse to pick up a fast running walk that quick. He was a natural at it. A running walk will carry a cowboy a lot of miles in a day and bring him back without his tonsils shook loose. Sittin' up there on him I felt just as good as an old coat that a feller's worn a long time and hates to throw away. He was already beginning to rein. The least pressure and he turned smooth as new grass, just where you wanted him.

"Now, listen, boy," Robert Ian said when I came back, "I owe Ed Young twenty dollars and I promised him this here horse in payment." My heart turned mighty cold at these words, for I thought he was giving the horse to me.

"You been wanting to go over on that San Cristobal outfit and hunt arrowheads, ain't you?"

I said, "Yeah."

"All right, here's your chance. You can leave about daylight in the mornin' and you'll be at the Indian ruins right around ten. I'll make out a bill of sale from me to Ed," he added. "You can stay at the old line camp across from Long Draw tomorrow night and make it in to Ed's the next day."

"Yeah," I said, not liking the sound of that bill of sale business.

"Something else," Robert Ian said. "If you keep your mouth shut, listen hard, and work like hell you might get a job later with the San Cristobal outfit. A regular payin' job."

That last sounded good because all I'd got in the way of pay around there was a dollar Robert Ian gave me when we went to Santa Fe one time. That seemed like a lot of money then but I was a year older now and wanted to put on the dog a little.

Me and Old Snip were out on a piñon-crowded trail heading lickety-split for the San Cristobal Ranch when the sun came up. Boy, it was a mighty fine morning. A bunch of deer jumped up out of some oak brush and went tearing up the hill. A coyote crossed our trail and the magpies started screaming. The blue jays flew from tree to tree.

By nine o'clock we crossed the highway between Cline's Corners and Lamy, New Mexico, and were well into the ranch property itself. The highway is fenced now, but then she was wide open. The August sun was warming up fast. I figured it was going to get hotter than blue blazes before noon. Sure enough, it did. I didn't care, though. Here I was mounted on a little animal that I figured the good Lord had made especially for me and I saw those sky-high, white and red bluffs sticking up like a bunch of cathedrals.

I took the worn-out catch rope Robert Ian had given me and tied Old Snip to a piñon tree with a knot that wouldn't slip and choke him later on if he got boogered at something. Then I started out across those ruins with my head down and my eyes peeled expecting any second to see a perfect arrowhead.

Some college feller told me years later that these ruins were five or six hundred years old. They were brand spanking new to me that day in August. You could still see the outlines of the sandstone houses built in a big square. Out in the middle was the round kiva—a sort of church for the Indians. Broken pottery with designs painted on them in real bright colors was scattered about everywhere. There were lots of broken arrowheads and pieces of flint all over.

Then I found what I'd been looking for, a great big perfect arrowhead made out of black glassy obsidian. Man! Chills ran all over me and I knew what a prospector must feel like when he pans a big gold nugget for the first time. I got to walking so fast trying to find another one that I probably stepped over several unseen. Boy, I had a pocket just smack full of flint pieces, arrowheads, and bright-colored pottery.

Then I saw another one, white and small, a bird point. Just as I bent to pick it up I noticed a shadow spread across the ground around me. It was a cloud. As I straightened up I looked into the sky. There were lots of clouds, black and heavy with water. They hadn't begun to get together yet so I figured I had plenty of time to hunt.

Between the cathedrals and the line camp where I aimed to spend the night was a lot of barren, badly eroded ground and one deep-cut arroyo called Long Draw. Flash floods in the mountains caused these to fill with water and sometimes made crossing impossible. I was so wrapped up in what I was doing, I didn't pay the clouds much attention.

Then she hit—an ear-bustin' clap of thunder! I raised up quick-like and looked over to where Snip was tied. He was so wide-eyed you could see the white showing. It's not natural for a cow pony to get excited over a little rainstorm brewing. But when Old Snip looked over at me and blasted out with a long, loud nicker, I figured it was time to leave. I still swear to this day that horse was smarter than me and was just giving warning it was high time to drag out of there before it was too late. Sure enough, it almost was.

Over to the east in the higher mountains, the clouds were having a family reunion and the more lively members were spitting out forked fire and deep-down, rumbling noises. I could see the blue-white sheets of rain pour out into the canyons and foothills. The storm was moving on out toward the flats and us, fast-like.

I buckled on my spurs, missing the hole with the buckle tongue a couple of times because I was getting a little excited. I untied Old Snip and mounted up. I leaned over in the saddle and away we went. Snip seemed to understand that the whole idea was to get across all that barren ground before the rain reached us. If it did, we might have to sleep out on this side of the arroyo all night without any shelter. He was really moving now, up and down . . . straining hard with his hindquarters on the upgrade and keeping his forelegs out in front on the downgrade.

We didn't quite make it. About a quarter of a mile out in the eroded flats, the rain caught us. I pulled up and took a look. There wasn't much to see, the rain was so heavy. As we moved out again I could feel the cold wetness already soaked through to the skin and the water running from the brim of my hat like it was coming off a tin roof.

Old Snip was beginning to slip and slide in the slick, muddy clay. We kept going just the same. I was so wet now I didn't feel the coldness so much. We finally made it to Long Draw. I reined down a gradual slope out into the gravel-covered bottom. Water was running in little muddy rivers every-where. Then all of a sudden I could see nothing but water. A solid stream of reddish, muddy churning water! We were in real trouble! The heavy rain up in the mountains was just now reaching this part of Long Draw.

Before I had time to think, the water swirled up around my boot heels. Then it hit, a great big wall of mud, water, piñon sticks, pine needles, and everything else that grows in the mountains. I dropped the reins and grabbed the saddle horn with both hands. My arms felt like they had been stretched out as long as a wagon tongue. I couldn't see and it felt like a whole ocean of water had spilled right on top of us. I knew for sure this was it. I wanted to do some praying but I couldn't get my mind on it for worrying about holding onto that saddle horn.

I began to strangle, and a lot of red, light, and black spaces seemed to jump out of my head. I got a big suck at a bunch of air. It was mighty wet air as far as that goes but there wasn't quite enough water in it to drown a feller. We went splashing under again, up and out, down and under, over and over. After this had gone on for what seemed like about two long years I hap-pened to remember hearing one old cowboy say a horse could swim better if you hung onto his tail instead of the saddle horn. They are only about two yards apart, but getting from that horn to that tail wasn't any simple act.

I had to take the gamble. If I missed I was a gone dog and I knew it. I turned loose and grabbed! One hand caught tail hair! I was washed side-ways and every other way. By this time I was sure there was as much water in me as there was out of me. Somehow I hung on and got hold with my other hand. Everything was muddy at this point, including my memory.

A long time later—at least it seemed a long time later—I noticed a horse's hind leg next to my face. I counted one, two, three, four horse's legs. Then

I realized I was lying in the mud and Old Snip was standing there with his head down, his sides bellowing in and out, breathing hard. I didn't mind that old sticky mud. No, sirree, not one bit. I rightly loved it. I got up and put my arm across that bay pony's neck. I didn't say anything. I didn't have to. I knew he understood.

We stayed all night over at the line camp. Even if we were hungry and a little cold I didn't mind and I hope Old Snip didn't.

The next day about noon I rode up to Ed Young's place and let out a yell. He walked out, or I should say a hat came out with him walking under it, because he wore the biggest hat I ever saw. It was a real, honest-to-goodness old-time cowboy hat.

I said, "Robert Ian sent you this here horse," and I handed him the bill of sale. The best eyes in the world couldn't have made out what that piece of paper said. That old Long Draw mud and water had seen to that. "Reckon you'll have to get him to make you out another one," I said, tickled plumb to death. I figured I still had a chance somehow to come up with the where-withal to own Old Snip for my very own. I told Ed what had happened, then I said, "Say, Robert Ian said you might be needing a hand."

"I might," he said, looking at me with those gleaming blue eyes across that hawk-looking, humped-up nose. "What can you do, boy?" he asked point-blank.

"Hell," I said, "I can do anything."

Several weeks later I knew that this was not exactly the whole truth. I know now that I stayed on at Ed's in the beginning because I wanted to be with Old Snip, but later on I liked it all the way around. That evening I helped him feed the horses and milk the cows. After supper I got up and helped his wife with the dishes.

This set real good with Mother. All the cowboys in the country called her Mother Young because she was such a top-notch cook, doctor, and anything else a woman had to be to make a good wife and mother thirty miles from town right smack-dab in the middle of all outdoors.

Ed had some good horses in his own right. He had broken broncs for the old Waggoner outfit in the early days and a lot of other big outfits, and he wouldn't have anything but good horses around him.

I got to ride and work with them all. There was Old Sut, a coal-black twelve-year-old. You could ride him all day and he'd never even break a sweat. Then there was Flax, the golden-maned sorrel—a good range roping horse; Apache, the big hard-bucking paint; Raggedy Ann, the little brown mustang that Ed had roped and broke himself; and Frosty, a blaze-faced chestnut—Ed's favorite. When the cowboys spoke about Frosty they would always say, "That Frosty's quite a horse, yep, he's one hell of a horse."

But none of them compared with Old Snip. As time went on he just got better and better. You could ride him all day without wearing him out because of his fast, easy gait. He reined like a regular cutting horse, quick, but smooth and easy. Boy, that stop he had! Those hind legs would slide way up under him with his forelegs shoved out in front and you didn't feel hardly any jar at all. He learned to work a rope. He kept his head looking down the rope all the time and the slack pulled out.

I learned to heel calves on him. Ed and I worked a lot just by ourselves. It sure makes a calf easier to throw and brand if you rope him by the heels. I was getting so I hardly missed a loop when riding Old Snip.

One day Ed said, "We're going down to Eldon Butler's and help him brand about fifty head. He's interested in buying Old Snip. We've got plenty of good horses around here and I need the money."

As we worked our way down out of the mountains toward Butler's I felt sort of sick. I cleared my throat and said, "Ed, how much you asking for Old Snip?"

"Aw, around a hundred I reckon the way he's turning out." He added, "Now, I really want you to show off what a heeling horse he is. That'll do more to sell him than anything else."

We cut the calves out from the mother cows and held them in a pole corral. The mothers bawled to beat sixty and stirred up a lot of dust. The branding irons were heating in an open fire. Eldon was getting the black leg vaccine ready and Ed was sharpening his knife getting ready to castrate the bull calves, except one they picked out for a breeding bull because of his good conformation and markings.

I was thinking, a hundred dollars, at the rate I was getting paid, I would be a hundred years old before I had it saved up. I really didn't feel any extra love in my heart right at that moment for Eldon Butler. He was a fine feller, too.

Ed yelled, "We're ready, boy."

I rode out among the calves on Old Snip. He eased in till we had one in the right position, then I dropped a slow loop under one of the big bull calves. Most fellers make the mistake of throwing too fast a loop to be good heelers. You've got to kinda let it float down. Then just as the hind legs move against the loop you pull the slack and you've got him. The big calf began bucking and bellering but I turned Old Snip and dragged it to the fire. Eldon ran up and got hold of his tail and over he went.

Pretty soon you could smell the hair burning where they put the brand to him. Ed castrated, earmarked, and vaccinated him while Eldon held. I let them have the slack, and the finished product got up shaking his head wondering what in the world had happened to him.

I caught four in a row and felt kind of proud of myself until I noticed Eldon looking at Old Snip with mighty admiring eyes. I don't know what happened after that but it was the worst branding I ever attended. It took me about nine loops to catch every calf and even when I did, it looked like Old Snip and me couldn't keep from getting tangled up in the rope.

It was something or other all the time. I reckon that's the sorriest work we ever did together. I could see the disgusted look on Eldon's face. Ed was downright pale after all the braggin' he'd done about Old Snip. I guess we were all glad to get the job over with.

It was after dark when we unsaddled that night. I told Ed to go on in the house and wash for supper if he wanted to, I'd take care of the horses. I shucked out several ears of corn and forked some hay in the manger. I stood there in the dark a while and smelled Old Snip. He smelled just like a horse, but not just any old horse.

There always seems to be just a little bit of fun mixed up with all the trouble we have, like the time I sat up on Old Snip and looked at a white-faced cow as if she were some sort of varmint. The fall before, we had moved all Ed's cows down out of the mountains to the home pasture for the winter. We didn't move them all at one time, I can tell you that.

Ed had a grazing permit on national forest land and those cows were scattered out in small bunches over about 200,000 acres of mountains, hills, canyons, rocks, and timber, but all the rest of his herd put together was easier to round up than this one old cow. She always took off into the thickest timber or down some rough canyon. She was nothing but trouble, so that's what we named her.

Now there she was out in the bog. There was plenty of grass on the outside but she had to go fall off in it, and now if I didn't drag her out pretty soon she'd sink out of sight. I took the leather loop from the saddle horn and unwound the three wraps from the catch rope. I tied one end of the rope to my saddle horn and built a loop in the other end.

I whirled it a couple or three times and let it go. I had to catch her horns if I was going to be able to let her loose by myself. The loop settled down just where I wanted it and I spurred Old Snip in the opposite direction. Nothing moved. Old Trouble was really bogged down. I began to do some solid cussin' and sweatin'.

After a while the old fool inched up out of the bog a little bit. "Now, Snip!" I yelled. "Now!" Old Snip threw all his weight against that rope and out she came. She struck dry ground running and hit the end of the rope hard. Old Snip was braced. I felt the back of the saddle raise and pull the flank cinch tight against Old Snip's belly.

Now, in the first place I should never have tried this by myself. In the second place I should never have got off Old Snip without somebody around, but that's exactly what I did. Old Snip backed fast, moving right and left trying to keep the rope tight. I worked in from the side trying to get to Trouble's head slightly behind her horns. She was slobbering at the mouth, shaking her head, and straining with all she had against the rope. Her main idea was to run one of those sharp horns right square through me.

I finally got to her and gripped down with all my strength on her muzzle with one hand, twisting and holding a horn with the other. She slung me around, but I stayed with her and pretty soon when she made a run forward there was some slack in the rope. I jerked hard and the loop came off her horns. I made a run for Old Snip and Trouble made a run for me. I could feel the breeze across my hind end as she went by.

To this day I've never mounted as fast. Even then I was a mite slow. Trouble turned back and ran her horns under Old Snip's flank. He leaped up and away! I almost fell off. She made a couple more wild passes at us before she turned and trotted. I reckon that was her way of thanking us for saving her life.

Old Snip learned to work in timber. It got so I could tell when and what he smelled even when we couldn't see it. For instance, if it was a coyote or some other varmint out in the brush, he would throw one ear forward and then the other while looking toward the scent. If it happened to be cattle hiding in the brush, his neck would arch and he would pull over toward them. This saved lots of riding and looking in rough country. If it was a bunch of horses, he got a little extra excited and quickened his gait.

One day we got lost. I did, anyway. Suddenly I didn't know exactly where we were. The country looked different than I'd ever seen it. I noticed the fast-moving clouds above. Then everything was solid gray.

The wind came first in big gusts, then the snow. It hit wet, cold, and mean. It was a blowing snow. I turned back down out of the high country, but I didn't really know where we were headed. First, the ground covered over; then the tree limbs began to pick it up. Every once in a while a big shower of snow would fall on us out of the trees when the wind shook it loose. My hands were getting numb in my thin leather gloves, and my nose and ears were beginning to sting. The snow came on thicker and thicker.

I reined Old Snip this way, then that. It just didn't do any good. I had to admit I was completely lost. The blizzard never let up; in fact, it was just getting started. Before long I could just barely see Old Snip's thick black mane out in front of me. He was plowing along with his head low. The snow was drifting. Sometimes we'd go in up over my boot tops.

Finally I let Old Snip have his head. I just sat in the saddle and hoped he didn't fall off a sheer bluff. Soon I didn't feel anything. It wasn't so bad. Then I remembered hearing that was the time of greatest danger. So I began to move my arms back and forth, back and forth, faster and faster, until I couldn't hold them up any longer. Then there was just a world of cold white, with Old Snip and me right in the middle of it.

I sat a long time wondering why Old Snip didn't keep moving. Maybe he'd frozen stiff standing up! Then there it was—a gate, by dogies. It was the horse pasture gate into Ed Young's Rafter EY Outfit.

After I fed Old Snip about three times as much as he could eat and stood with my hind end so close to the fireplace it just about scorched, I ate the biggest batch of Mother Young's hot biscuits, sowbelly, and pinto beans that a man ever wrapped himself around. That was twice Old Snip had saved my life. I don't know how he found his way down out of that world of frozen white, but he did.

I worked for the San Cristobal outfit off and on on a loan-out for a few years and then somebody got the idea I should go off and get some book learnin'. I had to leave Old Snip behind.

Ed sold him after I left to some rich Texas ranchers. Of course Ed didn't know him as well as I did or he'd never have done it.

I never did get a bill of sale to Old Snip, but I felt he was mine just the same. He belonged to me then and he does now—wherever he is.

The Cowboy and the Professor

It was Wyoming. It was June. It had snowed three inches the night before, but the sun was an hour above the mountains now and the snow was gone. The ground was still slightly damp beneath Luther Wilson's laced boots as he walked along the west bank of Crystal Creek looking for the right hole to cast his fishhook.

Sunlight darted across the creek sparkling like dancing diamonds. Damp ghosts of steam rose from the willow bottom in front of him. Luther decided to circle the willows and do his first fishing above them. About halfway around he heard a huge snort, a mighty whomping, splashing, and crashing noise. A monster was charging straight at him. He leapt aside, tripping on a cut bank. The creature's head looked to be about nine feet from the ground. It cascaded above and by him and must have weighed more than a ton. He reached for the .44 Magnum on his hip and felt a little foolish. He knew a moose can't hear or see very good, but they do have a needle-sharp sense of smell. For that reason Luther felt it would not return. He was certain he needed clean underwear.

With swiftly returning courage, he marched onward. He found the right spot and cast the number 12 Adams fly out on the blue-green ripples. On the third cast, he hooked a twelve-inch cutthroat and banked it. The fishing was good. In thirty minutes he had five ten- to fifteen-inchers in his creel. Then the toothless cowboy rode up. He and his horse wore only what they needed, chaps for the brush, hat for the sun, rope for the cows—utility personified. He dismounted. Luther guessed him to be about his age—late thirties—even though he looked about fifty.

Legend has it that cowboys don't speak unless spoken to. Some accountants and bulldozer mechanics are like that, too. This 'un wasn't. He introduced himself and right off wanted to know what Luther's line of work was. Luther didn't know how to tell him that he'd graduated from college when he was eighteen, that he'd been in the Peace Corps, was an editor at Cambridge, Harper and Row, the University of Oklahoma Press, and was now doing an outstanding job as the director of the University of New Mexico

Press. He was also a dead shot with a pistol and a right handy outdoors-man any way you looked at it. He had been raised in the Kentucky hills on a creek halfway between his aunt's cathouse and a preaching uncle's church. Luther told the cowboy none of this, even though he speaks seven languages fluently. He simply said in plain English, "I work for a school in Albuquerque."

The cowboy accepted this in his own way, replying, "Had any luck, professor?" obviously referring to the fishing. Luther proudly showed the creel of fish. "Welllll now, ain't that somethin'? Professor, you oughta be teachin' fishin.'"

Luther went on about his casting while they "visited."

The cowboy asked, "Say, what kinda pistol is that?"

Luther said, "It's a .44 Magnum. I'm wearing it because the game warden told me this is where they turn loose all the mean bears they remove from Yellowstone."

"Yep, that's right. I had a lot of trouble with 'em myself. Tore up our line camp twice . . . that is, they tore up what they didn't eat up. Headquarters sent us a big guard dog. Tied him to a stump right in front of the door. Thuh boss said he was a mean sucker. Never did know for sure."

Luther said, "How's that?"

"Rode in late one evenin' and that dog was plum gone. Welllll, not alto-gether—there was a little bit of hair stuck to the end of the rope."

Luther decided in mid-cast he'd change animals. He said, "Saw a moose this morning."

"A moose? Say, I did something a while back I been wantin' to do for years." Luther turned his head to him and waited expectantly. "By God, I roped one of 'em," he said, beaming through his squinty eyes and chomping his toothless gums in pure pride. Suddenly concentrating, he asked, "Say, professor, you didn't happen to notice if that sucker was still wearing my rope?"

Luther's negative answer brought a change of subject. "Say, did you spot our line camp down below here?"

Luther acknowledged that he had.

"Was there two pickups there? A blue 'un and a green 'un?"

"No. There was only a green one."

The cowboy tied his horse to a bush and shaking his head in a worried way, said, "That's what I was afraid of. You see, headquarters sent me a nine-teen-year-old kid name uh Jack a while back and I'll betcha a buffalo nickel he's over in Jackson Hole, a-gittin' drunk. I'm gonna fire him if he comes back—or hunt him up and kill him if he don't."

Luther said, "It sounds to me as if young Jack's a loser either way he goes."

"You got that zactly right, professor."

Luther caught several more fish and noticed it was about lunch time. He had sandwiches, an apple, a banana, and a bottle of wine for the mountain repast. He offered to share with the cowboy.

"Naw, thanks anyway. Outta the habit. Too much bother to carry a lunch where I ride."

"Well, some wine, then?"

"Naw, don't fool with it."

Luther was enjoying the lunch. He poured a plastic cup of wine. The cowboy stared at it like it was a rattlesnake and started another story.

"I was foreman of a jim-dandy outfit in Utah a while back. Had a good wife and bought a little house in town. The wife worked for the phone company . . . made good money. We was payin' everythang out, even the washin' machine and TV. Then me and ole Roger from the Cross W went on a three dayer . . . one of them knee-crawlin', table-grabbin', head-bustin' drunks. You know the kind I mean, professor?"

Luther nodded his head in affirmation. He'd seen people in that condition from Sardi's in New York to Baca's Restaurant in Albuquerque, New Mexico.

As Luther washed down a bite of turkey sandwich with a big swallow of Chablis, the cowboy continued, "Well, ole Roger run outta money right after I did. So we drove over to my house to get some more from the wife. I told Roger to jist wait in the pickup. I'd only be a minute. I knew the wife was home 'cause her car was and there was smoke comin'" out of the fireplace chimney. I knocked on the door till my knuckles was about to swell. Nobody came. I yelled. Nobody answered. I walked around the house trying to find a window to open. They was all locked tighter than a pucker string on a loan shark. The fact is, she was inside and I was out. So when I got to the pickup, Roger asked me if anythang was wrong. Welllll, I didn't want him to fret none so I told him, 'No, everthang is just fine and dandy. I got her locked in where she'll be safe and sound till I git back.'" The cowboy was quiet a minute, then added, "You know what I mean, professor?"

Luther acknowledged that not only did he have understanding, but also a great deal of sympathy.

The cowboy seemed to sense this honest compassion, for he soon went on with his story. "Well, there was a half bottle of whiskey in the pickup seat we thought was too sorry to drink earlier that morning, but we decided its time had come. A glass of water was settin' on the dash, and as I drove by a steep drop I just gave that water a good pitch out the window and told Roger to fill it with that good whiskey. A few days after I was fired, divorced, and had moved to Wyoming I figgered out that my teeth was in that glass of water."

Luther had decided that here was a man that could use some kindness. He caught three more fish and invited the cowboy down to the camp to meet his wife, Judy.

The cowboy took off his chaps and threw them across the saddle. He removed his spurs, buckled the leathers together, and slung them over his shoulder. He walked along beside Luther, leading his horse. This, of course, was utmost politeness because there could be no way he enjoyed this form of transportation. He was quietly thoughtful.

Luther took up the conversation. "You'll like Judy. She's lots of fun, a great cook, and she's sensible, too. She doesn't let any outdoor survival syndrome cloud her common sense. For instance, this morning I took a bath in that creek," Luther pointed to the stream, "but Judy drove into Moose, Wyoming, for a nice warm shower. Now that's sensible . . . because let me testify that creek water at seven o'clock in the morning, after a three-inch snow, will make your hair hurt and turn your blood to bone."

The cowboy gave Luther a long, lonesome look, then mumbled something about Jack being drunk and disgraceful in Jackson Hole. Obviously the runaway Jack was weighing heavily on his mind because he suddenly stopped and asked Luther if he'd teach him to shoot the .44.

He said, "I ain't never fired one like that before, so maybe you'll show me how."

Luther pulled the gun out to explain the basic facts about it. Then he pointed to a small rock under a bush about ninety feet distance, saying, "Not much chance, but we'll try for that."

Luther took the .44 in both hands, raised the sights above the rock, and as he came down to it, pulled the trigger. Although he knew he was a damned good shot he never expected to hit the small rock at that distance. To his pleasant surprise, the rock vanished. Having learned to think fast in many editorial meetings, Luther instantly handed the gun to the cowboy and said, "Your turn."

The cowboy tightened both hands on the bridle reins, thinking just as fast: "I better not. My horse is gettin' boogered."

Luther could have seen the truth in that from a mile away.

Finally they were in camp. The cowboy, the professor, and Judy hunkered around the late afternoon camp fire. Crystal Creek, now purple-black, gurgled by whispering in unknown tongues. Way off west, the snow-peaked Grand Tetons tore at the sky like a row of great shark's teeth. The falling sun blushed the mountain tips orange a moment before retiring. A coyote howled at eternity.

Luther was frying the fresh trout. Judy was getting a pan of sliced potatoes ready for the fire. The cowboy held a big mug of steaming coffee and
stared at the bottle of Jim Beam residing on a low camp table. Judy poured a
shot of bourbon into her glass of soda. Luther picked up the bottle, twirling
the liquid, studying it like a chemist, then tilted it up for three good gulps,
finishing with a satisfying "Aaaaaahh."

Judy and the cowboy hit it right off since they were both from Oklahoma.
He was born near Enid and she grew up on a stock farm at Chickasha.

The cowboy explained that he really needed his wayward hired hand
back, since they had to ride all the time to keep the cattle shoved back out
of the flats into the mountains. The high country was for summer grazing,
so when the snow came there would be grass left in the flats for winter forage. Young Jack was sure throwing everything in a bind and the cowboy was
worried about his double workload.

They ate and drank. Luther, warmed by the food, the fire, and the Jim
Beam, told Kentucky hillbilly stories of his childhood, and Judy, a much
sought-after CPA, chipped in with bits of her country background.

Luther kept the firewood coming while Judy cleaned up the dishes. She
turned to the cowboy and asked once more, "Are you sure you wouldn't like
a drink?"

The cowboy smiled, shook his head and replied, "No, thank you, ma'am,
but I am sorely tempted to let loose." He paused a moment before continuing. "This puts me in mind of my old Uncle Pete. He was one of the
fightin'est, drinkin'est, woman chasin'est rounders in that part of the hill
country, but what he was really known for was his cussin'. He could peel
the bark off trees and make a preacher go deaf. One day he was crossin' this
little river on the edge of town with a truckload of apples when the tailgate
came loose. The whole bed of apples went floating down the river. Uncle
Pete crawled out on the hood and stared at all that work and profit floating
away like autumn leaves. The town folks never seen him quiet like this when
he was mad. They commenced to gather around waiting for the explosion of
cussin' that was sure to shame all others before it. They waited till they was
in nervous shambles. Uncle Pete jist sat and sat. Then finally, he stood up on
the hood of the truck, took his hat off, and said, 'Sorry, folks, I jist ain't up

to the occasion.'" Having made his point, the cowboy's stare now alternated from the fire to the bottle.

Soon pickup gears could be heard grinding in the near distance. Finally the cowboy broke his silence as he reached over and picked up the bottle, saying, "Welllll . . . on second and third thought I might just . . ."

The gears ground close now and then lights flared luminous fingers through the trees. The cowboy held the bottle stiffly halfway to his mouth as if he'd been suddenly petrified in that position.

The lights moved up and stopped. A door slammed on the blue pickup and a young cowboy came forward at a strange gait. Here was a man who could walk, dance, and stumble all at the same time. It was young Jack and he looked like he'd been in dedicated training to commit suicide.

Jack moved right up to the fire with his hands out. He snorted and yelled at the cowboy, "Aha! There you go again!"

The cowboy lowered the bottle, giving Luther a sick "I told you so" look. Luther urgently removed the bottle from the cowboy's hand and passed it to an appreciative Jack who tilted it up in a toast, saying, "Thanks, pardner. We better drink this up before he ruins his life . . ." Jack took a long drink and then gasped out, "Again."

Luther smiled knowingly at the cowboy. "Might as well let the song play itself out."

The cowboy threw a pebble in the fire, tipped his hat back off his head, and scratched underneath it, saying, "I see what you mean, professor."

The night birds called. The dark mountains listened.

Showdown at Hollywood Park

T he race was at Hollywood Park, and it was a classic. In its excitement, color, conniving, and later importance it had to be one of the top-matched quarter horse races of all time. The head-on bet of one hundred thousand dollars by the owners was chicken sprinkling compared to the vast amounts gambled on the side by the country boys for their favorite brush-track quarter horse, Barbara B, and the city slickers for their imported thoroughbred, Fair Truckle.

It all began in Texas. Barbara B's trainer, Lyo Lee, was in Houston waiting to see if the Texas legislature would legalize pari-mutuel betting in the state. The racing crowd was eagerly anticipating success. Lyo was there to have his horses ready before anyone else, but the bill failed to pass, leaving Lyo with twenty-five good horses and not much to do but try to scare up a few match races. That's when the call came from Ray Bell that would start it all.

Ray was a commission buyer, mainly in Europe, for such stables as C. S. Howard, the wealthy San Francisco entrepreneur and owner of Fair Truckle; and Louis B. Mayer, the movie mogul head of MGM Studios. At that time, Mayer was the highest-paid corporate officer in America, drawing down over a million a year. He had many stars under contract—Clark Gable, Joan Crawford, Spencer Tracy, and Katharine Hepburn, to name a few. Just four years later the ironfisted Mr. Mayer would see his power begin to erode because of his love for horses and horse racing.

Lyo and Ray Bell were longtime friends, but even if they hadn't been, Mr. Lee would have given him a good listening. This man dealt with wheels . . . the kind that breathe the dust that money is made from.

Ray knew Lyo was looking for some races, so he passed on the comments C. S. Howard had made about his fancy horse, Fair Truckle, after winning a thoroughbred race and leading from wire to wire. "When you go all the way to Ireland to buy a horse you're going to race in the U.S.A., you expect him to be good, and I'd like to see some of those smart-ass quarter horse men try to take him." Fair Truckle was good. He was unbeaten. He'd shown the roots of his tail to all contestants.

After the phone conversation with Ray, Lyo got moving. He called Barbara B's owner, Roy Gill, and told him they had a good chance to get a big win here if they played it right.

Roy Gill's Arizona family had huge cattle feed lots and farms all over. They were big. Roy got into racing with Lyo as his trainer, buyer, and all-around man, so he could have extra money—lots of it—to play with. He didn't want to draw money from the family empire just to gamble with. He knew this would be heavily resented. He lived the highest life his winnings could buy wherever he was. There were always lots of lovely ladies in his presence, and some of these were escorted by men with much political muscle and moola.

Roy Gill didn't especially care about the art or sport of racing. It was a money machine to him. He expected to win and Lyo Lee delivered for him over 95 percent of the time. Gill wouldn't bet less than ten thousand a race. So, with anything below that Lyo was on his own. Gill took care of all expenses and Lyo received 10 percent of the winnings, including the side bets made by Gill. Since Lyo was one of the best trainers in the world (he finally wound up with over five thousand lifetime wins) and Roy was one of the finest spenders, it was a marriage made in horse heaven. At one time their stable had five of the top ten quarter horses listed in the Quarter Horse Journal. Among them were Tonta Gal and the great horse Pelican. When they cemented their partnership, Roy Gill had only one instruction for Lyo: "Win."

Lyo had some advice for Gill as well: "Anytime we find a horse that can outrun you, buy him. This rapidly eliminates the competition."

In further phone conversations with Ray Bell, Lyo learned that C. S. Howard wanted to run Fair Truckle at anything they had, but would bet no less than fifty thousand dollars with ten thousand up front as forfeit money. That put a lot of pressure on Lyo. He wasn't about to recommend to Gill they match the race until he'd done a thorough job of checking.

He went first to the Racing Year Book. Fair Truckle had been running at good West Coast tracks: Santa Anita, Golden Gate, and Hollywood Park. These tracks were all clocked with electric timers and the year book gave the exact time at every turn and quarter pole. These tracks all had a running start of twenty to seventy feet from the gate before the timer started. At Hollywood Park that distance was forty-nine feet. Fair Truckle was running the first quarter in 21.3 and 21.4 and had never been behind up to the three-quarter pole.

Barbara B had never been timed with a running start. So Lyo got ready and gave her a go with the forty-nine-foot advance. Well, guess what? Her time would make scavengers and gold watchmakers look wildly around and rub their hands together. Twenty-one flat, it was, and on a lot worse racetrack than the Irish-bred Fair Truckle had been using. Interest picked up around the Roy Gill and Lyo Lee stables like a banker's loan. Lyo didn't want this information spread around, but he wasn't worried. He said, "I had my help tied up so I could control 'em . . . not exactly a dictator, but close."

Lyo called Ray Bell and told him, "We'll run Fair Truckle in Texas for a hundred thousand." Gill was putting up fifty of this and a few close friends were picking up the other half.

Howard turned this down. He said he would only race at Hollywood Park under their rules and with their officials. He said he didn't want to risk such a valuable horse on rough country tracks. After further consultation with Lyo, Gill agreed to go to California. Then another of the many snags came up. California pari-mutuel racing was only for thoroughbreds, not quarter horses, so the racing commission refused to let them race during the meet or any other time. However, the go-between, Ray Bell, went to Louis B. Mayer and some of his rich, politically powerful cohorts, and an agreement was finally reached that the race could be run on Monday, August 6, 1947, the day after the big meet closed.

Gill, Lyo, jockey Tony Licata, Barbara B, and the rest of the crew arrived in California with everyone doing his own special job. Roy's was a little easier than the rest—he was there to gamble and have fun. He was a master at the latter and, with Lyo Lee's help, first-rate at the former.

Roy Gill had let his sixteen-year-old daughter come to the races with him. She wanted to be in on the thrill of mixing with the Hollywood celebrities and high rollers. She mixed a little too well to suit her father. One of the younger men of the thoroughbred group mesmerized her into falling in love with him. Gill tried, to no avail, to convince her that the young man only wanted inside information about the race. To prove it, Gill offered to bet the suitor five thousand dollars, headup. Surprisingly, he took the bet.

By now word was out all over the quarter horse world about the big race. Phones rang back and forth from the California stables to all points, concerning every little rumor and chip of gossip. The match-race crowd, the bookies, the habitual, and the part-time gamblers were all astir anticipating the day of action with almost a carnal craving. Finally the old, old question about the difference between a quarter horse and a thoroughbred had a chance to be answered. The press was picking up on the vast interest and excitement this race was creating. This put even more charge in the betting batteries.

C. S. Howard resided in San Francisco, so Lyo Lee drew up the contract himself and flew up to deliver it personally. The substance of it was that they'd use the seven and nine gates set exactly on the quarter pole. The post position would be decided in the paddock after the horses were saddled. This way no one would have the time or opportunity to alter the track to his own advantage. On a few rare occasions at match races, when the gate number had been decided in advance, the ground had been dug up soft and deep in front of it and then smoothed over to look untouched.

Howard admitted he was afraid that some of these match-race guys would attempt to trick him, so Lyo tried, in front, to make everything as up-and-up as possible. He included everything—the money, the track timer, the officials—that had already been verbally agreed. In spite of all Lyo's care, Howard refused the contract. He insisted the gates be left where they were— forty-nine feet back of an even quarter mile.

This would change the outside bettor's opinion of the race, most agreeing that the longer it was, the better chance Fair Truckle had. Howard and his people figured that Barbara B would slow at the quarter marker whether she was ahead or behind, and be slowing every foot after.

Lyo argued that this gate situation hadn't been mentioned until now and he complained, truthfully, that they would be out a lot of money in time, travel, and wages if the race was called off now. It did no good. Howard was adamant. He was what the town fellers call a "worthy adversary." Howard was a tough and clever man. He was also rich and powerful, having bailed

General Motors out of a hole after World War I. He got a large block of stock and a percentage of every GMC car sold in California.

Lyo flew back to see Gill in L.A. feeling like he'd swallowed a beehive—honey, bees, and all. He convinced Roy that they could beat Fair Truckle anyway, because he already knew that Barbara B could go three-eighths. Lyo had saved back this secret information to put with his other forty-nine-foot ace he had in the hole.

Lyo flew back to San Francisco and told Howard, "Well, it was tough, but I've finally convinced my people to go along with your terms."

Howard okayed the contract and they each deposited ten thousand dollars with the racing commission in L.A. If one defaulted before post time, he lost the money and, of course, there would be no race. The rest of the money was to be put up on race day. Then after they left the paddock everybody was on his own provided there wasn't an official foul in the actual race. The latter was included in the contract. They would take urine and saliva tests after the race as well. There would be no pari-mutuel betting, but the gates were open free to everyone.

The electricity was bouncing through the air. This race was crucial to advancing the status of the quarter horse, and could be the vital element needed for the legislature to pass the bill accepting the quarter horse into the pari-mutuel racetracks. At this time, the only places they could run under the pari-mutuel system were Tucson and Albuquerque.

It was in Albuquerque, in fact, that Lyo discovered Barbara B. She was entered in a handicap. Tom Snow owned her and they happened to be in the stall next to Lyo. He noticed, when they were shoeing her, that her feet were extra tender. She came in fourth, even with her feet in that condition. Lyo knew that here was a hell of a horse. He bought her for Roy Gill, at the extremely high price for the day of six thousand dollars. Barbara B was out of the stud B'ar Hunter II and a Wagonner ranch mare with rumors abounding that the dam had once sold for thirty dollars. Lyo patiently got her feet in shape and they started winning races.

Cal Kennedy, a horse trainer friend of Lyo's, came to him about a week before the "big 'un" with some information he thought Lyo might enjoy cogitating upon. Lyo knew Cal to be a knowledgeable man who would take every legal advantage to win a race—as who didn't in this world of worried inches.

Kennedy trained a horse named Three Bars. He'd run him three times against Fair Truckle at five-eighths. Each race Fair Truckle had taken him, but also each time Three Bars had been lapped onto him at the quarter-mile pole. Now Kennedy was all for his old friend Lyo, but he wanted to make a bunch of money by gobbling up a cinch. He explained that the only way to do this was to run Barbara B and Three Bars. If she couldn't take him, then the Gill and Lee stables better forfeit their ten grand and head for Texas, turning back a few thousand bettors on their way out. A dilemma, indeed. Lyo was under a glorious type of pressure from all angles.

"How much will she have to outrun Three Bars to be a contender against Fair Truckle?" Lyo asked Kennedy.

"A couple of lengths," he replied.

To keep Barbara B company, Lyo had hauled Tonto Gal out in the trailer and stabled her right next to the mare at Hollywood Park. Lyo didn't really want to give away any of his position, but when he made up his mind to go with something, he put all he had into it. He decided to run Tonto Gal with Barbara B and Three Bars.

Very early that morning, a lot of race barn folks saw the three horses heading for the quarter pole in front of the gate and being lined up for the run. People were yelling and looking for stopwatches to time the race. (Just what Lyo didn't want to happen.) Over a hundred of them watched the event.

Lyo decided to run Tonto Gal in case Barbara B got a bad start; he could still make a fair judgment because most of the time the two mares were only a head or neck apart.

Barbara B outran Three Bars by three lengths and Tonto Gal was lapped right on her. So now Lyo had what appeared to be a slick gut cinch . . . but instead of having twenty- or thirty-to-one odds, they were now dropping to even. Most of the track habituates knew Three Bars and a few seconds before had thought of Barbara B as a dog cow pony whom Fair Truckle could outrun like breaking sticks. That had all changed. The word flew out like a West Texas sandstorm.

The noted sportswriter Ned Cronin, who did stories for Pathe News and many large daily papers, dropped by the barn and asked Lyo, "Has she ever been in a starting gate?"

Lyo answered, "Think so—once or twice before we got her, but I'm not sure."

"Do you use a stock saddle or a racing saddle on her?"

"Oh, whatever's handy." Lyo knew that Cronin was only halfway putting him on, but he liked the reporter and played the game with him.

Cronin asked, "Did you ever rope any calves or steers on her?"

Lyo grinned and said truthfully, "Naw, I haven't rodeoed in years."

Lyo was having too many visitors around the barn now. Friends and acquaintances—hundreds of them—were beginning to arrive from all over the Southwest. The wealthier of these would be staying at the Coliseum Hotel on Figueroa Street in downtown L.A., because that's where Roy Gill and his "partying" party were headquartered. So were Lyo and his wife, but the last two nights he would stay at the barn with his horse. There were too many things that could happen to an unattended animal when hundreds of thousands of dollars were already laid down, and several million were yet to come. Lyo's pressures increased hourly.

Then another, more deadly form of squeeze play unexpectedly entered the game. Two finely dressed men came to the barn. One carried a large black leather folding bag. With extreme politeness they asked to speak with Lyo in private. He took them to the tack room.

The man placed the bag down, saying, "You see this? It contains five hundred thousand dollars. Now all we want is a guarantee. Just guarantee us which horse will win the race and this bag and its contents are yours."

Lyo felt like he'd been gored by a Spanish bull; and he heard the gates of heaven swing shut behind him at the same time. After a bit, he convinced the two money men that he'd need the night to think it over. They reluctantly agreed and left.

Now there was only one way he could guarantee the outcome of the race and that, of course, was to have the jockey hold the mare back. In spite of the race tests with Three Bars, where they were as close to a cinch as they could get, many strange things could happen to cost a man the race. Lyo had been in the game too long and too intensely not to know this.

He would spend a rough night. With half a million dollars, he could go to a tropical island and be a minor king. He could envision the dancing girls and feel the soft, warm sea breezes. Various temptations oscillated before his eyes, and he was truly entranced. On the other hand, he wouldn't be free to roam the country matching races anymore. The excitement of having a horse come from behind in the stretch and pound on to win with good odds would no longer be his. Doubt settled in like a Malibu fog. Then, too, there were all the people he'd dealt with over the years who'd had faith in his talents . . . most of them here at Hollywood Park now betting on his abilities as a trainer. The golden sparkling thoughts of the islands washed caressingly across him again. Indecision. Agony.

The next morning he told the bag men to forgive him, but he just couldn't go along. Surprisingly, they made only one more pitch, then left. Of course, Lyo would feel a chilled ghost over his shoulder until the race was run.

The flag was to fall at 2:25 that afternoon. By eleven o'clock that morning there were over five thousand people at the track to watch the only race for the day. The final number of the gathering was estimated by different writers to be between 7,000 and 25,000. Lyo Lee figured the unpaid attendance at about 20,000. It was a tentless circus. Heavy newspaper coverage had brought a lot of the spectators, but several thousand were there by word of mouth. The quarter horse enthusiasts from every southwestern state showed up to back their favorite Barbara B. The West Coast thoroughbred people and the rich, clubby followers of the financial wizard, C. S. Howard (justifiably known as Mr. Seabiscuit), arrived in even greater force. They didn't have as far to come, however.

This was an unofficial meet . . . two horses and one race. The money would either flow from the pockets of the booted, broganed, wrinkled-suit crowd to the Brooks Brothers and silk shirt set, or vice versa.

The Fair Truckle followers were almost smug in their betting—and why not? They'd never seen anything ahead of their hero in nine races from wire to wire. The quarter horse boosters were more enthusiastic. One was heard to say that the brown, four-year-old mare could beat that "Eurrrupeein' horse pullin' a plow." Another said, showing considerable confidence, that Barbara B could win by a length and stop twice to graze on the way.

The movement of mouths and tongues was matched by arms and hands reaching in and out of pockets counting money and layin' it down. There was a vast kaleidoscope of color, erratic and pulsating movement, and a chattering symphony of sound made up of laughter, bantering, bragging, and ridicule. It was almost as if two massive brains were in mortal money-crazed conflict: one controlling the Fair Truckle crowd and the other manipulating the Barbara B bunch. It would finally boil down, though, to the more concentrated gray matter of the city-sharpened Mr. Howard and the brush-and-bramble-seasoned Mr. Lee. The fact that Howard had bought the great horse Seabiscuit when he appeared to be no good and with his trainer had turned him into one of the fastest of all stake racers also enhanced this race.

The jockeys and horses are always expected to give their best in every race, but according to a perpetual racetrack yarn that started that day, Tony Licata could collect all honors for the most dedicated jockey of all. He was having trouble making the 114-pound weight for the race, so it was bandied about that he went out and had all his teeth pulled to lessen the pounds. (He did ride the race without his dentures.) Here was a racehorse man from the hocks to the gums. He was getting eight thousand dollars for the race, win or lose. He'd bet every penny of it.

The even money was changing hands by the barrel, and the only way to get odds was to bet on the length of the win. That's the way it was until the horses entered the paddock. It took two men to hold Fair Truckle while he was readied, while Barbara B, always the lady, took the money-changing madness around her with such calmness that she looked like a sleepy, dead-headed cow pony. Deception unlimited. Between the paddock and the starting gate the Barbara B clan got odds on hundreds of thousands of dollars at four or five to one. Lyo had held off betting until this moment. Again, figuring ahead, he had a friend get down ten thousand for him at three to one.

Billions of tiny bolts of lightning were heating the blood of thousands of people with the oldest passion in the world—contest fever. Unless there was a dead heat, one horse would have to chase the other.

As agreed in the contract, they had to flip a coin for the choice of a post position: gates nine and seven. Lyo was anxious to win the toss. Fair Truckle, having always come out of the gate ahead and leading all the way, naturally charged to the rail—the shortest route around the track. So if he had to cut across from the nine gate instead of the seven, he would have a little bit more ground to cover. Lyo Lee's mother had not raised an unthinking son. He had taken this into consideration. Neither had C. S. Howard's mama birthed a son without the thought process. Where Lyo was hoping to gain maybe a few feet with the gate choice, C. S. had already fudged in a forty-nine-yard head start. Lyo won the coin toss and picked the number seven gate.

Now the horses left the paddock and the thoroughbred crowd became more fired up because Fair Truckle was prancing and dancing, led by a pony horse whose rider was having a little trouble. Barbara B just strolled along with her head down and the reins slack like a worn-out ranch horse.

The track looked fast, but Lyo had tested it carefully and found it cushiony underneath. He told the groom that there'd be no timed records set today, but the money being bet would break all gambling records on a match race.

Because he'd won the seven gate, Lyo loaded the mare first. She stood there calmly. Fair Truckle, on the other hand, was really acting up. When they finally got him in, he hung a hock in the gate. So they had to let him out and walk him around to see if he was all right. Several thousand hearts froze! He didn't limp, so they decided to go ahead and run him. During this little ceremony, Barbara B seemed to be catnapping.

They were off! Barbara B was neither a fast starter nor a slow one. Fair Truckle came out of the gate a good neck in the lead. There was just one thing, though, as Lyo had said: "Barbara B reached full speed at the third jump and would be running faster at that point than any horse I'd ever seen. She was also hitting a stride of twenty-four and a half feet by then . . . I'd measured it many times. And that's how she won most of her races."

Because of the extra forty-nine feet, the gates were set back in a straightaway chute from the main track. By the time they hit that point, Barbara B had leaped out in front by a little over a length.

The great jockey, Johnny Longden, felt he now had a problem. He sure did! Fair Truckle had never been hit with the whip. Since he was always out front, there had never been a reason for it. Now there was, Longden figured. When he tapped Fair Truckle, he ducked in behind Barbara B and went to the rail. That move increased Barbara B's lead by another length as Lyo had anticipated.

The country crowd went slap-dab crazy. The stadium waltzed and the air was shredded into slivers by the roar. Fair Truckle really put out. He pulled up almost neck and neck and held there.

Now it was the thoroughbred's touts' turn to shake the earth and create vacuums in the air. The horses were sailing along on even terms, so that now everyone could go mad at once.

Then! Then Tony Licata smacked Barbara B right across her gearbox with the whip. Ned Cronin wrote about it in the Los Angeles Daily News the next day. "Somewhere in Barbara B's clouded past there is a jackrabbit among her forebears. There's got to be. How else could she cut loose with a jump that almost took her out of her hide? As that jackrabbit blood bubbled and boiled through her veins, she sprang with a few such prodigious leaps that they carried her under the wire an easy winner by two and a half lengths in the respectable time of 21 and 3/5ths seconds."

Payday at the mines! Wild and good times for the Barbara B's. Lyo Lee, Tony Licata, and the lady with four fast legs had delivered the baby full grown. Most of the winners had traveled hundreds of miles to bet and sweat their all on less than twenty-two seconds. They'd sliced up C. S. Howard's thoroughbred club elites like venison jerky. The final score: Country team—several million. City team—zero.

There was great rejoicing in and around the Coliseum Hotel that night. Other areas of Los Angeles rang out with resounding victory yells and toasts before the grass and plow folks headed back home.

Roy Gill patted his daughter's suitor on the back as he collected his five thousand, and said, "Why, you're a fine young feller. You come visit us in Arizona some year, you hear?"

Aside from the money, the real significance of the event was that it woke the racing world up to the fact that among all its other multiple and supreme abilities, the quarter horse was also a racehorse. The momentum this highly visible, publicized race gave to the entire quarter horse industry is incalculable.

Ned Cronin and a lot of other journalists broke this fact to the world the next day with satirical force. Too few people remember that this race was instrumental in the legislature legalizing quarter horse pari-mutuel racing in the state of California.

Barbara B went on winning races, but she lost one to Miss Princess in Del Rio, Texas, after stepping on a small round rock and falling to one knee with her nose touching the ground. She still got up and made the acknowledged King ranch Best in the World Champion run for it. In 1950, after Miss Princess retired, Lyo ran the seven-year-old Barbara B against the four-year-old mare Stella Moore for the generally agreed championship of the world at Sunshine Park, in Oldsmar, Florida. Again the national press, including Time magazine, picked up on the story and made several million more people aware of the quarter horse. Barbara B won the 330-yard race by a length and a half in 17.1 seconds.

All this is and should be recognized as a permanent part of quarter horse history. It was a vital part of the action that eventually led to the richest races in the world at Ruidoso Downs, New Mexico, and to the King ranch recently purchasing the two millionth registered quarter horse. Considering the involvement of the West Germans and other countries around the world, in breeding and using this very special breed, the number of three million or more will someday be announced. Even so, it will shower tubs full of hail in hell before a more momentous and exciting race will come along than the great matched shoot-out at Hollywood Park in August of 1947.

Lyo Lee and Barbara B—they made H-I-S-T-O-R-Y.

The Mare

It was the most fantastic story Forest Ranger Joe Healy had ever heard. "It just can't be," he said in stunned disbelief. "Don't you realize if she's over thirty years old, that would make her almost a hundred and twenty in human terms?"

"Yeah, something like that," Randy Lindsey answered. "She does truly exist. I first spotted her tracks about three years ago, and I felt just like you until I finally saw her for real a couple of months back. Yeah, she's up there, all right."

Randy was a young cowboy who worked for Jimmy Bason's F Cross ranch. Bason leased out most of the grassland on his hundred thousand acres, so he needed only his son, Brent, and one extra cowboy to help take care of his small herd. Jimmy was lucky . . . Randy was a "throwback" to the Old West. He liked living by himself in a line shack, and preferred to work with horses instead of a pickup truck. He wanted to carry on the old-time traditions.

The two men were sitting at a table in the one-bar, two-church town of Hillsboro in southwestern New Mexico. The bar also had the only restaurant available for thirty miles.

Ranger Healy knew that Randy would never lie to him about a thing like this, but he found it almost impossible to believe that a horse could have survived, totally alone, for all those years. He leaned forward across the plate of red chile burritos and the bottle of beer, saying softly, "Does anyone else know about this?"

The young cowboy said, "Only Jimmy Bason . . . and he don't want anybody to know. He says the do-gooders and the do-badders will both try to capitalize on her." He paused. "In fact, he'll probably fire me if he finds out I slipped up and told someone."

Joe laughed softly. "You don't have to worry, Randy, I won't tell anybody except my daughter. She's crazy nuts about animals, you know. That's why she's definitely decided to become a vet. And, by dogies, she'll never have another chance to see anything like this. That mare has to be some kind of miracle. My God, even gentle horses that are pampered and cared for don't live that long. I'd say this is about the rarest dang thing I ever heard of. It's like being first in line at the Second Coming. Yeah," Healy said as if to himself, "Pauline's got to see this horse."

Randy reluctantly agreed to describe the area the mare currently habituated. He was unaware that their conversation was being overheard by a vacationing young reporter for an El Paso, Texas, newspaper, who was sitting at the next table with his wife and two children. The young man hurriedly grabbed a pen and pad from his pocket and, with noticeable excitement, started scribbling.

———

Joe Healy drove the pickup, pulling a trailer containing two good saddle horses, as near as the rough terrain would allow, to the designated wilderness area. He and his fifteen-year-old daughter, Pauline, quickly set up camp. They had enough supplies to last over a month if that's what it took to find the wild mare. They had come prepared and totally dedicated.

They rode the piñon- and cedar-covered foothills then made their way up to the edge of the tall pines on the mountain. They roamed for five days looking at the ground, hoping to find a sign of the horse. Even in their anticipation of the latter, they still enjoyed the markings of the other wild creatures. They actually saw twenty or thirty deer, ten elk, a coyote, many kinds of birds, and even glimpsed a black bear disappearing into a patch of heavy timber.

On the sixth day they found her hoofprints. The tracks were at least a week old, but to the Healys, they were as new as first frost. The excitement of discovery surged through all the tissues, nerves, and thoughts of their bodies, but nevertheless, on the seventh day they rested themselves and their horses.

Pauline said, "Daddy, if she's never had a colt, she's still a filly no matter what her age, right?"

"Now don't get technical on me, Pauline. As old as she is, we're gonna call her a mare."

Pauline pushed her long, blond hair back from her face, and said in a soft voice filled with wonder, "She's really out there. We've found her unshod hoofprints. Poor thing . . . all alone. Just think of all the bad weather, and the predators, and the loneliness she has endured, and now she's so old. Wonder how she's done it?" Her blue eyes widened in astonishment at the frightening images.

Joe Healy searched for a special answer for this question, but he could only come up with "It does seem impossible. She must be blessed. That's the answer, Pauline. She's blessed."

Father and daughter rode out of camp at dawn the next day. The two had spent a restless night, but now they were keyed up and tuned in to the whole world. It was mid-afternoon when they found some more recent tracks—these were only a couple of days old. Joe recalled Randy saying, "I was ridin' old Birdie when I cut my first sign of her. I just knew she had to be the last of the wild ones. I never had a feelin' like it before. It was sorta like I'd just invented the first saddle." Healy was having some of the same feelings now. A sense of the primordial permeated his being. He couldn't have been more in awe if he'd just come face to face with a living dinosaur or the Loch Ness monster.

Pauline almost cried aloud, but instead she let the tears rivulet silently down her cheeks. To her it was a sacred moment and she looked up to the heavens. In the distance, she saw several buzzards circling. She lifted her wide, blue eyes above the birds to a patch of sky and then on above that, she saw something that caused her to cry out, "Daddy, look! Look way up there!"

He looked in the direction of her pointing, but his vision missed what she had so briefly seen. His eyes moved, by nature and training, back down to the tracks they had been following. Pauline reined her horse in line. Now her eyes were focused on a movement nearing a huge cumulus cloud. She stared in wonder.

———

The mare was born in the spring of the year the space age dawned. In October 1957 the Russians fired Sputnik I into the heavens. It circled the globe at altitudes ranging from 141 to 588 miles above Moscow and Washington, D.C. It traveled at 14,700 miles per hour. The people of the Soviet Union rejoiced and justifiably felt enormous pride. The Americans were embarrassed and scared. There was an outcry for more defense spending and the whole educational system of the free world to be altered. The emphasis was placed on science. Literature, all the arts, and old-time basic schooling were greatly neglected. The space age and the mare had been born.

Far below on the solid rocks of the Black Range, the colt frolicked, nursed, and grew stronger daily. She did not know, or care, about this monumental change in the world. From the beginning, she was more agile and faster than the other colts in one of the dozen or so scattered bands of wild horses. Her chestnut coat glistened in the sun and her large, dark eyes were full of adventure and mischief.

Her first winter was an easy one with little snow. The horses fared well in the rolling hills between the private ranches and the national forest area, but the springtime came dry and the grass was short.

The ranchers moved their cattle into the wild horses' domain under individual leases with the government. There was competition for the shriveling grass between the wildlife, the mustangs, and the domestic cattle. The ranchers and Forest Service joined forces to get rid of the wild horses.

They built log-pole traps around water holes in an attempt to capture them alive. They tried roping the young, the old, or the lame. This effort only delivered ten head of the wily bunch, and in the process they crippled three cowboys, one ranger, and twenty-two of their tame horses.

The ranchers and Forest Service executives argued over other means to dispose of this threat to the welfare of their cattle and consequently their families. During one of their meetings, word came of a forest fire in the area. It had been started by lightning from a small rain cloud. The flames caused the dry trees and vegetation to snap and pop like infantry machine guns.

One small band of horses was trapped and perished. All living things ran together now, to escape the inferno. Deer, elk, and cattle raced alongside coyotes, bears, and cougars. Rabbits dashed in and out of the flames until some caught fire and fell in kicking, smoking bundles. Everything attempted to escape in a terrible panic. Most small things like lizards, ants, grasshoppers, spiders, tree worms, squirrels, skunks, and nestlings were cooked as black as the forest floor.

The colt raced beside her mother as the dominant stallion of the band circled, squealing commands, kicking, biting, and trying to drive his harem and offspring to safety. The prevailing southwest wind joined in the chaos and whipped the flames in circles and drove them forward with destructive speed. The smoke could be seen one hundred aircraft miles away in El Paso, Texas. Firefighters tried to organize, but their efforts were futile against the raging force.

Then the winds suddenly quit as if on command from the gods and the fire died out at the banks of the North Percha Creek. It had decimated the five-mile width from the upper Animas drainage to the creek. The existing forage would be much sparser now.

The ranchers moved their cattle back to the home ranches with great effort and much loss of weight. The decision was made—the wild horses had to be destroyed. They organized and came with camping gear, horses, and rifles. They rode for weeks driving their prey into the burned areas where they killed them.

Joe Healy's father, John, who was a ranger at the time, led the onslaught. He instructed the rangers and cowboys to try to "bark" the wild horses. That is, shoot them through the top edge of the neck knocking them unconscious so they could be saved for live capture. It didn't work. The fire, followed by the cracking of rifles, the squeals and groans of dying animals, created a madness of desperation. The stallions lost control of their bands and ran about as erratically as their broods. Over a hundred and thirty horses were slaughtered.

The area became, and looked, like a battlefield. What with the dead horses scattered about through the massive burned area and the buzzards gathering from miles around to join the coyotes, bobcats, bears, mountain lions, and other meat-eating predators to feast on the carcasses.

The rangers and ranchers agreed there were none left to scatter the seed. They were wrong by one.

The yearling colt had been barked from a long distance and when she regained consciousness, she raced blindly across the scorched earth through the stench of the rotting bodies and kept on going up and up until the greenness of undefiled timber surrounded her. The sweat had turned to a lather over her entire body and her lungs bellowed in and out in painful gasps.

She kept going until she was deep into the high forest and her legs began to tremble and caused her to fall over and over. Then she stopped. She could move no more. She was sore and weak for several days before she found a spring and enough feed from brush and the scant grass to live. She was totally confused about where she was or what had happened to her world.

Then the late-summer rains came and the earth was soaked, cleansed, and revitalized, and so was the colt. The soreness and the gauntness disappeared. She was alone in several hundred thousand acres of wilderness. But she lived.

The rains made good feeding for the grazers, and the remains of the horses and the other burned animals gave plentiful food to the predators. This one winter, when she needed help so much, the fanged animals had no need of her flesh.

The spring grass and vegetation came again. She was feeding and nourishing her muscles and bones, and rapidly growing into a fine two-year-old equine specimen. She looked better than she felt. The flashes of fire still raced behind her eyes, and over and over she heard the death screams of her mother. Sometimes she would hold her head high, with nostrils straining wide, thinking she smelled the smoke from the scorched forest floor and the rotting flesh of her family and ancestors. After these flashbacks of horror, she would tremble and run about, trying to escape the imagined destruction. Finally, she'd calm and return to her normal watering, feeding, and exercising. The fearful images slowly grew dimmer as she grew older.

She was walking to her secret watering hole when the warning chatter of a tassel-eared squirrel become louder and more urgent. It was October the first, 1961. Roger Maris, who played baseball for the New York Yankees, had just hit his sixty-first home run of the season, breaking Babe Ruth's old record. Just as the standing ovation of the crowd drew him out of the dugout for the second tip of his cap, a heavy force hit the filly on the back.

The mountain lion had leapt from a limb above her and dug his front claws deep into her neck. His rear claws were locked into her hips. With powerful, open jaws and long, meat-ripping fangs he reached for the place where the neck bones join the skull. The instant she felt the force of the lion's weight, and the sharp pain of its claws, she bolted straight into a heavy growth of young trees. Before the lion could close his jaws on the death spot, a limb smashed into his forehead and dragged him off her back. In so doing, the claws raked through her hide and into raw flesh plowing permanent lines and eventual scars on both sides of her neck. The claw cuts were painful for a while, with the swelling and draining, but they healed. From then on, her mind was alerted to the warning sounds from other possible victims of predators.

The five-mile-wide and ten-mile-long burnt area had come back lush green. The grass and brush had fought the timber seedlings for space and won. The small surviving trees were scattered widely apart. All the new growth made, for a few years at least, lush summer grazing. For a long time she spent as much of her life here as possible. The trees were so far apart that

she could watch for the death drop from above and avoid the tearing claws of the lion. The deer felt as she did, and grazed right alongside her. In the fall and early winter she and the other foraging creatures would move high up, out of the healed area, and feast on the oak brush and mountain mahogany pine, putting on fat to hold them through the sometimes hard winters.

She wasn't so lonely anymore. She had the company of wild turkeys, band-tailed pigeons, quail, squirrels and chipmunks, blue jays and mountain grouse, hawks and eagles. Some of the creatures lived at all altitudes, changing locations with the seasons and the food growth, while others were found at only certain heights in special terrain. There were many creatures here she would have to study in order to live out her allotted span of years.

Fortunately, she had found a secluded spring soon after the earlier holocaust. The timber and rocks, while completely encircling it, sat well back from the watering hole. On this special terrain she could drink peacefully, knowing that she wouldn't suffer a sudden attack. She maintained a constant alertness as far as her knowledge at this point allowed.

In late September, she went to the spring and found it frozen over. This was a new surprise . . . another type of warning she must learn to heed. There was much more danger on this mountain than the long-toothed predators, and after this winter she would always remember that early ice and falling leaves, along with higher, more frigid winds, meant heavy storms soon. She didn't have that knowledge frozen into her genes at the time the great snow came.

The dark clouds moved in formation, low, caressing, over the peaks, like Alexander's legions. And underneath them the wind fought with the trees, thrashing them about in agony and sending the flying things coasting up and away on its mad currents. But below, where the wind was less, many of the four-footed animals failed to move out in time.

The snow stuck for a moment on the millions of branches and limbs before being shaken loose by the wind over and over, thousands and thousands of times. The white, frozen crystals were swept and piled into massive drifts higher than the mare's head. She was all right for a few days, pawing the snow down to the little clumps of bunchgrass and oak brush.

She rapidly consumed all edible food in the small radius she was able to control. Soon she had to struggle harder, pawing into the deeper drifts.

Her exertions caused rapid weight loss. Her lungs had to pump more warm air, which formed ice crystals around her nostrils and eyes, restricting her breathing and vision. She was in a white, frozen world and was quickly turning into an immobile ice sculpture.

She could only paw feebly now, and began to lose interest in making any effort at all. She was dozing. Her weakened neck allowed her head to drop down almost to knee level. She felt warm, dry, and totally without concern for food or anything else. Soon one foreleg slid out to the side. She was teetering with her whole body about to fall over, but she felt as if she was running in the summer warmth again with the gray male colt. They were jumping about, dodging and chasing each other with their short tails in the air, and heads up like the royal British mounts. They were full, free, and safe. It was a glorious moment.

Suddenly, then, she was certain that she smelled the smoke, envisioned the fire, and heard the squeals and screams again for the first time in months. The fear became so real she began actually running from it. Then she whirled and ran back toward it, craving its imagined warmth. After bursting through drift after drift, she began to feel the cold again, but kept plunging through the forest down, down, always down. Eternity returned. She now fought to reach lower ground as years before she had struggled for the high.

Her lungs pained terribly as she sucked in more and more frozen air, just as she had once breathed the hot ashes and fire-scorched winds. As before, there came a point where her afflicted lungs could not supply enough fuel to keep her body moving. She stood quivering, and made loud gasping sounds as she tried to take in the warmer air of the foothills.

When she could finally see again, she discovered that the drifts were much smaller here. There would be no problem pawing through to the grass and even some of the bushes could be reached with hardly any effort at all. She survived until spring once again. Never, not once, would she be trapped in the high country by the felonious storms.

By spring, she had gained back almost all her weight and strength when she spotted two black bear cubs climbing over and around a dead log, chasing and cuffing one another about in the purest of fun. One fell, hanging on just a moment before tumbling the short distance to the ground. The

mare, feeling good after the grinding winter, eased forward in a friendly gesture to the cub. They had barely touched noses when the little bear whirled and scampered away, and the mare heard the loud "whoof." The sound was followed by a blasting slap to her side and neck. The mama bear had been plunging downhill at such speed that her swipe at the mare was slightly off. The blow to the horse's neck and ribs had not been the solid finishing strike the bear had intended. Even so, it knocked the mare stumbling to the side. Her neck and ribcage were numbed where the mighty paw of the five-hundred-pound beast had struck.

As the bear whirled back to finish the mare off with her teeth and foreclaws, she received an unpleasant surprise. The mare's adrenaline had flushed up ancient resources of genes. An old experience imparted the knowledge to her brain that her numbed body could not outrun the bear. She whirled and started kicking back toward her attacker. The bear stuck her lower jaw right into one of the mare's hooves when it was at its apex of power. The bones cracked like a bull elk stepping on a tiny dry stick. The other hoof caught her on the left eye, chipping the skull around the socket in several places and knocking the bear's remaining vision askew. In a few weeks the coyotes got the cubs and the buzzards discovered the starved body of the mother bear.

The mare's left shoulder had torn tendons that caused her great pain as she traversed the uneven ground trying to feed. Another wide scar undulated with the muscles beneath the skin from the blow of the bear. Since she hadn't fully recovered from the decimation of the winter, it would be late summer before the scar healed and the soreness left her.

By early October, she was well and sufficient winter fat was already on her bones. With this recuperation also came a feeling of longing. Something was missing—something that was a part of her—something that she had every right to be sharing. The vacancy left an aching in her heart, her womb, and her animal soul.

She thought she saw a blur of her own kind, her own blood, in the bushes and trees, but no matter how hard she looked and searched, the images she ached to define would not come clear. This ineluctable feeling pervaded her all during, and past, the twenty-second of October, 1962, when the Cuban missile crisis began. President John F. Kennedy ordered the blockading of Cuba and revealed the discovery of Soviet missile bases on Cuban soil through air reconnaissance photos. The president went on television and gave media interviews in the Oval Office. The two leaders of the superpowers exchanged many accusations and threats. The hearts of the world stood still in dread.

For six days, the mighty powers threatened and blustered. U.S. bombers, loaded with atomic bombs, flew patterns up to the edge of Soviet territory by the hour. The warships were about to pair off for battle. The Russians, vastly outnumbered in the nuclear bomb category at the time, held out six days before they gave in. Never before had the world been so close to destruction in just a few minutes of madness. It has been debated ever since whether Kennedy saved the world by calling the Russians' bluff or gave it away by not taking Cuba while it was in his grasp.

During the six days of worldwide tension, the mare grazed contentedly and enjoyed the cool nights and warm days of autumn in peace. The forest has many eyes and ears, watching, listening, always aware, and now she knew how to use them to her advantage. These animals would voice the movements of danger to her instantly. She only had to listen and act to be safe.

As the other world started breathing again, but as yet looking over their collective shoulders, the mare spent a mild winter with plenty of forage. When spring came, some tiny bit of fat was still left under her long winter hair. She would soon be slick and shiny.

———

After many years of gaining knowledge through painful experiences and her natural force of observation, she finally chose her favorite spot for repose. About halfway down, between the jagged peaks of the high mountains and the lower meadows, there was a mesa with Mimbres Indian ruins on top. From here she could walk around the edges of the pueblito and observe the far-spreading wilderness in every direction, just as the Indian occupants once had.

Here in her part of southern New Mexico, hundreds of these ruins existed. Some archaeologists dated them back a thousand years, but the exact time period is as much in dispute as how an entire nation of mostly peaceful Indians vanished completely. They did leave behind their rock houses, burial grounds, stone and bone tools, arrowheads, and traces of jewelry. However, there were very few implements of actual war. Their main gifts to history were their wonderfully constructed and uniquely designed black-on-white pottery.

Here in the ancient ruins, the mare felt a comfort and peace greater than in any other spot in her domain. When the hidden blood longings and blurred visions came to her, she headed to this spot to share it with the ghosts of its former inhabitants like retreating to a Benedictine monastery. She heard drums and chants and sometimes saw incomplete images in the air, but she didn't know what they were—only that she was comforted.

After the time of the Mimbres and before the time of the satellites, there had been many battles in this part of her range. Geronimo, Chief Victorio, and Old Nana had made this area the last hideout from pursuing cavalry. Only half a mile below her, an isolated squad of buffalo soldiers from the Ninth Cavalry had encountered a small band of Apaches. It became a running battle. A black sergeant named Moses Williams, realizing two of his wounded buffalo soldiers were surrounded, charged back, catching the Apaches by surprise and saving the soldiers' lives. Sergeant Williams was awarded the Congressional Medal of Honor.

In 1963 President John F. Kennedy was assassinated by Lee Harvey Oswald in Dallas, Texas. It shocked a nation and a lot of the world into near paralysis. People will never forget where they were when they heard the news. The mare knew none of this, nor would she have cared, for hers was and had truly been another world. Much more would pass in both dimensions.

The mare was honored in the year of '67 by the weather. The forage was plentiful from the summer rains and the snow of the high country had melted early. She prospered . . . but in the cities of America the flower children came to full bloom, shouting peace and free love, while the rock music cascaded its battering and often deafening beat across the land, and cheap dope altered minds and history forever. In the Haight-Ashbury district of the lovely city of San Francisco, the children lay about the streets with minds bent and bodies so inert they could barely follow up on the prevalent misguided theory of love being free. They had presumably started out innocent and wound up tasting the refuse of the gutters, seeing visions of such complexity that for man there was nothing left but the accidental and sometimes purposeful ultimate quest—suicide.

That same fateful year ended in near tragedy for the aging mare, even more innocently than it had for the children of the streets. She wanted companionship . . . a direct communication of some kind. During one of those periods of deep loneliness, she was craving something like the image she saw reflected in the water as she drank from her favorite spring. That's when she followed and, in a friendly gesture, stuck her muzzle down to a porcupine. The animal with thirty thousand barbs swung its short tail and embedded fourteen of them into the left side of the mare's nostrils and face.

In a couple of days one passage was swelled completely shut and the other barely open so that she gasped for breath even while standing still. She started losing weight and strength immediately. The swelling and pain grew so great that she would rub her face against trees, rocks, bushes, the earth itself, and slink her head in circles trying to dislodge the darts.

Now the coyotes witnessed this and stalked her. They were far too smart to risk her deadly hooves, if she had been well. Due to their small size, they could only down big game when it was ill or injured. By her erratic actions, the coyotes knew she was both. So they patiently circled and watched, for days. Even with all her pain, the mare watched them, too. She turned her rear to them ready to strike out hard with her hind feet.

Slowly, some of the quills worked their way out, while only a few burst open the swelled spots at her rubbing. She was forced to graze solely on bush leaves. It was slow and painful. She was weakening fast.

Finally one coyote leapt at her nostrils. While she was busy with the first, the other tried to hamstring her. The coyote did manage to get hold of her muzzle just long enough to puncture it. This helped the poison ooze out, and the swelling started down. She kicked the other one in the side and sent it rolling down an embankment with three broken ribs. The wise coyotes left her alone and chose to dine, that day, on game already dead.

She could eat better now and gradually the barbs either worked themselves all the way out or a protective gristle formed around them. She became strong again. It seemed that no matter how long she lived and how much knowledge she acquired, there was still wisdom to be gained that could come only from pain. Just the same, she knew, and had survived, most of the deadly dangers of the wilderness at least once. She had paid a highly inflated price to gain a few years of relative tranquility.

The last year of the sixties was a good one for her. Most of her scars and injuries were healed. She spotted a bobcat on a rare daylight foray. It crouched in the grass stalking a quail. That same day Armstrong and Aldrin would complete one of humankind's most sought-after dreams. They landed a spaceship on the moon. Scores of millions of people worldwide were tied with invisible ropes, to their television sets. The bobcat didn't know any more about this than the mare. It was hungry and the solution to that problem hid motionless in the grass some ten feet ahead.

The cat's ears twitched ever so slightly, trying to catch any sound or movement from the intended victim. The soft, furry belly was actually touching the ground at its lowest point. Its short tail switched once as the cat leaped forward. The quail raised up, took three strides, and winged into flight. About four feet off the ground the bobcat's claws hooked into the bird's belly. As they fell back to earth, she locked her jaws on the last flutterings and crouched, holding it tightly as she looked about for any competition. As soon as the bird was dead, the cat took off toward its den in some rocks out of the mare's sight.

That same day, as the mare wandered browsing in the brush, a golden eagle dropped from the sky into an opening, hooked its powerful talons into a fat rabbit, and flew up to some bluffs to dine. The forest gave sudden voice with squirrels and birds chattering, then became cautiously silent again. This was all so natural in her life that the mare took only a cursory glance at the necessary killing. This golden eagle had landed, and so had the one on the moon—one in an action as old as animal history and the other as new as birth. New worlds had surrounded the old forever.

A mother elk tried to graze while her bull calf lunched greedily at her bag with switching tail. Three forest moths played in and out of a sunbeam like happy, little angels. The mare, witnessing all of this, would have fed in contentment except the yearning for something more of her own self struck her several times a month now.

She might have felt better about one human endeavor presently occurring if she had known about it. A lady known as Wild Horse Annie, from Nevada, had raised so much hell, enlisted so many supporters, and grabbed so much attention from the media that a federal law was passed protecting wild horses. Of course, it came far too late for the old mare's immediate ancestors. As her life moved in its eternal cycle of daily survival, the world around her was accelerating with a momentum that seemed to gain in speed like a great boulder rolling down a mighty mountain toward a tiny village.

In 1973 the Arabs put an embargo on oil, and while millions of Americans waited in line for hours at gas stations frustrated and unable to move, the mare browsed on luscious foliage and enjoyed an unhurried, uncluttered existence.

Oil prices escalated, and some poor nations became rich and many rich countries poorer. Wealth shifted about like the hearts of young lovers. The Watergate scandal dethroned a president and his men, changing the political attitudes and history of the free world for decades yet to come.

During these outside occurrences, the old mare had, on several occasions, seen a flash of gray in the timber and brush to the east of her Mimbres ruins lookout. She knew somehow that this was a replica of herself. She felt a kinship here at the ruins, and she had the same feeling for the glimpses of gray. She now took excursions trying to get a solid sight or smell of her illusory relation. But none came—no matter how long she wandered about on swiftly tiring legs, or stared with her dimming eyes, or sniffed with her knotted, scarred muzzle. The only place she could conjure up the flashing vision was from the same spot on the east side of the Mimbres ruins. There only. But she kept on searching, season following season. She would return to the magic spot and wait, sometimes hours, sometimes days, until forced to move away for food and water. But the gray thing began to appear more often. She felt warm and elated at each sighting, even if it was blurred and filmy.

Things had been working in her favor for several years now. A chief forester named Aldo Leopold had written an enormously influential essay titled "The Land Epic." It led to the creation of a huge official wilderness area named after the forester. The mighty Black Range was to the west of the free area. Gerald Lyda's Ladder Ranch, one of the largest and most famous in the Southwest, touched it on many sides. The Cross Triangle joined to the north and Jimmy Bason's to the east. The old mare lived, protected, right in the middle of it all.

Now that no private vehicles could ever enter her area, she sometimes watched the backpackers walking into the Animas Creek area to camp and relish nature. She would watch them through the bushes, standing as motionless as an oft-hunted buck deer. As long as they didn't carry cracking rifles, as did those who hunted yearly in the lower country, they were nothing but a pleasant curiosity to her. Many elk had migrated across the Black Range from the Gila Wilderness to hers. She enjoyed their presence and bugling calls, but it did little to allay the growing sense of an impending personal event.

Friday, September 18, 1987, the two-hundredth anniversary of the Constitution of the United States, the mare spent looking out the canyon from the ruins, hoping her gray companion would show. It was an anxious day for others as well.

The Polish pope John Paul II arrived in San Francisco toward the end of what would probably be his last junket to the United States, amidst about two hundred thousand picketing AIDS victims and sympathizers. The pope kept calm.

Headlines around the nation said that the United States and the Soviets had reached an accord on diminishing the number of missiles in the world.

When the mare had been born into the space age, America had far superior numbers of arms, but now on this day, the Soviets were ahead. Not many people on either side really believed the negotiations were being held for the good of all humankind.

As patriotic parades were held all across the land on this great day, the old mare went on, patiently looking. Then she saw it. Now the gray mist had taken on a little more solidity and form. Her heart beat faster. The figure didn't disappear this time but just inside the bushes as she strained harder than ever before to see and realize what part of her it was.

———

The year of the celebration of the Constitution passed with many wars in effect—in Lebanon, Afghanistan, all over Africa. The Iranians and the Iraqis went on butchering one another and the ships of the world filled up the Persian Gulf supposedly to protect oil tankers for the Western world market. While the old mare looked for her compatriot there were, in fact, over forty blasting, slashing, mind-numbing wars being fought, and oddly mostly ignored by the preponderance of the world population.

The calendar moved on into the presidential election year, with the candidates made up of preachers and lawyers. The old mare's body was as ravaged as the polluted and war-torn earth. The scars on her neck, ribs, and shoulders from the attacks of the lion and the bear looked like little erratically plowed firms. Her back was swayed, her eyes were dull and clouded over. Her once long, flowing mane and tail had been matted and stuck together with burrs and stickers of all kinds for years. The natural indentations above her eyes were sunken, creating round shadows. Her ribs looked like wagon bows sticking through thin, worn, chestnut-colored cloth. The old gunshot wound in her neck hardly mattered in comparison with all the rest. Her tattered ear bent over like one on a generations-old toy rabbit. She had spent her extended life searching for peace, hurting nothing except those who sought to destroy her breath and blood.

Unbeknownst to her, children of the cities, farms, and ranches ran around playing astronauts and aliens from outer space instead of cowboys and Indians as they had at the time of her birth, and most of their lives as well as those of their parents were hourly directed by computer buttons and little images on various screens. Her natural methods of survival had mostly remained the same through her decades here in the Aldo Leopold Wilderness. These ancient rhythms went back to the forest fire, to the conquistadors, to Spain and Egypt, and throughout history. Since the beginning of man, her ancestors were hunted for meat or used as beasts of burden, as creatures to make war with, and at times for racing, hunting, and even many forms of pure pleasure.

Her genes cried and tugged at her being, taking her back sixty million years to the Eocene epoch, or time of the Dawn Horse, when she would have been the size of a small fox terrier. Now as she strained ever harder to make the gray object clearer, she heard the Indian ruins and the accompanying chants become louder. The fuzzed objects were suddenly delineated. Some of the Mimbres Indians were dancing in a circle of spectators. Their brown legs and feet moved faster and faster as the drum's volume increased. Her heart beat in synchronization with them as she looked across the canyon and back to the Mimbres.

She was extremely excited, but a mellowness absorbed her at the same time. The drummer's hands, at their ultimate speed, pounded the hide drums and the moccasined feet thumped the earth with all the skill and power left in them. Intense vibrations filled the air and permeated everything. The sound and movement stopped at its peak—and for just a moment so did the universe, in total quiet and stillness.

Then four elders squatted in a rectangle. Each one took a turn standing and making a gesture with both hands in supplication to all four winds. A medicine man and a medicine woman stood before the mare now, and in contrast to the former solemnity of the ceremonies, radiated smiles of love and compassion toward her.

The medicine man reached into a doeskin pouch and gathered a handful of seeds from all the vegetation of the land. He leaped high in the air and hurled the seeds out over the mare. The seeds turned into uncountable bluebirds. They flew up, up, and dissolved the thin mists of clouds across the sky, and moved ever higher, growing into numbers so great they became a solid mass of blue. The birds moved past the sun and the bright land of the sky was reborn.

Just as the medicine man landed back on earth, the medicine woman leapt upward in a floating jump. She, too, reached into her doeskin bag for seeds, also throwing them above the mare as her compatriot had done. These turned into multitudes of white doves fluttering skyward, forming a great flat-bottomed, castle-domed cumulus cloud. She drifted back to earth standing next to the man. Both lifted their arms above their heads and yelled with all the force of their throats and lungs. Their cries were a mixture of all living things of the mountains—the lions and the insects, the bears and the bobcats, the hawks and the hares. All.

The mighty crescendo of sound moved up and became a symphony of drums and hand-carved flutes, spreading so wide it finally softened to a simple, sweet sigh. Instantly the Mimbres Indians vanished from her vision as they had so many centuries before from the earth.

And now, across the eons right to the present, she saw the grayness move out of the brush and become a circular movement. It was a great, shining, gray stallion who pranced with arched neck and high-tossed tail, back and forth directly across the canyon at about her level. Her scars were no longer felt, nor the stiff limbs, nor any of the lumps of the years. She was possessed with an inner feeling of permanent warmth and peace. Her eyes became so sharp she could see the nostrils of the stallion flare as he turned his head to nicker and squeal to her. She heard it as clearly as the bells of Notre Dame, and knew all its meaning as she always had and always would. She saw the stallion racing across the canyon, through space, toward her, mane and tail streaming. Then he sailed up and up above the grass, the brush, and the trees. She whirled agilely about, leaping down the rough terrain and then ascending sharply, racing in a soothing, golden vacuum straight toward her mate, at last. At the very moment Pauline Healy had yelled for her father to look in the sky above the descending buzzards, an El Paso reporter, a photographer, and three cowboys, who were expert ropers and trackers, were moving their pickups and gear toward the Healys' camp. If the ranger and his daughter had been listening into the quietness, they would have heard the truck engines straining uphill.

From another direction came the chawp, chawp, chawp of the helicopter as it passed over Jimmy Bason's ranch loaded with people from the Associated Press. The Healys didn't hear the sounds below because the discovery that lay before them blocked out all else.

The ranger felt his horse's muscles tense beneath him and saw three coyotes scatter away from a chestnut carcass.

He said with an infinite loss in his voice and a painful expulsion of breath, "Ohhhh . . . nooo. We're too late! The coyotes and buzzards have already beat us to her."

Pauline's wide, wondering eyes were locked on a movement in the sky. She did not hear her father, or see the signs and activity on the ground. Three tiny clouds, each one bigger than the other, raced across the blueness to the cumulus cloud and right up on top of it. There the girl saw a stallion, a mare, and a colt playing together in the upper mists and lights of the massive formation of white moisture. They were silhouetted proudly against the sky. Forever. Anyone could see them who knew how to look.

With an imponderable smile on her suddenly beatific face, the girl said softer than the whisper of a saint, "There will never be another her. Never."

An Equine Montage

The horse (and the mule—which is half horse) has given more to humankind than all the rocket scientists, presidents (all forms), dictators, and financial geniuses with all their billions of dollars combined. The horse's hold on humankind, joining in all the human glories and foibles, could actually fill many great libraries.

A small number of examples are:

Alexander the Great used his cavalry in brilliant support of his infantry to conquer all the known world, as did Genghis Khan and his Mongols. Napoleon came very close to dominating Europe until he overextended himself in the army-swallowing vastness of the Russian winter. Even then, the horses saved his great army from total annihilation by supplying meat from their own exhausted bodies for human survival food. Think of it.

When the Spanish explorers Onate and Cortez brought horses into the West, they never dreamed that the Apaches, the Comanches, and others would adopt, adapt, worship, and use the horse against them in some of the most brilliantly maneuvered battles ever fought. It would take the brave buffalo soldier cavalry, along with a gringo infantry far outnumbering the Indians, to finally bring the Apache and Comanche horse experts to a sort-of bloody peace.

All the hundreds of men on horseback who rode—with thirty-shot pistols blazing—through the dime novels and the Owen-Wister-spawned "B Western" movies, are unrivaled in a fifty-or-so-year reign as the epitome of the entertainment world. These are the American versions of the knights of the Round Table with everyone mounted on valiant steeds as they rescued fair maidens and saved the poor and downtrodden from greedy, gunslinging powers. These entertainment wonders never would have existed without the horse.

From the chariot races of the Ben Hur era, to the fashion show at the Kentucky Derby, or the American quarter horse two-million-dollar finals at Ruidoso Downs in New Mexico, the horse attracts class. The cutting horse addicts are more numerous and the sport is as expensive as polo.

And for entertainment, there are the plumed and prancing circus horses that delight all ages, or the polo ponies, or the almost pure white Austrian-bred Lipizzan horses who dance and do acrobatics beyond imagination as they perform, all over the world, for the most sophisticated and appreciative audiences.

Contrast these with the hardworking cow horse. A working cowboy will tell of the wonders, the lifesaving risks his cow horse has given him while chasing cantankerous bovines past rib-crushing rocks on mountainsides or hide-ripping brush in the canyons and flats. Even a horse that has bucked him off and nearly killed him, over and over, will still be spoken of with admiration, and his stories will be endless.

I must say that I appreciate the almost mystical colors of British painter J. M. H. Turner. I also love the convoluted and rippling landscapes Van Gogh did in Aries, France, and the "sky" period of Maynard Dixon's West has always sent my spirit soaring with the red-tailed hawks. However, as beautiful and stirring as the best of these artists' paintings are, they almost blanch in comparison to a young woman, her hair blowing as freely as the mane of the horse she is mounted on, racing across a rodeo arena or a dressage training course, or in a great, open pasture. This vision was, is, and always will be created by the greatest of gods. There is such joy between the horse and the female rider, such affinity, and a mutual understanding beyond words. Only the greatest of classical musical composers could capture the rhapsodic kinship here.

It comes to mind that our state capital of Santa Fe, as everyone knows—or should—is suffused with actual and movie history, and is always listed as one of the top art destinations in the nation per capita. It also ranks near the top as a horse-lover's paradise. One finds riders and trainers of pleasure, show, jumping, and mustangs everywhere. To observe a rider finely tuned to his mount coursing the foothills of Santa Fe is a perfect painting itself.

But this story is not a history of horses. This story is supposed to be a memoir of those horses who touched me—and a few of my friends—on a very personal level, beginning with my first horse, Cricket, and beyond. There will be all kinds of horses and a variety of attitudes of mine from age four to about forty, and even past.

In this montage, before the main stories and horses, I wish to mention a few—who for varied reasons I was associated with for only a short time, but nevertheless impacted my memory—even though I didn't write specific stories about them.

On Glorieta Mesa south of Santa Fe, I went to work on a cow ranch about three months before my twelfth birthday. Almost everyone—in this time and place—was so poor that it was a common practice for ranchers to loan themselves and/or their hired hands out to help each other—especially with big jobs like branding and roundups, and even fence building. It made survival possible.

I was on my way over to Pete Coleman's place to help him gather a few head of wild steers. I saw this horse standing at a gate entrance into Pete's horse pasture. He was a raw-boned gelding—brown with a crooked-lined, blaze face. He had that long-ago-used-up look about him—sunken holes above his eyes, loose lower lip, and old brands all over him. (None of which I recognized.) I opened the gate and let him into Pete's pasture. He followed me right up to the rock ranch house at Haney Springs where I saw Pete working a colt in the round corral.

As I rode up we exchanged "howdys," then he asked, "Where'd you get that?" pointing through the gate slabs at my new acquaintance.

I explained.

Pete grew curious. He came out of the corral, walked around the unconcerned animal, and studied its brands. He said, "The only one I recognize is the Lazy F E and that's way over into Arizona. Well, I guess we'll just put him over in a stall and feed him. We'll see if he'll do as a night horse."

It went unsaid for a while about how in heck that horse got over at least a thousand pasture fences to arrive way up here on lonesome, hardscrabble Glorieta Mesa. The grass sure wasn't greener. No answer came, but the fact remained that this old worn-out horse had belonged to a lot of different people and outfits. I decided to call him PDQ. Pretty Damn Quick was meant to be a satire, of course, for the laid-back animal.

Bill McDonald and his son, Little Joe, came over before daylight, and three days later we had worked the piñon/cedar-covered mesa and canyons to the east and penned six of the eight wild steers. Bill headed on back to the McDonald ranch over by the tiny Spanish village of Cow Springs, leaving his son to help finish the job.

Pete gave Little Joe and me a day off so we could go over to play and take a much-needed bath in the headwaters (Meadow Springs) of the San Cristobal Creek that splits that famous ranch, the San Cristobal, south of Lamy and Santa Fe. There was one little catch to our small holiday: Pete suggested I ride old PDQ.

We were riding along telling one another yarns and big dreams when we came upon a little bunch of mother Herefords and their calves.

I said to Little Joe, as I took down my catch rope, "Pete said I should try old PDQ out, didn't he?"

"Yeah," he answered, and his eyes got big. "But not on his calves."

Now, that really was against all the rules on a ranch. To run even one priceless pound of beef off an animal unnecessarily was an unforgivable sin, and the remote possibility of crippling one was criminal. A man, and especially a boy, could get himself fired for that.

Forbidden or not, I couldn't resist.

I took after a calf. Old PDQ built to him with surprising speed. I got just the right distance from him and threw the whirling loop. I caught the calf deep around the brisket and he really whacked the end of the rope as old PDQ set up like a well-trained, rodeo roping horse.

I was just looking around—hoping Little Joe had seen my performance of perfection—when PDQ went cloud hunting. I was a natural-born, "fairly" good roper, but I hadn't learned yet what a poor bronc rider I was always gonna be. However, I believe it was the third or fourth jump when I was bucked into a flock of flying birds. They flew on and I dropped like a ton of whatever. I didn't know if anything was broken, and in that moment of horror and excitement, I didn't care. I sat up, then staggered upright, watching PDQ still bucking and dragging that calf through the pasture.

Little Joe rode after them. He grabbed the bridle and PDQ stopped like he had been brain shot. I held what breath was left in me until the calf got up and I could see he wasn't crippled. Little Joe turned the calf loose and led PDQ back to me.

"Here's your rodeo ropin' horse," he said, flatly.

"No," I said, "here's my rodeo bucking horse."

Of course, we agreed there would be no mention of the cruddy old animal's various and unbelievable talents . . . or mine either, for that matter.

Three days later, Pete, Little Joe, and myself were still trying to gather the last two steers. We split up to cover more ground.

I found some fresh tracks, and had been following them for miles when I hit an opening and there he grazed. The wind was in my favor. I decided to try to rope him. Then the race began.

At my own stupid insistence, I was riding PDQ, and he was running like a greyhound with his ears laid back. A little bunch of piñon trees was heading at us fast. I threw the big old prayerful loop and durned if that big old steer didn't stick his head in it. As surprised as I was, I put a choke hold on that saddle horn. PDQ fooled me again. He set up and jerked that steer down even though I felt the back end of the saddle lift my butt about a foot upward. I was surprised the flank cinch had held.

The steer hit the ground so hard he was stunned. Jerking the piggin' string free where it was tied on the saddle, I bailed off and ran to him. I was actually dumb enough to try to tie that steer's feet, but he raised up, throwing me aside like a dried leaf off his back. While I regained my footing and got back in the saddle, PDQ kept the slack out, working that rope like a pro.

The steer started fighting the rope. He ran around a tree several times, each time shortening the rope and semi-securing himself for me. I dismounted after removing the honda loop from the saddle horn. With a great struggle and making a mess out of the catch rope, I finally, somehow, got him tied by the horns between two trees, so he wouldn't choke to death. That miracle is one piece of childhood foolishness that is still a blur to me, but the rest of it is as clear as bottled water.

I remounted PDQ and proudly rode off yelling and hunting for Pete and Little Joe to tell them about the miracle that just happened between myself and a rusty-looking old horse.

PDQ was turned out in a pasture with the rest of the usin' horses and we kept a different one for a wrangling horse. The next, and last, time I wrangled the horses before heading back to my home outfit—Ed Young's Rafter EY—I couldn't find PDQ among the horse herd. Pete and I rode the entire horse pasture twice. No fence was down, no gate was open, no horse tracks were outside them. Thinking the worst, we even futilely looked for bear or mountain lion tracks. None. He was gone as if he had sprouted wings and flown away.

That night at supper, Pete's Boston-raised and educated wife, Nancy, brought up the great mystery of PDQ's escape. She said he had to be part deer to jump a barbed-wire fence without touching it; or maybe rustlers had rustled him. Nah. We knew that hadn't happened. Maybe he just turned into a coyote and crawled under the fence. Nah. Or . . . maybe he turned into a ghost . . . they don't leave tracks. Well . . .

Several more scenarios passed between us before we let the subject die. Many rivers have flooded and dried up, and I still wonder about old PDQ every now and then. He was a mystery—one I'm blessed to have known. I always hoped I'd meet another one like him, but it never happened.

————

When I was still a teenager, I acquired a small, well-watered (with springs) ranch in northeastern New Mexico. It was located fourteen miles east of the village of Des Moines—which I would later call "Hi Lo" in many of my writings and a major film.

The first livestock I acquired was a five-year-old bay mare, Molly, from a Grenville neighbor. Molly was broke-out, but these people didn't know much about horse training, so she didn't know much, either, but I liked her anyway and set about putting a finish on her.

In those poor and struggling days, coyote hides each brought from five to fifteen dollars—a ton of money at the time. I found three running hounds to pursue the valuable coyote hides, and soon would team up with my all-time hunting partner, my uncle Tom Cresswell of a little stock farm between my ranch and Des Moines. He had an old dun gelding he used for horse and hound hunting.

Since most of these hunting stories have been printed in various other publications, we'll get to the real chase with Molly.

I must admit that I was having more trouble putting a rein, a stop, and instilling "rope and cow sense" in this horse than ever before. However difficult she was in those departments, she was just as expert and anxious to do right in another. She literally loved and lived to run after the dogs as they ran down one of the smartest creatures ever born. She must have had the ancient genes of some great general's best warhorse, for she had a true bloodlust. She liked to be in on the kill. Molly craved to watch the dogs' fangs still a freshly caught coyote.

Whenever I turned the dogs loose after a coyote, Molly would tear through brush as if it were Christmas wrapping paper. She would take me around and over jumbles of rocks that would have slowed a mountain lion to a careful creep and make an eagle fly carefully sideways. Downhill and uphill were all the same to her. She just went full cavalry charge all the time, all the way. It is amazing that I ever survived to write my own name, much less a million or so words.

Old Tom and his dun horse were far older than Molly and I. I had been living a rather reckless life since first memory; even so, Molly's rampaging runs were putting the years on me so fast I was going to be gray-headed and smooth-mouthed before I was twenty-one. Then my youth was spared—temporarily.

Silhouetted on a hill across a rock-strewn valley, I had seen, and figured Molly had as well, the dogs catch a coyote. I had my Model 62 .22 rifle out of its homemade scabbard because we had jumped four coyotes in a pack and I thought I might get a shot at one. Now that was daydreaming, right in the middle of a midday sunray bent by the Hi-Lo Country's wind, because Molly never would have slowed down enough for me to take a shot.

Before we could cross the rocky draw and get to the kill on the hill above, Molly flung us down that incline as if she had fallen or jumped off the white cliffs of Dover. Determined. Then . . . that old, overused, little-understood word—FATE—just jumped up and whacked us.

Molly hit an unseen rock in the grass and over and over she went. At her first flop, she propelled me out into space a distance, even then, I was too modest to mention. I broke my fall with my precious rifle butt so emphatically that it was nothing but lost splinters in the grass.

The ground had knocked me so goofy that I found myself standing, pulling the dogs from the coyote so they wouldn't ruin its valuable hide. I still held a piece of slightly bent steel that once had been a food-providing instrument of mercy for the coyotes. Then I saw Molly coming up the hill, straining mightily through the pain of a smashed shoulder, too late for the kill.

Tom and his dun horse were just now topping the opposite hill. I tried to explain what he had missed, but I was unclear and it was a month before he understood the rapid occurrences.

We hung the coyote on Tom's saddle. I told him to take the dogs on to his house and I would lead Molly home, if we could make it. I had a dislocated shoulder and smashed right hand myself. It was dark when I penned her. I rubbed some horse liniment on her shoulder and on myself. I mostly healed up; Molly didn't. I retired her to pasture and she never quit limping, but if a horse has memories and dreams she was full of wild ones.

It was a short, sweet, and almost deadly time with Molly, but as I write this I feel both my smashed hand and the same exhilaration that Molly and I felt racing after the hounds of the Hi-Lo Country. There is a little place saved in a corner of my heart where she'll never stop running healthy and free.

I left the heart of the Hi-Lo Country and went to Taos. I bought some subirrigated land and a house and moved there amongst the founders and old masters of the famed art colony. I also acquired my first Taos horse, Brownie. He was as plain as his name—just brown all over. There was nothing outstanding about him. However, for the thirty dollars I paid Horse Thief Shorty for him, he turned out to be quite a buy. Brownie was a good, solid cow horse, with good rein, fair stop, and some cow sense.

I tried to make a roping horse out of him as well, over the protests of my new wife, Pat. She was right. Brownie would lay his ears back and run as hard as he could to give me a loop at a calf, but it was mid-arena before I could whip it on one, and by the time I bailed off, ran to the calf, threw, and tied him, about the best time I could hope for was sixteen or eighteen seconds. Once in a while—in those days of long scores—that would get a roper in the money, but not often enough to show a profit.

Just the same, Brownie was pretty darn good at everything, outstanding at none, but a loyal friend all the way. A partner. As I look back now, I rank him mighty high for that priceless underrated loyalty. I even feel sorry I didn't see how all-around fine he was at the time.

Ah, beginnings and the forgetting of the same is the greatest of all human failings. My first Taos horse had given us more than we knew. I had forgotten that Brownie's companionship prize was when I would ride him for pure pleasure. We would move across the great sagebrush desert on top of the west mesa where the Taos Pueblo Indians held their annual, ancient horseback rabbit hunt. It was the sacred rite painted by some of the Taos art founders. I had also forgotten those times when Brownie and I were all alone out there with a 360-degree circle of the grandest, high-desert view on earth. Behind the pueblo, the sacred Taos Mountain loomed—as if it were the king of all earthly mountains—surrounded on each side by a great arc of timber-covered, mighty blue bulges that half encircled Taos to the north and east. The circle was completed by the seemingly endless expanse of sagebrush-covered desert on the south and west, across the Rio Grande Gorge—on and on and on. It was a time of peace and of absorbing the beauty of the visible high desert and all those wonders of the spirit unfortunately invisible to most. It was a special gift to share this majesty with Brownie. I must never forget about it again.

There were other fine horses during this period. I traded one of my original oil paintings for Clabber—also brownish, but nearer to a bay. He had been trained as a roping horse, and worked perfectly in the arena, but he, too, was a little slow for the faster times being developed by ropers. But . . . he had the best riding gait. I never was able to exactly define it—a cross between a running walk and a foxtrot is as close as I can come. Pat loved this horse as well, and since she had spent several summers at her grandparents' ranch in east-central New Mexico, she was a fine rider.

The Ramming family moved to Taos from back east to retire. They fell in love with Clabber. They kept trying to buy him for their teenage son and a daughter who, they felt, needed a horse to tie them to the earth. I took a liking to their son, John, and finally they caught me with my pockets empty of cash and my heart full of friendship. I sold Clabber to them, but we still had Brownie. Pat and I never regretted it because we would see Clabber often with different members of the family riding, loving, and caring for him. He was destined to be theirs and because of their good care, he lived an extra-long life—until his early twenties.

At that time, gambling was wide open, but illegal, in northern New Mexico and our neighbor, Curly Murray, who lived just up the road from us on the slope of the mesa, had recently taken charge of Long John Dunn's gambling operations. Now, nobody messed with Curly. Curly was tough. He had a widespread reputation as being that and also as being one of the most respected horse traders around. He was renowned as a judge of good horses and although tough, he had a reputation of being fair. He bought and sold horses for the Taos Indians and many of the other pueblos in several adjoining states.

Back in the 1930s the Bureau of Indian Affairs had bought a purebred Morgan stallion, along with some quality mares, to upgrade the quality of the Taos Pueblo horse population. Theirs was still a horse world in those days.

Anyway, Curly knew I wanted to get Pat a special riding horse and when he told me about one at the pueblo I went out there. I gave the four-year-old stallion a look and a tryout. I took him out in the pasture where the tribe would soon graze buffalo and aired him out. I was amazed and thrilled at the smoothness of his gait. I know it must be a cliché, but he floated when he walked. Just a suggestion from my knees or the reins and he turned so smoothly it seemed his joints were greased. Everything was almost too good, but he was just that special. I bought him for seventy-five dollars—a goodly sum in the early fifties—but one heck of a bargain just the same.

The horse's Indian name was Yuso. He was a rich, deep-red bay. His heavy black mane gleamed with bluish highlights and his black hooves and legs blended into his body like he had been painted with a master's brush. He was benevolent royalty. He knew it. Pat knew it, and both of them were made for each other. When I gave Pat her horse, it was as if they had known one another for . . . well, forever.

To this day it was one of the scenes of great beauty ever registered in my brain. Pat had great copper-brown hair, and whether it was loose or in a ponytail, to see her riding Yuso with the sun bringing out the red glints from both of them was a thing of awe. The way they silently communicated, the perfect rhythm they had together, was what the word "beauty" had been invented for.

She loved Yuso deeply, as he did her. I loved to watch them together. Old Brownie and I would ride with them occasionally, outclassed but proud to be along.

I have never, now or ever before, had such an animal incident to write about. My uncle Slim Evans had leased some land and was training horses a while before he acquired—with the help of his brother, Lloyd—a cow ranch on the second mesa west of Taos. Everyone in several states knew Slim as a cowboy, and a top-notch cowboy horse breaker (the PC world calls them horse trainers, horse whisperers, etc.) with few peers. So when he asked to borrow Yuso for some kind of work, Pat graciously lent him her love.

A few days later, Slim drove his old pickup out to our place. He didn't even knock, but came right on into the kitchen where Pat and I were having coffee. He paced the floor, clearing his throat, and his lean six-foot-three body shrunk about a foot as he told us that Yuso had drowned in the creek that split his leased land. There had been a flash flood there, but we were so stunned that I don't want to remember the implausible reason why.

Pat was beyond any feeling. I wanted to blow Slim's head off, but his own suffering defused that very natural thought. Slim got over this senseless loss. Pat never did. She would go on to like other horses and feed them, pet them, ride them, go to brandings and rodeos with me, but she never called another horse her own.

We were kids, really, but this was an ancient hurt. Somehow, in some way, in some now unknown world Pat and Yuso will enjoy moving out across a sunlit land together again with their hair sparkling like rubies. I know it.

Then there was Reno, a white Arabian. I traded an old slick-backed Chevy to an ex-cowboy-turned-car-salesman, Marion Minor, for him. Lord, he was a great riding horse. I could ride him all the way across the desert down to the Rio Grande Gorge and back uphill to our place without him breaking a sweat. He seemed fresher on the return than on the start. I began to understand about those legendary, long-distance, and running warhorses the Arabs had always seemed to brag about was, in fact, understated. A true pleasure horse, indeed, both for the ride and simply to look at.

In those days, I survived as a trader of anything including antiques, santos, cars, paintings, anything, and yes, horses. So when I had a chance to sell Reno to a rich Texas oilman as a gift for one of his lady loves, I did it. Two thousand dollars was a smart sum for a horse in those days. The most I ever got. I later missed Reno a million dollars' worth, but feeding the family and my artistic soul trumped everything then.

Just the same, Reno's great gift has always been with me—the gift of appreciation for the elegant beauty and durability of the Arabian horse. One of life's great pleasures has been the adventure of the Arabian Nationals, often held in my hometown of Albuquerque. The eloquence with which their performances speak to their riders, and audiences, is so unmistakable in its distinguished style and movement it actually elucidates this to all participants. The riders, male and female, feel this refinement. Their own beings emanate these courtly movements and feelings. Here the riders become so attuned, so much a part of the spirit of the horse that beauty seems like an inadequate word. Thanks to a car/horse trade and that blessed Arabian, Reno, my outer and inner eyes were opened so I could at least vicariously share this magic gift.

***

And then, along came an interim horse for several of us. I traded an ancient retablo of Christ on the cross and a worn ten-dollar bill for a ten-year-old buckskin mare. She was called Sleepy Kay because in the roping box instead of tensing up, muscles aquiver, ears working like a champion roping horse does, she just hung her head down and appeared to be asleep . . . a little unnerving to a tensed-up contestant.

However, in some unexplainable way, she knew when the roper nodded his head for the calf to be released. Instantly she would charge forward, all eleven hundred pounds of her with all she could give. She ran hard and heavy. And her stop! I tell you, she could have jerked a moose inside out with her stop.

Even as loyal and determined as she was, she sure made a guy work to get in the money. I really had to be ready to throw—even though she seldom gave me a shot before the middle of the arena. With all her drawbacks, I remember missing only one calf on her, and that was because it turned back just as I threw the loop. So, here's the deal—if I could get a matched roping of, say, four to ten calves against a faster, better-mounted, but erratic roper, I could win on average, and did so until folks caught on.

The mining business was beginning to take over my life and my art, and Pat's, too. I wasn't writing at all, but did keep on taking notes for what would become my major work decades later—Bluefeather Fellini.

My mentor's son, Woody Crumbo the Younger, and his best friend, a Modoc Indian named Sonny Jim, were protégé cowboys of my uncle Slim. So I gave them Sleepy Kay. We were all happy about that.

Slim had plenty of cow horses to tutor them on, but they started learning to rope on Sleepy Kay. She was exactly right for them, gentle and totally trustworthy, powerful but not so fast they couldn't keep up their learning. Eventually, they turned her into a steer-jerking horse. She seemed to have been born for it. She was so strong it was almost effortless for them to jerk a steer down, bail off, and tie.

In her own—often, seemingly ponderous—way, the buckskin mare was tutoring the blooming rodeo hands almost as much as Uncle Slim was training them in the surprisingly numbered and varied abilities it takes to be working cowboys.

Later, Woody the Younger went on to become a successful rodeo producer, realtor, and art dealer. Sonny was still riding bulls at age fifty in the PRCA but a bad and permanent shoulder injury made him finally quit. He still enters "doggin'" contests, but mainly he trains horses.

I think right here it would be fair to say that none of this would have happened without the faith and giving nature of the sleepy-looking mare. To show the power of her influence, all these great accomplishments happened after an incident beyond conjuring.

There were scattered cottonwood, elm, and evergreens along Taos Creek that sang and trilled their way through the Crumbo property southwest of Taos. The place would later become the noted cowboy singer Michael Martin Murphey's ranch. Whenever the boys wanted a break from their various forms of cowboy training, they would sometimes fish, and sometimes hunt squirrels with a .22 rifle.

Then it happened. Sonny missed a squirrel and the little bullet ricocheted into the soft temple of a grazing Sleepy Kay and killed her. There is no use going into the shock, pain, and great remorse everyone felt. However, the remembrance of her giving partnership most certainly carried the boys, yes, even drove them on to fulfill their many accomplishments. I myself go fuzzy headed when I try to remember our many close losses in calf roping, but the match roping wins are joyously clear as a spring sunbeam. I know that Sleepy Kay left a lot of lasting goodwill and a deeply felt forever thanks from us all.

———

Woody the Elder and I had gone into the mine-promoting business, with great initial success. Finally, way up into my thirties, I had the money to buy my one and only first-class roping horse, Powderface. I got him from a top professional roper named Hamm of Clovis, New Mexico, who had won a lot of PRCA roping contests on him. Powderface was a blaze-faced, strawberry roan, quartered up like a champion cutting horse. He was good. In fact, he was way better than I was.

We hauled him around to semilocal, community rodeos and jackpot ropings. These were the thing in those days because pros could enter with the ambitious amateurs in these winner-take-all contests. A lot of camaraderie was shared and the winner took home a real chunk of money.

I finally had a top-notch horse but no time to practice, since the mining endeavors were rapidly widening. Just the same, I got in the money more often than not and had a lot of fun doing it.

One morning, Pat and I took off from Taos for a Las Vegas, New Mexico, rodeo, had a flat tire, and got there too late to enter. An amateur action, for sure. So we drove back north to the Cimarron rodeo that was known in those days as the wildest working cowboy rodeo anywhere. And it was! Their bucking stock and the roping stock were brought in fresh off the range and they were scared and wild.

Their wild cow milking contest—later copied by the Calgary Stampede and a few others—was a Cimarron original. The cowboys pair up in teams—a roper and a foot-header—on one end of the arena. On the other end is a herd of sure-enough wild cows. The goal is: each team must catch a cow (any cow they can) and somehow get enough milk into a Coke bottle that it could be poured out—even a teaspoonful would qualify.

Cowboys on foot scare the cows out to the middle of the arena. At the signal, everything and everybody heads toward each other—all the cows, all the cowboys. When they all meet, total and outright chaos takes place.

It is the wildest, downright hilarious, most difficult event of the whole rodeo, and the most popular—at least it seems to be the audience's favorite. They scream and holler and encourage their favorite team until the whistle blows announcing that the first three bottles with milk have been delivered to the judges. Sometimes that takes a lot longer than expected.

I had picked as my foot-mugger a guy from Taos, Bob Mead, who worked for the telephone company but owned a few registered cows. I really wanted to win this crazy event. I held Powderface back while all the rest charged into the wildly milling mess. One cow broke out by herself and Powder built to her. I had her out in the arena all alone. The header was digging his heels deep in the dirt trying to slow her so I could get enough milk in the Coke bottle to pour out. Powder was working the rope, moving as best he could to slow the cow. It worked.

I mounted Powder and rode to the judge in the arena and poured the milk out at least a minute before second place showed up. I was as elated as if I had won the all-around in Las Vegas, Nevada.

I might as well have been on the rodeo circuit full time, because the copper ore Woody and I were profitably shipping by truck and rail to American Smelting and Refining at El Paso had dropped from forty-eight cents a pound to twenty-four cents in less than 120 days. We were going broke. The struggle trying to save this part of our world consumed every second of my time.

Powderface was turned out to graze and water. A waste of great horse talent. Then, my cousin, David Evans, from Meadow, Texas, and the Kinsolving ranch at Tatum, New Mexico, came into the picture. He had been a fine professional roper until he tore a knee apart. He wanted to borrow Powderface for a special match roping, but first he'd have to work the fat off of him and get him toughened up. He called him Roanie.

David won a saddle and a couple of rodeo ropings on Roanie as well. Before another match roping, he was practicing and just as he was ready to throw a quick loop, Roanie fell and rolled over dead. David escaped injury to his body, but his soul was somewhat bent. There could be no weeping here. In the little time I got to spend with Roanie/Powderface he had delivered the mail and one of my small but fondest wins. He did the same for David. His aging heart had more will than strength and he was gone, at full speed, without pain, in the middle of what he was born to do. Fulfilled . . . all of us.

These horses so briefly introduced here and so briefly in our lives are there as long as we have enough sense to both love and respect them. Now on to those who were lifetime friends and partners. Please open up and share the pain, the adventure, and the special joy of our equine brothers and sisters.

The Freak

For an animal that would eventually be registered and run as both a thoroughbred and a quarter horse, breaking several world records and called by many "the greatest potential all-around racehorse in the world," he was an odd-looking creature. He was awkwardly big, Roman-nosed, and had several white spots and streaks here and there among the overall reddish-brown. He grew long, ragged fetlocks like a Percheron workhorse. Considering how different he was from other running horses, it seemed altogether proper for him to get his name in a strange manner, too.

Rancher Marvin Ake, from Datil, New Mexico, had acquired the colt some time back but couldn't find a name that fit him. This particular early morning, Marvin and his wife were sitting at the breakfast table drinking coffee. They were having a struggle holding the then-modest-sized ranch together. Marvin was daydreaming about better cow prices and more rain when he looked out the kitchen window and spotted something totally out of place.

He cleared his throat and asked his wife, "Do you see what I think I see?"

She looked and answered, "If I don't you're in a bunch of trouble. And if I do we're both gonna need help."

It just couldn't be, but there on the rim of the round metal stock tank, many hundreds of miles from any ocean, sat a pelican. That's right. In the lonely, isolated, semidesert ranchlands of Datil, New Mexico, seeing the saltwater bird would be akin to climbing the Alps and finding a steaming pool full of Florida alligators.

Since he couldn't think of anything else to say that made any sense, Marvin told his wife, "That's it."

"That's what?"

"We'll call him Pelican." When his wife looked at him as if she was going to the rack for a gun, he added, "The horse, I mean . . . the new colt. We'll call him Pelican."

And so they did. To add more mystery to the situation, he had had a crippled wing. How did it get there in the first place? They fed it a couple of cans of sardines, but the next day it was dead. A mystic would have said it had come for no other purpose than to lend a name to greatness.

Marvin had once worked as a cowboy for A. D. Woofter, who owned Pelican as a yearling. When Marvin first saw the animal he decided he wanted to own him. He bought the colt for five hundred dollars and brought him back over the massive Magdalena Mountains.

When they first made the deal it was natural that Marvin should ask about the colt's breeding. Woofter hesitantly said he was almost certain he was out of Joe Hancock, Jr. (a great racing quarter horse sire from the famed Wagonner ranch at Vernon, Texas), and a little registered thoroughbred mare named Evelyn's Pride, but when Marvin went to pick up Pelican, Woofter changed his story and said the colt was out of Joe Hancock, Jr., and the mare Covollie. Marvin really didn't believe Woofter knew for sure and, at the time, didn't care, but he challenged him just for the hell of it. Woofter blew up and said he'd just keep the horse. It was too late. Woofter had five hundred dollars in his bank account and Marvin Ake had a horse that would eventually astound, entertain, and confuse the racing world. It's too bad that the horse's ancestry got mixed up in the passage of time, for even today most old-timers still give differing opinions. Probably the only one left who might really know is the great horse trainer Lyo Lee, currently of Ocala, Florida.

Marvin bought Pelican in the summer and that fall saddled him up but didn't ride him. The next spring he broke him out without any real problems. The horse was gentle by nature. Marvin did have a little trouble getting him to rein or stop properly like his other cow ponies.

One day he ran into a bunch of wild burros. He shook his loop down and took after them. Now, it takes a hell of a good cowboy and a better horse to get close enough to one of these creatures to throw a loop. Pelican built to one so fast Marvin didn't have a chance to get set properly. He threw the loop anyway and damned if it didn't fit right around the burro's neck slick as a Navajo necklace. The only trouble now was that Pelican just wanted to keep running right on over the top of the Magdalenas. Marvin was afraid they were going to drag the burro to death before he got Pelican stopped . . . but then everyone knows that a burro's neck is made out of stretchable, unbreakable rubber.

Right there Marvin Ake caught on to the fact that it didn't matter about the horse reining or stopping; Pelican's game was running, and how he loved it!

Up to now, Marvin had matched a lot of races with fast cow ponies around small rodeos and county fairs, but he'd never taken a horse to a real meet. He thought he just might have a meet horse on hand now.

Pelican had a few other unusual characteristics that showed up early. Besides being gentle, he just plain liked people. He seemed to care more for his human masters than for his own kind. Marvin could walk up to him out in a pasture and catch him anytime. Later, when Marvin started racing him, he was a novelty around the stables and barns because he didn't sleep standing up like all the other horses. He found it more comfortable to lie down flat on his side like a person or a dog. Pelican was peculiar. Marvin said he was strong enough to make a good plowhorse . . . the exact opposite of a great racing animal.

Marvin chewed Beechnut tobacco in those early racing days, and just for a joke he handed a wad to Pelican. Surprisingly, he took it and loved it. From then on, whenever Marvin came near, Pelican would nudge him

for a "chaw." The trainer said it wouldn't hurt him and added, "Shoot, everybody knows chewin' tobaccer kills worms."

Perhaps the key thing that altered Pelican's life, and the lives of a lot of sporting folks, was the illusion of his sleepy-headedness. The horse simply had an instinct to conserve energy and never waste the tiniest spark of it. Even as a two-year-old, Pelican never ran around and played like the other horses. As we shall see, this particular attitude, when improperly interpreted, would keep a lot of folks' money from burning a hole in their pockets, and send them back to digging postholes. Those few who knew would drive Cadillacs, eat the biggest, tenderest steaks, dampen their throats with the finest liquids, and occasionally giggle and do joyful little jigs here and there about the earth.

It all really started moving when Lloyd Crockett, a one-armed feller from over in the San Andres Mountains who really knew running horses, recommended Walter Harris of Artesia, New Mexico, as the trainer for Pelican. Marvin had nominated the horse for the Albuquerque Futurity in the upcoming fall meet at the New Mexico State Fair without having ever raced him on a track. Marvin must have been a strong believer in faith.

Since he had no horse trailer, Marvin and his wife loaded Pelican in the back of a wobbly old open-topped pickup and headed southeast for Artesia. So did the lovely, wet mountain clouds. Cold sheets of rain pelted the naked horse all the way down there. Pelican was wet, chilled, and shaking. He was drawn down and looked like a Calcutta dog when the trainer first took a look at him. They all thought he'd get pneumonia and die, but he didn't.

Marvin asked Walter Harris if he thought he could get Pelican registered with the Quarter Horse Association.

Walter Harris swallowed, turned half around, tipped his hat back, and finally said, "Tell you what . . . I believe I'd get him filled up real good fore I showed him to the inspector."

Marvin and his wife could tell that Harris didn't like the horse. Since they'd made a long, risky trip, they went ahead and made a deal for Harris to train the horse for a month before a small meet in Alamogordo, New Mexico.

On the long, muddy trip back that night, Mrs. Ake could tell that Marvin was feeling a little down. She said, "Now don't you worry, honey, we're gonna come out all right. That Pelican is an honest horse."

How right the woman was. The meet came off. Harris still didn't believe in the horse. He hired Frankie Nixon, a fifteen-year-old kid, as the jockey. The three-hundred-yard race was for two-year-olds only.

Tony Morrison showed up with a little bay stud, Joe Mac, that was really good. It was a big gamble for Marvin, considering his financial condition, to enter the untried Pelican against the fast and well-known Joe Mac. He figured he might as well find out right here if the horse could run. It would be less costly in the long run.

There were six horses in the race. At the gun Pelican broke last. Marvin was watching him closely and holding his breath. The horse was so green that he bent way out completely off the dirt track into a cow pasture. Even so, the kid did his best and got him angled back toward the track and the finish line. Pelican's long, ground-ripping strides pulled him on the bay and he finished second, only a head back. Now Marvin knew! He felt like throwing his hat about forty feet in the air and jumping up to grab it before it started down. Marvin's surface stayed as calm as an afternoon nap. Mrs. Ake, a smile almost ripping her face, patted Marvin on the arm, and said with soft control, "Stay inside your hide, honey."

That's what you call "jerking the fuse" or "capping the well."

Marvin was invisibly hilarious when George Foster, a horseman, said dryly, "That's gonna be a good'un."

Marvin greatly respected Foster's horse sense. He said, "George Foster was one of those rare men who could see deep into a horse."

They were both proved far more than right. Needless to say, Pelican's trainer now became an instant admirer.

The next small-town meet was at Truth or Consequences, a New Mexico desert town about half the size of its name. It does have grand hot-water springs and a large boating and fishing lake called Elephant Butte.

Now the trainer had renamed the horse Red Apple without consulting Marvin. The owner decided to keep quiet about the name until after the present race was run.

It was a 350-yard race. A ten-foot cut bank served as a rail on one side, but was still four or five yards from the track. Pelican had drawn the outside position next to the bank. They had the same jockey up. He was full of confidence after the race at Alamogordo. Marvin believed Pelican had a chance to take the race because they had fifty extra yards for distance, and maybe the cut bank would keep him on the track this time. He put down an additional hundred dollars, getting two-to-one odds. It was a lot of money for the Akes to gamble at the time.

The eight horses finally got lined up and were off. Again Pelican made his natural bad start and was eating the dust of every other horse in the race. Not only that, he arced out and was running almost up against the cut bank. Marvin was afraid he would drag the kid off and cripple him. The kid felt differently. He fought the horse back onto the track at about the 150-yard marker. Then Pelican straightened up and at two hundred yards swallowed the whole bunch and won by four lengths going away.

Walter Harris said, "Well, I got to admit it . . . I've never seen a horse jump the track and come back like that in my life. That Red Apple is . . ."

Marvin interrupted with, "His name is Pelican."

"Pelican! God almighty, that's the damndest, awfulest name I ever heard of for a horse."

Marvin closed the conversation with, "P-E-L-I-C-A-N. That's the way you spell it."

The next move was to the Albuquerque fairgrounds for the futurity. Marvin thought that Harris had Pelican in pretty good shape so about three days before the race he showed him to Ed Heller, the inspector for the American Quarter Horse Association. Heller hailed from Dundee, Texas, and traveled around to big meets looking for possible recruits for the organization. He wielded quite a bit of power and knew it. Marvin proudly held the halter of the shiny, brushed young stallion.

Heller circled Pelican several times expressionless. Marvin waited anxiously. Finally Heller said, "Well, you know, Marvin, that horse has got an odd conformity . . . I . . . just cain't put my finger on it. I think I better watch him for a year or two before we decide for sure."

After all the faith, hard money, and risk that the Akes had put in the horse, Marvin was deeply hurt. Again his wife came with the right words and correct prophecy: "Don't let it bother you, honey. They'll be coming to you before long."

Three days later, after the usual slow start, Pelican won the Albuquerque Futurity by six lengths and was going away again at the line. Heller dropped by the stables and asked Marvin if he could take another look at Pelican in the morning. Marvin, remembering his wife's words, simply nodded "yes."

The next morning Heller only circled the horse once and said, "That's an altogether different-looking horse today than he was yesterday. We'll register him."

Marvin said, "You know, Heller, I think we'll turn it down for now. I better talk to the National before we go ahead." The National was a rival quarter horse association.

Marvin took a big chew of Beechnut, gave Pelican a wad of the sweet tobacco, and they enjoyed the masticating together. Heller stared stunned for a moment before he walked silently away. That's what you call "pullin' the string."

Next stop, Tucson, where Marvin entered Pelican in several $500 purse races. At that time Tucson was the only track in the country to run quarter horses in the winter. The first race had a sure-enough fast horse named Jap. The odds were good on Pelican. Marvin put down $200 and got back over $2,500 when Pelican just blew the field away. They won three more races in the same easy manner, and then Marvin entered him in the Arizona Derby, which was a stud race against the best in the field. Pelican took them by three lengths.

Now the famous trainer Lyo Lee had been watching Pelican ever since Albuquerque. He represented a rich Arizona and California rancher and playboy, Roy Gill, who loved to gamble on horse races and usually won. According to Benny Binion, owner of the world-famous Horseshoe in Las Vegas, Gill was one of the winningest gamblers he had ever known. When a horse backed by Gill, Tonto Gal, beat another gambler's mare named Prissy, the irate loser had lost so often to Gill that he threw his ten thousand dollars in cash out on the ground in a high wind. Gill just laughed as the brush-track crowd helped him gather up his winnings. All but one hundred dollars was recovered and returned.

Coincidently, Marvin Ake and Lyo Lee had worked on some of the same cow ranches in Arizona and New Mexico when they were boys. So when trainer Harris brought Lyo to Pelican's stables it didn't take the two very long to get down to business. Lyo offered Marvin four thousand dollars for Pelican. The cash was a great temptation for Marvin, since the Akes' goal was improving and expanding their ranch holdings. Even though horse racing was only a side activity, the last thing he wanted to do was give up the horse.

Marvin said, "I'll take six." He never dreamed Lee would take him up on it, because six thousand dollars, at that moment, was the highest price ever asked for a quarter horse.

When Lyo Lee joined Roy Gill he told him, "If you see a horse that can beat you, buy him. That way you cut down the competition." Gill had totally agreed, and it sure worked. They had from five to seven of the top ten quarter horses in the world at any given time.

"You just sold him," Lyo said.

Marvin had a sick feeling way down deep, but there was no backing out. From that moment on he would have to enjoy secondhand the wondrous exploits of the horse he'd given so much to. As he handed over the bill of sale he told Lyo, "Just see to it that he gets his little chaw of Beechnut regularly."

Several decades later, after becoming a very successful and knowledgeable rancher, Marvin Ake said, "I believe at four years old Pelican could outrun any horse in the world from three hundred yards and all the distances in between, all the way up to a mile and a quarter—maybe a mile and a half. No other horse I've ever seen or heard of had that many distances. He was the top of his time."

The first thing Lyo Lee did was measure Pelican's stride. It was a phenomenal twenty-seven and one-half feet. He entered him in a race at Rillito Race Track in Tucson in a fast field. Included was the famous thoroughbred Piggin' String, whose owners were trying to turn him into a quarter horse, and doing a fair job of it.

At the latch, Pelican broke slow and awkwardly, rapidly flaring away from the bunch all the way to the outside rail. Even so he straightened up enough to come in a close second to Piggin' String. A week later Lyo Lee matched the same field at 660 yards. In the meantime he'd given Pelican a strong dose of schooling of the gate. This time the second-place Piggin' String was nine lengths behind, and Pelican set his first of many world track records. He ran the three-eighths in 34.1. He was so far ahead of the second-place horse that the photo shows Pelican hitting the finish line and there is nothing but empty track until you get to the far left of the photograph where you can barely see the top of Piggin' String's nose.

Now Lyo Lee was a trainer who would win over five thousand races in his long career, setting records with both quarter horses and thoroughbreds. He was the one to set up the famous race between their quarter horse mare, Barbara B, and C. S. Howard's thoroughbred, Fair Truckle, at Hollywood Park. The one-hundred-thousand-dollar match race made headlines all over the country and first launched the quarter horse into public racing prominence.

With all this first-rate professional background, Lyo soon found himself in a hell of a quandary with Pelican. He was beating everything on all the prominent brush tracks as well as the registered pari-mutuels. Now the owner, Roy Gill, didn't give a whoop about training horses or matching races. His game was to furnish the money for all this. His fun came in the minimum ten-thousand-dollar bets he loved to make. His order to Lyo Lee was, "I'll take care of all the costs, and your job is to win." And win they did—so much so they were having great difficulty getting a race set. About half the time Pelican was just turned out to pasture while they made the tour with the rest of their string. It was a terrible waste that a horse was so good that he had run himself out of both training, racing, and visiting his varied friends. It was a loss of love from a lot of Pelican's fans as well. They missed his antics around the stables. Besides chewing tobacco, he had a strange game he played with his best buddy, a mixed-breed dog named Guard. The dog would stand, in front of Pelican's stall and permit himself to be picked up by the scruff of the neck over and over. Up, down, up, down. The dog never flinched because Pelican knew just how to do it. They both loved their private game and would sometimes perform it for an hour at a time. "We coulda sold tickets," Lyo said. At night Guard was put on a long stretched wire with a loose ring and a short rope to its collar in front of the Gill stalls. He was free to run back and forth on the wire. Nothing strange ever came around their barn runway. Not ever. Sometimes Guard would lie down and sleep with Pelican, both stretched out in the same position. For a while one of the trainers had a pet raccoon. When he was walking Pelican, the ringtail would sit up on top holding onto the mane like a tiny jockey. Pelican didn't mind having his unique passenger.

Finally, by giving three to one odds, Roy Gill got his minimum at the famous Del Rio, Texas, brush track. The competition was a fast mare named Peggy. Lyo told Gill that they had to lose one if Pelican was ever going to get even a few more good races. Not racing was getting more and more frustrating for both trainer and owner, not to mention the people-loving Pelican. Neither Lyo nor Gill wanted to lose on purpose, but the mighty horse was getting fatter and older out in the pasture. This really galled them. Racing was their lives, and to see one of the greatest racers of all time just thrown away was more than they could take.

Lyo told the jockey, "Let's go fishin'." The jockey understood. He tied a piece of fishing line from the snaffle of the bit under the horse's lip against his gums. It was out of sight and only took a tiny pressure for the horse to feel it. Peggy won by a half length.

They rematched the race a month later, getting over twenty thousand dollars up, and Pelican buried Peggy by three lengths at four hundred yards.

They went to Silver Park, Silver City, New Mexico, with their string of horses. They took Pelican along as a pony horse. (For the uninitiated, a pony horse is the plain animal with the rider sitting on a stock saddle, leading the fancy racehorse to the gate.) Lyo didn't even dream he would get Pelican in a race here, much less make history, but by chance an opening came up for three-year-olds or older and he slipped Pelican in.

Lyo says, "Even so, the only reason they offered to let him in was because they'd seen him ponying horses and didn't figure anyone would enter a horse without proper training. I thought to myself, 'Well, lookee here, I found a bird's nest on the ground.'"

However, it was a three-eighths mile, where Pelican held the world record, so the odds were even. All Roy Gill could do was make side bets and put some heavy money on other horses to place and show.

It was a six-horse field. There was a palomino mare entered named My Question, owned by some Albuquerque people. They were wealthy folks and didn't run her except at their convenience, so little was known about her.

They were off. My Question took the lead right away and at about 150 yards Pelican was third by about a length and a half. Lyo wasn't worried at this point because even when Pelican got a slow start he didn't just play catch-up. With his twenty-seven-feet-and-over stride he'd just whip on by going away. It was "adios, amigos." However, Lyo got a sudden case of the shaky wobbles when the mare was still ahead at the four-hundred mark. Pelican, with a little inducement from jockey Tony Licata, made a move here and came head to head with her. But the mare just hung on. Pelican literally inched ahead to win by a neck. It was the only time he'd ever been legitimately crowded, and he set a new world record of 32.4.

Years later, Lyo said, "I've never heard of a horse running that fast before or since. It'll never be broken." In that race, the show (third) horse was Señor Bill, a fast horse that Lyo had trained for another owner. He was over three lengths behind the second place My Question.

One wonders what speed would have been attained that day if Pelican had been in training. Of course we'll never know, but plain judgment would make one think the mare would have pushed him to the one truly unbreakable record in all racing.

This race, sadly, cinched Pelican to become a white elephant in the Roy Gill and Lyo Lee stables. There was no one to race against. Out of frustration, the Gill Stables ran a large ad in the Quarter Horse Journal and other periodicals for over six months offering to take on any horse in the world from 300 to 660 or anything in between for $50,000 and up. There were no takers.

There was this majestic animal grazing out in a pasture away from the other horses, alone, as was his strange nature. It got so Lyo couldn't stand to have him around to pony on because he spent all his time trying to think of a way to run him. It was a hopeless, mad feeling. One of the great trainers of all time and probably the greatest all-around horse that was ever raced were tied to the ground like two dead trees because of quality. A paradox. A sadness. A shame. A great loss.

In desperation Lyo had a friend write to Ernest Lane, the trainer of Miss Princess. The mare was owned by the King ranch in South Texas, and was reputed to be the fastest quarter horse in the world at the time. She did hold the world record at 440 yards—three-tenths of a second faster than Pelican had been clocked at that specific distance. You have to consider here that Pelican had only run an exact quarter a few times and had never been crowded at all.

Lyo offered to bet $50,000 split evenly on three distances in one race: 350, 440, and 660 yards. They were still turned down.

He then called the man who had owned and developed Seabiscuit, C. S. Howard. Now, as earlier stated, Lyo and his mare Barbara B and half of western America had won millions when Barbara B blew Howard's unbeaten thoroughbred Fair Truckle off the track at 440 yards.

Lyo said, "Well, Mr. Howard, I've got a horse that would run a distance that would be more to Fair Truckle's liking, 660."

Howard replied, "I took care of all you cowboys last winter, and I don't have anything else I'd like to donate to you right now."

Lyo had missed the Albuquerque meet the last fall. This happenstance got him a race for Pelican. A good gambler and racehorse man named Stan Tanner had won the championship stud race there with his horse Be Seven. Out of the upcoming match race, half by chance, would come some partly accidental knowledge that would change the character and characters of quarter horse racing forever.

Up until the early 1940s, all quarter horse racing champions were mares. Even after that, for years the sport was dominated mostly by ladies such as Miss Princess, Tonto Gal, Barbara B, Miss Bank, and on and on. It was taken for granted in the industry that a stallion could seldom outrun a mare.

The only obstacle Stan Tanner had in Be Seven being recognized as the top quarter horse stallion was Pelican. Just one horse and one race separated him from this distinction. It came about by accident, or design, that Roy Gill and Stan Tanner got boozed up together in a Tucson hotel. As men have a tendency to do on these occasions, they brag about their money, physical and mental feats, women, cars, and/or horses. This usually leads to some kind of contest being set for later on with both parties wishing to hell they'd never made the bet. However, they usually stick it out because of that old infection, pride. This bet was for ten thousand dollars at 440 yards, thirty days later.

Roy Gill always left the matching of races up to Lyo. That was part of the deal between them. He was embarrassed to tell Lyo that he'd not only matched the race, but he and Tanner had already put up five thousand dollars apiece as forfeit money. The race was on.

Pelican had been turned out in a three-acre paddock with plenty of grass for sixty days, and Gill had gotten him matched with a very tough horse who was in training. Unlike earlier days when Lyo would get a rare bet and just pull the horse in, run him, and win easily, this would be a tough race even if Pelican had been in perfect shape. So Lyo started working him in the same manner they all did with mares, geldings, or stallions. Since he hadn't made the match, Lyo was worried a lot more than usual. About a week before the race, he decided to see where they were really at.

He took Pelican and Tonto Gal to the gate and really put the hammer down. The mare outran him by two lengths, and the time was only twenty-three. Lyo Lee started trying to fall dead and said, "Lord, what kind of a mess has Gill got me into this time?" Right there a ghostly thought came into Lyo's head.

He walked the stallion and breezed him a bit and ran him at Tonto Gal again. The time was 22.8, but Pelican was lapped on her. He walked him the next day and then the following morning ran him at Barbara B—a mare just a bit faster than Tonto Gal. The race went down in 22.1, with Pelican taking her by a neck. Lyo said, "Well, lookee here." In training a mare in those days all you did was walk her, breeze her slowly, walk her, and breeze her slowly, then a light blowout and you were ready to race. It worked on mares then, and it does now, to a degree. But everyone was training studs the same way. Lyo Lee learned and introduced another method right here.

At the old fairgrounds in Tucson, they ran the quarter mile against Be Seven, beating him by a lap in 22.2. They could have had a faster time but didn't want to look any better than it took to win, hoping they'd get another match.

They did. One more. A long year later, though.

The hard facts are that Lyo learned you have to work a stallion. Really work him to win. The word was passed around and handed down. Nowadays it's exactly the opposite of the 1940s; the studs usually dominate the quarter horse world instead of the mares. Lyo doesn't take credit for being smart; he was just doing anything he could to win that race. He does look back with some remorse and regret at the fine stud horses he handled. He says, "I didn't have enough good sense to work hell out of 'em."

Lyo Lee had the Gill Stable in Phoenix for the races at the state fairgrounds. It had been a year since they'd been able to race Pelican. The year of his prime. They alternately turned him out to pasture and used him as a pony horse.

Suddenly a friend of Lyo's came rushing down to the track, saying excitedly, "Say, Lyo, I think I got you a horse race matched. There's a feller staying at the Santa Rita Hotel that's got a little ol' mare that outran everything in California at three-eighths."

"Whoa, whoa, there," Lyo said, "does he know about Pelican?"

"Not yet, but you better get 'er down damn quick."

"Well, did you find out what this mare is?"

"Yeah, she's called Tidy Step, from a thoroughbred stallion named Tidy. I never got the name of the dam."

Lyo told his friend to go on back to the hotel and put up the forfeit money, and since he said he'd run anybody, he didn't have to tell him the name of our horse. "Just say you have a friend that'll run at him."

This is what you call "winding up the toy."

It worked, and the next day they drew up the contract stipulating that they'd use their own jockeys at an equal weight of 114 pounds, and they'd hire the state fair track starters and officials. The race was to come off a week from Saturday.

Lyo was glad that for a change he had Pelican with him ponying horses and occasionally walking him out. He'd give him a couple of good workouts, and, though that would be a short time for other horses, Pelican would be more ready to go than he'd been for 50 percent of his prior races.

Lyo called Roy Gill in Tucson and told him to get his ass and a bank full of money up here. He added, "We've found another bird's nest on the ground and it's full of golden eggs."

Now the owner of Tidy Step started talking around town and was told that he was crazy. He was informed several times that Pelican was undefeated at three-eighths and held the world record for that distance as well as a couple of others. The man began feeling that he might have overstepped a little. It was natural that he'd be nervous when everybody he talked to said he'd already lost his ten thousand dollars. The man wasn't stupid, but perhaps he was justifiably overconfident.

It turned out that the straightaway at the Phoenix track was 550 yards. So Lyo went to the man and said, "If we go the full 660 we're goin' to have to run on around the turn for another 110 yards. Whoever draws the post position has quite an advantage." The man agreed to the 550 distance.

The talk about the great qualities of Pelican never stopped, but the man also learned that Pelican was a slow starter about two times out of three. So he came to Lyo and said, "You're a gambler, Mr. Lee, a sportsman and a good sport to boot so I wish you'd give me a chance to win part of this race at the quarter pole. That'll make the race worth twenty thousand and if I could get lucky I could break even."

Lyo took it. Then Lyo's jockey came to him bubbling out, "Hey, boss, that man came to me and bet me two thousand against two hundred that he'd be ahead at three hundred yards. I took it."

Lyo blew up, "He's trying to sucker you into crowding our horse too early so we'll lose the big end of the race." Lyo went on more colorfully from there until the jockey was in tears, and then he added, "It's your money, but I'll tell you one thing, if you don't win the race, I'm gonna kill you."

The jockey had always been a strong believer in Lyo Lee and had never failed to listen carefully when he spoke. He said, "I shoulda known better, boss. Don't worry . . . we'll take him all the way."

The man had drawn the post position and was kicking himself for agreeing to the 550 yards when he could by contract have held Lyo to the 660. His trip on the jockey's mind hadn't worked, either.

Licata got Pelican out of the gate first and fast. Pelican was leading the mare a half length at three hundred, one and a half lengths at the quarter pole, and his twenty-seven-and-a-half-foot stride gave him a win of two and a half at the 550 finish.

Lyo said, "So we sent that good man back to California a little less jubilant than when he'd arrived."

That was the last quarter horse race they ever got down. Pelican stood high at twenty-six wins and two seconds, one of the latter being his loss to Piggin' String and the other time he'd been pulled at Del Rio. The word was out on Pelican all over the West now. At great expense and time, they probably could have had another pari-mutuel race or two, but there was no way it wouldn't be a losing proposition. The noble horse had won himself out of business once more.

However, there's more to the story. He would run again as a thoroughbred with astonishing results.

It came about long before the Tidy Step match that people had come to know Pelican and love him to the point that they'd drive or fly long distances just to see him run, even though they might not have a dollar down. To those who knew the horse, he was a major star. One of those was A. D. Woofter, the man who raised him.

A crowd was standing around watching and admiring Pelican as he was being walked after the Tidy Step race. Woofter accosted Lyo: "You know, everybody but me has got well off this horse. It's a dirty shame. I raised him and I deserve something more than the few hundred I got when I sold him to Marvin Ake."

This is what you call "regretting the deal" or "being pissed at the results."

Mr. Woofter went on, "Do you think this horse can run five-eighths?"

Lyo explained to him that he'd tested Pelican secretly several times at five-eighths to a mile and a quarter, and he could sure eat those distances up.

Woofter then wanted to know if there was anyplace they could run a thoroughbred at that distance. Lyo was kind of stupefied at the question for a minute and then he answered, "Yeah, there are a few places around, including Wheeling, West Virginia, and Lincoln Downs at Providence, Rhode Island."

Woofter went on to relate that Pelican was a registered thoroughbred and he had the papers. Only he and his son, Paul, knew about it. He was registered under the name Silent Partner. He told Lyo that if he thought the horse could win at five-eighths, he'd give him the papers. All he wanted was to be tipped off so he could get a good bet down. Lyo figured that Woofter had some counterfeit papers that he wanted to deal off on him, and that could sure get a man in a lot of trouble. Just the same Woofter told him he was going on back home and that he'd mail the papers to him.

Well, Lyo had forgotten about the incident and was surprised about a week later when the papers arrived. If he'd been subject to fainting spells Lyo would no doubt have bounced off the hard earth. The description was a page long and practically named every hair on the horse, including the gray spot on his hip, the gray spot on his mane, and the gray spot on his belly under the cinch. The right hind leg was white up to the hock in front sloping down to the back . . . the bald face that extended over his eyes but circled around the orbs, and on and on to the tiniest detail. Pelican had to be the horse that was described on the papers.

"The horse was registered before Marvin Ake ever bought him," Lyo said. Evidently the colt looked so bad, even though he'd registered him, that Woofter thought Marvin would like a quarter horse better for ranch work, never dreaming that he'd race him or even take him off the ranch. All things considered, Woofter can hardly be blamed for his actions, though it is reasonable to believe that as the horse's fame grew he sometimes gazed over the edge of sheer cliffs sorely tempted to test out his flying ability.

Woofter owned a thoroughbred stud named Montosa James. The stud was listed on the papers as the sire, and a mare called Covollie as the dam. It had been widely believed until now that Joe Hancock, Jr., was the quarter horse sire.

Melvin Haskell of Tucson, head of the American Quarter Horse Association and a writer on the breed for several magazines, used Pelican as the prime example of how a quarter horse could always outrun a thoroughbred. So Lyo quickly reasoned that he couldn't even run a matched five-eighths anywhere in that part of the country. It was a hairy situation. That wondrous, innocent animal named Silent Partner and/or Pelican was being cut off again because someone had messed with his ancestral papers.

Lyo talked to Roy Gill and told him, "Well, if we're ever gonna race this horse again as long as he lives we're gonna have to run him as a thoroughbred."

Gill agreed. Lyo explained about Haskell and a few other things and added that they better get as far from Tucson as possible. Gill agreed again. They had mostly thoroughbred speed horses in their stable now so they'd have some early action up there in Rhode Island until they could get the right situation set up for Pelican.

First they went to Hot Springs, Arkansas, because Lincoln Downs didn't open until after the Oak Lawn meet closed.

Lyo took a string of good, fresh horses that had been wintered in the fine climate of Arizona and hit the Arkansas boys who had to do a lot of their training in the snow and mud. It's called "gettin' the edge."

Lyo was using Pelican for a pony horse again. He met a man named Wills who was associated with track investigations across the country. Wills was actually an undercover agent for the FBI.

Lyo and Wills got to be pretty good friends—going out, drinking, playing, and dining together quite often.

Lyo said, "He drank quite a bit . . . in fact, he consumed a little too much." One night after dinner they were drinking and talking about horses. Lyo had just won a good race with a horse called Phantom Sea. Lyo told Wills he had a pony horse out there that could outrun most of the horses at Hot Springs. He had, in fact, secretly run Pelican at Phantom Sea for seven-eighths. Pelican had walked away from the ten-time stakes winner without having trained for a single day for that distance.

Anyway, Lyo continued and correctly told Wills that he'd won a lot of quarter-horse races with him, but he'd never had a chance to run him on a thoroughbred track. This is what you call "settin' up the deal."

The FBI man replied on schedule. "No problem. You've got the papers on him so I'll come back in the morning and take a look, and see if you want to go ahead and run him."

Lyo was quietly elated, but told Wills that the horse didn't have the required tattoo because he'd never needed it.

Wills said, "That's all right."

He came down the next morning and Lyo gave him the papers and led the horse out. Wills said, "Well, there's no doubt that this is the horse described on the papers. He's sure no ringer." So Wills called in the official tattoo people and they put it under Pelican's lip. He was now legal to run on a thoroughbred track, and Lyo was protected.

Lyo had never intended to run him at Hot Springs at seven-eighths. He wanted to get the five-eighths down, then move on up to seven and, step by step, to a mile and a quarter, taking down big bets as they escalated. Gill agreed once more. Of course, by previous testing, they'd already found out that Pelican was up to the enormous step-by-step challenge. This is what you call "justified ambition."

When the Hot Springs meet was over, Lyo loaded all their horses on a railroad car and shipped them to Lincoln Downs at Providence, Rhode Island.

Now, there wasn't any "form" on Silent Partner. He'd never raced as a thoroughbred so he was listed as a maiden (never won a race). However,

Lyo skipped the maiden race and put him in a handicap instead with a bunch of good horses. The distance was the required five-eighths. Lyo had his jockey hold him back so that Silent Partner was recorded as coming in sixth, with long odds of fifty to one. Of course the story was zapped around about these dumb southwestern cowboys coming up here and trying to make a pony horse compete with real racehorses. Lyo had left Pelican's mane naturally long and even a little shaggy, unlike the neatly pulled ones of the northeastern bluebloods. He looked pretty ragged amongst the city slickers and of course that drew extra attention to Pelican as he came in way back in the pack.

This is what you call "seeing what Lyo Lee wants you to."

Anyway, Lyo always liked to run a horse over a track before making any sizable bets on him. Different horses like different tracks. He did feel that Pelican could run on any kind of track, but he wanted to be sure. Also, the horse had never run around a turn in an official race.

Roy Gill was talking about laying down fifty thousand dollars on the race, so Lyo was under heavy pressure to set the proper music for the orchestra of which he was the sole conductor. The only way anyone could bet big money here was with the bookmakers and hope word didn't get back to the mutuels and kill the odds.

Gill put fifty thousand dollars down, over the phone, to his favorite and trusted bookmaker, who had assured him he'd not let the word get back to the race track and ruin the payoff. Talking of bookmakers—Lyo said Gill's trust was misplaced because bookmakers are not stupid or they couldn't stay in business. If too much money is on big odds they'll call a cohort and bet them down through the machines.

The night before the race Lyo called Mr. Woofter and tipped him off about the race. Then he tried to tell Gill he didn't feel the bookies would hold the money at the same price as when the horse would come out of the gate. Gill disagreed.

Pelican né Silent Partner came out on the board at twenty-to-one odds. If the price held, Gill's bet would return a million dollars. Just after the horse left the paddock the price dropped to nine to one and by the time they were about to head for the gate they were at four and a half to one.

Lyo's and Gill's spirits dropped down into their boot tops. As radical as the price change had already been, they were scared rootless the odds would wind up dead even by the time they closed the windows.

They didn't have any idea where the leak had come from—the bookies, Woofter, or from Gill's own stable. It didn't matter now anyway. The money was down. They were in line. They were off!

Pelican aka Silent Partner won easily, finishing just off a track record of fifty-eight seconds flat with a three-lap lead, coasting. The payoff wasn't so bad. They took down almost a quarter of a million dollars. Now they could move up through seven-eighths and a mile and sixteenths and "really tap 'em out."

"But, the splashy brown hit the fan in globs," Lyo said. "It created a disturbance in the racing business almost like a declaration of war. All the newspapers were full of the cowboys coming up there with a horse that looked like a wild mustang and taking them down the line. It was bad publicity for me and more so for this great horse. It was a big write-up in the *New York Times* that led to the real problem."

Bob Waldo wrote in part,

> A horse that looked more like a nice cow pony than a thoroughbred was a medium of a "killing" for the boys in the ten-gallon hats and high boots here yesterday afternoon. Mysterious money began showing up for Gill Ranch Stables. . . . The five-year-old son of little-known Montosa James and Covollie performed like the "good thing" he was supposed to be, winning handily by three lengths. . . . He is known to be one of the fastest quarter horse performers in the West, winning innumerable races against the "speedballs" in Texas and Arizona. In drubbing many of the horses that managed to beat him at this same track less than a week ago Silent Partner returned $8.40 to win. . . . Yesterday, however, he combined with the champion quarter horse rider, Tony Licata, to race the remaining eleven horses into the ground with his dazzling speed.

The aforementioned Melvin Haskell, president of the American Quarter Horse Association, who lived in Tucson, subscribed to the *New York Times* to keep up with the racing world. The paper was about four days late reaching Tucson, but there he saw the picture of Lyo and Pelican on the front

page of the sporting section. Now after all his support of Pelican and honest belief in the animal as an example of the perfect running quarter horse,
Haskell was understandably angry. He was also powerfully positioned and
personally wealthy. He did not take kindly to this horse being headlined as
a thoroughbred and making him look like an idiot.

Even though the head of the Jockey Club had told Lyo to go ahead and
run Silent Partner/Pelican because they weren't interested in quarter horses,
the situation instantly changed when Haskell got into it. Haskell pointed
out, accurately, that the registration papers around the country had two different sires: Joe Hancock, Jr., for the quarter horse Pelican, and Montosa
James for the thoroughbred Silent Partner.

Gill told Lyo that when the dust settled, he'd probably have a choice to
run Pelican as either a short- or long-distance horse, but not as both, and
in that case he was going to choose to go with him as a quarter horse. Well,
Lyo knew that decision put them out of business. Even before the new and
vast publicity, they were unable to get a short race matched. Now it would
be impossible. So with Gill's blessings he took the horse to Cleveland, Ohio,
for one last go.

He entered him in a seven-eighths with instructions for the jockey to pull
him. The odds were good because nobody except Lyo Lee, Roy Gill, and the
jockey Licata believed that Pelican was unusual enough to run and win at
seven-eighths. They pulled the horse and came in fourth. Since this was the
last go-around, Lyo decided to hold him again even though the odds were
at twelve to one. If the horse lost twice, the odds should be enormous on the
third and killer race.

Well, Pelican, with his natural love for people, must have temporarily
become disgusted with them. At the turn he took off and ran away from the
field in 1.23, still coasting.

Lyo said, "The only way the jockey could have held him would have been
to stand straight up in the saddle and rear back like he was trying to stop a
team of runaway mules."

The grand adventure was over. Pelican had taken control and ended it
running naturally and grandly several lengths ahead of the rest of the field.

They retired him to stud in Arizona and used him as a cow pony, just as
Marvin Ake had started him out. None of his colts amounted to anything.

Marvin Ake had bred a mare with Pelican before he sold him to Gill. The colt, which he named Penguin, won only one race before Marvin gelded him. Marvin used Penguin as a cow horse until he died.

Pelican was a freak. All the gene mappers in the world couldn't figure how this running marvel came about. He was crowded only once, and even then he set an unbeaten world record in the three-eighths. If you forget the four times he was pulled, his record was twenty-eight wins and two places. Even the great Australian horse Phar Lap and the mighty John Henry would be tested dearly to match his overall ability. He could run any distance, on any kind of track. He was sound as an anvil, better natured than a puppy, honest as Abe Lincoln, and, with reasoned consideration, probably the greatest all-around racehorse that ever lived.

Lyo said, "Pelican was a horseman's dream. He was what breeders had been trying to get since horses were first tamed. When you think of the small amount of training he received, the kind of tracks he ran on and the far greater methods of training, feeding, and doctoring we have today, as well as the mathematical odds of hundreds of thousands more horses to choose from, it's doubtful if we'll ever see anything to surpass him."

Yes, he was a joyful accident in history. He was so good that he was mostly idle and untrained for lack of competition. He chewed tobacco and slept stretched out like a dog, loved people and was loved by them. Among other things he was called Red Apple, Pelican, and Silent Partner, but for sure he must be called a creature of love and true greatness. Let's toast him and be thankful he passed our way—running.

Cricket

Little Horse of the Prairies

I don't remember when I started riding, playing, and working on Cricket. I was a four-year-old kid when I first got him, and he was a horse a year and a half younger than me, that's all. The little gelding was an odd horse in many ways. For one thing: his ears were the size of a much bigger horse— these gave him acute hearing ability. He was smaller than a quarter horse but built just as powerfully in the hindquarters as any show winner. This breed was called "Steel Dust" back then. The little bay had "bottom," as the saying goes about a horse that never quits, and delivers under the toughest conditions. Cricket always delivered. This formula applies to people, also. It's the only sure way to know a friend. Cricket didn't realize he was thriving in the era of the Great Depression and dust bowl of the thirties. I didn't, either. It seemed to have always been this way and I thought it always would be.

In 1928, the year before the biggest stock market crash in American history, my father, W. B. Evans, had founded a town, Humble City, on the west half of our modest-sized ranch. It was in the far southeast county (Lea) of New Mexico bordering West Texas. Our ranch land was located between the cow town of Lovington and the oil boomtown of Hobbs. My father envisioned Hobbs and Lovington growing to meet his town of Humble City. He had laid out a huge town site, fully expecting his town to be the center of a big city. He mailed circulars all over America. A few far-scattered lots sold, and eight or ten houses were built, but it still looked like what it was—a dried-up cow pasture. There was a small grocery and a filling station. He soon got a two-room schoolhouse built and an authorized post office, which was located in the front room of our home. My mother, Hazel, was the postmistress.

The crash of '29—and the far-reaching drought that created the dust bowl—put a whoa on all growth. Except, of course, myself, Cricket, and

Dolly, a bay saddle mare. Dolly was a much lighter, brownish-red color than Cricket, and had a starred face. We kept a fenced-in pasture west of our house for the milk cow and Cricket, but we let Dolly roam the entire town site—which was initially our ranch—with a mule and various colors and kinds of milk cows belonging to others.

It seems impossible, but nearly everyone became poor overnight, and more so as the weather and the business world deteriorated. Farmers, ranchers, and even most townsfolk tried to keep a milk cow, a few laying hens, a hog or two, and a vegetable garden to help them survive. So did our family.

But even before things got so tough, Cricket and I had started supplying meat for the Evans' table. I would cinch up my four-dollar saddle, mount, call my two dogs, and into the vast prairies we'd head. There were cottontails and jackrabbits to be had. And the approach to catching each was different. The compact cottontail rabbit averaged out being more tender and tasty than the more sinewy long-ears. Like a racing quarter horse, the cottontails were good for a short dash of great speed to their home hole. They never grazed farther than they felt safe from this protection. If we jumped a long-eared jackrabbit, the two dogs would race out after the quarry with Cricket and me following in pounding pursuit. If the jackrabbit was young or old, the dogs nearly always caught them. They seldom caught the in-between ones.

The moment of capture was critical. Everything had to be timed to precision. If Cricket and I were too far behind, the dogs would rip the rabbit into approximate halves and start devouring it. We had to be right on top of the chase-and-catch so I could bail off my horse yelling loudly, "No! No! No!" momentarily freezing the dogs' actions until I could retrieve the rabbit, gut it, and hang it safely from my saddle horn. The family's protein allotment was at stake, and it was my responsibility to supply it. It was fun. A lot of fun. It was a great game for all of us—except for the rabbits, of course.

More world-class rodeo ropers came from Lea County than anywhere else in the world, and I've often wondered if this sort of necessary activity of rabbit hunting in those great, arena-flat prairies was one of the reasons for that. It makes sense. When I'd hit the ground running to save the rabbit for the dinner table, Cricket had to come to a stop with his hind legs under his

belly. He'd stand waiting and watching, as if tied to the ground, with his ears working back and forth thinking silently about his own thrill at our mutual success—or failure.

The dogs, and Cricket, too, for that matter, never got over racing so near it they could almost touch the cottontail and then have it suddenly vanish underground while they were in full pursuit. It amazed and disappointed them every time.

Of course, we could have waited until the dogs dug it out, which often took two hours of pawing labor, until I learned how to twist them out with a strand of barbed wire. I would simply uncoil the wire, put a V at the end, bend a handle on the other end, stick it down in the hole, and start slowly twisting. It didn't take long until I felt when the V was solidly snared in the fur, and I'd simply pull them out. Fresh, unbruised meat for half-starved people and animals.

Yes, that is right. The dogs got the bones and gristle after we had the meat. They loved it. Unlike chicken bones, which break into dangerous sharp slivers in a dog's jaws, rabbit bones are safe and delicious as well as highly nutritious. On those unavoidable times when we'd tear and bruise a rabbit so it was unpleasant to humans, we'd profitably feed part to the dogs and all the rest to the hogs.

My mother had many ways of fixing rabbit. Stewed, baked, broiled, and she could fry and season them so many different ways that I never tired of it. Often she'd make hot biscuits and gravy to go with the little lifesaving creatures.

Later, when I was old enough to go to school, I'd sometimes have delicious fried rabbit to go with the sowbelly stuck between two halves of biscuit as well as peanut butter and jelly in the same manner. I loved it. I loved it all and was totally unaware that these were hard times.

Cricket benefited, too. Since Humble City was losing residents instead of gaining them, my dad was on the road in a Model T truck trading anything for anything. He knew how important Cricket was to the survival of all of us, and every chance he got, he would swap for whatever amounts of oats or shelled corn he could get, to help Cricket provide for the entire family.

My father had sold nearly everything to finance his dream of a bustling town. He sold all our riding gear, saddles, bridles, chaps, spurs, and anything that would bring a dime or a dollar. He let me keep my four-dollar saddle—bridle thrown in—that my mother had bought me with the pennies she somehow saved. The old leather reins kept breaking until I gave up and just used a piece of rope instead. It must have looked awful to some people but I didn't care. Survival was my game, not vanity.

The year was especially bad for the Evans family. The great blizzard froze to death every single cow they owned on their West Texas ranch, and their eldest son, Elbert, had been killed in World War I. Grandfather Evans never went back to ranching but became the first elected judge for Hockley County (Texas), for two terms, then was city judge at Ropes, Texas, for the rest of his life. When he'd come to visit us in humble Humble City, New Mexico, he always brought me a present. One day he brought me two half-grown shepherd-mix pups. He had already named them Depression and Proration. The first name was obvious, but the second name came from the government prorating oil production. People were so broke that they cut down on buying everything. This caused a glut of oil. It was selling for only a few cents a barrel. When the government cut pumping time to only a few days a month, oil went up to a dollar a barrel and finally became profitable.

Depression and Proration looked like twins, both dark chocolate with partial white faces. They grew big, strong, and fast. I became so close to them and Cricket that I would have done anything for them, and I mean anything.

The two dogs would often just lie down in the horse pasture and watch Cricket. He would graze right between them. They'd never move. Buddies. Well, after all they were the "chosen" and had permanent jobs taking care of our family.

My best friend was Wayne Simpson. His father had a ranch headquarters, corrals and all, about a mile and three-quarters southwest of town. Wayne really liked Dolly. We'd catch her up, and with me on Cricket, we'd ride the vast empty-appearing pastures, just talking horses, dogs, cows, and girls. Sometimes on our fun rides, Wayne would spot something ahead as a marker, and he and Dolly would challenge me and Cricket to a race. Now, on a real working outfit, this would get your tail fired. However, there was nothing left around there but survival places.

Anyway, we'd line up as even as we could and come to a stop and I'd count out loud, "One, two, three, go." Away we'd rip.

Dolly was a lot bigger than Cricket, and she was fast, but when I leaned over and touched Cricket on the neck and told him, "Now, Cricket. Now," the little bay always responded with an extra bit of heart and passed Dolly. Every time.

Sometimes, when I'd had a good day with the dogs and rabbits, I'd simply ride Cricket way out in a big circle either to the east or west of Humble City just to look at the prairie-so-flat that on a clear day—that was a day when the wind hid out—we could observe the horizon to the vanishing point and actually see the earth bend in the beginning of its great circle. And the cloudless sky—well, it was so big and blue that all I could measure in my little mind was forever and ever, up, down, and around. I'll never forget the wondrous feeling of the two of us being all alone way out there, at great peace and thankfulness for the magic of all that quiet space.

Just a few years later, I would get that same feeling looking at the many-colored mesas and blue-purple mountains of northern New Mexico and other vast spaces of the great Southwest.

At a chosen time during the summer, I'd ride Cricket out to visit Wayne at his ranch headquarters. You know, heckfire, everybody is aware of that old saw about timing is everything. Well, I learned that timing was food. I managed to arrive at the Simpsons' place when the sun was straight overhead, signifying the noon hour. I'd dismount and lead Cricket to water at the rock tank next to the Simpsons' windmill. Since it just happened to be on the side of the house where the kitchen was, I'd stand in an obvious place, looking all around, and whistling little tunes. If necessary I would try to get Cricket to drink more water than he wanted. I'd loosen the cinch on the saddle to make him more comfortable. I'd gaze at the sky looking for birds. It worked every time. Finally, Mrs. Simpson would spot me, come to the kitchen screen door, and yell out for me to come in and join them for the noon meal. Mrs. Simpson somehow managed to raise frying chickens all summer, and they had at least two or three for lunch almost every day. She could cook those things as delicious as my mom could rabbit. I never tasted anything better in my whole life. Not even later when I'd dine in the Beverly Hills Hotel or the late Russian Tea Room in New York City. Lordy, lordy, that Cricket horse had a happy pardner whether it was chasing after wild rabbits or Mrs. Simpson's fried chicken. I would have loved to share half my fried chicken with him, but he was a vegetarian . . . .

Here's the landscape as I recall it. There wasn't much of that life-sustaining element on top of the ground—swimming pools and fishing holes—where we lived, but Humble City did have a fine underground reservoir, and there weren't zillions of people then to deplete it. Windmills cost money—real money that folded or jingled. There were some good-producing windmills on all of the few, far-scattered ranches that were still inhabited. Everybody in Humble City had hand pumps. Even in the school yard. There was a solid reason for this. Although there was still a little money left over from oil and gambling in nearby Hobbs, Humble City townsfolk were as poor as a homeless person without pockets.

I was acutely aware of the best, biggest, and most available water in tanks. Three or so miles northeast of town, where Wayne and I used to set trot lines for the little catfish, there was a long dirt tank with a windmill at each end. And there was another one a couple of miles west of town made out of rocks. I can't remember these fortunate folks' last name, but I sure remember their daughter's first name. It was Lillian. These wise people actually built changing rooms—one for women on one side of the great tank and one for men on the other. They had diving boards at each end near the windmills that pumped the wonderful, pure cool water as long as the wind blew and that was 80 percent of the time. They cleaned the pool by emptying it into a large garden spot of corn, green beans, watermelons, and cantaloupes. There was enough extra water to miraculously have some green grass for their milk cows and a few beef cattle. I always figured they were the richest people in the whole world. Folks would come from all over to pay their dime to swim in the precious water and picnic on the lush grass.

During the school year, that beautiful, big-eyed, rich little Lillian would stop off at Curtis's store and buy me two or three Milky Way candy bars a week. Lordy, that gorgeous young girl got prettier by the day. She was a princess of the prairies. I just knew she'd be crowned queen of the earth someday. After Cricket and my dogs, little "Milky Way Lillian" was my first womanly love. Many years later I heard that someone made a commercial swimming pool at the northeast tank where our only sparse supply of catfish swam.

My dad had sold all the cattle off the east end of our ranch to help found his city on the west end. Then he moved his widowed sister, Pearl Nettles—mother of five daughters and a son, the eldest, named P. J.—from across the line in West Texas. They also had a little bunch of mixed-blood cows, a half-Jersey half-Hereford bull, chickens, and hogs. They were relocated to the house, which was formerly the headquarters, where there was still some old grass left. Even in times of great drought some spots would get rain. About half the rained-on, eastern pastures were in fair shape. My aunt Pearl didn't want to graze it down to the dirt. She wisely wanted some left for the winter.

As hard as her daughters worked, they didn't care much for cow punching, so it fell to me and Cricket to move a few head at a time around to outlying vacated homesteads. Sometimes we'd find a field of weeds or a little pasture that somehow had missed being grazed bare. Once in a while I could get my cousin Kaye, an eight-year-old, to ride Dolly and help me herd these cockeyed cows like sheep.

Since some of them had milk-cow blood in them—Jersey, Guernsey, Holstein—Aunt Pearl milked all of them that bore calves. She separated the cream and made butter to sell in Hobbs along with eggs from the hens. With me chousing them all over, hunting feed, they sure didn't get enough browsing to make any kind of surplus milk.

A man from Lovington and one from Hobbs and my dad had somehow gotten a highway right-of-way approved and fenced between the two towns with Humble City in between. There was a narrow fenced lane about a half mile from Aunt Pearl's to the highway right-of-way. So I figured out that Cricket and I could actually drive most of her motley herd down the lane along the fenced-in but as yet dirt highway. There was quite a bit of forage on each side of the road. It took a full day, leaving the ranch right after sunup and returning in the late afternoon with the cows better off than when we left.

At first, I nearly worked little Cricket to death before I got the cows trained to graze only on one side of the road going in the morning on the left and staying on the other side in the afternoon on the way back. About every third day I'd ride Dolly to work and let Cricket rest and feed on the home pasture. Of course, horses will graze at night if they're hungry enough. Their legs lock so that they can sleep standing up.

Everybody was doing their portion. Aunt Pearl and her covey of girls from four to thirteen in years seemed fairly happy and were healthy—growing and learning. P. J. was off somewhere working, sending her whatever he could spare to help out. Later on, he would be killed in the Battle of the Bulge during World War II.

Aunt Pearl had bright, brown eyes that, I was sure, could see through brick walls. She was small in stature, quick in movements, with the endurance of an Arabian warhorse, and she could somehow find something to laugh at even in a pen of dumb chickens. No matter how hard her labors, she was always kind with her firmness and I respected and loved her. So it is hard to understand—and especially to admit—how I could commit the sin against her that I did.

There was a family that lived on the corner where her lane ran into the

Hobbs-Lovington highway. I can't remember how many boys and girls the couple had. All I remember is only one of the skinny little boys, called Peter, went to school, and sometimes I had to share my lunch with him. He simply didn't have any. He was shy and seemed embarrassed about everything. Sometimes I'd take him by the house and my mother would scrounge up something for him to eat. He gulped whatever she could find without hardly chewing it. That boy was hungry. Peter told me his daddy was in California working on farms trying to save enough to move them to the state-of-all-dreams.

School was out for the summer and I'd been herding these cows right by Peter's house. His little sisters and brothers started coming out to the road and staring at me and Cricket as we worked hard to turn the cows down the right-of-way. They were all skinny right to the bone. I was afraid they were going to starve right before my eyes, and just fall down and blow away.

I don't know if I was asked or volunteered, I can't say, but one day it just started happening. Before returning the cattle to Aunt Pearl's, Cricket and I cut out a few cows that had milk in their bags and drove them around behind Peter's house where there was a barn and corral. I told Peter's mother that they could have a little milk from each one as long as they didn't take it all. They gathered ropes, or whatever they could find, to put around a cow's neck to tie them to the corral fence. Then the poor woman started ordering her kids to get clean buckets and pans—anything to hold milk. She, Peter, and the oldest girl started desperately milking the patient cows.

Well, I was feeling like a benevolent king after a few days because the whole family started perking up and looking like they might live. The mother thanked me and thanked me and said she was saying prayers for me to some saint I'd never heard of and I doubted ever heard of me. Oh, I felt like the Savior himself. I was the Salvation Army and Red Cross all in one. It was a good feeling, all right, but it wasn't gonna last long. This milk was not mine to give away.

I began to hear Aunt Pearl puzzling over the sudden drop in milk production. Half of it went to the calves. From the other half she extracted cream for butter and the "blue John" that was leftover was for her kids, chickens, and hogs. It barely went around as it was. Now, due to my generosity with someone else's property, I was possibly creating another health and welfare problem.

I might forget most names, and couldn't remember how many children the hungry lady on the corner had, but I'm here to tell you, I never forgot the silent looking-over Aunt Pearl gave me when she found out what was happening to the milk production. After the first stunned stare, she looked across her garden plot, up at the windmill wheel turning and clanking in the wind, took an extra-long, deep breath, and then she stared back into my suddenly-gone-blind, brown eyes, and said in a quiet, perfectly controlled voice,

"Maxie, you have to decide if you want to help strangers or your blood kin. It is your decision." She then bent over and started pulling weeds on her way to the garden.

I rode wonderful, faithful, honest little Cricket out into the prairie. My throat was swelled up with something mean. My chest seemed to have a badger in it trying to dig its way out with long, sharp claws, and my eyes were full of muddy water. Cricket circled and took me home.

Well, I recovered to a degree and felt guilty as a baby killer, as I worked poor Cricket half to death hurrying the cows past the corner place. The kids peeked around the house at me now; I couldn't stand to look. Then one morning I saw a rickety old truck beside the house and the whole family were busy loading it. The father had come for them after all. They were all working their skinny little tails off, joyously, chattering like a flock of week-old chicks. The mama said something to the papa, and he looked at me. He got something out of the seat of the old truck and, waving at me, said something I couldn't quite hear. I stopped Cricket and waited. He came on, this family man, and when he got close he looked Cricket over and said, "That's sure a nice looking little pony."

"He's a horse," I said.

"Yeah, yeah, I reckon he is." Then he handed me an orange he'd brought all the way from California and said, "Rosie told me how you helped. May God bless you, son." And he gave Cricket a pat on the neck and me one on my right leg. He turned back to finish loading the truck and taking his entire family way out west to the land of oranges.

I felt right keen for a while, and that orange was almost as delicious as little Lillian's Milky Way candy bars. I never did get all the way over my deceit to my precious Aunt Pearl. But I improved, and spent the rest of my life trying to be dead-on loyal to my friends whether they were kin or not.

Aunt Pearl and two neighbors got some rain. The rest of the country dried to dust, and there wasn't enough grass to fill up a dozen grasshoppers. The beef cows left were either dying or so weak they wobbled in a slight breeze. The government put up ten dollars a head and slaughtered around 80 percent of all the beef cattle in 1933. I tried not to think much on how lucky we were, even though I learned later in life how terrible times had been. Things seemed plumb natural to me.

Now the winds came even harder at times. I blamed that on the fact my granddad had given me a brand new dude hat. I immediately put a bend in the brim to make it look as much like a real western Stetson as I could. It gave me a whole new cowboy feeling as Cricket and I drove that string of cows halfway to Hobbs.

It seems that the same little bunch of clouds that had dropped rain on Aunt Pearl and her near neighbor's place had crossed the road, and there in the right-of-way for about a mile and a half some grass had actually turned green and grown.

There were three cows in estrus at the same time, and that half-Jersey bull was going crazier than he had been born to be, and that was a bunch. He'd given me two tons of trouble, turning back trying to find an opening in the fence, and I don't know what all. That bull had me out of sorts all day.

The wind just kept getting stronger, and the sun was only a light glow through the dust. I pulled my new hat down real tight and wrapped a handkerchief around my face to keep from strangling on the tiny pieces of the wind-borne earth.

Cricket and I finally got the little herd to the end of the lane and were within about a half mile or less of what had once been the horse pasture gate to the headquarters. I don't know how Cricket kept those cows moving in that truly blinding storm. He did it mostly on his own. I was having so much trouble keeping my new hat pulled down that I just gave the little horse his head.

That blasted bull kept quitting the herd. Cricket had to cut out with him and drive him back, over and over and over. I hope the wailing wind overcame the sounds of the words I used on that bull. If not, I was sure I knew which direction I'd be headed when the final trumpets blew.

I rode out ahead in a lope to open the home gate. I threw it back all the way to the fence so there'd be no excuse for the bull to turn back. I remounted and sure enough, I just barely returned in time to see the bull heading back for the lane. The cows were no trouble. They followed the wagon-rutted road. They knew there was water, some feed, and the windbreak of the barns to be had.

Cricket was working on that bull, his head down, his nose a couple of yards from the bull's rear, like a champion cutting horse. Even that didn't get the job done. The cockeyed bull would not go through the gate. Not only that, he got mad. Real mad. He whirled, charging us.

Just as Cricket sidestepped him with about a strand of hair to spare, I felt my hat go. I grabbed at my head, but it was too late. I somehow saw in that blur of brown, my hat sailing and bouncing off the earth ten feet high. At the same time, Cricket had whirled after the bull and had him going in a dead run.

It was a moment of decision. Did I rein Cricket after my hat or let him pursue the bull? The bull was heading full speed away from the gate but straight at the horse pasture fence with us after him desperately trying to turn him back. I let my precious hat go on toward Texas, or even possibly Louisiana, and concentrated my thoughts with Cricket's on the bull.

Too late again! That sucker had run right smack into a fence post, smashing its middle into splinters and taking out about forty or fifty yards of wire. I was barely able to rein Cricket sideways to keep him from getting badly cut with the barbed wire. We just kept on going, running half blind trying to see the bull. We couldn't find him in the thick brown hide-lashing storm. I eased Cricket into a walk and felt the thoughtless wind tearing the hair on my hatless head out by the roots.

When we got to the corral, Aunt Pearl and a couple of her girls were just closing the corral gate on the cows as they shoved together at the water trough. There stood the bull. I was shocked numb; Cricket paid no attention. He'd done his job. As soon as the bull saw us, he crowded out some of the cows and took three places at the trough for himself. The calves were bawling in an adjoining pen for their mamas and I wanted to leave for mine, but it would not be understood why, so I held it back.

The wind growled all night and then clouds followed, but it only rained in a few little spots again. But once more, Pearl got nearly a half inch of the lifesaving wet. A couple of days later, my dad and a couple of the Curtis boys roped and snubbed up the bull and put a ring in his nose. I've heard the old saw about "a horse laugh" a zillion times just like everybody else, but I never could hear Cricket laughing out loud. I'm pretty sure he was chuckling silently all the time because that bull got easier to handle than a baby chick.

I never did find my hat, but I'm sure somebody did who needed it worse than I did. It ended up okay because my dad traded for me a real working wide-brimmed hat that had proven itself for about a decade on the head of one of the Curtis boys. It was sort of greasy and too big, but I folded paper inside the band and felt like I was wearing a crown of pure gold. I could tell Cricket was happy for my new-old acquisition because of the extra zing in his running walk. After all, he was a world champion bull chaser himself.

Because of Cricket—and Dolly—and our creative grazing practices, we had given Aunt Pearl's pasture some rest, and with the blessed spot rains the Great Mystery in the Sky had sent her, she had enough grass to run her cows through the fall and winter without damaging the land. That would free up Cricket and myself to pursue other activities.

Dad had given Aunt Pearl and her hardworking brood of girls his saddle-and-work mule. The family enlarged their garden to practically field-size, and had worked all summer putting up jars of all sorts of vegetables—enough for the year ahead. The hog they butchered was already hanging in the smokehouse, all salted down. Eating pretty well was further ensured by the chickens for meat and eggs, and the milk cows supplying dairy products.

However, other citizens of Humble City hadn't planned as well and the town was slowly losing its citizens. They were starving out and leaving the houses empty. That meant school enrollments were dropping. My mother's post office in our home was losing business, and she didn't seem to be doing so well, either. I don't think that was what was mainly on her mind, though. She had been with child for about nine months. Dad took her over to stay with our friends, the Mannings, southwest of Lovington.

The Manning family, with their three boys, had tried to make it at Humble City, believing in my dad's vision, but were forced to move temporarily back to their father-in-law's homestead. So my mother stayed with them near a doctor until my sister Glenda was born. For whatever reason, she couldn't breast feed Glenda. So Cricket and I were enlisted to drive a milk cow—Aunt Pearl had donated her best milk producer—the nine miles to Lovington to, as my dad so cleverly put it, "save your sister's life."

Cricket and I had made drives back and forth so many times on the right-of-way that I was actually looking forward to this honor. Herding the lone cow wasn't so bad from Aunt Pearl's house down the narrow lane, but the minute we hit the right-of-way and I got the old mixed-blood headed toward our desperate destination, Cricket had already broken a little sweat where his neck joined his shoulders. Driving this one animal was a whole lot harder than driving a herd. She wasn't as big or as mean as the bull, but for the first couple of miles she tried to turn back what seemed to me like a thousand times. Finally she quit trying that and started going from one side of the dirt highway to the other to graze, just as she'd been allowed to do for months with the rest of the herd. Each of the nine miles seemed like a month. We were all three beginning to wear out before we were halfway there.

If I hadn't been "chosen" to ride Cricket half to death chasing one cow, I might have thought that, maybe, she would have been more use being butchered for beef rather than milking—and I would have happily volunteered to do the deed. Driving her was like pushing a long chain up a mountain highway.

The sun moved slowly on over the sky, into a hazy sunset. We were still a piece of hard ground from the little cattle town. Cricket was actually lathering a little at the mouth, and his flanks sweated and were drawn down. For the first time I could remember he quit working his ears. This was another worry. And me? After all the riding I'd done lately I figured this drive would be a song, but my butt was so numb I could no longer feel my four-dollar saddle under me.

It was way after dark when we got there, but my dad greeted us with a big smile, along with giving instructions. Feed and water the cow. He would fill the bucket he was carrying with milk.

As for Cricket and me? Well, I watered both of us at the stock tank, put him in a stall, and fed him some shelled corn Mr. Manning had furnished.

He also threw him a shock of grain hay from a stack. My dad was finished milking. My mom was heating baby bottles, and I got in just in time to see my sister take her first swallow of cow's milk. I told my mom several dozen times how pretty her new baby was and how glad I was that my new sister was saved.

All I wanted then was a little bit to eat and some sleep. I didn't even wait for them to show me where I was to bed down. I just jerked a blanket from one of the boys' cots and wrapped myself in it on the floor. I slept. If I dreamed at all it would have been about a dirt highway stretching all the millions of miles to the planet Mars.

I was still sort of numb the next day. I checked out Cricket and he had made a miraculous recovery. He was grazing in a small adjoining pasture on weeds and dry grass. My dad had to leave on some trades involved with trying to save his town. He was to return in a week. I had fun with the Manning boys playing baseball, marbles, mumblety-peg, and a bunch of games we made up as we went.

Dad returned from his business trip and said that he and I were going back to Humble City, leaving Mom at the Manning's for a couple or three weeks. But Mr. Manning convinced Dad to stay over Saturday for a bunch of jackpot horse races being held only a short distance between them and town. I was really excited when he agreed. I can't explain it exactly, but I wanted to ride Cricket over and show him off. Later, I admitted, only to myself, that I was secretly hoping I'd somehow get to enter a horse race.

Seemed to me like everyone in the world came to the Lovington races that day. A free event always draws crowds. In the great drought and depression, "free" was a magic word. The sun could actually be seen through the dusty haze, mainly, I think, because the wind was quiet. Well, no wonder—I don't believe it was blowing much over twenty miles an hour.

The track was just raw ground with a graded straightaway about a mile long. Some of the crowd—mainly the ones who were going to enter horses in a race or make bets—were at the starting place. This consisted of more open ground at the end of the graded track. The big crowd was down at the finish. My dad, myself, Cricket, and the Manning boys were at the finish line. The race distances were marked: quarter mile, half mile, and mile. They were all full of betting, yelling, and sure enough fun for me.

Then it came time for the oddest horse race I ever saw. A hundred-yard dash. I started breathing hard and walking Cricket back and forth, then slow-lapping him to warm him up.

My dad asked, "What're you doing, Max? You're not in the race."

It took all the courage I had left and more than I would ever need again, but I croaked out through a suddenly drought-stricken throat, "We can win at a hundred, Dad." It was like a fervent prayer. It was answered. Dad looked at us, then he smiled so small and quick you could hardly see it, and said, "Keep him moving and let me talk to the officials."

Lordy, lordy, and lordy again. I was continuing my automatic praying that Dad had enough money to get me entered. He came back in a little while and said, "There are nine horses entered, all told." I waited while my heart turned to cold, rusty nails. "You and Cricket are one of 'em. I'll be waiting for you at the finish line."

Nine miles to Lovington. Nine horses to heaven. Or . . . well . . .

The officials had quite a bit of trouble getting us all in line so the starter could fire the Colt .45 he used as a starting gun. To the day I change universes I'll wonder why he didn't use a smaller gun with less expensive and less booming bullets.

I was a skinny little kid on a well-muscled but very small horse. As we crowded into the number seven spot, I felt like we were two midgets. I tried to take comfort in remembering the wins I'd had on Cricket when Wayne Simpson was riding the much bigger mare, Dolly. I was as scared as I could remember—not only because we were outsized and outclassed, but I couldn't lose Dad's money. The entry fee was probably all he had and this odd race was winner-take-all.

The hammer of the frontier gun had gone down on the shell. It exploded. We were off. No one had told me that racing a hundred yards could take a hundred years or a fraction of a second. Or both. I learned this that day all on my own.

I was ahead of the horse on my right, but the big sorrel gelding had half a length on me to my left. It was a slow-motion blur. I leaned over even closer down Cricket's bobbing neck and said, as before, "Go, go, Cricket, go!" and patted him on the right side of his neck.

It was over. Some of the horses ran on to the end of the track. But Cricket and I stopped and turned around pretty quick. Then I saw my dad, Mr. Manning, and the three boys coming at us, laughing and saying great things none of which I really heard, but I knew we'd won. People crowded around, all congratulating me and the little bay mule-eared gelding called Cricket. Later Dad handed me three one-dollar bills—the most money I'd ever had in my life. I would have given it all to Cricket, but he didn't have a pocket to carry it in. We were rich.

My dad had scrabbled up five whole dollars for the race entry fee. So he won forty dollars. A cockeyed fortune in those days. As badly as he needed the money for other things, he bought me a model 62 Winchester .22 pump. This was a dream gun. More people survived through hard times supplying hungry bellies with this rifle than any other. Things were moving in several directions now. And up and down as well.

Aunt Pearl's son P. J. had come home for a ten-day visit. He did a lot of work around the place for his mom and also brought her a little money. He had a part-time job in the oil fields somewhere besides Hobbs and was hiring out to different baseball teams as a pitcher at five dollars a game. He was that good, and people started talking about him trying out for the Fort Worth Cats. He never did get to, though, for the biggest of all wars came along and took him away before too long.

Even though Aunt Pearl was doing backbreaking work for sixteen hours a day, she still needed a little financial help. She got it from Granddad Evans and her brother Lloyd. Her cows were giving a lot more milk now and the calves were actually growing so she could butcher and sell a few head.

I was really proud of my new gun. I built a scabbard out of an old piece of canvas for the .22 and tied it with binder twine under the saddle skirt at just the right angle. It didn't look like much, but it worked.

In the area surrounding Aunt Pearl's outfit, I could hunt quail and doves as well as rabbits. Where the grass and water grew, so did the wild meat. I soon learned that rabbits weren't very scared of a horse. I could get right up on them. Another thing I caught onto was never to shoot anywhere near a horse's head. It hurts their ears real bad. I'd shoot to the side and Cricket would hardly flinch. Bullets were money—and that was scarce as new hats. I soon learned how to make every shot count by easing the sights onto a critter's head and pulling the trigger softly. This not only killed our food instantly, but it saved damaging edible meat or having a wounded animal to run down.

It took me a while to figure out how to hunt doves with the .22. The main thing was patience. I'd tie Cricket to the offside of a mesquite bush a distance from a spill or dirt water tank. I'd ease up and find a bush to hide behind as close to the water hole as I could. Then I'd wait. Doves water in larger numbers in the morning and late afternoon. But they also come singly, sometimes in pairs, and water all day. They have very small heads and quick movements when they drink and so I'd carefully study where the head was going to be when they raised it from the water and when they dipped their bill back in again. Then I learned to put my sight right on the water where the head would meet the liquid when they ducked their bills in. Plink. Meat for the table.

The blue quail took even more study. They'll run instead of flushing into the air if you work it just right. Walk at them very slowly toward whatever bushes they are using for cover. Then one will see you, then two, three, and they'll all move out until they have a little wash or cow trail to run in. If you give them the proper amount of time, they will run in single file down a cow path. The trick is to lie down when they are at the right distance and aim. As they run, their heads move to the side about an inch each way. So for just a fraction of a second you have a two-inch target and if you fire in that instant you can often get three or four head shots with one round. Clean meat. The best there is. I was having fun supplying two households with rabbits, doves, and quail. Cricket always waited, giving me a close eyeballing, to see if I was going to have enough bounty to hang from the saddle horn.

I swear, he knew when I'd had a good hunt. His running walk got faster, smoother, and, I do believe, prouder.

I thought that my dad and mother had my baby sister and me, Aunt Pearl, and her fine daughters all doing fine, but I realized later they must have been dancing barefoot through hellfire themselves. My mother, who was so gratified to be able to deliver letters and packages to the poor folk of the prairies, was about out of a job. Now, where she'd once taken in nickels it was pennies. Soon the government papers would come that would close her post office forever.

My dad, with the help of Pete Manning, dug the first irrigation well in that country. We raised one crop of watermelons, green beans, and straw-berries before we moved to Andrews, Texas. We harvested them and sold them in Hobbs. Dad was the driver and I was the peddler. It was too late to save his town, but I didn't know it. My folks never complained where I could hear them. I was enjoying all these struggles so much I failed to see the signs. I occasionally took my dogs hunting, just for fun now, because I had the rifle for necessary food gathering. I should have sensed that with everything going so good for me that the Great Equalizer would show up.

I was sitting out on the edge of our front porch with Depression asleep at my feet. Proration had wandered off around the emptying town site and was walking along with Dolly as she grazed. Suddenly I looked up and saw the dog after a grown jackrabbit. They were racing about a hundred yards paral-lel to the front porch. I had a tough time keeping still. I didn't want Depres-sion to wake up and waste his energy so far behind the chase. Even so, my heart started thump-thumping like hands clapping to a church song. Old Proration was gaining. I thought he was going to catch that rabbit. Cricket was grazing at best a half mile away in the horse pasture and my dad was gone in the old truck.

Then I saw it. A Model T was moving along the road between Curtis's little store heading for the Lovington/Hobbs right-of-way. It was the only thing moving in all that huge country to be seen. Proration stretched closer and closer to the rabbit. I was so sure he was going to catch him, I wondered why the driver of the Model T didn't stop to watch the thrilling action. I jumped up, waking Depression, who also stood up, looking around, trying to find the source of my excitement.

Then . . . then a mighty coldness grabbed all my insides and I couldn't let loose my breath. Proration's attention was totally concentrated on the flying meat—as he was born to do. Trained to do. Loved to do. This moment in eternity was his world. His entire life.

I stood right there and watched the rabbit miss the wheels of the car by inches, but my beloved Proration smashed into it at full speed, stretching to grab his prey.

I will never be able to recall exactly what I did. In just a moment, though, I, my mom, and Depression were running across the empty lots toward the spot of the collision. The rabbit and the car had both moved on, but there lay Proration with his head turned back from a broken neck and his muzzle a bloody mess.

I yanked his head straight, screaming for him to get up. My mother pulled at me to get me away from the terrible scene. It took some doing. However, when Depression started smelling different parts of his brother in confusion, I started bawling so that I couldn't even see. After a while, my mom told me to wait, and she went to the house and got a pick and shovel. We pulled him off next to a big mesquite and we dug his grave. It helped, a little, but my mother later told me that I bawled for two days and nights. The odds against this terrible happening were just too great for me to handle. Old Depression would all of a sudden just start up howling and I'd start crying again for about a week. Then my dad came home and I had to shape up. I could tell something big was about to happen.

About a week before my dog's impossible wreck, I used a morral with grain in it to catch Dolly. I put a bridle on her and was riding her bareback along a Humble City street that was turning to weeds.

There was an oilman from Hobbs who had bought two of the vacated houses. He was driving a new Model A sedan to check on the crew stripping all the lumber to move and rebuild something in Hobbs. He stopped and asked me about Dolly. I told him what a fine horse she was.

I could tell he admired her, and to my surprise he got out of the car asking if he could take a short ride. I slid off and handed him the reins. He knew how to mount a bareback horse, jumping up with his belly over her back first and then swinging his right leg over.

He looked good on her all right and reined her around a bit, pretty pleased.

"How much you take for her, son?"

I told him, "She's not really mine. She's my dad's."

He looked over at the house and saw Dad's truck and said, "I'll drop by in a little and see what your pa has to say."

I remounted and rode over to the Curtis store tying Dolly around back, thinking foolishly that if nobody could see her, they'd forget about her—just like a dumb kid to think like that.

I fooled around faking shopping, watching out the window, and visiting with Mr. Curtis.

Sure enough, the oilman went into the P.O. part of our house, then he and Dad visited a little on the porch, shook hands, and the man drove away.

I was scared to death, but I rode Dolly over and told Dad what he already knew.

"That man wants to buy Dolly."

"Yeah, yeah, he does. But I told him not now. He'd have to wait and bid at the Lubbock sale."

"Sale? Lubbock?"

"I was going to tell you in the morning, Max, but we might as well face it now. Me and Uncle Pit are putting on a sale over at Lubbock." My dad's uncle Pit Emery was an auctioneer from Lubbock. A good one. "We've been gathering stuff over there for weeks. Furniture, farm equipment, a few cows, and horses."

"Horses?"

"Well, yes, son, all our horses."

Since we only owned two, that word "horses" meant Cricket, too. I came as close to dying right there as I ever would till it really happened.

"We're gonna lose Humble City," my dad said, looking across its emptiness. "Don't you worry, though. We've got some good, solid plans for the future. Just trust me that I'm doing what's right for all of us."

I heard him. The whole world whirled before my eyes. It wasn't just me. It was our own family, and Aunt Pearl and hers, and a whale of a lot more.

I caught up Cricket, called Depression, and rode out across the prairie. I couldn't cry now. Heck, I'd done a lifetime of that over Proration anyway. I thought beyond my dog's death, though, to Aunt Pearl's husband getting killed from a hammer falling off a windmill deck and bashing his brains out right in front of her. I thought many, many things—most of them not good. It must have been even worse for my dad because he was losing a whole town and all the people who had believed in his dream. The worst of all was that his dream was as dead as a dinosaur bone.

By the time I reined Cricket back toward the remains of our town, I'd made up my mind to take whatever happened without a complaint. I rode by the little schoolhouse my dad had built, and I couldn't look straight at it no matter how hard I tried.

My granddad Evans and my uncles Roland and Lloyd came over, loaded, and hauled all of Aunt Pearl's household belongings—her chickens, hogs, and daughters—away. My dad had traded the little ranch Aunt Pearl now occupied for a stock farm two or three miles north of Brownfield, Texas, toward Lubbock. Then he made a deal with the Curtis cowboys to drive her cows across country to her. She spent the rest of her life there, putting all her girls through school in spite of losing her husband to a hammer and her only son to the bullets of an SS soldier's machine gun.

Well, there we were a few days later at the big sale on a farm northwest of Lubbock. I was amazed at the people who came in various modes of transportation, even on horseback. They were walking about, checking out all the farm equipment and endless household items—tables, chairs, even a four-poster bed.

Dolly and Cricket stood tied to the back of the truck. I had already brushed them till their red coats shone like new pennies in the sun, and now I was wandering around looking at stuff, but I wasn't really seeing it.

The sale began and my uncle was fast and expert. Time had vanished from the earth. Well, it was probably still there but I didn't know if it was moving backward or forward. Maybe it was just still—motionless—like a broken clock.

Then I felt my dad's hand on my shoulder.

"It's time."

I saddled Dolly first and reined her around, showing her off. I was stunned, as I'm sure my dad and his uncle Pit were, when the Hobbs oilman bid her all the way up to seventy-five dollars and bought her. He loaded her in a trailer behind his new Model A and took off in the dust for Hobbs. Well, she'd have a good home for sure. I hid the vacancy left somewhere in my little gut and saddled Cricket for the last time. I'd taken my rifle scabbard off the saddle. At least I'd have that. An empty leftover.

I wanted to gig him and spur him till he was acting silly and everyone would think he'd been eating loco weed. I probably could have used a dose of that myself. But I heard the rhythmic chant of Uncle Pit saying: "Looky, looky, looky, what a horse. Small and gentle enough for the kids, and powerful enough for the best grown-up hands. See that rein. A true cutting horse if there ever was one. Look at that smooth stop. Isn't that something? Run him out a ways, Max, and show these fine folks how you won the nine-horse jackpot race at Lovington, New Mexico."

I kicked him out and for the last time I leaned over and choked out, "Go, Cricket, go!"

He did. He scorched the dry earth drier. I couldn't help it. I had to make my dad proud and Cricket show his heart. There was no other choice.

Then Uncle Pit went into his selling chatter and the bidding went up and up, but I didn't want to hear. So I went deaf, and just circled my partner smoothly before the eyes of the bidders.

My dad took the reins, then, and stopped me and Cricket. I stepped down. My dad said, "You did good, son. Real good."

I never saw who bought him, and I was glad when he was gone. I could feel the water building behind my eyes, but I kept it there somehow. It seemed like hours, and I reckon it really was before all the money was collected, paid out, divided, and all the things they do with money were finished.

That night, Dad drove us back to Humble City. Then he talked to me like I was grown up, as he explained what our next move was going to be in this insecure world.

He told me that up at Guymon, in the Oklahoma panhandle, they had a big spot of good rain—enough to plow and plant farms again, and run cattle on the pastureland. During the worst of the dust bowl, their plow horses and cow horses had either been sold for a pittance or starved out. So now, they were going to need horses to work that wet land.

He also knew of a ranch down at Jal, in the southernmost corner of New Mexico, south of Hobbs. This big outfit had tried to keep their remuda intact, but the animals were so poor and bony, they were going to be forced to sell them all before they died of starvation.

He continued to explain that an old one-eyed cowboy friend of his named Boggs and I were going to make the horse drive from Jal to Guymon. Since it might take us as long as three months to get them there, we'd have time to "borrow" feed along the way and fatten them up for the big sale.

I had no idea that lonely night in that bouncy, groaning old Model T truck that my dad's idea would work and all our families would somehow make a go of it ever after.

The next morning I got up, milked the cow, gathered the eggs, pumped, and carried all the water my mother would need for the house before breakfast. She fed the baby and cooked us a good breakfast of fried eggs, biscuits, and gravy. She even had a new jar of grape jelly she opened so we could spread it over the butter melting in our hot biscuits.

Dad said, as he got up from the table, "I gotta get goin' and settle up some accounts, and I won't be back till late. I'm gonna go down to that ranch and sew up our horse deal, Max. Here's some change. You might want to buy yourself a bar or two of candy."

"Naw, thanks," I said. "I still got some of my three-dollar winnings left."

When he was gone and mom was busy, I yelled at her I was goin' hunting. I took the lifesaving Model 62 out of the horseback scabbard and went out the back door. I didn't have to call old Depression. He was already waiting for me. We walked to the Curtis store, but they didn't have much left on the shelves. Mr. Curtis was selling down, getting ready to close for good, just like our town. I was sure worried he wouldn't have any Milky Way candy bars left, but he had three. I splurged and bought them all. I surprised the old man by asking for a paper bag. He found one. I thanked him and he thanked me, and we started hoofing it out to little Lillian's swimming hole.

She had a little pinto pony, and I had had Cricket. Once in a while we snuck off riding. We'd ride and talk about our dreams of the future and race across the prairies with her hair blowing in the wind and sun, like tiny strings of polished gold. Lillian had given me a lot— what with the candy and all—but the thing that made me look at a girl on a horse racing the wind was priceless. It still is.

I knocked on the door, figuring I'd have to ask her folks where she was. It was wonderful luck she answered it, saying, "I saw you coming," and stepped out.

We moseyed out along a rock path toward the rock swimming pool, two small people making small talk. Then we sat down and old Depression did, too. We all three looked into the beautiful blue water as it sparkled like a tub full of diamonds and pearls in Lillian's great big blue, blue eyes.

I reached in the sack and handed her a Milky Way, and then I took one and we unwrapped them and ate away, getting chocolate all over our mouths. We tried to wipe it off with the back of our hands, but it didn't quite work. We sat a spell, getting the last of the luscious taste off our teeth with our tongues. Then I handed her the sack with the third Milky Way in it, and I leaned over and gave her a big chocolate kiss. It was the most delicious thing I'd ever tasted.

I got up. Old Depression and I walked in a wide circle out across the prairies where I had ridden so many wonderful miles on Cricket. I carried the rifle on my shoulder. Depression made out like he was looking and smelling for a rabbit, but I knew he wasn't, any more than I brought the gun to shoot one. I could feel little Lillian standing there watching us grow smaller. I loved her very much, but just like Cricket, I knew I'd never see her again. I didn't look back.

Flax

Flax was as beautiful as a Taos sunset in deep summer, as faithful as your grandmother, as smart as a border collie, and his dark-as-shoe-polish eyes shined with intelligence. Pull the stray hairs from his flaxen tail, curry his blondish mane, brush his light sorrel body with his muscles reflecting rippling lights and shadows as he moved, and he'd shine all over in appreciation. At another time, in another place, decked out with a black leather, silver-studded bridle and saddle to match, he could have been a parade horse that anyone would have been proud to show off.

But Flax was mainly a cow horse, and it was a privilege and a pleasure to work cattle with him. I never could tell how many hands tall a horse is, but I knew Flax was just exactly the right size to handle any job I rode him at—because he always delivered. He kept his eyes on whatever number of cattle we were driving, working his ears all the time. He could tell if a cow was a real bunch-quitter and be on her before she got started. Or he could read the body motions of bluffers and ignore them. He could make the sorriest cowboy look good. He instilled a green kid like me with the confidence of a top hand—even though I had a lot of long trails to ride before that term could be used about me—if ever.

Up there—just south of Santa Fe—on sixty-mile-long, fifty-mile-wide Glorieta Mesa, people were impoverished. The recovery from the great drought and the Depression had hardly gotten a toehold. Everyone borrowed hands from one another for roundups, brandings, and sometimes even fixing fences and windmills. Often I was the only hand working for Ed Young on the Rafter EY. Those were the times I liked best, because Ed was one heck of an old-time cowboy and he knew I wanted to learn. I felt honored. No kid before me had ever lasted as a hand with him. I didn't know if I'd make it either, but I was gonna give it a hide-stretching try.

The one place I didn't mind being loaned out to was the great San Cristobal ranch—part of Ed's land joined it on the west side. Mr. Gould, the ranch manager, was kind to horses, dogs, and kids and was a real hand. Of course, the San Cristobal had eastern money backing it, and was the only outfit around that could afford its own crew. Part of Mr. Gould's fine fettle came, I'm sure, from drawing good wages, being fed well, and knowing all his hands would be paid every month. I only got paid in the fall after shipping time—at least for the first two years I was on the Rafter EY.

The San Cristobal ran black Angus cattle, the first I'd ever seen. Their eastern fence line was partially along the west edge of Glorieta Mesa where it joined the Rafter EY. There were a few scattered water holes among the miles of boulders and tall untouched grass in secluded little meadows. The San Cristobal cattle had plenty of range on the flats and it was against their nature to climb uphill—in jumbles of boulders—to graze. So, we did a strange type of "ridin' fence" in those days—nature, you see, will give you help if you let it. We looked for places where the barbed wire was loose and down, but instead of repairing it we'd drive little bunches of cattle along those places. Flax and I would circle around and sort of get in their way, until finally one of them would discover the downed fence and stray off the rocky slopes of the mesa onto San Cristobal's grassland. If we were patient, the other cows would soon follow. Ed called this "borrowing grass."

In order to give me time to do my cowboy job, we had worked it out so I could go to school in Andrews, Texas, just across the New Mexico line, during football season, then back to the EY in the late spring. I was a fair halfback and punter so I was allowed certain privileges. I could take textbooks and library books from the school to the ranch. I chose Balzac, Tolstoy, Chekhov—and Shakespeare by assignment—and stuff like that to continue my education. However, ol' Flax was going to educate me in a different manner the next spring.

Ed had cattle scattered about the mesa in different pastures so we had to have at least three roundups and three brandings. First the cattle had to be gathered and penned.

I was on Flax and Ed rode a black-legged bay—his favorite.

We had already moved ten or fifteen cows and calves into the biggest meadow at Chico Flats where the windmill and corrals were—and where we would hold our first branding. But now we were working the rocky slopes of Glorieta Mesa finishing up a hard gather.

I was tracking a "dry" cow who hadn't calved that year. She charged into a bunch of brush below me and headed back north instead of southwest to

Chico Flats. Flax was after her, working his way through the rocks at considerable speed. I could hear the brush popping below, but I couldn't see the critter. I had a fleeting panic shock as I reined Flax hard to the right to head the cow off. He didn't want to go, but I spurred him in my chosen direction anyway. Well, I had just that second returned to cowboy kindergarten . . . me, not Flax.

I had reined him out on some big, flat rocks that dropped off at a pretty steep slope. I tried to pull the horse up and he tried to obey, but the slope and the momentum, along with the speed and weight, carried us right over the edge of about an eight- or ten-foot drop. Flax's steel horseshoes had to have made sparks on the rocks as he shoved his hind legs under his belly in a desperate attempt to save a bone-busting fall.

Instead of letting the momentum and gravity take us smashing and rolling to our doom, the horse launched us with his powerful hind legs way out into space and we came down on almost level ground, tearing through some small cedar limbs as he struggled mightily to stay upright. He did. A miracle. Even though my tailbone felt like it had been driven right up between my ears, I somehow stayed on. Flax just kept going with me trying to tear the horn out of the saddle because I'd lost a stirrup. Durned if he didn't turn that ol' cow and line her out southwest. He knew, all the time, what we were supposed to do and where we were going.

I had learned—in that ripped-apart second—that you rein a horse in the best direction your instantaneous judgment tells you to and then leave it up to the animal to pick his own way through the rocks. There is no other reasonable way. In spite of knowing this, I figured I'd never work in rocks enough to know if I'd make a real hand at it or not. Since then, I've talked to lots of cowboys who were raised in rock country, and every one of them told me, "Just leave it up to the horse, that's all you can do."

Ed came in on his bay with two more cows and calves. We started bunching them and then the dry cow that had nearly got us in a permanent fix hit the trail down to Chico Flats and the rest followed. It was smooth going, downhill all the way to water now. I wanted real bad to brag about Flax's brilliance to my boss, but I had to pass because I couldn't figure a way to conceal my own ignorance.

At just the right moment I circled around and down to the flats to open the corral gate. We'd been so busy on the rocky slopes that we hadn't noticed the thunderclouds gathering overhead, herded together by some mighty force in the sky not unlike the way we had rounded up the scattered mother cows and calves.

Flax and I made it across the half-mile flat and had taken a flank position. We could hear the cattle coming and Ed yelling them on: "Ho cattle, ho cattle, hoooo."

They left the trail and hit the flats headed for the water they could smell. The windmill tank was half in the corral and half out, convenient watering for both loose cows and confined ones. They were beginning to spread out a little and most of the mother cows were breaking into a trot, the calves, running and bawling, trying to keep up. Then it hit.

The lightning bolt came down and split a cedar tree into splinters not over a quarter mile to our north. That bolt had shredded the hugging clouds as well, I reckoned, because the rain just dropped like a waterfall and the lightning and its thunder roar came as fast as a World War II artillery barrage and just as loud.

Here was the deal. During the great drought, most of the springs had dried up forcing wild game and cattle to come to this good water from all around. They had tromped the grass, and all other vegetation, except for the scattered cedar trees, into barren ground, and now, as the rain sheathed it like a huge mirror, it really turned slick.

The cows were scattering more as their calves lost track and smell and sight of them. The lightning made a vast glow of the earth every time it flashed and addled the little herd.

Flax and I were working back and forth. He had his head down, spinning with every breakaway cow just like a cutting horse. There was nothing I could do but just give him his head and let him work. I half expected him to lose footing on the glassy world and land right on top of me any flashing second. Sometimes he'd slide sideways several feet, other times he'd almost go down, but by some power of will and skill, we put the last of the cattle in the corral just as I heard Ed yell off to the south. He and his bay were coming out of a gully after a cow.

I reined Flax around and moved back, trying to get the distance exact so we could maneuver to block the corralled cattle at the gate if any decided to break out. At the same time I had to leave an opening for Ed's bunch-quitter. When she heard the calves bawling, instead of trying to turn back, she raced toward the corral gate. I leaned forward and touched Flax lightly with the spurs. He moved at a cautious speed now. When we reached the corral, I bailed off and shut the gate behind the last cow just as Ed rode up.

The sudden thundercloud had moved on, raising about a half square mile of hell up on the mesa. Our slickers were still on the back of our saddles, but I felt so proud of our work my chest felt plumb puffy and I didn't even notice that I was soaked to the liver.

When I remounted Flax I reached down and patted him on the neck— the side away from Ed. He was standing up in the stirrups making a count. He eased back in the saddle, saying softly, "We got 'em all." I waited for more words, but none came.

We had to head home if we were to make it before dark, but we'd be back tomorrow morning at sunup. It was a mile up to the trail and about three more to headquarters. At first the ground was slick, then the mud started drying, and it just got sticky.

Eldon Butler, who had a little outfit that joined the south end of the San Cristobal—just across the Clines Corner/Lamy dirt highway to the west of Chico Flats—would come help us brand the calves. I was thinking how I would love to heel and drag 'em to the branding fire from the back of Flax, but he'd had an Olympian day of performing and no matter how great and tough he was, he'd be stiff and sore as hell by morning. I would have to use a lesser mount. Of course, the way I felt right then, every horse in the world was second place to the golden-maned warrior.

We left the trail when we finally found a wood hauler's wagon road allowing me to ride side by side with the boss like I'd been trained to do. My mind drifted back to that mighty leap from the flat rock that Flax had taken, and I suddenly wanted to tell Ed how much I admired Flax's great feat and feet. But, you see, words were for other purposes to these old-time, rough-butted cowboys.

Ed Young spoke one sentence all the way home. Suddenly, almost under his breath I heard, "You and ol' Flax did a perty good job today."

That was it, but that was a bunch. Even if ol' Flax might not have understood the words, I knew my bent tailbone was sending him proud messages right through the saddle seat into his valiant heart.

Actually, I was a little uneasy about bragging too much about Flax due to the shock I had suffered the year before when I returned from school to work on the EY. I didn't want a repeat happening.

I had ridden a horse called Old Snip—who was also a "young learner"—to apply for a job with Ed Young, and was instructed to turn Snip over to Ed in return for a debt from the cowboy/horse trainer superb, Robert Ian. Ed let me ride Snip as often as possible because I was putting a good neck rein on him and perfecting the proper hind-legs-stuck-way-under-stop on this horse. We worked great together. We fit. I loved him, and he at least respected me.

One must try to understand the times. The family food and sparse clothing came before all else. In the '30s, those who didn't go on relief survived in any manner they could.

We all shipped cattle to Kansas City, Missouri, in those days, and it seems an authority was scouting for special horses to work in the Kansas City Stockyards. He had seen, and tried, Old Snip and of course, the horse was perfection. Ed had sold him for the almost-unheard-of amount of two hundred dollars. A true fortune for a cow horse in those days.

When Ed told me about selling Snip, all I could say was, "Oh."

This horse had saved my life once and probably twice and my fourteen-year-old heart was broken, but I couldn't let on. These people were tough by circumstance and tender by nature. They just took the blows and moved instantly onto something else. I had to be like them. There was no other way, but now, Flax had filled in the hollow spot. A loss had been turned into a gain. Ed let me work with him more than ever. I guess he knew.

The area cowboys liked being loaned to the Rafter EY just as much as I liked going to help out at the San Cristobal. First, Mrs. Young—everyone called her Mother Young—was a truly great cook. Next, Ed had a fine string of top horses, and the bunkhouse had been built adjoining the main house, making them feel welcome and at home.

Two hands from White Lakes ranch and I had just finished about a mile and a half, or more, of fencing, so, they had returned to their home base. I regained my position as "the hired help." That's when Ed assigned me and Flax the second toughest adventure we were to share.

Right after breakfast, Ed lit up a "town cigarette"—the one luxury he allowed himself besides a single big swallow of whiskey at night just before supper—then he spoke at great length, for him.

"Max, go wrangle the horses and saddle Flax. You're going on a trip. Get a morral out of the tack room and put a pint of corn in it."

I went to the corral and got the night horse, wrangled the horses, roped and saddled Flax and led him out the corral gate toward the backyard where Ed stood waiting.

"All right now," he said with the authority of General Patton, and he gave me instructions on how to get to a big pasture on the south end of the San Cristobal. He had loaned one of his mules to Mr. Gould to pack some of the Eastern owners into the Pecos wilderness for a camping and trout fishing trip. Ed had told him not to worry about returning it. He would come get him when he needed the animal. That time was now.

Ed had contracted to deliver a couple of hundred cedar fence posts to a well-to-do person in Santa Fe who was going to use them placed side by side for a rustic and long-lasting yard fence. He needed the Jack mule to work with his other mule, Mary. They would pull the wagonloads of cedar posts I was going to be assigned to cut. These survival moves of Ed's were an inspiration to me throughout my long life. Right now I was anxious to see what he had planned for Flax and me that was so special.

Ed said, moving to Flax and taking the catch rope and morral from the saddle, "I'm just going to show you this one time."

A morral is a canvas feeding bag you hang over a horse's or mule's head and they eat the grain in the bottom. We used corn that we raised ourselves. Only the San Cristobal could afford the preferred oats. Ed put the "tie hard and fast" honda knot over the saddle horn and formed a roping loop. He held it out in front of him with one hand and with the other he rattled the grains of corn in the center of the loop.

"Listen up. When ol' Jack gets his head close enough to smell that corn and figures he's gonna get a bite, you whip this loop over his head and jerk it tight in the same motion. If you miss you'll never get him, and if you don't bring him home, just ride on to Arizona." He went on out to the corrals without looking back.

I mounted Flax and rode off down the trail to Chico Flats on the way to the big pasture. I can still feel the pressure in my gut all these years later. My belly felt like there were two regiments of scorpions doing battle with swords and axes as sharp as the edge of freshly broken glass. These were unpleasant sensations, but those words, "Just ride on to Arizona," were amplified in repetitious echoes pounding through my brain until I was sure my head was gonna spin right off my body into space.

I got to that fated pasture about mid-afternoon. It had sounded easy, but this pasture was big—somewhere around ten or fifteen thousand acres. The biggest on the ranch. I had helped gather cattle there, so I knew how big it was. And now here I was, trying to gather one mule with my life's travel itinerary at stake.

I started looking as far as I could see. However, as good as my eyes were in those youthful days I couldn't see through a single one of the thousands of hills, mesas, and clustered clumps of piñon and cedar. So I started riding in a big circle, checking the ground for sign. I stopped every now and then to search inside the circle. I saw the tracks and spoor of coyotes, deer, bobcats, skunks, rabbits, birds, cows, and calves, but no mule.

About an hour short of sundown, I crossed a little open patch and there were scattered tracks of a whole remuda of horses. It took me a while, but finally I found the smaller, sharper tracks of the mule Jack, who was also a jack mule, or for the layman, a stud. I felt a bunch better. I had a chance of missing a long, lonely, probably hungry horseback trip to Arizona.

I tried to follow the general trend of their directional grazing. A remuda of loose horses moves in all directions hunting for the best grass, but they were generally en masse heading north.

Suddenly I felt Flax bunch under me and his steps quicken. He sort of danced. When he heard or smelled out-of-sight horses, he threw both ears forward at the same time.

I rode expectantly up to the top of a long rise. There they were. It took me a spell to spot Jack, but he was the first one to raise his head and spot us. Then one after the other, about thirty head of cow horses from newly saddle

broken to some that were pretty near worn out, were looking at us in curiosity. It looked like I might get my one chance after all.

As I was planning my move, the sun was setting. I failed to enjoy the
orange bronzed blazes across the thousands of miles of space as I usually
did. I was staring at a mule slowly fading into darkness just like the sunset
was doing.

The night came quickly. I shuddered at the suddenly cold air and the full
realization that I was going to spend the night here with no food and only a
saddle blanket for warmth. It bothered me even more that I hadn't brought
any hobbles for Flax so at least he could have grazed and not gone hungry
like ol' dumb-butted me. There is no use going on or regretting ignorance. It
only multiplies the problems.

I unsaddled Flax and tied him to a tree with a no-slip, no-choking knot. I
turned the saddle upside down, got half the folded saddle blanket under me
and the other half over my legs, and lay back staring at the stars. As dumb
as I felt, it shouldn't have been any trouble not to think. After counting past
a hundred thousand stars and listening to coyotes howling to one another
into the soft distance that seemed as far away as Arizona, I must have slept
more than I thought, because when I woke up with the sun, I was raring to
go.

First I had to get Flax to water. I could see a windmill about a mile back
to the southwest. I hated to backtrack, so for once I broke Flax into an easy
lope. We both watered up at the tank and I forgot about being hungry. Flax
didn't let on one way or the other. I rode back up on the long rise and the
horses were gone.

Of course, they were gone. Horses graze on at night, just like deer browse.
There was a little panic but I could see tracks under us and as long as tracks
were visible we'd have a chance.

Flax found them with his ears before my eyes spotted them. We, by some
unknown instinct, moved slowly back and forth about a hundred yards
from the closest horse. It took about thirty minutes. They were mostly grazing and ignoring us as I dismounted and slowly led Flax back and forth to
where we'd just ridden. This created a little curiosity, but they soon went
back to feeding.

I hooked the honda over the saddle horn, got the loop out, and hung the morral over my left shoulder. I led Flax ever so slowly toward them. He kept trying to graze with his bridle on, flipping the bits back to get a bite or two.

Three or four of the horses had become nervous and were watching us with heads high, ready to break away in a run. If they did, all the others would go with them. I stopped about fifty yards from the grazing remuda.

I love Arizona. It is my second- or third-favorite state, but at that moment the thought of it turned my blood to hardening cement.

I waited motionless as Flax grazed around me. A year whizzed by. A decade. A century. At the millennium mark, I eased Flax's head up and set my loop with the morral in its center slowly shaking it. One horse heard and looked, then another, and another. Then Jack. Five or six took tentative steps forward. I increased the corn's rattle. Jack was paying attention, but not enough. However, when six or seven horses slowly moved toward me, his interest began to grow. He started following them.

When they neared us, the lead horse stuck his head out, smelling, watching, almost to the morral. I'd have to pull it back very slowly and silently. I had already stopped breathing. Then I'd shake it some more. Six or seven of the horses had gotten so close I might have snared one if that was what I was after. Then Jack inched through the animals in his turn. Everything fused together now, the horses in front, Flax in back. Jack. Hello, dear Jack. Come on, sweet Jack. Just six more inches, beautiful Jack. Three more inches, handsome Jack. Hungry all the way to Arizona or Mother Young's delicious cooking on the Rafter EY was only a rattle away.

Now!

I made my one move just as the velvet nose of the Jack mule touched the morral, nostrils wide, smelling the luscious corn. The loop went around his neck. I jerked it tight and moved to get hold of Flax's reins. I didn't have to worry about Flax; he had felt me hook the honda on the saddle horn. He was ready—braced and looking down the rope—when the Jack mule hit the end of it sideways. The mule leapt backward, spun in a circle to run, but the rope straightened and jerked him around facing Flax.

The instant the Jack mule started choking, he eased up and actually took two or three steps toward us to loosen the loop proving that mules are smarter than most animals. I mounted Flax, took the first breath since the catch, and rode up toward Jack, taking coils. When there were about four or

five feet of rope left, I made a good half hitch on the saddle horn and rode toward the Rafter EY. It was a great surprise to me that Jack moved out with us as if he had trained all his life for this moment of polite relief.

I couldn't believe how events had turned our way. I'd hooked that prize long-eared fish and was reeling him into the home corral. We were almost halfway up the Chico Flats trail, only an hour and a half from headquarters and some of Mother Young's biscuits and trimmings. I could imagine Ed grinning all over even though I was a day late getting back.

Then we came to a sudden stop. I tapped ol' Flax with the spurs and he dug in for about five or six yards, literally dragging Jack mule, who had all

four legs stiff as iron pipes. Flax knew a lot more about mules than I did. And he knew there was no way he could ever drag that mule to the top of the mesa. Gravity was all in Jack's favor.

I reined Flax all the way in a circle, a rough one because of the brush beside the hill. The mule sort of turned with us but we hadn't gained an inch. I rode up to him and then spurred Flax, trying to jerk him sideways. It didn't bother Jack at all. In fact, I started believing he was enjoying this. For a fleeting moment I wished I'd left the choking loop as it was instead of making a hackamore loop over his nose. Then I remembered Ed needed Jack healthy to join his gray mule to pull wagonloads of posts.

I dismounted. I left Flax and Jack staring at one another down a short length of rope while I looked around in the brush for a dead but strong pole. Finally I found one. I walked over to Jack, looked him in one eye and said—paraphrasing here—"See the cedar pole, Jack? Well, I'm going to knock your cockeyed eyeballs right out your long ears. You hear me, you . . . ?"

I raised the pole high over one shoulder and then the most unbelievable thing happened. Flax stepped forward head to head with Jack and if I'd have come down with the pole I would have smashed my beloved sorrel. I held the silly pose with the post for a moment, then hurled it off into the brush. I mounted Flax, and Jack followed us home like a calf follows its mama to water. I don't know how horses and mules know the same silent language, but the gorgeous golden-maned cow horse had either threatened or sweet-talked that mule into doing his duty. I prefer to think it was the latter, and to this day I still believe it without any doubt whatsoever.

We all three rode up in front of that ranch house and I just couldn't help it. I reared back and let out a yell that would have woken every hibernating bear in the Rocky Mountains if it'd been winter, but it was early summer and the grass was green and growing for the first time in a long spell.

Ed came around the corner from the work shed and Mother Young came out of the house. She was smiling and spoke first. "Well, Max, get 'em watered and in the barn and fed. I've got a big meal just about ready."

We all three moved right past Ed who was studying the condition of the mule. He was soberly puzzled. Heck, I knew Jack was in perfect shape. I had only threatened to kill him. When I dismounted at the corral gate and was pulling it open, I took another quick glance back at Ed. He sure didn't want anybody to see it, but he was grinning so wide his ears were practically touching on the back of his head.

The two animals were out in the corral eating hay. Jack finally got those few bites of corn that had led to his capture. It had taken two days of playing cow-pasture roulette, but there were winners all around. We had fried chicken with our biscuits and gravy that special night on this rocky earth. Oh yeah, I almost forgot. We had sweet potato pie for dessert. Don't try to tell me anything about heaven, I've done been there.

Ed sure gave me the right advice about one thing to look for whenever

I hooked Jack up to the wagon: "Watch that hind foot." Sure enough, every time he was being hooked up alongside the gray mule, Mary, he lifted a hind foot and would leave the hoof tipped right on the edge just waiting for me to get careless. Then he was gonna kick my brains out. Once in the traces, he worked perfectly, balancing out the pulling ability of the ginny with precision. No doubt about it, some human had unforgettably mistreated him in his youth, and like all mules, they never forget the good or the bad.

I selected and cut posts out of big cedar trees for days before I finally got two hundred straight ones. Ed told me to resharpen the ax, because he'd had word from the Santa Fe buyer it was going to take three hundred posts for his yard fence. When I had cut, trimmed, loaded, hauled to headquarters, and unloaded all three hundred, it formed quite a pile. Ed hauled them to town in a cattle trailer pulled by a little Chevy coupe.

After he returned from delivering the last load, he seemed pretty pepped up. He and Mother Young decided to throw their once-a-year dance and party for the few far-flung people of the mesa. That afternoon about sundown, just before the first ranch folk began to arrive, he told me some good news—he had decided to raise my pay from twenty dollars a month to thirty.

I said, "That's right keen."

If you think that was not enough elation, you are right. But here I was, still a fourteen-year-old kid and I was going to be drawing equal wages to all the other full-grown, working cowboys of the American West. It was a great moment in my life and it's a miracle I could speak at all. The dance was a dandy. I wanted to tell the entire citizenry of Glorieta Mesa that was gathered here about my raise, but I couldn't tell anyone. It would have seemed like bragging. Anyway, I owed at least a third of the thirty dollars a month to ol' Flax.

Instead of cowboying, Ed temporarily turned me into a corn farmer. Every outfit—except the San Cristobal—had to raise a patch of corn for horse feed. So, I daily walked twenty—seemed like a hundred—miles behind a two-horse, two-mule harrow. I cultivated, killed weeds, and aerated the soil around the dry land shoots of cornstalks. I was consoled by the fact that ol' Flax would get to enjoy part of the harvest—if it rained, that is.

Well, one thing was for sure—the axing of three hundred cedar posts and the twenty-mile walk in plowed ground had sure as shootin' got me in shape for the football season down southeast at Andrews, Texas.

Each summer Ed Young leased a section of land—640 acres—from an elderly couple, Mr. and Mrs. Curry, eight miles to the north. They had left a starvation farm in Texas and homesteaded the 160 acres, which they eventually traded into a section of starvation ranch land. They had been there since somewhere around the turn of the century. They kept the grass idle except for three or four horses owned by their off-to-work sons, Shorty and Francis, so it was pretty good grazing. Every couple of weeks, Ed would send me over there to make a count on the thirty cows and calves he ran there from July until shipping time in late October.

The vast Glorieta Mesa also held many, many little mesas and canyons on its massive deck. There were a few windmills and only a precious few springs. The elderly Currys had one of the best of the latter located at the foot of a cream-colored sandstone mesa.

The Currys had dug a cavelike house into part of the bluff about thirty feet from their spring. Then they used the rocks they found in the ruins of an ancient Indian hunting camp to build a good sized extension in front of their cave home so they could have a wood cookstove with a chimney. The surrounding mesa was covered heavily with piñon and cedar trees, furnishing them plenty of firewood. The location of their home didn't seem to make much sense, at first glance, because they had to pack all the household water, and water for the chickens, hog, and garden, up a crooked path to their dugout. Seemed unhandy, but it was obviously what they wanted.

This strange little home was insulated by the whole world. They were, themselves, insulated and isolated beyond the reach of most of society. About every two months, one or the other of their sons would show up with their sparse mail, some staples such as pinto beans, flour, salt and pepper, and some canned milk. They had a milk cow or two, at one time, but could no longer handle the feeding, gathering, watering, and care to have their own milk and butter, but as I would learn, the old couple were ultimate survivors.

Mrs. Curry was about five feet and filled out even from her shoulders to her 1890s hemline. Mr. Curry had once been about six feet, but the years of carrying two big buckets of water at a time, up the steep, cutback trail had bent him like wire, so he was probably about five foot eight now. It was strong wire for sure, and his large knuckled hands looked like they could crush granite. When I shook hands with him, I couldn't help but try to flex my fingers to see if they were still there. One thing, though, that I'll never forget—no matter the shape of their bodies, they both had black eyes that shined right into your heart with good, honest feelings.

It took Flax and me from before sunup to twilight to make this trip to the Currys. This was the only time I'd break him into an easy lope so we'd have time to have a meal and a visit with these gracious people. This total of around a twenty-mile ride was my picture show, my ice cream soda, my Sunday picnic of fried chicken and biscuits and gravy dinner at grandmother's all rolled into one. The wildlife was scarce, but once in a while I'd see a coyote or a deer or a mountain lion track. There were two things I could count on, though: the blue jays and magpies were always flickering from tree to tree and the chipmunks chattered both a greeting and a warning to all the unseen listeners, that you were present.

It was a joy to slow lope across that mile of sparse pasture. Flax made it so easy after the first time. I could watch his ears working and tell when we were near cattle, even in the sometimes timbered hills. That horse had a memory better than an elephant or almost as good as a mule. When I had finished the cattle count, usually by straight-up sun, I'd water him at the Curry spring. Then we'd ease on around to where the mesa flattened and open a gate, riding the hundred-yard trail to the front of the Currys' dugout. Their old black dog had already told them I was there.

"Well, I'll be," was Mrs. Curry's greeting every time, and Mr. Curry was just as brief, with "There you are," as if I'd somehow mailed them a message ahead. Maybe I had, without knowing, in some wonderful way of the wilderness.

As I dismounted, Mr. Curry always commented on how good both Flax and I looked. He'd walk out with me to his little shed and corral and insist we give Flax a morral of corn. I knew his sons had to deliver this priceless commodity to them, as their little garden would never supply their chickens and the butchering hog, much less a horse. I felt sort of guilty, but I didn't want to hurt their feelings and Flax certainly appreciated it. He had—for two summers now—looked forward to this treat.

It wouldn't be long until Mrs. Curry had the biscuits baking, the great permanent pot of pinto beans warming, and she was stirring up gravy and slicing some sowbelly. I swear she would have cheerfully cooked their last bite for company.

Long years back Mr. Curry had helped Ed work on the Rafter EY and he knew Chico Flats, Wild Horse Mesa, the name of every pasture and water hole, so we had plenty to talk about. In later years, when I thought back on it, I was awed that they never asked me about the outside world . . . things like war, politics, or the price of cattle. We simply visited about the mesa land he knew, but Mrs. Curry always wanted to know about Mother Young's house and if she still painted pictures and raised flowers.

The old black dog stood with head through the open doorway listening and smelling the food, but he never set a paw in the house. Just as soon as the old half-gallon blue-enameled coffeepot boiled, we were ready to eat.

Flax and I had already covered about twelve to fourteen miles, so I was plenty hungry. That feeling was soon cured. We all three had a ceremonial cup of coffee strong enough to dig a water well in solid rock. Then me 'n Flax left. I don't think it was possible to feel more at home than we did in the Curry cave. They were polite enough not to insist we stay longer, even though they may have desired it. I surely loved those two old folks. Their kind made the good part of the world and they are all that holds it together. They also understood how long the eight or nine miles would stretch out that Flax and I still had to cover, returning to the ranch.

To my excited surprise, on the next cattle count, Ed decided to go with me. The Currys would be inundated with visitors this month enough to do them for an entire year.

Ed Young was the only gringo I ever worked with who used the Spanish spade bit. Few riders could handle it without cruelly tearing up and eventually permanently numbing a horse's mouth. It had a spade mouthpiece of the bit that could tear a horse's mouth if used improperly. The cowboy had to use it with great delicacy and knowledge. Ed could do it. I could only marvel.

Every now and then Ed would mention a little bit about working with Ysidro Sandoval, who was now the last of the real vaqueros in this part of the country. I could hear the awe in his voice when he spoke of him. Since

Ed was such a knowledgeable and skilled cowboy/cowman himself, I dreamed of someday meeting Ysidro. I'm here to tell you, miracles do happen.

We—Ed on his bay, I was on Flax—were in an open pasture about three miles from the Curry place when we heard these crashing noises on the edge of a long brush- and timber-covered hill about a quarter mile from us. We reined up. All four of us were wondering what kind of critters were tearing up the world and making all that racket. I could feel Flax's muscles bunching under me and his ears were working so hard I thought they might tear loose from his head.

Talk about witnessing a happening. First there were ten, maybe more, head of steers that came ripping out of the timber. These were followed by a little dog working, back and forth, nipping at their heels, and the whole crashing thing was followed up by a tall man on a tall, dusty-colored horse. We could see they were trying to pen the stampeding cattle at one of the few working windmills and adjoining corrals down in the flats.

We spurred forward to help hold the flank nearest us, but the tall man and the tall horse and the little black-and-white heeling dog penned them before we got there. He had dismounted smoothly, shutting the gate and remounting before we could join him.

We pulled up. Ed spoke a greeting in Spanish and it was returned the same way. Then in English, he said "Ysidro, this is Max Evans. He lives with us."

I was really proud of the "lives with us" instead of "he works for us" stuff, but I forgot that as I finally got to meet the last of the greatest of all cowboy lines in our part of the country. I went a little blind, but I can still remember that one and only handshake with "the greatest" as if I'd been invited to join Babe Ruth in the dugout when he hit his sixtieth home run. The blur cleared up and I regained full control and soaked in everything about this living legend from his black flat-brimmed hat, the silky bandana around his neck, to his leather catch rope. I could tell by the coils that the riata was at least forty feet long.

Ysidro had an elegance in the straight but relaxed way he sat in the saddle rolling a cigarette while he visited with Ed. The dog lay down in the shade of the corral, but he watched every move and listened to every sound his master made.

Suddenly, Ysidro turned his head to Flax, examining him. And in English better than mine, said, "I remember when Ed Young was first reining that sorrel. He is beautiful. How does he work the rocks and brush, Max?"

It was my turn to talk. I choked and then it poured out, "He's just the best . . . he knows cows better'n me. I just let him do most of the thinkin'."

This seemed to please Ysidro. He lightly touched his own mount on the roots of the mane, smiled broadly under that perfectly chiseled face and said, "A good horse knows when you give him freedom. A great horse knows how to use it." I never have had to paraphrase that last statement. It is indelible. I felt as honored as if Flax had just won the Kentucky Derby.

Ysidro's land had been divided up so many ways among his children that his once-large holdings had shrunk to small leases and some original ownership near Cow Springs between the Coleman outfit and Haney Springs.

We said our good-byes to Ysidro and finished making the count. To this day I can visualize Ysidro riding off away from us, straight as a shovel handle but soft in the saddle. The little heeling dog trotted along beside the horse as if he was harnessed in the traces with the tall, slightly burnt sienna sorrel. That team could do more cow work than five good cowboys . . . if it was in rough country. I felt so privileged that Flax sensed his importance and headed out with a running walk as smooth as the first swallow of vanilla ice cream in summer.

When we arrived at the Currys', Ed told them about seeing Ysidro Sandoval, his horse, and his dog. They announced proudly that once or twice a year Mr. Sandoval stopped by and had coffee with them.

Ever since I was four years old, I thought of myself as a grown man and joined in the conversation with the grown-ups like I was one of them, but during that lunch break that day, with Ed and the Currys, I just listened. They were telling stories about the last of the true vaqueros. I didn't want to miss a single word. I knew this was a day, riding Flax beside my cowboy mentor and boss, and meeting the legendary vaquero, I would always remember.

The following week, Flax and I were making a count, looking for sick cattle, and riding a fence line. We had watered at the well near Chico Flats and read sign around the tank. Six mother cows were grazing off about a half mile and four of their calves were lying down, and two of them raced away, playing, bucking, whirling, tails up. Their white faces stood out like big snowballs.

I sat there on ol' Flax with his velvet muzzle in the water taking in long drafts of the cool, high-altitude water. I was thirsty myself, but you never dismount a horse while he's drinking. They'll run backward and maybe cause a hell of a wreck. Their ancient genes still make them feel vulnerable to a tiger or a lion creeping up on them while they are watering with their heads down.

We moved up the Chico Flats trail east toward headquarters as we'd done so many times before. A good breeze whispered through the piñon and cedars. I had some hopes for rain. Down on the southeastern plains of New Mexico, a good east wind meant, quite often, that moisture from the Gulf of Mexico was accompanying it. Today, however, this wind would create a different kind of storm.

About a hundred or so yards from the rim of the mesa there was a tiny meadow where I always reined off if I was alone. I looked back west across Chico Flats, the Lamy/Clines Corner highway, the rolling hills, and endless mesas of the San Cristobal. On across a million acres, up into the dark blue Jemez Mountains, I could even see a section of my beloved White Bluff Anasazi ruins. I've since this time seen paintings of some of the world's great landscapes, many by immortal artists, and even brushed a few fair ones myself, but this canvas before my young eyes colored and patterned by the Great Mystery in the Sky is etched into my being forever.

I was in an unexplainable trance, and then I was pulled back to the moment by the unmistakable tensing of Flax's muscles under me. His ears were thrown forward and stayed there. A sure sign, and his flared nostrils revealed he not only heard but smelled horseflesh. There was a salt lick just as one topped out on the trail. The east wind was sending Flax signals and blowing our sound and scent away from whatever was partaking of the salt.

I rode ol' Flax around rocks in the trail the best I could to soften our sounds. Then I saw the backs of some horses through the brush. Wild mustangs.

I eased Flax to a stop. I took my catch rope loose from the tie and slipped the honda knot over the horn. I built a big Mother Hubbard loop and leaned a little forward, signaling Flax to move on up. He did. I could feel the excitement surging through him. He was almost dancing. My heart whammed against my chest like a wild eagle trying to escape a cage.

There it was! A colt from an old mother in the front of five or six others. There was no time to check whether they were stallions or mares for they all spied us at the same time, whirling and racing for the part of Glorieta that was called Wild Horse Mesa. The old mare and what would probably be her last colt were behind. A dream realized.

Flax and I were flat running and riding with all the strength we had and we were slowly gaining. Forty, thirty, twenty feet. Now contrary to many written and filmed tales, I've never heard of a cowboy catching up to and roping a full-grown, healthy mustang. The weight of the saddle and the rider is just too great a disadvantage.

I leaned forward and started whirling the big loop. Flax was stretched out in a dead run. He was giving me all he had when I saw a big opening through some piñons. On the other side the timber really thickened. It had to be now.

Flax moved through the scattered trees expertly. We were within about ten feet. I was ready to rope the bay colt when I had to duck a little for a limb. I had unintentionally let the loop drop as we dodged a tree limb, getting ready to rope the colt. Instantly thereafter I was gazing for a brief moment into the blue, blue domain of birds, billions of planets, and, some say, heaven. Oh, this vision was brief and just before I lost sight of the endless blue, something like a kind of monstrous prehistoric bird flew across my line of sight. Then nothing. Blank. Nada.

The first thing I saw when I came around was a mountain with red monsters moving back and forth on a road. They were coming and going like . . . like . . . ANTS. My vision cleared before my weak mind did and I realized I was full length on the ground, face sideways, staring at a very active anthill. This revelation caused me to move, even though I was amazed I still could. As I sat up, I was certain every bone in my body would snap apart like dry kindling. I struggled over and started analyzing the scene—the happening—the wreck.

Flax was standing, shaking. I knew he had gone down when I spotted the big tree stump with about half my rope around it. The other half draped down to the ground still attached to the saddle. I sat there until I knew most of what happened. Somehow, instead of the wild colt's neck, I had dropped the loop around a stump. We had jerked it out of the ground at the full speed of a thousand-pound horse. It had yanked Flax and me both into the air. What saved us was the fact the stump was old and somewhat rotted, and at the same time, the overly used catch rope had snapped. That monstrous bird flying over me just before I whammed into the earth was the stump.

I finally gathered the guts to try standing. I made it. Next I ventured walking. Amazingly I could with little pain. Now that it looked like Flax and I would both live, I walked over to him, rubbed his neck, and said, "Forgive me, old pard."

I saw where the torn skin of the earth marked the spot where he, too, had greeted the ground in a maladroit manner. To my continued amazement, the saddle and the front cinch were still intact. In some unfathomable happenstance the flank cinch had broken without disemboweling poor, faithful Flax.

I led him over to the stump. He didn't even limp and had quit shaking. I took the half rope from the stump and the other half from the saddle horn, coiled them together, and draped them over the horn and swells of the saddle. I wanted some evidence when I would have to try explaining to Ed Young the inexplicable series of events.

Before I reined back toward home, we followed the wild horse tracks all the way to the heavier timber where they disappeared. I stared and stared. I have no idea why. All I saw was trees. Then Flax and I moved toward the Rafter EY to whatever interesting events might await us there. I don't know what made me look back, but I did. A coyote was following us, about forty paces back. When we stopped, he did. This little show was repeated a dozen times before I got down and opened the horse pasture gate a half mile from home. When I mounted up, the coyote had turned around and was moving away down the trail. Then he stopped and looked back at me. We locked long-distance eyes. I swear I could see a grin on that sucker's face. I felt right then that the canny little critter had observed and enjoyed our recent wreck and was relishing the thoughts of how stiff, sore, and foolish we were going to feel tomorrow. The wind was wrong or I'm sure we could have heard him giggling out loud.

A couple years later, I miraculously acquired a small ranch of my own in northeastern New Mexico; fought in the Great Ground War and survived; and surrendered to the obsession of becoming an artist, which moved me to Taos and many other things.

I was living with my new wife, Pat, in Taos, New Mexico, when we got the letter inviting us back to the mesa for the once-or-twice-a-year dance and a lot of catch-up gossip. Those gatherings were famous on the mesa.

We drove over the dirt road and purposely got there right after lunch. We knew the Youngs would be overworked preparing for the grande balle.

It was a very welcome sight to enter Ed and Mother Young's living room and see the rock fireplace Ed had built back in the 1920s with his own hands. No matter what the season, he kept two or three piñon logs going. It was the strobe light of its time and the pride of his construction life. In preparation for the party the room was stripped bare except for the fireplace and a couple of benches. These were soon filled by the Youngs' close friends, some of which were the Witte family, the Macdonalds, the Colemans, the Curry boys, the Sandovals, the Cozarts, the Eldon Butlers, and the Tapias. They arrived in old cars, trucks, wagons and teams, and on horseback. The women all brought food and the men came with a hidden bottle, mostly pints. Also furnished by the guests was the music—usually a fiddle, a banjo, and a guitar or two. They alternated between the waltz, the two-step, and the cowboy stomp, and it went almost nonstop. The kids joined in. Some danced with other kids and some with grownups. Everyone had a great time.

There was an unwritten law of the land: no hats worn indoors, and all thirst quenching was done outside the yard fence. No exceptions ever appeared. The visiting, the dancing, the teenage sparking went on all night until the roosters truly crowed. No fights. No arguments. Just plain conviviality and pure fun. I would never see it again like this anywhere in the world.

Just about everything was the same except Flax. When Flax had reached eighteen years he could still work a branding and was a good night horse, but Ed decided to retire him while he was in good enough shape to enjoy the long grass and fresh water. He'd long ago paid his way and a whole lot more. He had four precious horse years of total freedom left to make his own choices.

He had given me, an unskilled kid, five human years of his vast earthly and spiritual knowledge. It was priceless. And all I ever had to give back to him was my loving memories. Everlasting.

Ghost Horses of Tulsa

Does a trip from Taos to Tulsa to find twenty thousand dollars in buried gold coins with a great guy like Woody Crumbo the Elder seem like a worthwhile trip? Well . . . yes, it does. And, it was.

But I must start at the beginning.

I had left the heart of the Hi-Lo Country to live in Taos hoping to become a professional artist and had been fortunate enough to be accepted by the great pioneer Potawatomi Indian artist Woody Crumbo as his sole pupil. During his lifetime he placed over five hundred paintings in museums around the world including the Corcoran, the Metropolitan, and the Gilcrease in Tulsa. His work was also collected by hundreds of accomplished individuals like Wort Phillips of Phillips Petroleum—the founder of the famed Philmont Boy Scout ranch at Cimarron, New Mexico—Winston Churchill, Queen Elizabeth II, and many other notables.

. . . And he was my mentor. So when he told me of his knowledge and interest in the location of this coined yellow metal I accepted his words as if he had simply said, "The sun is hot." Anyway, this trip would be a welcome relief from covering canvas with images for a while.

To attempt an understanding of the equine adventure to come, a few earlier actualities about Woody must be revealed. He was orphaned at the age of seven and ran wild for a time along the Arkansas River, surviving on small game and fish.

The summer he was ten years old, a Creek/Muskogee outlaw, George Island, talked him into staying a couple months with him in the woods at his cabin near Sapulpa, Oklahoma, mainly to do chores during the two and a half months left before school started.

It was a time of revelatory horror for the great artist-to-be. The child was in fear for his life every second because George Island was a robber, a killer, and just plain born as mean as a stepped-on rattlesnake. Not only that, he was crude, unkempt, and missed the coffee can three out of four times when he spit tobacco juice.

The one thing Woody gained from this stay was that ol' George had him ride out a couple of broncs. In spite of being thrown over and over in the beginning, his fear of the murderer made his natural trepidation of gentling the bucking horses as negligible as being forced to eat a candy bar. When the horses were finally working, reining, and stopping right, the outlaw took the saddle away from him, saying he needed to learn to ride Indian style, which to George Island was bareback.

Crumbo continued riding until he entered college. Much later in Taos, he was a fine horseman and I rode with him many times.

Woody retold the story that Ol' George kept telling him—that he should ride west of Tulsa a piece (designating a location) where all this yellow coin was buried. An outlawed friend of George's had robbed a bank just north of Tulsa and mounted on a fine gray gelding had outrun a posse and buried the money near this sandstone bluff west of the city. With a spur he had chipped a fishhook sign on the rock face about ten inches tall. The money was buried fourteen steps south of the sign. As George related, the friend had been waiting for a safe return to get the money when some unknown enemy had waylaid him outside Tulsa and put a .45 bullet through the back side of his heart. George claimed he was too stiff and sore to ever retrieve the wasted treasure. He gave no other reason. All he asked of Woody was to bring it back to him just to enjoy the sight—then . . . young Woody could do with it as he pleased. After George's insistence that he tame spoiled horses at the age of ten, Woody had one of those feelings often referred to as "sneaky." He was dead certain that somehow Ol' George would make him dead as well, and take the money for whatever uses natural-born murderers feel necessary.

George Island became famous during those days for escaping being hanged after three different murders, three times by the infamous and implacable Hanging Judge Parker. The first two misses have never been fully explained, except both medicine men and women gathered and made medicine and danced dances to save him. One can't help wondering why and what for. Maybe to make a horseman out of Crumbo will have to suffice.

The third time is a horse of many different colors. George Island was in a cell with the notorious Cherokee Bill—both scheduled to be hanged a day apart—Bill first.

Someone had smuggled a pistol and shells to Bill. He told George that there was no way he could make it out because the guards were too numerous. He gave George a plan. George took it. Bill started shooting out the food slot, up and down the walkway of the jail, screaming obscenities.

As instructed, George took the gun away from him and was pistol-whipping the wadding out of Bill when a horde of armed guards opened the door.

The unbelievable actually came to pass. Multiple robber/murderer George Island was pardoned for his valiant efforts to prevent Cherokee Bill's escape. It would seem that frontier justice was confused—for George, in truth, was meaner than Bill, and that was mean.

One can easily understand why young Woody sneaked off to school a day or so early. In a few years he went on a scholarship to the main Indian college in America, Bacone at Muskogee, capital of the Creek Nation, to study art. He was so good, the day after he graduated, he was made head of the art department. Only a short while later he won the right to do the large murals in the new Department of Interior building in Washington, D.C. His accomplishments after that would take a book all its own to list.

Woody was the main buyer for Thomas Gilcrease and his great art museum. He acquired artwork from all the Taos Founders, and of Remington, Russell, and most of the leading Indian artists of the day. More than eighty-five of those in the museum collections were painted by the hand of Woody Crumbo. Gilcrease purchased everything Woody painted including six of his nocturnals in oil.

So it is totally understandable why I instantly agreed to go with him to Tulsa on his long-delayed search for the buried, golden treasure, and it also should be easy to understand why we were slightly taken aback when we arrived at Tulsa and discovered that this land that held the gold was owned by Mr. Gilcrease himself. This very fact would necessitate that our search would be in the darkness of night.

Woody was sure he had found the gate west of town that led up a wooded draw toward our spot. We drove my station wagon as far as it seemed feasible. With a metal and glass coal-oil lantern, a pick and shovel, and nervously growling insides, we made our way back toward Tulsa up the draw.

I whispered to Woody, "Why didn't we come on the full moon?"

"Because gold is not a thinking man's metal," he stated matter-of-factly.

It was at the very least a small miracle that we found the fishhook chipping in less than half an hour. But it was there! Woody stared speechlessly at the revelation mouthed to him so long ago by Ol' George the multiple murderer, who was so mean his own son-in-law had killed him out of fear. But one thing for sure, George Island was not a liar. There it was.

Our amazement subsided and we stepped off the fourteen steps and started digging—I with the pick and my artistic/spiritual mentor shoveling by the light of a lantern.

Suddenly a crack of lightning hitting the ground a quarter mile or so away jarred us into reality. We were amazed again as the fiery shafts from the heaven's arc lighted. We expected the woods to be afire. Instead, huge drops of rain fell. We had earlier seen, by the lantern light, a shelf of rocks sticking out slightly up the bluff. We clambered up, almost at the top of the rimrock, and took shelter in the cavelike space beneath the ledge. Woody extinguished the lantern to save fuel. It became as dark as the insides of a vein of coal.

The lightning quit as suddenly as it had fired, and the cloud that created it moved silently on. Our eyes adjusted. We could see the universe of stars out beyond the earth that we were pinpricking, looking for a few pieces of gold, as humankind, it seems, had always done.

The silence was so profound it became noise. It was impossible—one would think, but we sure as all angels did think—that we heard chains rattling, clanking, and moving up the erratic slope toward us. The noises would go away, making muffled sounds as they left. Then they would come almost to us again, then retreat again. I was truly paralyzed, except for the shaking the cold chills created.

Woody began chanting a Kiowa prayer song. He had been adopted first by the Creek, then the Kiowa, as well as by the Sioux Nations, but it was a Kiowa medicine man, Opetone, who was his spiritual guide in more than one dimension and now he sang from his gift. Opetone (Wooden Lance) had broken out of imprisonment at Fort Sill and led the very last Indian raid on Texas. Opetone had given Woody the wherewithal to cause the retreat of the chains of evil. The chains moved on down and away from us into the great silence.

Woody struck a match, lit the lantern, and said, "Let's get this job done, Max."

I agreed. My fear had dissipated—just like the strange little storm and the terrifying sounds on the side of the small mesa. I swung the pick frantically. Woody shoveled furiously. After a short time, we stopped to catch a little more air in our overpumped lungs. We sat on the dirt pile and looked into the hole. It was about two feet deep, three feet wide, and four feet long, I would have guessed.

We foolishly smoked in those days, so we lit up. Soon it was my turn to say, "Let's get the gold."

"We should be about there," Woody figured.

"Yeah," I said, swinging the pick hard at the earth. It struck far quicker than I had judged and with a loud clang. My hands, my arms, my whole body were jarred so hard I dropped the pick. In pain I leaned over, picked up the lantern, and held it directly above our diggings. Instead of being hollowed out, the hole bulged up in the shape of a human and a liquid slowly oozed out of it in a slow stream. My first thought was of blood, but it was darker. I looked up intending to query my mentor, but the lamplight showed his downward staring eyes of such intensity that I grabbed the pick with my still slightly numb hands and scrambled out of the hole without looking down again.

Woody had already begun shoveling the dirt pile back into the hole without letup. He finished. He walked back and forth on it, then using the shovel, tamped it down with some ferocity.

He said, "Mother Earth is not ready to give us this gold . . . yet."

There is no use going into detail here. We got out of there. We almost ran back to the station wagon and rapidly headed it toward the safety of a highway. We drove until we found a small motel on the way back to Taos.

All I can remember about the conversation later that night was when I asked him, "What in hell was that?"

"A person," he answered.

"A rock person? How could that be?" I asked. "My pick hit something as solid as rock."

"I don't know right now."

We had dug where the miracle of the fishhook sign was found under George Island's instructions from years back. It had been delivered there on horseback, but our real equine adventures were still ahead of us as we both went on with the various phases of our art careers. We occasionally had a few discussions about the happenings at the wooded bluff west of Tulsa, but we always arrived at the decision Mother Earth had made for us.

We slowly regained confidence and the feeling we were being tested, that night, to see if we deserved the unearthing of the precious metal. We sacrificed some funds and bought a rather expensive metal detector. Testing it around old adobe Spanish ruins, we discovered it found—to perfection—ancient horseshoes, rusted cans, pans, buckets, and nails. This boosted our already high expectations in pursuing our treasure hunting.

Both of us being born optimists, we soon decided the time was nearing when the great Mother Earth would release the booty to us.

Many changes would be made in our plans before the next trip took place.

First, we decided to take the horse trailer and our two horses and ride them to the treasure site. Woody's horse, Felix, was a horse that came to him by an Idaho cowboy who simply pulled up at his place southwest of Taos, unloaded the horse from his trailer, visited a while about Idaho, then said in terms of absolute certainty, "I'm supposed to go to Arizona. Felix is yours, Woody, no matter what. But . . . I'd like to sell you the horse trailer so I can eat and gas up to be sure I'll make it to where I've got to go."

Woody bought the trailer and inherited a magic horse. He was almost all black except for an odd white streak that wrapped across his face and down part of his left side. He had the glassy, light blue eyes of a full-blown pinto. The horse could cut, stop, work cattle, pleasure ride, and I'm sure add and subtract into the fifth dimension.

I had Powderface, the first combined top roping and riding horse of my life. This roan was later renamed Roanic by my cousin, David Evans. He had been a professional roper until he tore up his knee. Now he only did matched ropings. Much later I gave him the roan and while training him for a big match roping, Powderface—while in a dead run—just fell dead. I think he did it because I gave him away. He got even.

It is no strain to understand why Woody and I actually made plans and were preparing to take the best horses of our lives—or so we felt at the time—to a place where the gold had been delivered on a horse, and the man delivering it, had later been ridden down by men on good horses and shot dead as last year's dream. It made sense, both common and spiritual. I was all for our new plan.

We were having after-lunch coffee at Foster's Cafe when Woody's brother-in-law, Tom Tune, walked in and joined us. Of course there was no way we could possibly know this would be a fateful meeting. Tom was a mechanic, a durn good one. He saw the world as held together by tools, tightening nuts and bolts, and the careful adjustment of various timed motors. He had part of it right.

People who are involved in many other dimensions often forget that some other people may not see things the way they do. Tom was one of those people. So, as Woody and I were discussing the elusive gold coins underground near Tulsa, Oklahoma, Tom sat down within hearing distance of us and ignored such talk as fanciful and foolish—anyway, as far as he was concerned. However, when we started discussing the wondrous merits of our new metal detector, his attention span increased immeasurably. If he had been a fox his ears would have been standing above his head like the pointed radar disks of today.

Before the coffee session was ended, Tom agreed to accompany us and handle the metal detector with long-trained precision. It was decided that he would test the metal detector over and over until he felt a part of it—even in darkness.

After another cup of coffee and a piece of pie, the return to Tulsa had been settled—with some changes. We let Tom Tune's ability with machinery influence us into a different vision. A well-worn path that didn't fit.

We would take disbelieving Tom with us. We would not take our horses. We changed the date for the Oklahoma trip so we would arrive at the Tulsa site on the full moon.

We both watched Tom as he left for work. When he had disappeared from sight, Woody said, "He's going to use that machine to prove us wrong—and stupid."

"He is unable to see past his eyes," I added.

"Maybe this trip will give him a different line of sight. Maybe." Woody was seeing many things as he uttered these words that have remained indelible even amid my complicated memory cells.

He said, in an aside to me, "We will find it this time."

The blue moonlight was electric when we arrived in Tulsa. The wondrously soft breezes were inhaling our growing expectations like the lungs of a mastodon . . . I could feel the earth beneath me pulsating, breathing, waiting with massive ease for our beginning.

We parted a little brush so Tom could see the fishhook indention in the sandstone bluff. He showed no emotion, but whispered to Woody, "Step off the fourteen steps and stand there." It was an order. Tom had mistakenly thought he was in charge of the precious blue night.

Woody obeyed and stepped it off. He stood on the spot, upright as a flagpole, his big chest stuck out like a rooster's, and he waited with great patience.

Tom picked up a stick and scraped a big square with Woody in the center. Then with the precision of an army parade sergeant he turned on the metal finder and plugged in the sound phones and mathematically, mechanically walked across the square north to south until he had covered the square. He stopped behind Woody about four feet to the south and we could hear the machine buzzing with greatly increased volume. My heart reached the same tempo, notifying my entire chest of discovery. Gold fever!

Then to our dismay he did the same calculated parade from east to west, finally arriving at the same place with the same shattering sound in the quietness of a night that was beyond painting, photography, or recording in any other way but the part of your soul that savors beauty. Contrasts.

Tom stood up like Charles de Gaulle and scratched an X in the ground, saying as if he had taken a swallow from a bad cup of coffee, "It's probably some old rusty horseshoes or a slop jar."

We ignored him and dug as before, only faster. Hadn't the high-tech world given us a certainty of rare collector's gold coins? Ah, the red brown Oklahoma soil was picked and shoveled by two dumb artists faster than a badger or a backhoe, except, of course, when Tom intruded to insert the knowledge of the machine with his own in a superior movement. The deeper we dug the louder the buzz and the faster the needle whammed and held against the peg.

As we reached about three feet and the same test held up, I had a combination of high anticipation and doubt. First, because we had the treasured coins almost trickling through our fingers, and at the same time I tried not to reason that the bank robber had buried the wealth intending to retrieve it later. So why go deeper than his trove?

I sat down on the abundant pile of disturbed earth and pulled out a pack of cigarettes and passed them to Woody and Tom. You've heard the old saying "Three on a match" . . . ? Well, I didn't let it happen. I lit Woody's and Tom had to dig out his perfectly performing metal lighter.

As Woody and I deteriorated our lungs and breathed in the pure blue air to counteract it, we were all three looking up at the ledge. The moon had moved over to light part of the cave where the dark entities had come to put us in chains. It all seemed so far away now. So unimportant.

Woody broke our triple reveries with, "The next shovel will get it."

Tom said, in a quiet but superior rebuttal, "Probably a vein of iron."

We were all silent. The only sounds in the night were the low buzz of a few unknown insects and the haunting cry of some night bird in the midst of the woods. The world was big. The sky that held the stars, dimmed by the moonlight, was bigger. The backward and forward and sideways and up-and-down movement of time stopped. All motion ceased.

Then it came from the distance above the rimrock. A thunder of four mighty hooves. We all stared into the sound. Invisible sound. It was coming above but straight at us and then it leaped. We all three fell over south off the dirt pile waiting to be smashed by the mighty hooves, but there was only a sound I'd never really heard before. That of a horse displacing air as it hurtled through space, right over us.

The human mind will always offer up many surprises. I wondered if this horse was blue like the great oil painting of the dappled blue spirit horses Woody had invented and so many others emulated later. Or maybe it was his painting of the rainbow horse that delivered souls through the cosmos, avoiding wayward angels, to safely deliver its chosen spirit rider safely to the next dimension. All of this, and more, plunged through me as the horse pierced the sky above us. Then we heard it land in a great clattering of rocks and race on and vanish in silence far, far faster than it had come. Instantly.

We all three sat slowly up staring south now away from the rimrock, but full on our faces and even glinting in our eyes was the light of the blue, blue moon. Oh, what a silence it was. All the more profound when it was replaced by a far-distant unmistakable sound of horses coming toward the rimrock at full speed. Close as before, but much louder. We could feel the skin of the earth quivering under the terrible pounding of all the racing hooves. I knew, and I looked at Woody, and knew that he knew as well. The posse of horses pounded to the edge and in ones, twos, and threes, they leapt into space above us.

Tom had jerked his head back to the rimrock, but Woody and I looked on south waiting for the horses to land. To our surprise it was so far away it was only a few soft thuds and a softer sound of exiting into another time—another place. All the horses had evanesced into the place from which they had come.

The silent moon stared down one-eyed at the three of us who were unmoving, and I do believe until now unthinking for a time without calculation.

Tom broke the multidimensional spell by standing up abruptly, stiffly bending down to gather up the pick and shovel, then walking with his Lincolnesque stride—long and swift—toward our vehicle.

Woody said, picking up the metal detector that Tom had seemed to worship only a while back and had now abandoned, "We better go before he drives off and leaves us."

He might have done it, too, because the motor was just catching the first sparks of fire to gasoline when we arrived. Tom drove all the way home, the entire distance back to Taos, only stopping for gasoline. No talking, no coffee, no good-just-getting-the-heck-out-of-Oklahoma.

Woody and I slept some, but we didn't talk, either. What we would have to say could only be to each other. Tom never said a single word ever again about our journey. I often thought that he denied to himself it ever happened—any of it—and it couldn't be fixed with even the finest amalgamated steel wrench ever made.

Late the next day Woody and I met at the Sagebrush Inn and, after many beginnings with no ends, decided we had been blessed with the ghost horses of the gold robber and the posse that ran him down. We believed this was true, and I added with a laugh that the coins had probably turned to ghosts as well and we would never have been able to feel them or spend them or even have the pleasure of giving them away.

In later years, we grew to accept that a billion dollars in rare coins could never replace the oh-so-rare golden moments gifted us and shared with human ghosts as well as with the ghost horses of Tulsa.

The Horse Who Wrote the Stories

Yeah, that is right, it was a horse that started it all—the stories, the books, the movies, the paintings, and he came close to ending it for me, as well.

I was back home at my little ranch in northeastern Union County, New Mexico, after recently spending six and a half months of straight infantry combat from Normandy's Omaha Beach, to the Brest campaign in Brittany, to the Ardennes forest in Belgium and Germany.

Before leaving for the dogface days of World War II, I'd sold all my horses and cows at auction. Upon returning, I wanted to acquire *one* good horse to start over. Since I was a lousy bronc rider to begin with, I wanted a gentle, well-trained horse.

I had "broken out"—or rather, as the PC'ers insist—*trained,* a string of rough broncs for Pete and Ben Jones, neighboring ranchers, just before leaving my wife, daughter, and the land I loved more than tequila gold or homemade ice cream to get shot at by SS men. Not much of a swap when I think about it right now.

I had chosen the village of Des Moines, New Mexico, as my new headquarters. George Larkin had a grocery store in town and a big cow ranch southeast of town. In his store he sold on credit—especially to the small ranchers whose land adjoined his. With the ranchers' unpaid grocery bills, he obtained considerably more land and livestock. So when I inquired about getting a fine horse, he obliged me.

Mr. Larkin had a foreman I was later to fictionalize as "Les" in *The Hi-Lo Country* novel and film. Les was a fine horse trainer. George took me, and my gear, down to his ranch. He had called Les ahead on the party phone line, and the foreman had a horse waiting in the round corral. I didn't even have to rope him. He walked toward me as I stood in the middle of the corral with the bridle over my shoulders.

Now, in the novel, I made him a sorrel, but in actuality he was as shiny black as newly mined coal. I named him Blackie right there. He took the bit like it was a handful of sugar. I hand-brushed him down and saddled him up. I led him up three steps, gathered the reins in his mane with one hand and the saddle horn with the other, and mounted.

Les had put a fine rein on him. All I had to do was touch his neck with one rein and push my leg a little against the shoulder on the same side, and he turned like a cutting horse. I spurred him slightly and he took off in a run, and I set back on him before we hit the corral. Talk about a stop! He slid those hind legs underneath him with his front legs forward, and it was all I could do to stay on him. Three years away and a rider can lose his seat; of course, it usually comes back in a little while. I rode him out in the horse pasture and tried everything I would need him to do for starters. He was a hell of a good horse, coming five years old, and just right.

Now my wife and I had quite a bit of personal business to attend to—furniture to acquire, repairs on the house, and corrals for the home place—before I even thought about going into debt again for some cattle. So I paid Larkin the seventy-five dollars he asked, and it was agreed I'd get the horse in a month. I was thrilled. So was George Larkin.

Even though my small ranch was about fourteen miles south of his, it was spring-fed and Larkin knew he could trade it to anybody if I defaulted on any bills, because he also knew that by the time I got the place in shape and went into debt to stock it, I'd probably be buying groceries on credit. That was slick planning, except I traded with the only other grocer in town, Toby Smith.

There was a car dealer in Morton, Texas, who owed my dad some favors, and he sold me the very first new Dodge pickup delivered to his postwar dealership. I had the only new pickup in Union County. It was black and shiny, like my horse. When my wife drove me down in our new Dodge pickup to claim my horse, I was feeling pretty damn sassy.

I decided instead of loading him in the pickup, I would ride Blackie home. I was hand-brushing him before saddling when I felt some new scars on his neck that had mostly healed over. Might as well get to it. Les really liked this horse and didn't want to give him up, so he had spurred scars in his shoulder to spoil him. I knew how he felt about giving up an animal. When I was younger, working for Ed Young on Glorieta Mesa, I'd been certain I'd owned a horse named Flax—but I didn't. Flax was Ed Young's horse by title, and now this horse was mine by bill of sale.

Despite my fears of what had taken place, I proudly rode him to my ranch. His smooth running walk kept the tender skin on my tail and inner legs from peeling. I was sore, but pleased with Blackie even though I'd already figured that Les had done his best to spoil him for me without letting his boss Larkin know. Oh, what suckers we *trusters* can turn out to be.

I was enjoying the moment—thankful to just be alive—as I rode over my *malpais- and* mesa-surrounded outfit checking fences, watching for coyote and bobcat tracks, trying to figure how many blue quail there were to draw from for part of our sustenance. I'd forgotten all about the new scars in Blackie's neck, even though, when I had saddled him, he humped up enough to make the back skirts of the saddle stand up a couple of inches, but not enough to figure he'd buck. Anyway, he had such a smooth gait, I was lured into a little laxness.

I rode up to the big spring half a mile downhill from the main house. Blackie walked out into the mud to water. I just reared back in the saddle enjoying the plentiful water and the grama and buffalo grass growing across my pastures as lush as a Bel Air carpet. Blackie pulled his muzzle up from the cool water and turned to move on. When he raised the first hind foot out of the muck, the suction caused it to make a popping noise. That was the excuse he'd been waiting for. I'm still here to tell you that horse could buck. I lost one stirrup, then two, and all I could see was his black mane flying. He'd sure swallowed his head.

Blackie was hitting the ground hard and kicking backward before he turned in midair. It felt like my spine had been replaced by peanut butter. I tried to fall off but he bucked right under me for about three more jumps—each one felt like he'd ripped me in half, right up between my legs and out the top of my head, which was the appurtenance I failed to drive into the ground when I finally bucked off. At last the world slowed its spinning and I was able to sit up and look for my hat. It took a while, but I finally discovered it was mashed flat on top of my numb scalp.

I spotted Blackie who was already up the hill past the house and heading for a barbed-wire gate—a *shut* gate. The stirrups were flopping up above the level of the saddle seat when he slammed on the brakes. He turned and just stood there looking back down the hill for Ol' Max.

I cursed him with all the epithets I could get breath enough to yell. Then

I decided to check out how many of my bones had been broken. I did that by standing up. To my amazement, I could move every one of my limbs. So the next chore was pulling my smashed hat from my head, putting it back on, and walking uphill over a half mile past the house to congratulate my noble steed.

As I went past the house, my wife yelled from the porch, "What happened?"

I didn't even look her way, but I said, "Walking and falling zigzag across France and half of Belgium/Germany just wasn't enough exercise for me." And I'm sure, neither one of us knew what I meant.

Blackie was not smiling over his triumph. Nor was I. One rein was broken in half where he had somehow stepped on it in his one-horse race up the hill. I took out my pocketknife and cut the bridle off the bit. Then I took the end of the other leather rein and tied it in its place, and pulled it over his head and neck. It was too short, but it was all I had.

I was ready for him this time. I mounted, squeezing the saddle horn till it yelled "ouch," and rode to the gate of the round corral. I managed to open it without dismounting. Then I rode him around and around inside those poles spurring him faster and faster. Hell, he seemed to enjoy it, so I gave up, fed him some hay and oats, and stumbled for the house.

The next time he got me was when I dismounted to open a gate into one of the big eastern pastures of the adjoining A. D. Weatherly outfit. I was cutting across to the Jones boys' place to help them build some fence, when I saw where a really big old coyote had gone right through the wires of the gate without leaving a particle of fur. I was amazed almost every day of my cowboying and ranching life enjoying and observing the multiple, often magical, talents of these creatures. That's where my mind was as I led Blackie through the gate at the Joneses'. I shut it, mounted, and tapped him lightly with my spurs as he headed downhill to a long draw, headed north.

I think I must explain that Blackie could read minds, and when a simple mind like mine went blank or wandered into some foreign subject, such as the brilliance of coyotes, he knew it.

The next thing I became aware of was the fact that he had jumped up into the realm of eagles and when he came jarringly down, I myself learned to fly. My new skill was short-lived. I hit the ground so hard I saw heavenly bodies sparkling all around my prone one. This time, however, I stayed with my Glorieta Mesa training and held the reins. Ol' Blackie was bending down and his dark, soft muzzle touched me in false sympathy. When I finally retrieved my breath well enough to mount him again, I decided to contest him all the way, so I would know if it was ever going to be possible for me to ride this wonderfully gaited, reined animal that so resented my presence on his back.

In spite of what Les had done to him, I pulled my hat way down, took as deep a seat as the saddle and Blackie's backbone would allow, choked the moisture out of the saddle horn and spurred him right in the healed-over scars ol' Les had given him. He answered by turning twice to the left and whipping back to the right as he left the ground. I somehow stayed with him until he came down trying to tear holes, big holes, in the skin of Mother Earth. Then I departed again, trying to hold on to at least one rein. However, after doing the impossible, by staying up in the fresh mountain air for a magic spell, gravity finally moved the entire world up to wham me in the butt and the back side of my body with such force that my fingers flew apart and the reins went downhill with the runaway horse.

It took me longer than I wanted to discover my breath this time. I was also very slow getting up, as I was busy praying my bones were still in my body and connected. I was also pleading to the Great Mystery in the Sky to arrange for Blackie to dive off a bluff into oblivion when he got to the bottom of the slope where there was a little rock-strewn creek and some steep sandstone bluffs.

I had been thrown without mercy at the earth's gravitational center and then left to die, and the powers I so beseeched for favors had either ignored me or were busy with more important things.

Blackie raised his head from the creek water as it dripped from the bits. The reins were intact, and I'll be a one-eyed goat if he didn't snicker a welcome at me.

Now there is not a lot of benefit that I can see in revealing how Blackie was smarter and meaner than I was. The outwitting and unloading continued at times of his choosing. He had dislocated a knee, an elbow, and a shoulder twice—mine. Several times I thought my neck was broken and my head caved in as well. I was wrong about the last, I think, but he had forever reshaped my hat. There were uncountable minor things such as bruising, torn tendons, pulled muscles, and other extreme inconveniences; but flip the pancake over, and that sucker could work the outside circle from sun to sun on a roundup, and take me to cattle like a professional roping horse when I had to educate a bunch-quitter or doctor a bovine critter for fixable ailments. Above all he was a hellacious heeling horse at a branding. He seemed to enjoy dragging calves to the fire, and it was a pure pleasure for the both of us because that had been all that got me by in those kid days on and around Glorieta Mesa.

I did put a ride on him one time. Once. I was taking my two best wolfhounds over to loan to my hunting partner, Uncle Tom Creswell. I rode along scanning for coyotes. Each of the hounds wore a ring on its collar, which I ran a rope through. I held both loose ends in my free hand. All I had to do was drop one end of the rope and it would slide slickly through the rings as the dogs took off after a coyote. Today, I didn't spot one and got to Tom's without a problem from Blackie. Tom knew I had some day labor coming up on neighboring ranches and wanted to get in some fun hunting with our hounds before I went back to slaving for a living.

When I got there, Tom and his wife had gone to town or were visiting somewhere. Since our dogs were well acquainted from previous hunts, I put my hounds in the pen with his, tied the gate shut, and started the eight-mile ride back home.

I could tell by Blackie's ears trying to see me backward—yeah, ask any working cowboy—most good horses have eyes in their ears. He was waiting for me to doze off or let my mind wander before he fired. And sure enough, he caught me off guard an inch or two when a covey of blue quail ran across the road ahead, but it wasn't a total disaster this time. Right there the barbed-wire lane narrowed for about a half a mile. He went up and out and the third jump came mighty close to the flesh-ripping fence. However, he was like a mule about barbed wire—he understood its danger and avoided it even when his mind was set on driving me into the ground like a five-foot eleven-inch nail.

The fourth or fifth jump, my head was snapping back hard and I'd lost a stirrup. Miraculously, I got it back and this gave me a spurt of confidence. If I could head him west with the lane and keep from pulling the saddle horn loose, I had a chance.

That's when I learned something new. It was easier to whop the ground *once* with my body than to have him jar me in the saddle a *dozen* times or more. Just as I was straining to straighten up and pull myself back into the saddle at every jump, and my entire body had been turned into a well-shaken martini, the black sucker just quit and took up his running walk as if nothing had happened. It had, though. Blackie's sides were heaving and there was heavy sweat on his flanks and shoulders. I was so weak I nearly fell off. But my ego would not allow that. It was my one great victory, and I looked all around hoping somebody had seen this mighty deed. There wasn't a pair of human eyes to be found. I might as well have made the ride on top of Mount Everest or in the middle of the Sahara.

If I'd had a gun, a coin would have been flipped to see which one I shot—him or me. I understood at last that I couldn't handle this horse. He knew I had lucked out on this single ride and I knew it even better.

No matter how things are planned, they are destined to change.

It was shipping time. Farrel Smith, whose big ranch headquarters were only five or so miles northeast of me, had gotten rich during the rainy war years running Corriente steers imported from Mexico. This year he was experimenting with fifteen hundred head of Black Angus steers. He sent a hand over to get me to help them with the roundup and the fourteen-mile trail drive into Grenville to the shipping pens there. I wasn't feeling too well from an inner-ear problem and I said "no" with regrets.

Well now, Ol' Farrel hadn't gotten rich because of the inability to think, so he sent Bill Caperton, an old-time cowboy—who I really liked—over to ask me again. I thought Bill was still foreman as he had been when I left for the war. Naturally, this time I said yes.

At this time, there was a shortage of any regular crews in that part of the country, so a bunch of old *worn-outs* and *reluctants* like me spent three days on the roundup. I used Farrel's horses on the roundup and saved Blackie for the drive to Grenville.

Fortunately, I'd never met the big old overbearing foreman now in charge. He knew horses and cattle pretty well, but a sparrow splatter would have smothered his knowledge of human beings. I resented his taking old Bill's well-earned place, I suppose.

We started on the big drive so early in the morning that we left by the light of the moon. For about seven or eight miles we had barbed-wire fence lanes. We could use a pickup's headlight beams rolling past the point rider. Blackie and I along with Bill and another hand named Max something-or-other were put on the drag. It didn't matter. I'd used up my dizzy medicine the day before and wondered if I'd make it anyway.

We were halfway there before noon and nobody I knew ever served a noonday meal while working cattle in those days except at a neighborhood branding where all the women brought food and a visiting picnic was made out of the work.

Farrel had prepared ahead as usual and several old semiretired, broken-up hands that lived in Grenville were waiting down at the shipping pens to help us. We were slowed a while because for three or four miles there was a stretch of open country and the herd was harder to keep gathered and moving. Soon, though, we got another lane and shoved the last steer into the pens at around midafternoon. The bawling, the dust, the yelling, the cattle prods, and all made a hell of a mess as cattle car after cattle car was loaded to transport the stock to buyers in Kansas for feeding, fattening, and then steak dinners around the world.

Suddenly that cockeyed inner-ear problem hit me and I snuck off hoping nobody would see me heaving up an unfed stomach. Then I sat down on some boards along an already emptied pen trying to ride the whirling world. I must have dozed off as my battered brain went back momentarily to the irony that a five-hundred-pound railroad shell had created this problem a short while back at St. Vire, France. Here I was trying to work cattle at another railroad thousands of miles from the site of the exploding shell.

I heard words. I don't remember them exactly, but they were harsh. As I fully awakened I saw the big foreman looming above me like a movie monster. I instantly felt the board I sat on and it had been split. So I stood up probably trembling and lifted the smallest part of the board at the same time. It was far too long, but I examined it like I was going to use it to strike a baseball. To my relief the monster stomped away, still cursing with words I do not care to remember.

I felt cold. It was. An early north wind was gathering force and seemed to me as if it was straight out of the arctic. I ambled over and saw that all the cattle were loaded. A couple of pickups and a car were pulling out and a bobtail truck followed carrying all the horses but one—Blackie. The foreman had ordered that I be left behind to ride the eleven miles north from the Grenville shipping pens to my front gate.

I had somehow forgotten that every few years an October storm whams the Hi-Lo Country. If I'd had any sense at all I would have stayed in Grenville. Anyway, a determined storm was gathering in me to make the ride home.

About three or four miles out of Grenville, the wind picked up in velocity. I could see a huge bank of clouds coming our way blanking the setting sun. There was a little hotel and restaurant still open in Grenville during those days, but I can't recall having the slightest sensible thought of turning back.

I had foolishly made the drive without a bandana. I took out a handkerchief and tied it around my face.

Blackie's tail and mane were whipping around like they might be blown out by the roots. He had his neck and head down as low as he could and still walk straight into the growing wind. First it started to sleet. Then the small snowflakes came and before you could say "stop" the flakes became huge and ground-covering even in the breath-stealing wind.

I kept looking for the graded road, but soon it was night and I couldn't see it at all. It wouldn't have made any difference if it had been straight-up noon, the clouds were down on the ground, it seemed, and made up of one great solid snowflake. We were blind and I was helpless. I'm sure I must have prayed out loud, but I doubted any higher powers could see or hear in the weird moaning of the storm that had swallowed Blackie and me like a burial shroud.

The only way one can understand the lost blindness, the nonbeing where there are no compass points—not even up or down—is being there. I do not recommend the experience of suddenly being nowhere at all in a pulsating, white darkness.

I held onto the saddle horn as a newborn does its mother's breast. That was all that kept me anchored, as long as my hands didn't get so numb I couldn't feel it. Luckily, I had brought a pair of cloth-lined leather gloves in my chaps pocket. These kept my hands from getting so numb I'd lose the reins or the saddle horn. There was nothing left but to try to stay atop Blackie.

I know it seems extreme to say that, eternities later; I sort of gathered my senses and realized we weren't moving. Nevertheless, when time ceases to exist for you, what else is there to feel?

Gradually I realized that we weren't moving. I reached down and touched Blackie's neck. He was holding his head up not far from the ground. Sure enough, we were in front of my home gate. I was so stiff that I just sort of fell off him, and did in fact fall down in about a three-foot drift, but the elation of the possible continuation of life gave me a charge of energy. It was a mile uphill from the gate to the ranch house where my wife and four-year-old daughter must be envisioning me well fed, warm, and content in the Grenville Hotel.

If Blackie had brought me this far in total blindness, one more mile in a suddenly softening wind should be a cinch. It was.

Now, before we reached the house, the adrenaline had not only caused me to move but also to think for a change. I've heard many different stories about this mythical ability of horses that I don't think we humans are meant to know. I believe we lost the ability to understand this seeming phenomenon eons ago. This was the second time already in my young life that a horse had unbelievably delivered me home in a blind blizzard: Ol' Snip, up on Glorieta Mesa, and now Blackie in the Hi-Lo Country.

Even though the storm had been vicious, and in places created drifts several feet deep, it soon dissolved or melted away before real winter came. I don't remember hearing about any livestock losses.

I have to give Farrel Smith credit; when he found out about the monster foreman leaving me behind to face the threatening storm, he instantly fired him, and the critter quit the country. I had not told anyone, but I was sincerely relieved since I dreaded the chore of eventually being forced to use him for batting practice.

I'd forgotten that I'd put the word out that I wanted to sell Blackie. Then one day I was having a cup of coffee at the kitchen table when I heard a yell outside. I got up to check it out. There were two horseback riders dismounting as they saw me coming toward them.

It was Wiley "Big Boy" Hittson and his younger brother Tiny. I later called Tiny "Little Boy" in *The Hi-Lo Country* novel and movie. We shook hands, had a few "how you doin's," and Big Boy got to it. He looked out in the corral at Blackie and said, "I hear you want to sell that ol' pony."

A lot of surprising emotions shot through me, as if I'd been plugged into a high-voltage light socket. The horse had saved my life. He had also entertained me quite often by bucking me off in cactus beds, rock piles, plain old hard ground, and twice in clumps of spear like yucca bunches. Being a fallible human being with faster-than-light-itself thinking ability, I reasoned that Blackie had saved me so he could enjoy finishing me off at a time of his own choice.

"Yeah," I said.

"How much you want?"

"Just what I gave for him. Seventy-five bucks."

"Tiny, take your catch rope and go get him."

He wrote me a check. It was good.

Tiny led Blackie up. Big Boy unsaddled his sorrel and threw his rig on Blackie and rode off leading his horse with Tiny riding even with him. It may sound strange, but unexpected tears welled up in my eyes as I just stood there and watched the three horses and two men become smaller and smaller on their nine-mile ride back to the Hittson place.

I sensed something for sure. Buying the horse from George Larkin, and his foreman getting jealous and spoiling him for me, got the beginning going. Many unusual events were launched at the moment I said "Yeah" to the horse sale. It would all grow and grow. First into a killing, then a great doomed romance, then a novel, and new acquaintances with some of the world's wildest and most noted people, a motion picture actually shot in the country where the horse deal started. The movie would include Woody Harrelson, Patricia Arquette, Billy Crudup, Sam Elliott, James Gammon, and Penélope Cruz in her American debut and brought thirty million dollars into the poor state of New Mexico that didn't somehow come from even poorer taxpayers' pockets. But those stories have been told in hundreds of other places over the long, long years and are still going on. This is Blackie's story.

From what I gathered, Blackie only tried unloading Big Boy twice, and then with no choice given he settled down and made Wiley an outstanding cow horse. Blackie was quartered up and fast enough that Big Boy could easily have made a calf roping horse out of him, sold him, and even way back in the late forties tripled his money. Big Boy was a good amateur bareback bronc, bull rider and "dogger," steer wrestler, but the nearest he ever moved ol' Blackie to a rodeo arena was once when he decided to get all duded up in old-timers' real garb and ride him in the Des Moines (Hi Lo) rodeo parade.

Whenever Big Boy was working for Hoover, or Farrel Smith, or the T.O. or other big outfits, I'd sometimes help with roundups and branding. He generously let me use Blackie to heel and drag calves to the branding fire. It was a great pleasure just to sit on him as he moved with a fluidity only the best athletes have. Besides, I knew he wouldn't dare toss me over a low-flying bird in front of Big Boy. Despite all of our early misadventures, I still felt a kinship to him and of course I always will.

I sold my ranch, my family left for Texas, and I went to Taos to become an artist. Big Boy helped move my belongings and me in his old Chevy pickup. The Larkins' cowboy—the one who had deliberately spoiled Blackie—had a lovely wife, but she was leaving him. So it only seemed right that Big Boy give her his respect and his companionship. When he left me there in Taos to head back to the heart of the Hi-Lo Country, I said, "Tell Mona [fictional name] and ol' Blackie hello and give them my love."

His face showed one of his rare grins, and he said, "You betcha."

Later Wiley was at the home place. His mother, Tiny, and two even younger brothers were branding. Big Boy and Tiny got in an argument over the way the home place was being kept up. Tiny knew he didn't have a chance fistfighting Big Boy, so he shot my best friend to death.

Pat and I drove over the Rocky Mountain range from Taos to Des Moines. We were late because we had been informed late. The doors to the church were opened for the pallbearers to carry him out. The Marine Hymn floated out across the little town and the vast lands around it, which he had represented and become part of and would now be covered by.

We drove up to the graveyard on the hill behind Hi Lo. Folks broke off in small groups. Strange. I only heard the droning of the preacher, not his words. My mind was on the good times we'd shared and one of those was a horse named Blackie.

Afterward, only a few of us were invited out to Mrs. Hittson's. It was hard for me to be nice to Tiny, but I think I was. I owed it to the family and Mrs. Hittson had enough to face holding the place together without any added trouble.

We got ready to go back to Taos and continue in our world of art, horses, and a million other things that wouldn't have existed except for the cowboy ex-Marine just placed six feet under the top of the first hill north of the little town . . . and . . . the black horse in a corral behind the Hittson place.

Mrs. Hittson wanted me to have Big Boy's .30-30 rifle. I took it. She handed me the big hat he'd been wearing when he was killed. I was honored to have it. Then she offered me Blackie.

I said, "No, thank you, ma'am. He belongs here in the country where he and Big Boy worked. Besides, a smart horse like Blackie will still remember that I'm not much of a bronc rider."

Decades later, the fine actor James Gammon, who played Hoover—the old-time rancher that Big Boy respected so much—wore Big Boy's hat in *The Hi-Lo Country* film.

He said, sincerely, "I'm much honored."

I know I was, as well, and wherever the spirit of ol' Blackie was, I feel sure he bucked about ten feet straight up in full agreement. He could buck all over horse heaven if he wished. He had sure earned the right. After all, Blackie was the horse who wrote all those stories.

Acknowledgments

The stories in this collection appeared in previous publications, as follows:

1. "The Old One"
   Southwest Wind. San Antonio: Naylor, 1958.
2. "The One-Eyed Sky"
   Contact Magazine (literary magazine, San Francisco), 1962.
   Three Short Novels: The Great Wedding, The One-Eyed Sky, My Pardner.
      Boston: Houghton Mifflin, 1963.
   The One Eyed Sky. Los Angeles: Nash Publishing Co., 1974.
   Xavier's Folly and Other Stories. Albuquerque: University of New Mexico
      Press, 1984.
   Shining Sun, Grinning Moon. Santa Fe: Red Crane Publishing, 1995.
   Hi Lo to Hollywood: A Max Evans Reader. Lubbock: Texas Tech University
      Press, 1998.
3. "Don't Kill My Dog"
   Super Bull. Albuquerque: University of New Mexico Press, 1986.
4. "The Matched Race"
   Southwest Wind. San Antonio: Naylor, 1958.
5. "The Heart of the Matter"
   American West, a Short Story Collection. New York: Forge Books, 2001.
6. "Blizzard"
   Southwest Wind. San Antonio: Naylor, 1958.
   Tierra: Contemporary Short Fiction of New Mexico. Edited by Rudolfo Anaya.
      El Paso: Cinco Puntos Press, 1989.
7. "A Man Who Never Missed"
   Southwest Wind. San Antonio: Naylor, 1958.
8. "Old Bum"
   South Dakota Review, Spring 1993.
   Shining Sun, Grinning Moon. Santa Fe: Red Crane Publishing, 1995.
9. "Once a Cowboy"
   Hot Biscuits: Eighteen Stories by Women and Men of the Ranching West.
      Albuquerque: University of New Mexico Press, 2002.
10. "The Far Cry"

The Pick of the Roundup. New York: Avon Books, 1963.

Hi Lo to Hollywood: A Max Evans Reader. Lubbock: Texas Tech University Press, 1998.

11. "My Pardner"

Three Short Novels: The Great Wedding, The One-Eyed Sky, My Pardner. Boston: Houghton Mifflin, 1963.

My Pardner. Boston: Houghton Mifflin, 1972.

"Mein Partner." Dortmund, Germany: Der Übersetzung Hermann Schaffstein Verlag, 1974.

Shining Sun, Grinning Moon. Santa Fe: Red Crane Publishing, 1995.

For the Love of a Horse. Albuquerque: University of New Mexico Press, 2007.

12. "The Sky of Gold"

South Dakota Review, Spring 1995.

Hi Lo to Hollywood: A Max Evans Reader. Lubbock: Texas Tech University Press, 1998.

13. "The Orange County Cowboys"

"Three Southwest Novellas," *South Dakota Review,* Winter 1987.

Rounders 3. New York: Doubleday, 1990.

Rounders 3. New York: Bantam Books, 1990.

Rounders 3. Boulder, Colo.: University Press of Colorado, 1997.

14. "The Call"

South Dakota Review, Summer 1968.

Hi Lo to Hollywood: A Max Evans Reader. Lubbock: Texas Tech University Press, 1998.

15. "The World's Strangest Creature"

Super Bull and Other True Escapades. Albuquerque: University of New Mexico Press, 1986.

Hi Lo to Hollywood: A Max Evans Reader. Lubbock: Texas Tech University Press, 1998.

16. "Super Bull"

Super Bull and Other True Escapades. Albuquerque: University of New Mexico Press, 1986.

Southern Horseman Magazine, 1995.

Hi Lo to Hollywood: A Max Evans Reader. Lubbock: Texas Tech University Press, 1998.

For the Love of a Horse. Albuquerque: University of New Mexico Press, 2007.

17. "A Horse to Brag About"

Horse Tales Annual, 1972.

Super Bull and Other True Escapades. Albuquerque: University of New
   Mexico Press, 1986.

For the Love of a Horse. Albuquerque: University of New Mexico Press, 2007.

18. "The Cowboy and the Professor"

Super Bull and Other True Escapades. Albuquerque: University of New
   Mexico Press, 1986.

Hi Lo to Hollywood: A Max Evans Reader. Lubbock: Texas Tech University
   Press, 1998.

19. "Showdown at Hollywood Park"

Southern Horseman Magazine, 1985.

Super Bull and Other True Escapades. Albuquerque: University of New
   Mexico Press, 1986.

Hi Lo to Hollywood: A Max Evans Reader. Lubbock: Texas Tech University
   Press, 1998.

For the Love of a Horse. Albuquerque: University of New Mexico Press, 2007.

20. "The Mare"

(under the title "The Wild One") *The New Frontier—The Best of Today's
   Western Fiction.* Edited by Joe R. Lansdale. New York: Doubleday, 1989.

Hi Lo to Hollywood: A Max Evans Reader. Lubbock: Texas Tech University
   Press, 1998.

For the Love of a Horse. Albuquerque: University of New Mexico Press, 2007.

21. "An Equine Montage"

For the Love of a Horse. Albuquerque: University of New Mexico Press, 2007.

22. "The Freak"

Southern Horseman Magazine, 1985.

Super Bull and Other True Escapades. Albuquerque: University of New
   Mexico Press, 1986.

For the Love of a Horse. Albuquerque: University of New Mexico Press, 2007.

23. "Cricket"

For the Love of a Horse. Albuquerque: University of New Mexico Press, 2007.

24. "Flax"

For the Love of a Horse. Albuquerque: University of New Mexico Press, 2007.

25. "Ghost Horses of Tulsa"

For the Love of a Horse. Albuquerque: University of New Mexico Press, 2007.

26. "The Horse Who Wrote the Stories"

For the Love of a Horse. Albuquerque: University of New Mexico Press, 2007.